SHARI'A &
CONSTITUTIONAL
REFORM
IN INDONESIA

The **Institute of Southeast Asian Studies (ISEAS)** was established as an autonomous organization in 1968. It is a regional research centre dedicated to the study of socio-political, security and economic trends and developments in Southeast Asia and its wider geostrategic and economic environment.

The Institute's research programmes are the Regional Economic Studies (RES, including ASEAN and APEC), Regional Strategic and Political Studies (RSPS), and Regional Social and Cultural Studies (RSCS).

ISEAS Publishing, an established academic press, has issued almost 2,000 books and journals. It is the largest scholarly publisher of research about Southeast Asia from within the region. ISEAS Publishing works with many other academic and trade publishers and distributors to disseminate important research and analyses from and about Southeast Asia to the rest of the world.

ISEAS Series on Islam

SHARI'A & CONSTITUTIONAL REFORM
IN INDONESIA

Nadirsyah Hosen

ISEAS

INSTITUTE OF SOUTHEAST ASIAN STUDIES
Singapore

First published in Singapore in 2007 by
Institute of Southeast Asian Studies
30 Heng Mui Keng Terrace
Pasir Panjang
Singapore 119614

E-mail: publish@iseas.edu.sg
Website: http://bookshop.iseas.edu.sg

ISEAS Library Cataloguing-in-Publication Data

Hosen, Nadirsyah.
    Shari'a and constitutional reform in Indonesia.
    1. Islamic law—Indonesia.
    2. Constitutional amendments—Indonesia.
    3. Islam and politics—Indonesia.
    4. Islam and state—Indonesia.
    I. Title
KNW479 H82   2007

ISBN 978-981-230-399-8 (soft cover)
ISBN 978-981-230-402-5 (hard cover)
ISBN 978-981-230-570-1 (PDF)

Typeset by Superskill Graphics Pte Ltd
Printed in Singapore by Utopia Press Pte Ltd

CONTENTS

LIST OF TABLES

ACKNOWLEDGEMENTS

This book is based on my Ph.D. thesis at the Faculty of Law, National University of Singapore (NUS). It was submitted on 20 February 2005. Credit is due to the Institute of Southeast Asian Studies (ISEAS) for publishing this book and making it available to a wider audience.

While being written, this work has accumulated a few debts along the way. To start with, I owe a great debt of gratitude to Associate Professor Gary F. Bell. Without his continuous guidance and invaluable help, the completion of this work would not have been possible. He has offered many insightful comments and frequent words of encouragement over the years.

The earlier stages of this work also benefited from Associate Professor Thio Li-Ann and Associate Professor Victor Ramraj. During my Doctoral Candidate Qualifying Examination (DCQE), they have opened my eyes with their questions and suggestions. I was delighted that after the DCQE Professor Ramraj appointed me as his research assistant in 2003. I would also like to give my special thanks to the Thesis Examination Committee: Teo Keang Sood (Chair), Victor Ramraj, Hikmahanto Juwana and Priyambudi Sulistiyanto for their comments and feedback.

Acknowledgements also go to other professors at NUS: Simon Tay, Lim Chin Leng, Michael Ewing-Chow, Dora Neo and Robert Beckman. My wholehearted thanks are due to Professor Wael Hallaq (McGill University) and Associate Professor Tim Lindsey (University of Melbourne) who visited NUS in 2004. Their insightful suggestions and encouragement will always be appreciated.

I would like to express my gratitude to my Indonesian sources. They provided invaluable assistance and friendship. The information I gathered from them is essential and critical to the thesis. I also wish to express my appreciation for the support granted by NUS. From Research Scholarship to President's Graduate Fellowship, the University has been unfailingly generous. I am also grateful to the Asia Research Institute (ARI) for providing Graduate Fieldwork Fund for my research in Indonesia.

In preparing this book, I have been assisted in different ways by friends and family. While friends from around the world are too many to list here, I would like to thank Taiwo Oriola for reminding me that at least one chapter of the thesis was publishable. I am also grateful to my old friends, Rudi

Irawan and Ahmad Ali Nurdin, for helping me and my family during our stay (and struggle) in Singapore. I am also indebted to Ian Usman Lewis who lent a helping hand in editing and proofreading. Arskal Salim was always ready to share his thoughts, stories and jokes. I thank him for his friendship. I am also very grateful to Dr I.B. Watson for his careful readings of the draft. I wish to thank the library staff at the NUS and the secretarial staff of Graduate Division at the Law Faculty (Zana, Normah, Chin Yee) for their assistance and for being courteous and helpful.

I devote my immense gratitude to my beloved wife, Rd. Ina Inayah. This work is only a small token of my appreciation of her devotion, sacrifices, and infinite forbearance. My daughters, Hamamatul Haramain Hosen (born in 1998) and Nurul Haramain Hosen (born in 2000), deserve separate mention for so patiently tolerating all the piles of clippings, files and books, decorating and taking up a lot of space in our small apartment. In addition, the support from my brothers and sisters have given me the strength to make it thus far.

Finally, I wish to express my sincerest gratitude to my late father, Professor KH. Ibrahim Hosen and my mother Hj. Zatiah Kadir whose love of knowledge has motivated me to pursue further education. My father (born in 1917) passed away in 2001, two months before I started my course at NUS. He was my first comparative law teacher. He provided the daily example of being an exceptional and extraordinary person, who inspired me to push on in pursuit of my own extraordinary ambitions. It is my hope that he would have been proud of his youngest son's work.

My mother (born in 1928) suffers from breast and lymphoma cancers. Every night she prays for me. Every word typed in this work was inspired by her love, which is the fuel that enables me, a normal human being, to do the impossible. All that I am or ever hope to be, I owe to my mother. It is to her that I dedicate this work.

1

INTRODUCTION

Shortly after Independence in 1945, Indonesian Muslims demanded that the Constitution guarantee an Islamic state in Indonesia. Reference was made to the draft of the preamble of the Indonesian Constitution (known as the Jakarta Charter), which contained the following religious principle: "Belief in one Supreme God with the obligation for adherents of Islam to perform *shari'a* (Islamic law)." However, the last seven words (*dengan kewajiban menjalankan syariat Islam bagi pemeluknya*) [with the obligation to carry out Islamic *shari'a* for its adherents] were removed on 18 August 1945 after protests were made by some Christian Indonesians. They argued that this clause amounted to discrimination against other religions.[1] Therefore, the first principle of the Indonesian state ideology became "Belief in one Supreme God", without the mention of Islamic *shari'a*.

It should be noted that many Muslims expressed disappointment at the omission of this seven-word clause, and since then the desire to have an Islamic state in place and to remove Pancasila, the five principles of the Indonesian state ideology, continues to resurface from time to time. In 1985, President Soeharto succeeded in enforcing the adoption of Pancasila as the sole foundation (*asas tunggal*) of all political parties and social and religious organizations in Indonesia. Any aspiration to restore the Jakarta Charter was seen as an attack on the ideological foundation of the state. Many Muslim activists were jailed because of their ideas on the Islamic state.

1

By the end of the 1980s, the Soeharto government was trying to get closer to the Islamic community. The President signed Law No. 7 of 1989 on Islamic Courts which allowed the formation of ICMI (Association of Indonesian Muslim Intellectuals), headed by Professor B. J. Habibie. The President then went to Mecca for a pilgrimage. The effect was that many government officials adopted Islamic attributes, and the government involved itself in some Islamic issues in a much more positive way. For example, Muslim women were allowed to wear the *jilbab* (veil) at schools and at government offices, the government supported the building of new mosques and prayer houses, and many Ministers attended Friday services in mosques and celebrated the Ramadan rituals.[2] However, Pancasila remained the ideology of the state.

Following the resignation of President Soeharto on 21 May 1998, Indonesia, the largest Muslim country in the world, entered a new era of political, legal, and economic reforms. While the Soeharto government recognized only three political parties, President Habibie allowed the Indonesian people to establish new political parties.[3] On 7 June 1999, forty-eight political parties took part in the elections, with twenty-one parties winning at least one of the 462 contested seats in Parliament. There are several Islamic-oriented political parties among those who won.[4] It may safely be stated that Islamic political parties are in a favourable position to make a contribution to Islamic teachings, including those dealing with poverty, corruption, development, and good governance issues.

A significant step in Indonesian law reform is the reform of the 1945 Constitution. When Soeharto was in power, he forbade any attempt to propose amendments to the 1945 Constitution since this Constitution accorded him greater authority than the legislative and judicial bodies. However, since the end of Soeharto's presidency in 1998, Indonesia has amended the Constitution four times between 1999 and 2002.

This achievement is notable for a number of reasons. Firstly, it has broken "the sacred statement" of former President Soeharto that people must not change their Constitution. Secondly, constitutional reform is a critical aspect of Indonesia's transition since the original form of the 1945 Constitution was an inadequate foundation for democracy. Constitutional reform was also one of the basic demands of the student movement, which was instrumental in leading to President Soeharto's resignation in 1998, and the Indonesian political elites have been struggling with the issue ever since.

Thirdly, the amendments have altered the basis of the political structure in Indonesia. For instance, the first amendment limits a President to serve a maximum of two terms only.[5] A new chapter, comprising ten articles regarding human rights, was introduced in the second amendment.[6] The structure and the power of the executive, legislative, and judiciary bodies were reformed.[7] In all, thirty-one articles (or 83.79 per cent) have been amended or modified and only six articles (6.21 per cent) have not been changed at all.[8]

Meanwhile, Soeharto's departure had also opened the opportunity for several Muslim groups and political parties to propose the introduction of *shari'a* into the Constitution. This process is important from the perspective of democracy since it accommodated different and conflicting views in a constitutional way. For more than half a century, Indonesia has not been able to conduct an uninterrupted dialogue concerning the position of *shari'a* in the Constitution. In 1945 and 1955, efforts were hampered by the pressure of time and political manoeuvrings by Soekarno and the military. Under Soeharto, debate was forbidden, since his government was afraid of its disruptive potential. The moment for free dialogue and debate, through constitutional mechanisms, came after Soeharto's resignation.

Some Muslim groups only demand the modification of Article 29 of the 1945 Constitution, which would mandate the practice of *shari'a* for Muslims. The Islam Defence Front (FPI) mobilized thousands of its supporters outside the Parliament Building to demand the 1945 stipulation on Islamic law be included in any Constitutional amendment.[9] In addition, the first Indonesian Mujahidin Congress in November 2000 called for the inclusion of the Jakarta Charter in the Constitution and for *shari'a* to be applied as state law.[10]

However, others went further by proposing that Indonesia becomes an Islamic state and Pancasila be replaced. The periodical *Tempo* reported the existence of student cells in the Bogor Agricultural Institute (Institut Pertanian Bogor, or IPB) and the Bandung Institute of Technology (Institut Teknologi Bandung, or ITB). These leading Indonesian state universities had earlier sworn oaths of allegiance to the Proclamation of the Islamic State of Indonesia, which was declared in 1948 by Kartosoewirjo, the leader of the Darul Islam rebellion. These student cells considered the Soekarno-Hatta declaration of an independent republic in August 1945 as null and void.[11]

Although these groups have different opinions, strategies and goals, they share the common view that *shari'a* should contribute to constitutional reform in Indonesia. Their slogan is "Save Indonesia with *Shari'a*!". They are of the view that implementing an Islamic legal system will bring Indonesia out of crisis.[12] They opine that the government's inability to deal with corruption, collusion, nepotism (popularly known as KKN, or *Korupsi, Kolusi, Nepotisme*) has led them to provide another solution: the adoption of *hudud* law, which entails amputating the hand of persons who commit corruption.[13] They believe that the objective of introducing *hudud* law is to punish the perpetrator of a crime, which would generally push the criminal towards repentance. This can act as a deterrent, so that he/she becomes wary from experience, and also for others who have the intention to commit crime. In this sense, the implementation of this kind of Islamic law would protect the public.

However, in August 2002, the People's Consultative Assembly (Majelis Permusyawaratan Rakyat, or MPR)[14] officially rejected the call for the inclusion of *shari'a* in Article 29 of the Constitution. Partai Persatuan Pembangunan (PPP, or United Development Party) and Partai Bulan Bintang (PBB, or Crescent Star Party) failed to convince other parties to support the inclusion of *shari'a* into the Constitution. These two parties only occupied 71 seats in Parliament, which translates to 12 per cent of seats.

The study of *shari'a* and constitutional reform in Indonesia in the years 1999 to 2002 had been a heated and controversial topic among Muslims and legal scholars in Indonesia. It invited attention from all levels of society with mass demonstrations, petitions from various religious leaders (including Christians and Hindus), political statements from the Chief of the Army, and public debate influenced the "atmosphere" of the annual sessions of the MPR in those years.

In the context of the Muslim world, this study is also important since after the events of 11 September 2001, world leaders are wondering whether democracy would be made to flourish in the lands where Islam prevails. Perhaps, this might be the single most pressing question for American foreign policy. The Bush administration has played its role in "helping" Iraq and Afghanistan rewrite their constitutions. Behind all these lies a basic question: can a state be truly democratic and Islamic in character at the same time?

In some other Muslim countries, the alternative to democracy is autocracy, in the form of secular dictatorship or religious monarchy. However, the process of constitutional reform in Indonesia during 1999–2002 was different. The process began before September 11. The tumultuous chain of events that ultimately led to the fall of Soeharto, the re-establishment of free and open elections in 1999, and the rise of political parties and the Parliament were the product of domestic political dynamics rather than any policy initiative by the Bush administration. One of the key differences between Indonesia and Iraq and Afghanistan is that Indonesia has reformed its Constitution without "assistance" from other democratic countries. On the other hand, the constitutional reform in Iraq and Afghanistan might be seen as a form of American economic, legal, cultural, and political hegemony as the processes did not originate locally, but were externally imposed.

This book will investigate how law reform in Indonesia deals with the issues of democracy, rules of law, and human rights. It will cover not only the legal aspects, but also the historical, socio-cultural, and political aspects. Therefore, this study will make a contribution to *fiqh siyasa* or Islamic constitutionalism, Indonesian constitutional law, and law reform in the post-Soeharto era.

The situation in Indonesia can also be explained by looking at other Muslim countries and other scholarly works on this matter. Several Muslim scholars, such as Muhammad Asad and Abul A'la al-Maududi,[15] have written on several aspects of constitutional issues such as human rights and the separation of powers. In addition, several scholars take the view that Islamic law became increasingly rigid and set in its final mould[16] following the call to close the door of *ijtihad* (independent legal reasoning).[17] The fall of the Ottoman Empire also contributed to the lack of Islamic constitutional thought since the empire was the last caliphate. Even books on political law (*fiqh siyasa*) written in the twentieth century by Abdurrahman Taj and Abd al-Wahhab Khallaf,[18] for instance, refer to the idea and the practice of Islamic state more than a thousand years earlier.[19] Their works are undoubtedly useful in understanding the practice of Islamic states in the past and examining Muslims' political thought.

Western scholars and Muslim scholars who graduated from Western universities have addressed the various issues of Islam and public law;[20] state, politics and Islam;[21] and democracy, the rule of law and Islam.[22] However, these works do not look at the case of Indonesia.

Meanwhile, several scholars have written on Indonesian Islam and its relation to constitutional issues. The works of Ahmad Shafi'i Ma'arif and Adnan Buyung Nasution[23] discussed the debate in the Konstituante (Indonesian Parliament in 1955) on Islam vis-à-vis the state. Prior to that, Endang Saifuddin Anshari wrote a Masters thesis at McGill University, which examines the Jakarta Charter.[24] Although their works are important for understanding the historical context of the issue, they do not cover the new debate and recent developments in the post-Soeharto era.

Munawir Syadzali's 1991 book addresses several important topics in Islam and the governmental system.[25] He summarizes the opinion of major thinkers in Islamic historical thought. In conclusion, he argues that the Pancasila state is the best available option for Indonesia. Four years after the publication of Syadzali's work, Ahmad Sukardja of the State Institute of Islamic Studies (Institut Agama Islam Negeri, or IAIN) Syarif Hidayatullah, Jakarta, published his Ph.D. dissertation on the comparison of the Medina Charter[26] with the 1945 Constitution. He concludes that the 1945 Constitution does not conflict with the Medina Charter and consists of Islamic views of a plural society as expressed in the Medina Charter.[27] The implication of his study is that Pancasila and the 1945 Constitution are in line with Islamic teachings and, therefore, Muslims do not have to replace them with Islamic ideology or *shari'a* constitutional law. In 1997, Masykuri Abdillah's Ph.D. thesis[28] outlined the responses of Indonesian Muslim scholars to the concepts of democracy and human rights, democratic values and democracy in Indonesia from 1966 to 1993. The study provides evidence that Indonesian Muslims recognize the concept of democracy. In 1999, Suzaina Abdul Kadir wrote a dissertation that focused on the behaviour, choices, and strategies of the Nahdlatul Ulama (the biggest Islamic organization in Indonesia) in its interaction with the state.[29]

However, Syadzali, Sukardja, Abdillah, and Kadir did not relate their studies to constitutional issues in the post-Soeharto era, nor do they cover the significant developments in recent Indonesian constitutional law. Since their data and argumentation predate 1999, they are inappropriate for the analysis of recent developments.

A new development occurred when Gary F. Bell's article on the amendments to the 1945 Constitution was published in *Van Zorge Report on Indonesia* in 2001.[30] Bell analysed the temporary outcome and the ongoing debate of this constitutional reform. It should be noted that the process of constitutional debate in the MPR was ongoing when this article was written. This explains why the article does not analyse the final outcome of the amendments. It provides room for more investigation. Blair King wrote an interesting Ph.D. thesis on presidential power in the Third Amendment.[31] This suggests that he analyses only one aspect of the new Indonesian political structure. It is worth noting that while King used a political science approach, I use a legal approach.

Bivitri Susanti also examined one aspect of the amendments regarding human rights.[32] Since human rights provisions are in the Second Amendment, she did not discuss other issues covered in the First, Third and Fourth Amendments. The same applies to another of Bell's article concerning minority rights.[33] He examined individual rights and collective rights (exercised individually or collectively) in the Second Amendment to the Constitution. In short, the works of these scholars examined only one aspect of the amendments whereas this study examines not only human rights provisions, but also the rule of law and the position of religion.

Timothy Lindsey's article is quite different. He published his article after the process of constitutional reform was finalized.[34] This gave him plenty of time to explain the main issues of the amendments. However, he did not specifically report the stories (or the stories behind some stories), the debate and political compromise since his work was written in the form of an article, which naturally prevents him from writing more on these issues. In addition, the work of Todung Mulya Lubis, a prominent lawyer, deserves attention. He criticizes the outcome of the constitutional reform. He holds the view that the new Constitution should be prepared and drafted by an independent constitutional commission; not by members of the MPR since they could be influenced by party interests. In taking this position, parallels were drawn with the new Constitutions adopted in recent years by Thailand, the Philippines and South Africa, all of which were established by independent commissions. Lubis's work suggests that the MPR solicited citizens' input on only a limited basis, preferring to reserve the final decision on amendments for itself. The MPR rejected all calls for a popular referendum on amendments.[35]

In the Indonesian language, there were many books and even drafts of the Constitution produced by scholars, research institutions and political parties during the 1999–2002 constitutional debate.[36] Jimly Asshiddiqie, now the Chief Justice of the Constitutional Court (Mahkamah Konstitusi), also provided academic analysis on the amendments.[37] Another development is the works of Slamet Effendy Yusuf (member of the MPR from Golkar Party) and Umar Basalim (Secretary General of the MPR) which compiles minutes of meetings, views of members of the MPR and political statements of all political parties in relation to the First Amendment.[38] Basalim also produced a new compilation that focused on the proposal to adopt the famous seven words of the Jakarta Charter.[39] The last two works are useful as a short-cut to understanding the process and the debates arising from the Amendments, but they do not offer a critical analysis on this subject.

This book is designed to further contribute to the work undertaken by Indonesian legal scholars — by analysing *shari'a* and the amendments to the 1945 Constitution, which previously have not been the subject of detailed examination. It aims to fill a gap in the literature by examining the *shari'a* dimensions of human rights provisions, the relationship between the executive, the legislative and the judicial branches of the state, and the position of religion in the Constitution. It investigates the response, the debate and the contributions of *shari'a* in constitutional reform in Indonesia in the post-Soeharto era.

Most Muslims agree that their religion provides guidance on a whole range of matters, from the personal to the political. Since Islam provides guidance, political systems in the Muslim world should reflect the moral and religious teachings of Islam. The guidance is embodied by the Islamic *shari'a*. However, as Nathan J. Brown points out, there are some differences between Western and Islamic forms of constitutionalism. Firstly, while *shari'a* is based on the will of God, Western constitutionalism is reflected in the idea of popular sovereignty. Secondly, Western constitutionalism has focused on the principle and the procedure of limiting government, whereas *shari'a* provides the principles of governance.[40]

Several Islamic countries have attempted to write constitutions that are based on the principles of the *shari'a* and, at the same time, they have borrowed procedural forms from Western constitutionalism. However, combining two different systems in a constitution is not an easy task. It is possible that there are some compromising and even conflicting views and values. This leads to the first question addressed in the book: Is *shari'a* compatible with the principles and procedural form of constitutionalism?

The above question is important as the September 11 events have sparked extensive debates about Islam. Stereotypical images about the religion and its teachings have been openly discussed in the media, citing as examples the undemocratic and oppressive regimes in most Muslim countries. Dictatorial and tyrannical governments are anything but Islamic. Therefore, in order to answer the above question, I will not only look at Islamic teachings on the substance and principles of government, but will also discuss the historical development of Islamic constitutional thought from the classical period to the modern era.

Egypt is an interesting model of how a country manages to incorporate *shari'a* provisions into the amendment of its Constitution.[41] In 1980, Egypt amended Article 2 of its Constitution so that it now reads: "The principles of the Islamic *Shari'a* are the principal source of legislation". According to Adel Omar Sherif, Egypt demonstrates how an emerging democracy can proceed towards increased rule of law. Democratic developments have advanced significantly within Egypt in the past two decades.[42]

While Egypt could be seen as a model of the combination between Islamic and Western constitutionalism, Saudi Arabia could be seen as a model of a state that believes that *shari'a* is above the constitution.[43] Another difference between these two countries is that the majority of Egyptians follow the Hanafi and Shafi'i schools of thought, whereas Saudi Arabia follows the Hanbali school.

On 1 March 1992, King Fahd ibn 'Abd al-'Aziz of Saudi Arabia issued three major laws: the Basic Law of Government, the Consultative Council Law, and the Law of Provinces. The first formalized several aspects of the constitutional framework of the country; the second replaced the council that was established in 1926 with a new council appointed by the king; and the third aimed at regulating the relationship between central government agencies and regional governors, thereby replacing a 1963 law. These laws constitute significant steps towards codifying the largely unwritten legal system of the country.[44]

Unlike Saudi Arabia, Iran is a republic and it follows the Shi'a school of thought.[45] The foundation for the Islamic Republic of Iran is based on a new Constitution (after the Islamic revolution), which was established in 1979 and was amended in 1989. According to Article 4 of the Constitution, all laws and regulations in civil, criminal, political and other aspects shall be based on Islamic principles. The Iranian Constitution is based on the concept of *Wilayat al-Faqih* (governance of the Islamic jurist introduced and coined by Ayatollah Khomeini).[46]

When compared with those Islamic countries, Islam in Indonesia is unique. At the theological-doctrinal level,[47] generally speaking, Indonesian Muslims are the followers of Ahli Sunnah Wal-Jamaah theology, which consists of the Ash'ari[48] and the Salaf schools of thought. Although the schools have different opinions on several aspects, Muslim tradition recognizes them as Ahli Sunnah Wal-Jamaah. It stands in between the *mu'tazila* (rationalist) and *jabariya* (non-rationalist) positions.

At the legal-doctrinal level, Indonesian Muslims generally are followers of the Shafi'i school of Islamic law, although they recognize the existence of other schools (*madhhab*) such as Maliki, Hanafi and Hanbali.[49] The Shafi'i school stands between the Hanafi school (rationalist) and the Maliki school (traditionalist). It should be noted that some Muslims in Indonesia follow none of these schools strictly, but pick and choose the opinions of the schools eclectically. Others go further by referring directly to the Qur'an and Sunna and avoiding the opinions of the schools. However, the followers of the Shafi'i school, which is represented by the Nahdlatul Ulama (NU), form the majority in Indonesia.

Normative, historical, legal and comparative approaches will be used to answer the question regarding the compatibility of *shari'a* with the principles and procedural form of constitutionalism. I will outline a solid introduction and foundation for arguments on an analysis of *shari'a*, Indonesia and the Constitution.

The second question will be: How have the Indonesian people linked the *shari'a* and the Constitution historically? Again, a historical approach will be used in order to answer this question. I will re-evaluate the debates arising in 1945 and 1955. The evaluation of the events of those years is important in understanding the debate in the period 1999–2002. The shifting positions of two largest Islamic organizations, that is, Muhammadiyah and the NU between 1955 and 2002 will also be critically analysed.

An analysis of political reform in the post-Soeharto era will be provided in order to understand the political compromises and interests of Muslim political parties and other parties. The political impact of the *shari'a* debate in constitutional reform is also an interesting topic in this part. Political and legal approaches will contribute to these discussions.

It is expected that the answer to the second question will provide some arguments for the main sections: How does *shari'a* relate to three critical issues of human rights, rule of law, and religion vis-à-vis the state? Incidentally, this is the third question addressed in the book.

Human rights have been chosen as a case study since both Indonesia and Islamic law have faced criticism in the areas of human rights protection. Islamic thinkers often repeat that human rights are part of the essence of their beliefs. It seems that they make no clear distinction between human rights in the modern nation-state and human rights in Islam. When a right is recognized in Islam, it is often an ethical and spiritual assertion in an abstract religious discourse. When a right is recognized in a state, it is a fundamental entitlement enabling the individual to make specific legal claims, based on constitutional demands on the public authority.

Those rights that do exist in Islam remain pious assertions by the faithful unless they are embedded in the constitution of a particular state, creating a legal framework arrived at without resort to political coercion. The experiences of the existing Islamic states, both in their legal construction and their own legal enforcement have been the target of criticism. The implementation of *shari'a* in Saudi Arabia in the case of Islamic criminal law (*hudud*) and the role of women could be seen as examples in this context.

Ann Mayer devotes a large part of her book, *Islam and Human Rights: Tradition and Politics*, to a critical analysis of specific aspects of Islamic human rights schemes developed by traditionalist Muslims. Mayer shows that the authors of Islamic human rights schemes have failed to create a comprehensive formulation of the philosophical and logical foundation for their rights' standards.[50]

Meanwhile, according to Human Rights World Report, Amnesty International Report, and the U.S. Department of State, Indonesia has a record of abusing human rights. It was thus reported in 2000:

> The Government's human rights record was poor, and the overall human rights situation worsened during the year, despite the Wahid Government's efforts to continue the country's democratic transition and permit the exercise of basic freedoms. Security forces were responsible for numerous instances of, at times indiscriminate, shooting of civilians, torture, rape, beatings and other abuse, and arbitrary detention in Aceh, West Timor, Irian Jaya (also known as Papua or West Papua), the Moluccas, Sulawesi, and elsewhere in the country. TNI personnel often responded with

indiscriminate violence after physical attacks on soldiers. They also continued to conduct "sweeps" which led to killing of civilians and property destruction. The Government and the leaders of the Free Aceh Movement members signed an agreement in May providing for a humanitarian pause in the fighting between them, beginning on June 2. During the pause, both sides agreed not to undertake offensive operations or maneuvers. Initially the humanitarian pause greatly reduced violence in Aceh, but by September violence had returned to roughly pre-pause levels. Army forces, police, and GAM members committed numerous extrajudicial killings. In Irian Jaya (Papua) police shot and killed persons involved in Papuan independence flag-raisings or demonstrations on a number of occasions, even when these demonstrations were nonviolent. There continued to be credible reports of the disappearance of dozens of civilians, including Jafar Siddiq Hamzah, a non-governmental organization (NGO) activist, and Tengku Hashiruddin Daud, an Acehnese Member of Parliament. Both later were found dead with indications of torture.[51]

Since both *shari'a* and Indonesia have been the target of criticism regarding human right issues, it will be instructive to discuss them in the light of human rights provisions in the second amendment to the 1945 Constitution.

The rule of law is another interesting subject to be discussed. The modern conception of the rule of law derives from the late nineteenth and early twentieth century movements in Anglo-American legal scholarship to convey the operation of law, law-making, and functioning of the legal system as scientific processes governed by ascertainable and predictable rules.[52] The rule of law, as the embodiment of governance by fixed principles rather than the discretion of political expediency, fits into this mode by serving, in the view of its best-known exponent of that period, Albert Venn Dicey, three functions. These are (a) supremacy of the law and absence of arbitrariness, (b) equality before the law, and (c) constitutional law as part of the ordinary law of the land.[53]

Since then, the exposition of the concept has largely revolved around subjecting the government and in particular the lawmakers to the same laws as ordinary people. That is, the law effectively restrains and where necessary punishes the abuse of political powers. Considering the historical context in which the concept was propounded, it is not surprising that its focus was political.[54]

It is worth noting that Indonesia does not follow the common law tradition. In practice, the term *Negara Hukum* or *rechtsstaat* is used in Indonesia as an equivalent to the common law notion of the rule of law. However, as Lindsey has correctly pointed out, "the use of common law traditions of 'rule of law' to understand Negara Hukum is problematic" since no consensus has been reached on the exact meaning of Negara Hukum.[55] The debate over Negara Hukum in Indonesian legal history is reflected in the writings of (to name but a few):[56] Sunaryati Haryono who interpreted Negara Hukum in the light of the rule of law; Oemar Seno Adji who opined that Negara Hukum has its own Indonesian characteristics based on family principle; Padmo Wahyono who related the concept of Negara Hukum with the political philosophy of organic statism (integralism or *integralistik*); Ismail Suny who adhered to the literal meaning of Negara Hukum as rechtsstaat; and Hartono Mardjono who took the view that elements of Negara Hukum are supremacy of law, equality before the law and due process of law.[57]

Although the concepts of rule of law, *rechtsstaat*, and Negara Hukum have different meanings,[58] they share the common views that the government and the state apparatus would be subject to the law, that areas of discretionary power would be defined and limited, and that citizens could turn to the courts to defend themselves against the state and its officials.[59]

Meanwhile, the topic of the rule of law in Islam is controversial. The image is that Islamic law allows the ruler (King, Prime Minister, or President) to govern as a dictator: whatever his decision, it is always right. This goes with other images that *shari'a* does not provide procedural regulations to control the government, *shari'a* does not have a clear rule on how to elect the government and how to limit the powers of the government, and there is no judicial independence in the countries that perform *shari'a*. These criticisms and images of Indonesia and *shari'a* lead this book to relate *shari'a* and Indonesian Constitution as a case study.

The next important case study is the relationship between the state and religion. According to Ira Lapidus, "Islamic societies are said to be fundamentally different from Western societies. The European societies are presumed to be built upon a profound separation of state and religious institutions" and therefore:

Western societies, with their inherent separation of secular and sacred, church and state, civil and religious law, are said to have promoted an autonomous domain of secular culture and civil society which are the bases of modernity. Conversely, Islamic societies, lacking a differentiation of secular and sacred, have been tied to binding religious norms, inhibiting their potential for secularization and development.[60]

Prophet Muhammad himself did not leave behind any comprehensive theory of the Islamic state. Therefore there is no single answer in defining the Islamic state. For example, as Asghar Ali Engineer has pointed out, some of the countries have declared themselves as Islamic states not by restoring the essence of Islam, but by enforcing certain punishments prescribed such as cutting off hands of thieves or stoning adulterers to death. Thus, one may see countries governed by military dictatorship or those ruled by monarchs considering themselves to be Islamic states.[61]

Indonesia is not an Islamic state, but Indonesia also rejects the secular state which requires the government to distance itself in the affairs of religious institutions, by keeping religious beliefs out of the motivations of public policies, preventing interference from religious authorities into state affairs, and disapproving of political leaders expressing religious preferences in the course of their duties. However, this does not mean that no Islamic law is practised in Indonesia. Indonesia recognizes the Religious Courts as one of the four components in its court system.[62] How both *shari'a* and the 1945 Constitution respond to this relationship between state and religion will be discussed in this book.

In order to answer the third question above, three case studies will be discussed in detail in three separate chapters. In the chapter on analysing human rights, the focus will be given to the second amendment of the 1945 Constitution. The background, significance and the text of human rights protection in the Constitution will be highlighted. The opinions of some Muslim scholars' on human rights issues will be analysed. It will proceed further by comparing the 1948 Universal Declaration of Human Rights (UDHR), the 1981 Universal Islamic Declaration of Human Rights (UIDHR), issued by the Islamic Council for Europe, the 1990 Cairo Declaration on Human Rights in Islam adopted by the Organization of the Islamic Conference (OIC), along with the Bills of Rights (if any) of the Egyptian, Saudi Arabian and Iranian Constitutions, and the 1945 Indonesian Constitution. Lastly, the ideas and political statements of Muslim political parties in Indonesia will be discussed in order to see their interests, opinions and contributions on the human right articles in the Constitution.

The second section of the three case studies will be the discussion on *shari'a* and the rule of law. It is essential that the rule of law must determine the offices to be filled by election, the procedures to elect those office-holders, and the definition of, and limits to, their powers, in order for the people to be willing to participate in, and to accept, the outcomes of the democratic regime. The rule of law in this context is also understood to include the rules of "separation of powers", in which mechanisms for checks and balances are guaranteed and the independence of the judiciary is secured. How did *shari'a* and the 1945 Constitution respond to those issues? A critical analysis will be provided in examining and comparing the rule of law in Egypt, Saudi Arabia, Iran and Indonesia. Prior to this, the works of Muslim scholars' from the classical period until recent times on the concept of the rule of law will be consulted. The history, the significance, and the idea of the rule of law, *rechtstaat*, and Negara Hukum will also be analysed.

The third and last section is on the role, function, and position of religion and the state. I will look at state–religion relationship in terms of Islamic law and Western constitutional and political thought and draw some comparisons. This examination will influence the discussion on the possibility of Indonesia fully imposing *shari'a* and/or becoming an Islamic state.

All these lead to the fourth and central question of the book: To what extent did *shari'a* contribute to constitutional reform in Indonesia in 1999– 2002? All the answers to previous questions will provide data, evidence and argument on what and how *shari'a* has contributed, responded and influenced the process and the result of the amendment of the 1945 Constitution. However, inspired by Charles Kurzman's work, this book also defines the type of *shari'a* that has played a role in the debate on Indonesian constitutional reform.

Kurzman takes the view that, within the Islamic discourse, there are three main tropes of *shari'a*. The first one is the liberal *shari'a* which argues that the Qur'an and the tradition of the Prophet order Muslims to pursue liberal positions. The second trope, the silent *shari'a*, holds that *shari'a* is soundless on certain issues, not because it was unfinished or defective, but because God intentionally left certain subjects for humans to choose their own way. This suggests that while the first trope of liberal Islam asserts that *shari'a* requires democracy, the second trope takes the view that *shari'a* allows democracy.

The third approach is the interpreted *shari'a* or Islam. This third trope argues that religious diversity is unavoidable, not only among religious communities but also within Islam itself. This view admits that the revelation is divine, but "interpretation is human and fallible and inevitably plural".[63]

Despite their different opinions, those tropes of *shari'a* can simply be classified as *substantive shari'a*. In this book, I describe the substantive group as follows: they formulate their ideas by consulting not only the text of the Qur'an and the Hadith, but also the textual treasury of classical Islam as they find it a valuable instrument in arriving at answers to questions and problems important in the Islamic world today. However, the substantive *shari'a* does not treat the classical authors and Muslim scholars who have interpreted the Qur'an and the Hadith as absolute authorities. It proposes the development of a contextualized *ijtihad* (independent legal reasoning) to reach a universal interpretation of Islam. It also holds that *shari'a* should be reinterpreted in the line of democracy and constitutionalism. Their views can be summarized as attempting to "maintain that which is old and good, and embrace that which is new and better" (*al-muhafazah 'ala al-qadim al-salih wa al-akhz bi al-jadid al-aslah*). They hold the views that substance or content of belief and practice is more important than its outer form. I have labelled them as the "substantive group". This group takes the view that, in the context of a constitution, the *shari'a* is seen as an "inspiration" and a "moral or ethical guideline".

I would add another type of thought in contrast to substantive *shari'a*: *formal shari'a*. This group believes that Islamic constitutional law has been theorized under classic works of Muslim scholars, and they tend not to modify these conceptions. The main reason is that all constitutional issues should be based on *shari'a* practised by the Prophet and his companions in Medina fifteen centuries ago. In other words, they see *shari'a* as a formal source of their constitutional elements. This suggests that human rights protection, checks and balances mechanisms, independence of the judiciary and the separation of powers are accepted in their constitutional theory as long as these elements of constitutionalism are in line with their formal interpretation of *shari'a*.

In Islamic tradition, the validity of the two groups is illustrated by a story of how companions of the Prophet have interpreted the Prophet's direct instruction to them:

> One example of such an incident has been recorded by both al Bukhaaree and Muslim. During the Battle of the Confederates, the Prophet is reported to have said to his Companions: "Do not perform the mid-afternoon ('asr) salaah until you get to the [place of] Banoo Qurayzah." While still on their way, the time of the salaah came. Some of the companions said, "We will not perform the salaah until we get to the [place of] Banoo Qurayzah" while some others said, "We shall pray. That [saying of the Prophet] will not prevent us [from praying now]." The matter was later brought before the Prophet and he did not disapprove of either group.[64]

Taha Jabir al-Alwani explains the significance of this story:

> It is clear from this incident that the Companions of the Prophet had split into two groups over the interpretation of the Prophet's instructions — one group adopting the literal or explicit meaning of the injunction (*'ibaarat al nass*) while the other group derived a meaning from the injunction which they considered suitable for that situation. The fact that the Prophet approved of both groups showed that each position was legally just as valid as the other. Thus, a Muslim who is faced with a particular injunction or text (*nass*) can either adopt the literal or manifest (*zaahir*) meaning of the text or he may derive interpretations which are appropriate to the text by using his reason.[65]

However, it is worth noting that the categorization into formal and substantive *shari'a* is not entirely new. The attempts to define, classify and identify differences among Muslims have been reflected in many works. In general, they have tried to explain two main approaches: textualist and contextualist. In Islamic history, one may find two groups: *ahl al-hadith* and *ahl al-ra'y*. While the first group tried to limit the use of reason, opinion, *aql* or *ra'y*, the latter tended to liberally use *ra'y* in interpreting and applying the law. However, this does not mean that the latter has never considered the text of the Qur'an and the Hadith, and it is also misleading to state that the first group has never performed their independent legal reasoning. The existence of both schools has been justified in Islamic tradition since Imam Abu Hanifah was attributed to the *ahl al-ra'y* camp, whereas the other three Imams (Shafi'i, Malik and Hanbal) stood on the *ahl al-hadith* side.[66]

Scholars in the contemporary era have used the terms "modern" and "traditional"; "conservative" and "moderate"; and "fundamentalist" and "liberal".[67] To some extent, the demarcation between these terms are often blurred. One scholar may agree with a liberal approach in a case (for instance, allowing a woman to become the president), but strongly disagrees with another (for instance, allowing a Muslim woman to marry a non-Muslim man). In other words, they might share common visions, but when it came to the details of the *shari'a* agenda, they took different positions.

However, this fact should not be overstated. I take the view that one should not abandon these terms or classifications and the values they embody simply because they are contested. These categorizations, including the one that I use in this book, are a useful way of highlighting the tensions and competing influences that are central to the process of constitutional reform in Indonesia.[68]

As a summary, here are four main questions addressed in the book:

1. Is *shari'a* compatible with the principles and procedural forms of constitutionalism?
2. How have the Indonesian people linked *shari'a* and the Constitution historically?
3. How does *shari'a* relate to three critical issues of human rights, rule of law, and religion vis-à-vis the state?
4. To what extent did *shari'a* contribute to constitutional reform in Indonesia in 1999–2002?

This book refers to documents (archival data) such as the Amendments of the 1945 Constitution, Indonesian laws and regulations, reports of conferences, meetings or studies, articles in the mass media, papers written by individuals or groups, and other books regarding this issue. Some members of the MPR were interviewed to capture their opinions and feelings regarding specific issues. Through the primary sources and the interviews both the process and the product of constitutional reform will be considered. This book also obtained the benefit of interviews with several political actors, some of which have been published in the mass media.

Although the study analyses the process and the outcome of Indonesian constitutional amendments, it will be limited by giving special focus on provisions of human rights, the rule of law and religion in the Constitution. In this regard, the Constitutions of Egypt and Iran, and the Basic Laws of Saudi Arabia will also be analysed. Scholars' comments on those Constitutions will contribute to the understanding of broad issues of *shari'a* and constitution in the Muslim world.

The book also uses a comparative approach. Although there is a debate as to whether comparative law is a method, a discipline or a science,[69] it can be stated that several scholars have asserted that comparative law is a method of comparison. Schlesinger et al. dedicate the introduction of their casebook to the topic of comparative methods.[70] These authors define comparative law as a "method, a way of looking at legal problems, legal institutions, and entire legal systems, … [which can be used for] a wide variety of practical or scholarly purposes."[71]

I adopt H. Patrick Glenn's approach on comparative law in *Legal Traditions of the World*. In Glenn's work, comparative law goes beyond the legal problem-based approach mentioned above. Glenn goes further by looking at legal traditions. Glenn takes the view that all traditions contain elements of the other traditions, for example, Western legal traditions may contain elements of the Eastern legal traditions. "There are always common elements and common subjects of discussion."[72] Therefore, Glenn rejects the claim that a religious legal tradition is incompatible or incommensurable with a secular legal tradition. However, at the same time, Glenn does not suggest that in all traditions everything is subject to negotiation. He concludes that traditions may absorb foreign elements, as they contain many internal elements of variance or dissidence. Tradition should be defined as information, and information is not dominating.

As a comparison, Alan Watson argues that "political, moral, social and economic values which exist between any two societies make it hard to believe that many legal problems are the same for both except on a technical level." He draws a clear line between a comparison of these factors and more technical legal comparisons when he states: "when the starting point is the problem the weight of investigation will always be primarily on the comparability of the problem, only secondarily on the comparability of the law; and any discipline founded on such a starting point will be sociology rather than law."[73]

In addition, Zweigert and Kötz claim that because explanations of legal systems are often stated in terms internally unique to each system, one must "free" these explanations "from the context of [each] system".[74] Arguably, they support creating an abstract heuristic conceptual framework within which contrasts of chosen variables can be understood.

Glenn's approach differs with that of Alan Watson and Zweigert and Kötz. According to Glenn, comparative legal tradition is also beyond technical things. One does not need to be free from the context of each system. One can compare different versions of law with criteria drawn from themselves, with internal criteria. There is no *tertio comparationis*; it is all internal debate, which is what gives it its sense. Glenn rejects the proposition that "you can't have your cake and eat it too".[75] He offers multivalent views that everything would be a matter of degree. It is possible to compare apples and oranges. In other words, according to Glenn, "you can have your cake and eat it too, if you eat only half of it."[76] Moreover, comparative reasoning allows and facilitates judgement. "Not only is contextual judgment possible, the judgment based on criteria of existing traditions, juxtaposed with other criteria, is the only judgment which can possibly exist."[77]

Glenn explains further:

> Multivalent thinking tells you to keep in mind the sources of conflict, that is, the large, inconsistent principles, the sources of alleged incommensurability, the ideas which people use to (differently) identify themselves. This is not hard to do, since these are the terms by which conflict is usually defined, and the parties to disputes will often want to talk about little else. Multivalent thinking tells you, however, that these opposing principles really only serve to define the field of play. They tell you where to find the middle ground, and there is always a middle ground. To find the middle ground you need more information. You need the detailed information which disintegrates boundaries (it's just like quantum physics).[78]

Multivalent thinking is used in analysing four Constitutions (Indonesia, Egypt, Iran and Saudi Arabia) in three cases (human rights, rule of law, and position of religion in the Constitution). Glenn's legal tradition approach is also used when analysing constitutional law in two different legal systems: Islamic law and Western law. I also use comparative method *within* Islamic legal schools of thoughts (*fiqh muqarin*) since Indonesia, Egypt, Saudi Arabia and Iran follow different schools.

Three sets of data are collected to answer the research questions: classical and modern Arabic Islamic books on *shari'a*, the Constitutions of Indonesia, Egypt, Iran and Saudi Arabia, and the opinions of Indonesian scholars and political parties.

Having examined all research questions, data and evidence, the overall argument of this book is that the formal *shari'a* approach has failed to influence the process of constitutional reform, not only in the issue of religion vis-à-vis the state (Article 29 of the 1945 Constitution), but also in the issue of human rights and the rule of law. *Shari'a* has contributed to constitutional reform in Indonesia (1999–2002) through substantive *shari'a*. Indonesian constitutional reform reflects the ability to deal with a modern Constitution without abandoning the principles and the objectives of *shari'a*. In the Muslim world, this model is important since the Indonesian experience has demonstrated that substantive *shari'a* does provide a basis for constitutionalism.

Thus far the topic "*shari'a* and Constitutional Reform in Indonesia" has been described from a number of viewpoints: the background and the significance of the study, literature review, research questions, and methodology. I will now describe the outline of the book.

The book comprises seven chapters including the introduction and conclusion. This chapter discusses the background, topic, significance, question, method and aim of the study. An analysis on the theoretical background of Islamic constitutional law and its relation to constitutionalism is presented in Chapter 2. It also describes the approaches of substantive *shari'a* and formal *shari'a* and goes further to examine specific aspects of Iranian, Saudi Arabian and Egyptian Constitutions as a comparison to the 1945 Indonesian Constitution.

The third chapter deals with constitutional reform in the Indonesian context. A brief historical background will be given as well as a brief outline of the Indonesian legal systems. In addition, this chapter demonstrates the attempt of the Indonesia people to link *shari'a* and the Indonesian Constitution from historical perspectives (1945, 1955 and 1999–2002). Controversial issues such as the establishment of a constitutional commission, the method used for constitutional reform and the debate on three fundamental elements of choice (direct presidential election versus indirect/representation system; presidentialism versus parliamentarism; and unitary versus federalized government) in both the process and the result of the amendment of the Constitution will also be discussed. This will assist the understanding of the complete picture of the problems and the arguments before moving forward to specific cases or issues.

Chapter 4 provides a critical analysis on constitutional reform in human rights. Islamic legal opinions, the Constitution of three Islamic countries, the Cairo Declaration, the Universal Declaration of Human Rights and the Second Amendment of the 1945 Constitution will be analysed and compared critically.

Chapter 5 analyses the rule of law in the 1945 Constitution. As mentioned earlier, the concept of the rule of law, Negara Hukum, and *rechtstaat* in the 1945 Constitution before and after the amendments are discussed. The aim of Chapter 5 is to discuss the contribution of *shari'a* (if any) in the debate of the accountability of the government, the independence of the judiciary and the executive–legislative relations. The amendments have transformed the Constitution from a vague and incomplete document rooted in anti-democratic political philosophy of organic statism into a more coherent, complete, democratic framework for a pure presidential system with significant separation of powers and checks and balances. The stand of *shari'a* (formal and substantive) on these issues becomes the main discussion in this chapter.

Chapter 6 critically looks at the issue of religion vis-à-vis the state by embarking on an analysis of the theory of state-religion in Islamic law and Western constitutional and political thought. It focuses specifically on the debate over Article 29 of the 1945 Constitution.

Finally, the conclusion presents a summary of the study, the answers to the key questions addressed in Chapter 1, and a reflection of the establishment of *shari'a* in Indonesia. In particular, it considers how the debate, process and outcome of constitutional reform during 1999–2002 might influence the current and future situation. This reflection is necessary to show the relation between the results of the past and the hopes for the future.

Notes

1. For the history of the Jakarta Charter, see Endang Saifuddin Anshari, "The Jakarta Charter of June 1945: A History of the Gentleman's Agreement between the Islamic and the Secular Nationalist in Modern Indonesia" (M.A. thesis, McGill University, Montreal, 1976).

2. See Nies Mulder, *Inside Indonesian Society* (Bangkok: Editions Duang Kamol, 1994), p. 128.

3. See Bilveer Singh, *Habibie and the Democratisation of Indonesia* (Sydney: Book House, 2001); Ahmad Watik Pratiknya, Umar Juoro, Indria Samego et al., *Reform in Indonesia: Vision and Achievements of President Habibie*, Vol. 1 (Jakarta: The Habibie Centre, 1999); Nadirsyah Hosen, "Reform of Indonesian Law in the Post-Soeharto Era (1998–1999)" (Ph.D. thesis, University of Wollongong, 2003).

4. See Edward Masters, "Indonesia's 1999 Elections: A Second Chance for Democracy", available at http://www.asiasociety.org/publications/indonesia/.
5. See Article 7 of the First Amendment of the 1945 Constitution: "The President and the Vice-President hold their office term for five years, and afterwards, can be re-elected for the same position, for only one office term."
6. See Chapter XA, Articles 28A–28J of the Second Amendment of the 1945 Constitution.
7. See the Third and the Fourth Amendments of the 1945 Constitution.
8. Articles 4, 10, 12, 21, 29 and 35 are not changed.
9. See "UUD Bukan Kitab Suci" [The Constitution is not the Holy Book], *Sabili*, No. 23, 16 May 2002.
10. Documents of Kongres Mujahidin (Yogyakarta, 5–7 August 2000) is available at http://www.geocities.com/kongresmujahidin/.
11. See *Tempo Interaktif*, 28 February 2000.
12. *Kompas*, 3 August 2002.
13. "Men who steal and women who steal, cut off the hand of either of them (as) retribution for what they have done and as a torment from Allah. And Allah is Almighty, Most Wise." (Qur'an, 5:38).
14. MPR was constitutionally the highest authority of the state and was charged with meeting every five years to elect the President and Vice-President and to set the broad guidelines of state policy.
15. Muhammad Asad, *The Principles of State and Government in Islam* (Kuala Lumpur: Islamic Book Trust, 1980); Abul A'la al-Maududi, *Political Theory of Islam* (Lahore: Islamic Publications, 1985).
16. Joseph Schacht, *An Introduction to Islamic Law* (Oxford: Clarendon Press, 1998), p. 75. Shaista P. Ali-Karamali and Fiona Dunne, "The Ijtihad Controversy", *Arab Law Quarterly* 9 (1994): 238–57; M. Hobink, *Two Halves of the Same Truth: Schacht, Hallaq, and the Gate of Ijtihad* (Amsterdam: Middle East Research Associates, 1994); Frank E.Vogel, "The Closing of the Door of Ijtihad and the Application of the Law", paper delivered at the American Oriental Society Conference, Cambridge, Massachusetts, 13 March 1992.
17. *Ijtihad* in Islamic law can be defined simply as "interpretation". The main difference between *ijtihad* and both the Qur'an and Sunna is that *ijtihad* is a continuous process of development whereas the Qur'an and Sunna are fixed sources of authority and were not altered or added to after the death of the Prophet. See Mohammad Hashim Kamali, *Principles of Islamic Jurisprudence* (Cambridge: Islamic Text Society, 1991), p. 366.
18. 'Abdurrahman Taj, *al-Siyasa al-Shar'iya wa al-Fiqh al-Islami* (Cairo: Dar al-Ta'rif, 1953); 'Abd al-Wahhab Khallaf, *Al-Siyasa al-Shar'iyya* (Cairo: Salafiyah, 1350 A.H.).
19. The common sources are Abu Hasan al-Mawardi, *al-Ahkam as-Sultaniya* (Cairo: Mustafa Babi al-Halabi wa Auladuh, 1996); Ibn Khaldun, *Muqaddima* (Beirut: Dar al-Fikr, n.d).

20. Chibli Mallat, ed., *Islam and Public Law: Classical and Contemporary Studies* (London: Graham & Trotman, 1993).
21. See Mumtaz Ahmad, ed., *State, Politics and Islam* (Washington: American Trust Publications, 1986); also Mohamed S. El-Awa, *On the Political System of the Islamic State* (Indianapolis: American Trust Publications, 1980); P.J. Vatikiotis, *Islam and the State* (London: Routledge, 1991); Olivier Roy, *The Failure of Political Islam* (Cambridge: Harvard University Press,1996); Asghar Ali Engineer, *Theory and Practise of the Islamic State* (Lahore: Vanguard Books, 1985); Nathan J. Brown, *Constitutions in a Non-Constitutional World: Arab Basic Laws and the Prospects for Accountable Government* (Albany, NY : State University of New York Press, 2002); Andrew Harding, "The Keris, the Crescent and the Blind Goddess: The State, Islam and the Constitution in Malaysia", *Singapore Journal of International and Comparative Law* 6 (2002): 154.
22. Eugene Cotran and Adel Omar Sherif, eds., *Democracy, the Rule of Law and Islam* (London: Kluwer Law International, 1999); L. Carl Brown, *Religion and State: The Muslim Approach to Politics* (New York: Columbia University Press, 2000); Anthony Shadid, *Legacy of the Prophet: Despots, Democrats, and the New Politics of Islam* (Boulder, CO: Westview Press, 2002); John L Esposito and Azzam Tamimi, eds., *Islam and Secularism in the Middle East* (New York: New York University Press, 2000); Abdulaziz Sachedina, *The Islamic Roots of Democratic Pluralism* (New York: Oxford University Press, 2001).
23. Ahmad Sayfi'i Ma'arif, *Islam dan Masalah Kenegaraan: Studi tentang Percaturan dalam Konstituante* (Jakarta: Lembaga Penelitian Pendidikan dan Penerangan Ekonomi dan Sosial, 1985) (this work is based on his Ph.D. thesis at the University of Chicago); Adnan Buyung Nasution, *The Aspiration for Constitutional Goverment in Indonesia: A socio-legal study of the Indonesian Konstituante 1956–1959* (Jakarta: Pustaka Sinar Harapan, 1992).
24. Anshari, "The Jakarta Charter".
25. Munawir Syadzali, *Islam and Governmental System: Teachings, History, and Reflections* (Jakarta: INIS, 1991). Syadzali served as Minister for Religious Affairs (1988–97) under the Soeharto government.
26. Full text of the Medina Charter can be found in http://islamic-world.net/islamic-state/macharter.htm.
27. Ahmad Sukardja, *Piagam Madinah dan Undang-Undang Dasar 1945: Kajian Perbandingan tentang Dasar Hidup Bersama dalam Masyarakat yang Majemuk* (Jakarta: UI-Press, 1995). Currently, Sukardja is a Professor of *fiqh siyasah* at the State University of Islamic Studies, Syarif Hidayatullah, Jakarta and has recently been appointed as Judge at Supreme Court (Mahkamah Agung).
28. Masykuri Abdillah, *Responses of Indonesian Muslim Intellectuals to the Concept of Democracy* (1966–1993) (Hamburg: Abera Verl, 1997).
29. Suzaina Abdul Kadir, "Traditional Islamic Society and the State in Indonesia: The Nahdlatul Ulama, Political Accommodation and the Preservation of Autonomy" (Ph.D. dissertation, University of Wisconsin-Madison, 1999).

30. Gary F. Bell, "Obstacles to Reform the 1945 Constitution: Constitutions Do Not Perform Miracles", *Van Zorge Report on Indonesia — Commentary and Analysis on Indonesian Politics and Economics* III, no. 6 (2001): 4–13.
31. Blair A. King, "Empowering the Presidency: Interests and perceptions in Indonesia's constitutional reforms, 1999–2002" (Ph.D. thesis, Ohio State University, 2004). See also Priyambudi Sulistiyanto, "The 2004 General Elections in Indonesia and the Virtues of Indonesian Presidentialism", *Kasarinlan: Philippine Journal of Third World Studies* 19, no. 2 (2004): 4–24.
32. Bivitri Susanti, "Constitution and Human Rights Provisions in Indonesia: An Unfinished Task in the Transitional Process", in *Constitutions and Human Rights in a Global Age: An Asia-Pacific Perspective*, edited by Tessa Morris-Suzuki (Canberra: Australian National University, 2003), pp. 5–14.
33. Gary F. Bell, "Minority Rights and Regionalism in Indonesia: Will Constitutional Recognition Lead to Disintegration and Discrimination?", *Singapore Journal of International and Comparative Law* 5 (2001): 784.
34. Tim Lindsey, "Indonesian Constitutional Reform: Mud Towards Democracy", *Singapore Journal of International and Comparative Law* 6 (2002): 244–301; Tim Lindsey, "Indonesia: Devaluing Asian Values, Rewriting Rule of Law", in *Asian Discourses of Rule of Law*, edited by Randall Peerenboom (London: RoutledgeCurzon, 2004).
35. Todung Mulya Lubis, "Constitutional Reforms", in *Governance in Indonesia: Challenges Facing the Megawati Presidency*, edited by Hadi Soesastro (Singapore: Institute of Southeast Asian Studies, 2003).
36. For a full account, see, for instance, Harun Alrasid, *Naskah UUD 1945 Sesudah Tiga Kali Diubah oleh MPR* (Jakarta: UI Press, 2002); Didit Hariadi Estiko, ed., *Amandemen UUD 1945 dan Implikasinya terhadap Pembangunan Sistem Hukum Nasional* (Jakarta: Tim Hukum Pusat Pengkajian dan Pelayanan Informasi Sekretariat Jenderal DPR-RI, 2001); Suwarno Adiwijoyo, *Amandemen UUD 1945* (Jakarta: Intermasa, 2000); Habibie Centre, *Naskah Akademis dan Draf Rancangan Naskah Undang-Undang Dasar Republik Indonesia* (Jakarta: Habibie Centre, 2001); Anhar Gonggong, *Amandemen Konstitusi, Otonomi Daerah dan Federalisme: Solusi untuk Masa Depan* (Yogyakarta: Media Presindo, 2001); Hendarmin Ramadireksa, *Visi Politik Amandemen UUD 1945 Menuju Konstitusi yang Berkedaulatan Rakyat* (Jakarta: Yayasan Pancur Siwah, 2002).
37. Jimly Asshiddiqie, "Telaah Akademis atas Perubahan UUD 1945", *Jurnal Demokrasi & HAM* 1, no. 4 (2001): 17.
38. Slamet Effendy Yusuf and Umar Basalim, *Reformasi Konstitusi Indonesia: Perubahan Pertama UUD 1945* (Jakarta: Pustaka Indonesia Satu, 2000).
39. Umar Basalim, *Pro-Kontra Piagam Jakarta di Era Reformasi* (Jakarta: Pustaka Indonesia Satu, 2002).
40. Nathan J. Brown, "Islamic Constitutionalism in Theory and Practice", in *Democracy*, edited by Cotran and Sherif, p. 492.
41. See, for example, Kevin Boyle and Adel Omar Sherif, eds., *Human Rights and*

Democracy: The Role of the Supreme Constitutional Court of Egypt (London: Kluwer Law International, 1996).

42. Adel Omar Sherif, "Separation of Powers and Judicial Independence in Constitutional Democracies: The Egyptian and American Experiences", in *Human Rights and Democracy*, edited by Boyle and Sherif, pp. 25–44. It is interesting to note that others may disagree with Sherif's views. According to a Freedom House report, the Egyptian government has increased its suppression of domestic opposition and "many worry that the Egyptian government's antidemocratic behavior, concessions to Islam, and failure to address poverty work to promote Islamic fundamentalism". See http://www.freedomhouse.org/research/ freeworld/ 2002/countryratings/egypt.htm.

43. More information on Saudi Arabia can be found in Frank Edward Vogel, "Islamic Law and Legal System Studies of Saudi Arabia" (Ph.D. dissertation, Harvard University, 1993).

44. See James T. McHugh, *Comparative Constitutional Traditions* (New York: Peter Lang, 2002), pp. 193–211.

45. More information can be found in Asghar Schirazi, *The Constitution of Iran: Politics and the State in the Islamic Republic* (London: I. B. Tauris, 1997).

46. See Abdulaziz Abdulhussein Sachedina, *The Just Ruler (al-Sultan al-Adil) in Shiite Islam: The Comprehensive Authority of the Jurist in Imamite Jurisprudence* (New York: Oxford University Press, 1988).

47. For basic information regarding theology in Islam, it is recommended to read W. Montgomery Watt, *The Formative Period of Islamic Thought* (U.K.: Edinburgh University, 1973); Ignaz Goldziher, *Introduction to Islamic Theology and Law* (New York: Princeton University Press, 1981); and Hasan Qasim Murad, *"Jabr* and *Qadr* in Early Islam: A Reappraisal of their Political and Religious Implications", in *Islamic Studies Presented to Charles J. Adams*, edited by Wael Hallaq and Donald P. Little (Leiden: Brill, 1991), pp. 117–32.

48. As an introduction, see George Makdisi, "Ash'ari and the Ash'arites in Islamic Religious History", *Studia Islamica* XVII and XVIII (1962 & 1963).

49. The Hanafi school is well represented in Iraq, Egypt and Syria. It had earlier spread to Afghanistan and Turkish central Asia. The Maliki school spread westwards from its first centre, Medina, over practically the whole of North Africa and over Central and West Africa as far as it is Muslim. The Shafi'i school is followed by Muslims in Indonesia, Malaya and the rest of Southeast Asia, whereas the Hanbali school is followed by Muslims in Saudi Arabia and Qatar. More information on schools of Islamic law can be found in Muhammad Salam Madkur, *Manahij al-Ijtihad fi al-Islam* (Kuwait: al-Matba'ah al-'Ashriyah al-Kuwait, 1974); Mohammad Hashim Kamali, *Principles of Islamic Jurisprudence* (Cambridge: Islamic Text Society, 1991); Noel.J. Coulson, *A History of Islamic Law* (U.K.: Edinburgh University Press, 1964); Taha Jabir al-Alwani, *Source of Methodology in Islamic Jurisprudence* (Virginia: International Institute of Islamic Thought, 1993).

50. See Ann Elizabeth Mayer, *Islam and Human Rights: Tradition and Politics* (Boulder: Westview Press, 1991).

51. U.S. Department of State, "Indonesia: Country Reports on Human Rights Practices — 2000", released by the Bureau of Democracy, Human Rights, and Labor, 23 February 2001.

52. Information on the origins of the rule of law can be obtained from F. A. Hayek, *The Rule of Law* (California: Institute for Humane Studies, 1975); See also Robert S. Summers, "A Formal Theory of the Rule of Law", *Ratio Juris* 6, no. 2 (1993): 127–42.

53. See A. V. Dicey, *Introduction to the Study of the Law of the Constitution* (London: Macmillan, 1959).

54. For more information, see Judith N. Shklar, "Political Theory and the Rule of Law", in *The Rule of Law: Ideal or Ideology*, edited by Allan C. Hutchinson and Patrick Monahan (Vancouver: Carswell, 1987), pp. 2–16.

55. Lindsey, "Indonesia: Devaluing Asian Values", p. 299.

56. Other views can be read in Herbert Feith and Lance Castles, eds., *Indonesian Political Thinking (1945–1965)* (Ithaca: Cornell University Press, 1970); Nasution, *Aspiration for Constitutional Government*; and Daniel S. Lev, *Legal Evolution and Political Authority in Indonesia: Selected Essays* (Boston: Kluwer Law International, 2000).

57. Sunaryati Hartono, *Apakah Rule of Law Itu?* (Bandung: Alumni, 1982), Chapter 5; Oemar Seno Adji, *Peradilan Bebas Negara Hukum* (Jakarta: Erlangga, 1980), pp. 24–58; and Oemar Seno Adji, "An Indonesian Perspective on the American Constitutional Influence", in *Constitutionalism in Asia: Asian Views of the American Influence*, edited by Lawrence Ward Beer (Berkeley: University of California Press, 1979), pp. 102–10. His view is supported by Tahir Azhary, *Negara Hukum* (Jakarta: Bulan Bintang, 1992), p. 99; Padmo Wahyono, "Konsep Yuridis Negara Hukum Indonesia", unpublished paper, September 1988; see also Padmo Wahyono, *Guru Pinandita: Sumbangsih untuk Prof. Djokosoetono, SH* (Jakarta: Lembaga Penerbit Fakultas Ekonomi Universitas Indonesia, 1984); Ismail Suny, *Mekanisme Demokrasi Pancasila* (Jakarta: Aksara Baru, 1978), pp. 10–12; Hartono Mardjono, *Negara Hukum yang Demokratis* (Jakarta: Yayasan Koridor Pengabdian, 2001), p. 139.

58. See Gottfried Dietze, *Two Concepts of the Rule of Law* (Indianapolis: Liberty Fund, 1973).

59. Stern distinguishes the following elements of the *rechtstaat* principles: The constitutional state, liberty and equality, the separation and control of government authority, legality, judicial protection, a system of reparation and a prohibition of excessive use of government authority. See Francois Venter, *Constitutional Comparison: Japan, Germany, Canada and South Africa as Constitutional States* (Cape Town: Juta & Co., 2000), p. 49.

60. Ira Lapidus, "State and Religion in Islamic Societies", *Past and Present* 151 (1996): 3.

61. See Asghar Ali Engineer, *The Islamic State* (New York: Advent Books, 1980), pp. 1–2.

62. For more information about Religious/Islamic Courts in Indonesia, see Daniel S. Lev, *Islamic Courts in Indonesia: A Study in the Political Bases of Legal Institutions* (Berkeley: University of California Press, 1972); M. Cammack, "Islamic Law in Indonesia's New Order", *International and Comparative Law Quarterly* 38 (1989); also Nur Ahmad Fadhil Lubis, "Institutionalization and the Unification of Islamic Courts Under the New Order", *Studia Islamika* 2, no. 1 (1995): 1–52; M.B. Hooker, *Islamic Law in South-East Asia* (Singapore: Oxford University Press, 1984), p. 258; Busthanul Arifin, *Pelembagaan Hukum Islam di Indonesia* (Jakarta: Gema Insani Press, 1996); Moh. Mahfud MD, Sidik Tono and Dadan Muttaqien, eds., *Peradilan Agama dan Kompilasi Hukum Islam dalam Tata Hukum Indonesia* (Yogyakarta: UII Press, 1993); Ibnu Qayim Isma'il, *Kiai Penghulu Jawa Peranannya di Masa Kolonial* (Jakarta: Gema Insani Press, 1997); Karel A. Steenbrink, *Beberapa Aspek tentang Islam di Indonesia Abad ke-19* (Jakarta: Bulan Bintang, 1984), pp. 211–33.

63. Charles Kurzman, "Liberal Islam: Prospects and Challenges", *Journal Middle East Review of International Affairs* 3, no. 3 (September 1999), available at http://www.biu.ac.il/SOC/besa/meria/journal/1999/issue3/jv3n3a2.html. This paper draws and expands on his book *Liberal Islam: A Source-Book* (New York: Oxford University Press, 1988).

64. Taha Jabir al-Alwani, *The Ethics of Disagreement in Islam* (Herndon, Virginia: The International Institute of Islamic Thought, n.d.), available at http://www.usc.edu/dept/MSA/ humanrelations/alalwani_disagreement/chapter3.html.

65. Ibid.

66. See Taha Jabir al-Alwani, *Usul Al Fiqh Al Islami: Source Methodology In Islamic Jurisprudence* (Herndon, Virginia: International Institute of Islamic Thought, 1990), available at http://www.usc.edu/dept/MSA/law/alalwani_usulalfiqh/ch3.html; Muhammad bin al-Hasan al-Hajawi al-Sa'alibi al-Fasi, *al-Fikr al-Sami fi Tarikh al-Fiqh al-Islami* (Medina: al-Maktabah al-'Ilmiyah, 1396 H); Muhammad Salam Madkur, *Manahij al-Ijtihad fi al-Islam* (Kuwait: al-Matba'ah al-'Ashriyah al-Kuwait, 1974); Muhammad Yusuf Musa, *Tarikh al-Fiqh al-Islami* (Cairo: Dar al-Ma'rifah, n.d).

67. For a full account, see Deliar Noer, *The Modernist Muslim Movement in Indonesia 1900–1942* (Singapore: Oxford University Press, 1973); Ira M. Lapidus, *A History of Islamic Societies* (Cambridge: Cambridge University Press, 1993), pp. 765–67; Nurcholish Madjid, "The Issue of Modernization among Muslims in Indonesia: From a Participant Point of View", in *Readings on Islam in Southeast Asia*, edited by Ahmad Ibrahim, Sharon Siddique and Yasmin Hussain (Singapore: Institute of Southeast Asian Studies, 1985); Saiful Muzani, "Mu'tazila Theology and the Modernization of the Indonesian Muslim Community: Intellectual Portrait of Harun Nasution", *Studia Islamika* 1 (1994); Fazlur Rahman, *Islam and Modernity: Transformation of an Intellectual Tradition* (Chicago: University

of Chicago Press, 1982); Abdullah Saeed, "Ijtihad and Innovation in Neo-Modernist Islamic Thought in Indonesia", *Islam and Christian-Muslim Relations* 8, no. 3 (1997); Greg Barton, "Indonesia's Nurcholish Madjid and Abdurrahman Wahid as intellectual ulama: The meeting of Islamic traditionalism and Modernism in neo-Modernist thought", *Islam and Christian-Muslim Relations* 8, no. 3 (1997); Greg Barton, "Neo-Modernism: A Vital Synthesis of Traditionalism and Modernism in Indonesian Islam", *Studia Islamika* 2, no. 3 (1995): 1–75.

68. In this context, Peter Beyer has examined the terms *religious function* and *religious performance*. According to Beyer, religious function refers to "pure" religious action: the cure for souls, the search for enlightenment or salvation and so on. Religious performance is the strategy that uses religion to solve social, political or economical problems and not religious in the sense of "personal piety". According to Beyer there are two versions of religious performance — "liberal" and "conservative". Representatives of "liberal" performance are advocates of ecumenism, inclusivism and tolerance towards plurality regarding religious function, and respecting the individual choice. They also view religion as a moral or ethical guideline able to solve social problems. Advocates for the "conservative" version accentuate the need of putting holism above pluralism and exclusion above inclusion. They stress the authority of one specific religious tradition over all other spheres of society. They also demand that religious norm should be enforced by law. See Peter Beyer, *Religion and Globalization* (London: Sage Publication Ltd, 1994), pp. 70–71, 79–93.

69. See, for example, Venter, *Constitutional Comparison*, pp. 15–19.

70. See Rudolf B. Schlesinger et al., *Comparative Law: Cases, Text, Materials*, 6th ed. (Mineola, NY: Foundation Press, 1998), pp. 1–43.

71. Ibid., p. 2.

72. H. Patrick Glenn, *Legal Traditions of the World* (New York: Oxford University Press, 2000), p. 35.

73. See Alan Watson, *Legal Transplant: An Approach to Comparative Law*, 2nd ed. (Athens, GA: 1993), pp. 4–5. Pierre Legrand criticizes this book in "The Impossibility of Legal Transplants", *Maastricht Journal of European and Comparative Law* 4 (1997).

74. See K. Zweigert and H. Kötz, *An Introduction to Comparative Law*, 3rd ed. (Oxford: Clarendon Press, 1998), p. 36.

75. Glenn, *Legal Traditions*, p. 325.

76. H. Patrick Glenn, "The Capture, Reconstruction and Marginalization of 'Custom' ", *American Journal of Comparative Law* 45 (1997): 613.

77. Glenn, *Legal Traditions*, p. 44.

78. Ibid., p. 334.

2

SHARI'A AND CONSTITUTIONALISM

Constitutionalism in the West is mostly identified with secular thought.[1] In recent years, there has been a growing interest in Islamic constitutionalism. For instance, the Bush administration's response to the 11 September 2001 attacks on New York and Washington has radically transformed the situation in Iraq and Afghanistan as both countries are rewriting their Constitutions.[2] Ann Elizabeth Mayer has pointed out that Islamic constitutionalism is "constitutionalism which is in some form based on Islamic principles".[3]

Several Muslim scholars such as Muhammad Asad and Abul A'la al-Maududi[4] have written on several aspects of constitutional issues such as human rights and the separation of powers. However, in general their works fall into apologetics, as Chibli Mallat points out:

> Whether for the classical age or for the contemporary Muslim world, scholarly research on public law must respect a set of axiomatic requirements. First, the perusal of the tradition cannot be construed as a mere retrospective reading. By simply projecting present-day concepts backwards, it is all too easy to force the present into the past either in an apologetically contrived or haughtily dismissive manner. The approach is apologetic and contrived when Bills of Rights are read into, say, the Caliphate of 'Umar, with the presupposition that the 'just' qualities of 'Umar included the complex and articulate precepts of constitutional balance one finds in modern texts.[5]

Going further back in history, the fall of the Ottoman Empire also contributes to the lack of Islamic constitutional thought since the empire was the last caliph state. It is also worth considering that books on political law (*fiqh siyasa*) written in the twentieth century, such as those by 'Abdurrahman Taj, and Ahmad Syalabi,[6] refer to the idea and the practice of the Islamic state more than a thousand years ago.[7] This suggests that their works are simply repetitions of opinions from *fiqh* books written several centuries ago without making modification through *ijtihad* (reinterpretation) and without trying to link the revelation, which was sent down fifteen centuries ago, to modern problems in a nation-state. In other words, what Islamic constitutionalism entails remains contested among Muslims and also Western scholars who study the topics.[8]

Constitutional law can be defined simply as law that regulates the government of a state. It is concerned with the struggle between rival contenders for power and the question of the limits to be imposed on the government. In a minimalist sense of the term, a constitution consists of a set of rules or norms creating, structuring and defining the limits of governmental power or authority. In this sense, all states that have constitutions are constitutional states. However, it should be noted that having a constitution — written or unwritten — does not necessarily mean that a state follows constitutionalism.

Louis Henkin defines constitutionalism as constituted of the following elements: (1) government according to the constitution; (2) separation of power; (3) sovereignty of the people and democratic government; (4) constitutional review; (5) independent judiciary; (6) limited government subject to a bill of individual rights; (7) controlling the police; (8) civilian control of the military; and (9) no state power, or very limited and strictly circumscribed state power, to suspend the operation of some parts of, or the entire, constitution.[9]

In other words, constitutionalism has evolved to mean the legal limitations placed upon the rightful power of government in its relation to citizens. It includes the doctrine of official accountability to the people or to its legitimate representatives within the framework of fundamental law for better securing the citizens' rights.[10] The philosophy behind the doctrine is that the people are the best judges about what is and what is not in their own interest.[11] Therefore, a constitution which has the spirit of constitutionalism must, at least, limit the power of the state; guarantee and protect the rights of the citizenry; and regulate the process and procedural paths of authority and accountability.

The main question in this chapter is: "Is *shari'a* compatible with the principle and procedural form of constitutionalism?". This chapter answers this question by looking at the arguments put forth by the opponents of Islamic constitutional law and the counter-arguments. One group takes the view that not only is *shari'a* sufficient to meet Muslims' needs, and therefore Muslims do not need constitutionalism, but also that *shari'a* as God's law is above the Constitution. *Shari'a* has already provided a unique system of government or politics. Another group believes that Islam (including *shari'a*) has no relationship with state affairs. According to this group, the Constitution should not be used to enforce *shari'a*.

Although both groups have different arguments, they share the same conclusion that the nature of *shari'a* does not permit them to acknowledge the compatibility of *shari'a* with constitutionalism. This chapter offers a different position on this issue. It argues that *shari'a* is neither above nor outside the Constitution. Instead, the principles of *shari'a* and constitutionalism can co-exist, but reinterpretation of *shari'a* is needed to articulate the procedural and institutional mechanisms of Islamic constitutional law, particularly to draw a clear line of authority and accountability.

AUTHORITARIANISM AND SECULARISM

This section discusses the arguments against the compatibility of *shari'a* with constitutionalism. The first four arguments are pointed out by fundamentalist groups, while the rest are provided by secularist groups. Although each group has its own reasons, they take the similar view that *shari'a* is not compatible with constitutionalism.

THE ARGUMENTS OF THE FUNDAMENTALISTS

Firstly, there is the view that Islamic law is immutable because the authoritarian, divine and absolute concept of law in Islam does not allow change in legal concepts and institutions. *Shari'a* is immutable, regardless of history, time, culture, and location. Muslims may change but Islam will not change. This means that the rulings pronounced by *shari'a* are static, final, eternal, absolute and unalterable. In other words, its idealistic and religious nature, its rigidity and its casuistic nature lead to the immutability of *shari'a*.[12] This position is not compatible with the nature of a constitution, which can be amended, modified, reformed or even replaced by a new one.

Secondly, *shari'a* is based on the revelation of God. The source of Islamic law is the will of God, which is absolute and unchangeable. There has always been a close connection between Islamic law and theology. This means that the laws that do exist must operate within the boundaries set by *shari'a*. In other words, real power is in the hand of Allah.[13] This condition contradicts the nature of constitutionalism, which is based on the will of man. Under *shari'a*, sovereignty belongs to God, not to man.[14] This means that the government must act according to *shari'a*. It is argued that even though a legislative measure has been supported by a majority, it does not necessarily imply that it is a "right" measure. It is always possible that the majority, however large and well intentioned, might be mistaken, while the minority might be right. What is right and what is wrong should be based on *shari'a*, not on the popular vote.[15]

Thirdly, constitutionalism is not drawn originally from Islam. It is a Western product and is part of hegemony. The tension between the church and the state in Western tradition is evident in most European constitutional traditions and also in the constitutions of colonial states such as the United States and Australia.[16] It is argued that adopting constitutionalism, which is outside of Islamic discourse, will lead Muslims to separate Islam from politics, thus abandoning their religion. Moreover, in Islam democracy and the rule of law are concepts introduced by Western traditions. In *shari'a*, there is no distinction and separation between religion and state. Islam is a religion and at the same time a state (*din wa dawla*).[17] Politics of the state is a part of Islamic teachings since Islam is a religion as much as it is a legal system.

Secularization, or the separation of religion and politics, is seen as the product of Western colonialism.[18] During the colonial era, the concept of secularization was introduced into Muslim societies in order to maintain Western power. With the separation of religion and politics, *jihad* becomes meaningless. The word and the idea of secularization become pejorative terms. Any Muslim scholar who supports this concept would allegedly be seen as a supporter of Western hegemony, since constitutionalism is the product of this Western idea.[19]

Fourthly, it is argued that, based on the Qur'an (5:3),[20] *shari'a* is perfect and covers broad topics such as ritual, social interaction, criminal law, and political law. Every single problem can be answered by *shari'a*. It was designed for all times and places and for universal application to all peoples. It is comprehensive and encompasses all aspects of law — personal, societal, governmental, constitutional, criminal, mercantile, war and peace, and international treaties. Hence, Islam is an ideology addressing all of life's affairs.[21] Meanwhile, constitutionalism will not (and cannot) provide answers for all the problems of humankind.

The arguments above are supported by the fundamentalist groups. These groups take the view that *shari'a* is not compatible with constitutionalism in the modern, legal and secular sense. Instead, the Qur'an and Hadith should be used as the Islamic constitution.

Saudi Arabia

Saudi Arabia adopts a fundamentalist position. The Qur'an and the Sunna became the Constitution, and *shari'a* is the basic law, implemented by the *shari'a* courts with *ulama* as judges and legal advisors. The head of state is the king, who is elected by and is a member of the Saudi family. The King, assisted by a council of ministers, supervises legislative and executive institutions, and the judiciary. It has no House of Representatives whose members are elected by the people, and also no political parties.[22]

It is worth noting that demands for reform initiatives led the Saudi rulers to promulgate their 1992 Basic Law, which has been loosely referred to as a kind of constitution, even though it carefully avoids calling itself one. Having discussed the Basic Law, Mayer comments that "the Basic Law does not set down constitutional limitations on government or establish a genuine system of separation of powers and protection for the rights of citizens."[23]

The evidence comes from Article 1 which states: "The Kingdom of Saudi Arabia is a sovereign Arab Islamic state with Islam as its religion. The Holy Qur'an and the Prophet's Sunna are its constitution. Its language is Arabic, and its capital Riyadh." Article 44 further stipulates: "The authorities of the state consist of the following: the judicial authority; the executive authority; the regulatory authority. These authorities co-operate in the performance of their duties, in accordance with this and other laws. The King shall be the point of reference for all these authorities."

The national Consultative Council, known as *majlis al-shura*, was established pursuant to Article 68. All the council members are appointed by the King and have powers to give advice to the government on issues of public interest. Through Article 46 the Constitution recognizes the judicial authority as "an independent organ and nobody has authority over the judges except the authority of the Islamic *shari'a*". Article 8 offers a different picture of the basis of the Saudi state, providing: "Government in the Kingdom of Saudi Arabia is based on the premise of justice, consultation, and equality, in accordance with the Islamic *Shari'a*."

THE ARGUMENTS OF THE SECULARISTS

At the other end of the spectrum, the secular group rejects the constitutionalization of *shari'a*. According to this group, in Islamic history, *shari'a* was never the constitution of the traditional Islamic caliphate, which was in fact an "absolute monarchy". It is not possible to enforce *shari'a* in a constitutional way, since *shari'a* and constitutionalism contradict each other.

Shari'a is not compatible with constitutionalism since *shari'a* is a matter for individual compliance. States do not have the right to intervene nor to enforce *shari'a* law on the public. One may observe that Islamic law began with the activities of jurists owing to religious motives, it was not created by state legislation. This results in the jurists' conviction of the independence of Islamic law from state control. States could encourage their citizens to comply with *shari'a* (for example, the payment of zakat, fasting, making the pilgrimage to Mecca), but the state cannot force its people to comply. Unlike the authoritarians' view, this group believe in the secular state and, therefore say *shari'a* cannot (and should not) take the place of the Constitution. They introduce the idea of de-politicizing Islam, and determine it solely as a religious faith, as once articulated by the Islamic scholar 'Ali 'Abd al-Raziq.[24]

Shari'a was sent down fifteen centuries ago, and it is fit only for the conditional, political and institutional conditions of that time. *Shari'a* could be operated only in a traditional state (or city-state) which is based on a personal charisma of the leader; not based on the constitutional system. Fifteen centuries ago, there was no parliament, no check-and-balance system, no judicial review, no good governance, and no separation of powers. The implementation of *shari'a* is, therefore, in contradiction with modern institutions and concepts. Moreover, constitutions cannot be viable documents in the absence of the ideological, cultural and political prerequisites for constitutional life. How can constitutionalism emerge in societies in which liberalism and secularism is so far from hegemonic?

If constitutionalism is defined as a set of ideologies and institutions, predicated on the idea of the limitation and regulation of government authority by law, according to this view, *shari'a* does not limit the power of governments. In the Islamic tradition, the Caliph could do anything he wanted without the fear of facing the opposition party or even impeachment procedures. The power of the Caliph was unlimited. The implementation of *shari'a* would lead to an undemocratic state. In the words of Bassam Tibi, "none of them was a legal ruler in the modern constitutional sense".[25] One of the reasons was that there existed no institutional authority able to control the Caliph's compliance with *shari'a*.

Historically, the decision of the Caliph would be based heavily on his discretion, or his political interest or his interpretations of *shari'a*, not on the rule of law. Discretion can be inimical to efficiency, stability and transparency. Discretion is prone to ad hoc decision-making. In that case, it does not lend itself to long-term planning and certainty. It is in such circumstances that it runs counter to the doctrine of rule of law. Besides, it can confer too much power that could corrupt and be abused. Factors other than transparent scientific considerations could infect the decision-making process.

Another argument is discrimination among people if *shari'a* is enforced through a constitution. According to Islamic history, the world was split into two divisions: the territory of Islam (*dar al-Islam*), comprising Islamic and non-Islamic communities which accepted Islamic sovereignty, and the rest of the world, called the *dar al-harb* or the territory of war.[26] Muslims enjoyed full rights of citizenship while others enjoyed only partial civil rights. For instance, a non-Muslim could not be appointed as a caliph or a president. The fear of non-Muslims on their status under *shari'a* can be understood by looking at the concept of *dhimmi*, which does not give non-Muslims the governing rights, and while guaranteeing them security of life and property, does not permit them to become an integral part of the ruling class.[27] The treatment of non-Muslims under the concept of *dhimmi* will violate religious freedom under international human rights instruments.

This means that there would be no equality before the law, should *shari'a* be implemented. In other words, *shari'a* does not guarantee and protect the rights of minority groups. The problem of equality in Islamic society is centred around, as pointed out by Esposito and Piscatori, "unequal status between Muslims and non-Muslims as well as between men and women".[28] For instance, in civil matters the testimony of Muslim women is accepted, but it takes two women to make a single witness. A Muslim male is always a fully competent witness under *shari'a*.[29] This discrimination should be seen as being against the spirit of constitutionalism. Accordingly, these examples provide evidence that *shari'a* should not be put into a constitution.

Turkey

The best model of secular state in the Muslim world is Turkey. The republic that Kemal Ataturk founded and subsequent leaders have shaped is radically different from the imperial society of the Islamic Ottoman Empire. The fifth constitution was established in 1982 by the last military regime after its seized power in 1980. The 1995 amendments abolish about twenty articles and the preamble, which stated the people's will to accept military rule. Civil servants are allowed to engage in collective bargaining and unions may take part in politics.[30]

Turkey is a parliamentary democracy. Although the population is 99 per cent Muslim, the Turkish constitution establishes the Republic of

Turkey as a democratic, secular and social state, governed by the rule of law and respecting fundamental human rights and freedoms.[31] Legislative power is vested in the 550-member Turkish Grand National Assembly (TBMM), whose members are elected to five-year terms by the votes of Turkish citizens over the age of 18.[32] Internationally recognized human rights are protected but can be limited in times of emergency and cannot be used to violate the integrity of the state or to impose a non-secular or non-democratic system of government. Turkish women gained the right to vote in 1934, well ahead of women in many other European countries. Many Turkish women do not wear chadors, burkas, or any of the head-to-toe coverings.

According to the Constitution, the president and the prime minister divide the functions and executive power of government in a way similar to the system of government in France. The Turkish president is the country's head of state, but he also has important governmental powers. He is commander-in-chief of the armed forces. He signs bills passed by the Grand National Assembly or may return them for reconsideration. He may call a referendum on certain issues relating to the Constitution. He decides who among the members of the Grand National Assembly should have the right to seek to form a government as prime minister. The president is elected by the Grand National Assembly for one term of seven years.[33]

The prime minister appoints the members of the Council of Ministers. The prime minister and the Council of Ministers share executive power, taking care of such matters as foreign policy, defence, public works, internal revenue, customs, health, education, and welfare. As in most European democracies, the prime minister is the head of the majority party in Parliament.

According to the Constitution, the judiciary is independent and includes a system of lower courts, the national Court of Appeals and the Constitutional Court. The Constitutional Court has the task of ensuring the compatibility of laws and administrative acts with the constitution. It may also act as Supreme Court in hearing cases against high public officials. The first woman judge was appointed to the Turkish Constitutional Court in 1932. The Council of State is the highest administrative court.

Turkish law is codified based on various European systems: civil and commercial law originally based on the Swiss system, administrative law on the French system, and criminal law on the Italian system. Turkey today is a secular state.[34] Turkey has mosques, churches, and synagogues open to all, and politicians are forbidden to exploit religion for political purposes.

COUNTER ARGUMENTS: FORMAL AND SUBSTANTIVE *SHARI'A*

As can be seen from the discussion above, both authoritarian and secularist groups believe that *shari'a* is not compatible with constitutionalism. Although both have similar views, they have different arguments in support of these views. While the authoritarians believe that *shari'a* is better than constitutionalism, the secularists take the position that *shari'a* is part of a religious faith and not a system of government. It seems that both groups put different interpretations on the word and the meaning of *shari'a*. Therefore, the notions of *shari'a* and its relationship with the idea of constitutionalism will be examined critically.

At the outset of this book, I mentioned Kurzman's thought on three main tropes of *shari'a*: the liberal *shari'a*, the silent *shari'a*, and the interpreted *shari'a*.[35] Despite their different opinions, these tropes of *shari'a* can simply be classified as *substantive shari'a*. It holds that *shari'a* should be reinterpreted in the line of democracy and constitutionalism. Using this substantive *shari'a* approach, I would take the position that no inherent contradiction exists between the principles of *shari'a* and constitutionalism.

In this context, I have mentioned another type of *shari'a's* thought in contrast to substantive *shari'a*: *formal shari'a*. The formal *shari'a* approach holds the view that *shari'a* is also compatible with constitutionalism. However, unlike the substantive approach, it takes the view that all constitutional issues should be based on *shari'a* practised by the Prophet and the companions in Medina fifteen centuries ago. It refers to the textual meaning of the Qur'an, the tradition of the Prophet and even the Medina Charter. While the fundamentalist group believes that *shari'a* is above the constitution and, therefore, it is incompatible with constitutionalism, the formal *shari'a* group takes the view that *shari'a* can have a place in a constitution and become the source of such constitution.

Egypt

Egypt is an interesting model of how a country put *shari'a* provisions in its constitution through amendment of its constitution.[36] From the Arab Republic of Egypt's Constitution of 1980, it can be said that Egypt is a democratic socialist state in which Islam is the state religion. *Shari'a* has been made the main source of law. However, sovereignty belongs to the people, and the people are the source of the state's power. Egypt follows a multi-party system. All citizens have equal legal status. They have equal rights and responsibilities, without distinction on race, heredity, language, religion or belief. According to the Constitution, the state assures freedom of expression, and of establishing or joining associations or political parties. On the requirements for those elected as Head of State, aspirants for the presidency shall be citizens of Egypt, progeny of an Egyptian father and mother, not have lost their civilian and political rights, and be at least forty years of age. The condition of being Muslim is not included.

In 1980, Egypt amended Article 2 of its Constitution. The wording of Article 2 was thus changed from *mabadi' al-shari'a al-Islamiyya masdar ra'isi li al-tashri'* (the principles of the Islamic *shari'a* are *a* principal source of legislation) to the more forceful statement, *mabadi' al-shari'a al-Islamiyya al-masdar al-ra'isi li al-tashri'* (the principles of the Islamic *shari'a* are *the* principal source of legislation). The act of amending Article 2 was a concession by the government to Islamists, and it implied that the Islamic *shari'a* was henceforth to have a more important role in Egyptian society.[37]

Iran

Another example of a formal *shari'a* group is Iran. The foundation for the Islamic Republic of Iran is based on a new Constitution, which was established in 1979 (after the Islamic revolution) and was amended in 1989. According to Article 4 of the Constitution, all laws and regulations in civil, criminal, political and other aspects shall be based on Islamic principles.

The 1979 Iranian Constitution is based on religious sovereignty in terms of the doctrine of *wilayat al-faqih* (governance of the Islamic jurist) introduced and coined by Ayatulla Khumayni.[38] However, one could find borrowed Western elements that lack Islamic background, such as the republican form of government, the division of the government into three separate branches (separation of powers), a directly elected president who functions as chief executive, a prime minister and cabinet, the ideas of the independence of the judiciary and judicial review, the concept of legality, the notion of an elected legislative body, the need for the cabinet to obtain votes of confidence from the legislative branch, and the concept of national sovereignty. Such rules have counterparts in Western political systems. Therefore one could argue that they bear no relation to the traditional function of the Shi'a School.[39]

Ann Mayer examines further that:

> In many facets, and its general format, the Iranian constitution resembles the 1958 French constitution. The way Islamic content has been injected into provisions with French antecedents can be illustrated by comparing the treatment of national sovereignty in article 56 of the Iranian constitution with article 3 of the French constitution. The French version establishes

that sovereignty rests on the will of the people as expressed through referendums and enjoins interference with the exercise of popular sovereignty. It begins: "National sovereignty belongs to the people, which shall exercise this sovereignty through its representatives by means of referendums. No section of the people, nor any individual, may attribute to themselves or himself the exercise thereof." In Chapter 5 of the Iranian constitution under the heading "The Right of National Sovereignty and the Powers Derived from It" one sees in article 56 the Islamized version of the same provision, in which the theological tenet that God is Supreme Ruler is inserted and the French provisions enjoining interferences — this time with Divine Sovereignty — have been incongruously retained: "Absolute sovereignty over the world and mankind is God's and He alone has determined the social destiny of human beings. None shall take away this God-given right from another person or make use of it to serve his special personal or group interest." Wanting to retain the provision for popular referendums, the authors of the Iranian constitution relegated it to article 59, by which placement the clash between the idea that national sovereignty is exercised by the people via referendums and the idea that sovereignty is the exclusive province of the deity has been rendered less obvious. The incongruity remains: there is no room for popular sovereignty exercised via referendum in a system based on the theological premise of divine rule, which at the very least should mean that God's laws are binding and not subject to modification by any human agency, such as popular referendums involve.[40]

However, the 1979 Iranian Constitution contains some startling new elements. Alongside a popularly elected Assembly and President, the Constitution designated a Leader and a Council of Guardians. The authority of these new institutions is such that Chibli Mallat has described them as forming a second tier of the separation of powers, on top of the more traditional separation between the executive, legislative, and judicial powers.[41] According to Article 91 of the Iranian Constitution, the Guardian Council's role is to examine the compatibility of the legislation passed by the Assembly with Islam. The council consists of twelve members (six *ulama* and six jurists).

SUBSTANTIVE *SHARI'A*

Contrary to the formal *shari'a* views above, other Muslim scholars such as Abdullahi Ahmed An-Na'im and Muhammad Sa'id Al-Ashmawy[42] advocate an emancipated understanding of *shari'a*, stressing its original meaning as a "path" or guide, rather than a detailed legal code. *Shari'a* must involve human interpretation. Islamic law is, in fact, the product of a very slow and gradual process of interpretation of the Qur'an and the collection, verification and interpretation of the Sunna during the first three centuries of Islam (the seventh to the ninth centuries). This process took place among scholars and jurist who developed their own methodology for classification of sources, derivation of specific rules from general principles, and so forth.

This led the scholars to distinguish between *shari'a* and *fiqh*. While *shari'a* can be seen as the totality of divine categorizations of human acts, *fiqh* might be described as the articulation of the divine categorizations by human scholars. These articulations represent or express the scholars' understanding of the *shari'a*. This means that jurists or scholars in the Islamic tradition, however highly respected they may be, can present only their own personal views or understanding of what *shari'a* is on any given matter. Moreover, the Qur'an and the Sunna cannot be understood or have any influence on human behaviour except through the efforts of (fallible) human beings.

Bernard Weiss has correctly pointed out that:

> Although the law is of divine provenance, the actual construction of the law is a human activity, and its results represent the law of God as *humanly understood*. Since the law does not descend from heaven ready-made, it is the human understanding of the law — the human *fiqh* (literally meaning understanding) — that must be normative for society.[43]

Therefore, even though *shari'a* is based on the revelations of God, it cannot possibly be drawn up except through human understanding, which means both the inevitability of differences of opinion and the possibility of error, whether among scholars, or the community in general. Khaled Abou El Fadl explains further:

> All laws articulated and applied in a state are thoroughly human, and should be treated as such. Consequently, any codification of *shari'ah* law produces a set of laws that are thoroughly and fundamentally human. These laws are a part of *shari'ah* law only to the extent that any set of human legal opinions is arguably a part of *shari'ah*. A code, even if inspired by *shari'ah*, is not *shari'ah* — a code is simply a set of positive commandments that were informed by an ideal but do not represent the ideal. In my view, human legislation or codifications, regardless of their basis or quality, can never represent the Divine ideal.[44]

Since *shari'a* involves human understanding, the social norms of *shari'a* follow the nature of human beings because they are derived from specific historical circumstances. For instance, the caliphate was the product of history, an institution of human, rather than divine, origin, a temporary convenience, and therefore a purely political office. This means that most of the regulations in Islamic law, including the status of non-Muslims and women in Islamic societies, may be amended, changed, altered, and adapted to social change.[45]

Whilst the Qur'an contains a variety of elements, such as stories, moral injunctions, and general, as well as specific, legal principles, it should be noted that the Qur'an prescribes only those details that are essential. It thus leaves considerable room for development, and safeguards against restrictive rigidity. The universality of Islam lies not in its political structure, but in its faith and religious guidance.

Another source of Islamic jurisprudence, secondary only to the Qur'an, is the examples and words of the Prophet Muhammad, or his Sunna. Not only do both the Qur'an and the Sunna not cover all issues, but quite often they also use words which have speculative meanings. They are interpretable and debatable.

Ijtihad

This leads to the third source. *Ijtihad* in Islamic law can be defined simply as "interpretation". The main difference between *ijtihad* and both the Qur'an and the Sunna is that *ijtihad* is a continuous process of development whereas the Qur'an and the Sunna are fixed sources of authority and were not altered or added to after the death of the Prophet.[46]

Ijtihad literally means "striving, or self-exertion in any activity which entails a measure of hardship".[47] According to al-Amidi, *ijtihad* is defined as "the total expenditure of effort made by a jurist to infer, with a degree of probability, the rules of Islamic law".[48] In this sense, al-Ghazali defined *ijtihad* as "the expending, on the part of a *Mujtahid*, of all that he is capable of in order to seek knowledge of the injunctions of Islamic law".[49]

Ijtihad can be conducted in one of at least three ways: *ijtihad bayani, ijtihad qiyasi* and *ijtihad istislahi*.[50] The first (*ijtihad bayani*) may be applied to cases that are explicitly mentioned in the Qur'an or Hadith but need further explanation. The second (*ijtihad qiyasi*) may be applied to cases that are not mentioned in these two sources, but are similar to cases mentioned in either of them. The third method, *ijtihad istislahi*, may be applied to those cases that are not regulated by the Qur'an or Hadith, and cannot be solved by using analogical reasoning. In this case, *maslahah* (utilities) is considered to be the basis for legal decisions.

It is commonly stated that in the Sunni schools, the "gate of *ijtihad*" was closed (*insidad bab al-ijtihad*) at some stage, often assumed to be the third or fourth century. The formation of the four schools and the recognition of their canonical status (to the detriment of others), it is assumed, "fixed" the main contours of *fiqh* and substantive law, and left no room for *ijtihad*. Jurists from then on would follow the authority of the founders (*taqlid*), their canons being contained in the major texts and early commentaries. Rather than independent *ijtihad*, arguments and rulings would have to be sought in the existing corpus. It is further argued that the authoritative *'ijma* (consensus) of previous generations was binding on jurists, thus further restricting the scope of *ijtihad*. It is in this context that Joseph Schacht claims that Islamic law became increasingly rigid and set in its final mould.[51]

Contrary to this proclamation of the closure of *ijtihad*, one may find many jurists throughout the history of *fiqh* who exercised independent judgement to reach novel theoretical as well as substantive formulations. Wael Hallaq, for instance, refutes Schacht's claim. In analysing this problem, Hallaq has come to the conclusion that Islamic law was still dynamic even after the establishment of the orthodox legal schools in the fourth century. He argues that the consistent emergence of *mujtahids* (jurists), the existence throughout this period of those qualified to issue legal opinions, and the availability of works on legal opinion (*fatwa*) supports this interpretation.[52] Hallaq traces the controversy that resulted in the generalization of this position to the sixth century, when some Hanafi and Maliki jurists argued that there were no longer any persons qualified to engage in *ijtihad*, and that the practitioners of each school must follow authority. Their arguments were opposed by Hanbalis and some Shafi'is, who insisted on the necessity of *ijtihad* at all time, indeed on the religious duty (*fard kifaya*) of the learned to practise it on behalf of the community.[53] Hallaq puts the case that the activity of *fatwa* in dealing with new issues proves that the gate of *ijtihad* was never closed.[54] In other words, there is always room or space for Muslim scholars to exercise their legal reasoning.

The issue is still the subject of considerable debate. It is interesting to note that nowadays even many *ulama* believe that the gate of *ijtihad* is closed. Some of them try to open it; others take the view that none can open it. For the *ulama* who try to open it, some of them make the restriction that, although *ijtihad* is open, it cannot be applied in the cases of making a new *Usul al-Fiqh* and new rules (*qawa'id*); *ijtihad* is open only in *furu'* (*fiqh* cases) not the methodology. In other words, it is not possible to have *al-mujtahid al-mustaqil*.[55] However, others take the view that the door of *ijithad* is open fully and there is no restriction on its use.[56]

I take the position that the door of *ijtihad* is always open. I argue that *ijtihad* is a tool for Muslims to understand and practise *shari'a* (God's law) in line with the nature and the characteristics of human beings. Having performed *ijtihad*, Muslim scholars can build a fresh theoretical construct and a contextual approach to legal language and legal interpretation, to follow the dynamic character of human beings. The secularist views discussed above — that *shari'a* fits only with the conditional, political and the institutional occasions of fifteen centuries ago — can be rejected.

Moreover, I also argue that the rule of *ijtihad* might also be seen to indicate "the imperfectness of the *shari'a*". This means that *shari'a* alone does not cover all issues, as claimed by authoritarian groups. The authoritarian's interpretation of Qur'an 5:3, as has been mentioned above, could be criticized. The verse is only about the complete and perfect teachings of Islamic ritual; from prayers to pilgrimage. After Allah sent down this verse, there were other verses such as the verse on *kalalah* (4:176).[57] This means that, "This day, I have perfected your religion for you", should be read in the context of this verse alone. Qur'an 5:3 actually talks about prohibitions against the eating of certain food, prohibitions against using arrows to seek luck or decisions, and prohibitions against fearing unbelievers. Accordingly, the word "perfect" should be understood to refer only to the mandates and prohibitions of Islam. The word "perfect" in this verse does not regulate the establishment of the caliphate.

In other words, from this verse, one could not argue that *shari'a* deals with any specific form of government. In fact, there is no single verse in the Qur'an which directly regulates the power of a state. If the Qur'an is a comprehensive compendium of knowledge on every issue, then why does the Qur'an leave this issue without further clarification? As will be explained below, the Qur'an provides only some basic principles on this matter.

Scholars who believe that Islam was meant to be a political order have performed their *ijtihad* on this matter based on their understanding and interpretation of the rule of *shari'a*. While their interpretations should be respected as intellectual exercises, their *ijtihad* is not legally binding on all Muslims, nor is it regarded as *shari'a* itself. This means that scholars who have different opinions on this matter have also performed their *ijtihad*, and whatever the outcome of their intellectual activities could not be seen as against the Divine Law. The issue of whether or not *shari'a* is compatible with constitutionalism is an issue of *ijtihad*.

Following on the point above, one may come to argue that the understanding of *shari'a* is not perfect in the sense that it is changeable through the *ijtihad* of Muslim scholars; according to the requirements of different places and times. For instance, Muhammad b. Idris al-Shafi'i (the founding father of the Shafi'i school) changed several of the views he held in Iraq (*qaul qadim*) when he moved to Cairo (*qaul jadid*). Much earlier, before al-Shafi'i, Umar bin Khattab is known as the caliph who practised *ijtihad* on

several occasions, not only when there was no guidance in both the Qur'an
and the Sunna, but also when he thought that the law mentioned in both
sources was no longer suitable for dealing with the circumstances of his era.
The two texts below provide examples of how the result of Umar's *ijtihad*
differs from the Prophet's decision:

> 1. Narrated Imran: 'We performed *Hajj al-Tamattu'* in the lifetime of Allah's
> Apostle and then the Qur'an was revealed (regarding *Hajj al-Tamattu*) and
> somebody [Umar] said what he wished (regarding *Hajj al-Tamattu*) according
> to his own opinion (*ra'y*)'.[58]

> 2. Yahya related to me from Malik, from Ibn Shihab, that Muhammad ibn
> Abdillah ibn al-Haris ibn Nawfal ibn Abd al-Muttalib told him that he had
> heard Sa'd ibn Abi Waqqas and al-Dahhak ibn Qays discussing *tamattu'*
> (performing *umrah* first, then *Hajj*) in between *umrah* and *Hajj*. Al-Dahhak
> ibn Qays said, "Only someone who is ignorant of what Allah, the Exalted
> and Glorified, says would do that." Whereupon Sa'd said, "How wrong is
> what you have just said, son of my brother!" al-Dahhak said, "Umar ibn al-
> Khattab forbade that," and Sa'd said, "The Messenger of Allah, may Allah
> bless him and grant him peace, did it, and we did it with him".[59]

Umar believed that the situation had changed and this forced him to
apply *ijtihad* which, in several cases, caused him to differ from the position
adopted by the Prophet. Umar's decision not to distribute the lands of Iraq
and Syria among the companions furnishes another example. Muslims insisted
on distributing the land among them according to the Prophet's practice. To
all their contentions Umar replied that if he kept on distributing the lands,
where would he maintain the army to protect the borders and the newly
conquered towns. The companions, therefore, finally agreed with him and
remarked, "*al-ra'y ra'yuka*" (yours is the correct opinion). Umar later found
the justification for this decision in the Qur'an (59: 6–10).[60] Umar actually
preferred actions which benefited Muslims in general, rather than individuals.
Social justice, in Umar's time, demanded that conquered lands should not be
distributed among the army. Another interesting example occurred when a
man was found guilty of theft but Umar, as a Caliph, did not amputate his
hand, because at that time famine ravaged his territory.[61] In deciding this, it
seems that Umar contravened the formal Qur'anic injunction.[62] However,
Umar was still regarded and respected as one of the four rightly-guided
caliphs. The Umar cases above suggest that *shari'a* is not unchangeable.

Shari'a is also considered not to be "perfect" on the grounds that there
is much disagreement and disputation among scholars concerning the
meaning and significance of different aspects of the sources with which they

are working. For example, one School takes the view that analogy (*qiyas*) is one of the sources of Islamic law, while others reject it. It is worth noting that, as has been mentioned earlier, in the case of al-Shafi'i, the scholars' work cannot be in isolation from the prevailing conditions of their communities in local as well as broader regional contexts. The interpretations of scholars, *ulama* and *mujtahid* would reflect the state of their human and political consciousness, and usually that of their people, at that particular time and place. Disagreements between Schools (and even among scholars of the same School), as history tells us, provide other evidence that the understanding of *shari'a*, as humanly understood, is not static, final, eternal, absolute and unalterable.

The Qur'an encourages ethnic and other types of diversity as blessings from God. Consequently, classic Muslim jurists recognized the fact that what may suit one culture may not be quite suitable for another. For this reason, they encouraged each country to introduce its own customs into its laws, provided that these customs do not contradict basic Islamic principles. As a result, even today, the Islamic laws of Muslim countries differ significantly on various matters.

While rejecting the Qur'an and Hadith as the Islamic Constitution (authoritarian view), at the same time, I also reject the secularist view that in the secular sense Islam is a religion that regulates it only to the relationship between man and the Supreme Creator. The Qur'an and Hadith cannot be seen as the Islamic Constitution, but perhaps as its Code of High Constitutional Principles. They comprise guidance on legislation, morality, and meaningful stories which, unlike other constitutions and laws, were unsystematically recorded. Although both the Qur'an and Hadith do not give their preferences for a definite political system, both primary sources have laid down a set of principles, or ethical values and political morals, to be followed by Muslims in developing life within a state.

For instance, Muhammad Husayn Haikal takes the view that Islam does not provide direct and detailed guidance on how the Islamic community shall manage state affairs. According to him, Islam does lay down the basic principles for human civilization, not basic provisions to regulate human behaviour in life and in association with fellow humans, which, in turn, will characterize the pattern of politics. In short, according to Haikal, there is no standard government system in Islam. The Islamic community is free to follow any government system, as long as it assures equality among its citizens, both in rights and responsibilities, and also in the sight of the law, and manages affairs of state based on the *shura* or consultation, by adhering to the moral and ethical values taught by Islam for mankind's civilization.

Haikal believes that a governmental system according to Islamic provisions is a system assuring freedom, based on the principle of the appointment of a head of state having the people's approval, and that the people have the right to control the implementation of government and to call on the government to give account of its actions. Islam appeals to mankind, especially Muslims, to make an effort to carry out those above-mentioned principles as far as possible. This position is a middle position between authoritarian and secularist views. In this context, one may see that Haikal's views clearly oppose the strict opinions raised by authoritarian groups, that sovereignty belongs to Allah, not to the people. However, at the same time, Haikal also opposes the view that Islam does not teach methods of living within a community and within a state.[63]

PRINCIPLES OF ISLAMIC CONSTITUTIONALISM

The counter-arguments above specifically reject some ideas of the incompatibility of the nature and the characteristics of *shari'a* and constitutionalism. The following arguments will be focused on examining the principles of *shari'a* in relation to constitutionalism. Simultaneously, the arguments below are presented to counter secular views on this matter.

The secularist views mentioned earlier hold that historically the powers of the caliphs were unlimited and that, therefore, *shari'a* is not compatible with constitutionalism could be rejected on the grounds that Islam has provided *wilaya al-mazalim* (the redress of wrongs). It is the embryo of the administrative tribunal or constitutional court in the modern sense. Al-Mawardi has outlined ten areas that can be reported to this tribunal, including the oppression and maltreatment of the public by government officials, and the implementation of sentences when judges are too weak to enforce them due to the sentenced person's power or social standing.[64]

Abd al-Wahhab Khallaf goes further by stating that an Islamic government is a constitutional government; not a tyrannical one.[65] In other words, based on Khallaf's understanding of *shari'a*, the government in Islam is not based on the charisma of the person. He also takes the view that Islam guarantees individual rights and provides the separation of powers into *al-sulta al-tashri'iya* (legislative), *al-sulta al-qada'iya* (judiciary), and *al-sulta al-tanfidhiya* (executive).[66] Khallaf's views can be justified on the grounds that the Qur'an provided the basic principles for a constitutional democracy without providing the details of a specific system. Muslims were to interpret these basic principles in the light of their customs and the demands of their historical consciousness.

Once again, this partly explains why Muslims currently need a new reinterpretation or *ijtihad*.

In addition, advocates of Islamic constitutional law have sought to broaden the classic understanding of *ijma'* (consensus). Only Muslim scholars had a role in reaching consensus; the general public had little significance.[67] Fazlur Rahman argues that the classical doctrine of consultation was in error because it presented consultation as the process of one person, the ruler, asking subordinates for advice; in fact, the Qur'an calls for "mutual advice through mutual discussions on an equal footing".[68] In this context, the doctrine of *ijma'* is closely related to the concept of *shura* (consultation), and therefore can be implemented as a legislative power in modern sense. Louay M. Safi also notes that the "legitimacy of the state ... depends upon the extent to which state organization and power reflect the will of the *ummah* [the Muslim community], for as classical jurists have insisted, the legitimacy of state institutions is not derived from textual sources but is based primarily on the principle of *ijma'*."[69] In this understanding, an Islamic constitution is a human product of legislation based on the practice of consultation and consensus, and thus, virtually, no longer a result of divine act. It is set by the people and approved by them. In other words, consensus and consultation offer a justification of Islamic constitutional law.

In addition, the claim that *shari'a* refutes the majority principle — what is right and what is wrong should be based on *shari'a*, not on the popular vote — is actually open to discussion. For instance, Ermin Sinanovic has shown that key concepts of *ijma'*, *al-sawad al-a'zham*, *jumhur*, *al-tarjih bi al-katsrah* and legal maxims *al-qawa'id al-fiqhiyya* could strengthen the case for the legitimization of the majority principle in Islamic political thought and decision-making processes.[70]

I would also add that Muslims agree about the primacy of *Hadith Mutawatir*, which is reported by such a large number of people that they cannot all be expected to agree upon a lie.[71] But, how does one define "a large number of people"? Although Muslims agree about the primacy of *Mutawatir*, they hold different opinions about the number of narrators for a Hadith to be accepted as *Mutawatir*. Some believe four persons are needed; others insist that a Hadith will achieve the degree of *Mutawatir* only when seventy or more narrate it. Actually, the number of reporters required to define "a group" for *Hadith Mutawatir* is derived by analogy. The requirement of four is based on the similar number of witnesses required for legal proof; the requirement for twenty is derived from the Qur'an (8:65) (the number required to vanquish unbelievers). The next number seventy represents an analogy to another text of the Qur'an (7:115) referring to the seventy companions of Moses. Others scholars have drawn analogy from the number of participants in the battle of Badr (313 persons).[72] Despite this debate, the point is that the number in Islamic tradition does matter. Therefore, it is essential to note that deciding a case through the majority or popular vote is permitted. One of the justifications comes from the sayings of the Prophet:

> "I (Ali bin Abi Talib) said to the Prophet, 'O, Prophet, [what if] there is a case among us, while neither revelation comes, nor the Sunna exists." The Prophet replied, "[you should] have meetings with the scholars — or in another version: the pious servants — and consult with them. Do not make a decision only by a single opinion."[73]

In this sense, Nathan J. Brown points out that *shari'a* does provide a basis for constitutionalism and that Islamic political thought is increasingly inclined towards constitutionalist ideas. According to him, "while it is true that attempts to put these ideas into practice have not so far been successful, the problem could be seen to lie in the lack of attention to the structures of political accountability, rather than flaws in the concept of Islamic constitutionalism".[74]

Azizah Y. al-Hibri explains some key concepts of Islamic law in order to support the view that *shari'a* is compatible with constitutionalism. A state must satisfy two basic conditions to meet Islamic standards: the political process must be based on "elections", or *bay'at*; and the elective and governing process must be based on "broad deliberation", or *shura*.[75] These two principles are part of the criteria employed to determine or to judge Islamic constitutional law. According to al-Hibri, these two principles, together with other factors (the ruler in a Muslim state has no divine attributes and there is no ecclesiastical structure in an Islamic setting), indicate that there is, in fact, little difference between an Islamic constitutional setting and a secular one.[76]

Given the alleged parallels she discovers between the Constitution of Medina and the U.S. Constitution, al-Hibri considers the possibility that the founding fathers of the United States were directly or indirectly influenced by the Islamic precedent. She notes that Thomas Jefferson was aware of Islam since he had in his library a copy of George Sale's translation of the Qur'an. Al-Hibri suggests that Sale presented Islam in as fair a light as possible, under the circumstances of the eighteenth century, thereby making the Prophet's precedent amenable to Jefferson. Al-Hibri argues that if the founding fathers were, in fact, influenced by the Islamic model of constitutionalism, then this would "support the argument that American constitutional principles have a lot in common with Islamic principles.

Such a conclusion would be helpful in evaluating the possibility of exporting American democracy to Muslim countries".[77]

Although her argument could be considered apologetic,[78] it seems that Al-Hibri has attempted to show some similarities between the two traditions, using the American standard as the standard of evaluation. The comparison between two legal traditions is, borrowing Patrick Glenn's term, a multivalent thinking. Glenn takes the view that all traditions contain elements of others. Western legal traditions may contain some of Eastern legal traditions. In other words, "there are always common elements and common subjects of discussion".[79] Glenn rejects the proposition that "you can't have your cake and eat it too".[80] He offers multivalent views that everything would be a matter of degree. It is possible to compare apples and oranges. In other words, Glenn takes the position that "you can have your cake and eat it too, if you eat only half of it".[81] Therefore, Glenn rejects the claim that a religious legal tradition is incompatible or incommensurable with secular legal tradition.

In addition, a Muslim scholar could readily conclude that a Muslim country may choose to be a republic and still be in compliance with *shari'a*, as long as the vote for the president is genuinely free, and the consultation among all branches of government is broad. Furthermore, the existence of a House of Representatives would ensure that the people's voice is heard in legislative matters, even if indirectly. Another scholar, however, may make similar arguments for a constitutional monarchy based on the British example. One can see that Muslim countries may, or may not, satisfy the two criteria above, in their constitutions.

In relation to the protection of the rights of the citizen, despite some rights which are established in the Qur'an and the Sunna,[82] *maqasid al-shari'a* (the objectives of Islamic law) should become another principle or criterion of Islamic constitutional law. This view is supported by UCLA Professor of Islamic Law, Khaled Abou El Fadl.[83] According to Muhammad Husein Kamali, *maqasid al-shari'a* is an important but neglected aspect in the discourse of *shari'a*. Kamali claims that even today many highly regarded textbooks on *Usul al-Fiqh* (Islamic legal theory) do not comprise *maqasid al-shari'a* in their descriptions. Generally those textbooks are more concerned with conformity to the letter of the divine text. Accordingly, this, directly or not, has contributed to the literalist direction of juristic thought.[84]

The *maqasid al-shari'a* consists of the five juristic core values of protection (*al-dharuriya al-khams*) for religion, life, intellect, honour or lineage, and property. Basically, *shari'a*, on the whole, seeks primarily to protect and promote these essential values, and validates all measures necessary for their preservation and advancement. El Fadl argues that the protection of religion would have to mean protecting the freedom of religious belief; the protection of life would mean that the taking of life must be for a just reason, and the result of a just process; the protection of the intellect would have to mean the right to freedom of thought, expression and belief; the protection of honour would have to mean the protection of the dignity of a human being; and the protection of property would ensure the right to compensation for the taking of property.[85]

It is essential to note that these five core values are not divine, but human values, since they are developed by Muslim jurists based on their interpretations of the Qur'an and Sunna. This could mean that the *maqasid al-shari'a* is not limited to the five core values. Ibn Taimiyah, for instance, departs from the notion of confining the *maqasid al-shari'a* to a specific number of values.[86] Yusuf al-Qaradawi takes a similar approach. He extends the list of the *maqasid al-shari'a* to include "human dignity, freedom, social welfare, and human fraternity among the higher *maqasid* of the *shari'a*".[87] The existence of additional objectives is upheld by the weight of both general and detailed evidence, in the Qur'an and Sunna.

A new *ijtihad* could be performed by considering the theory of the *maqasid al-shari'a*, examining *shari'a* as a unity in which the detailed rules are to be read in the light of their broader premises, substantives, and objectives. This means that by looking at the *maqasid al-shari'a*, *shari'a* could be analysed beyond the particularities of the text. In Kamali's words, "the focus is not so much on the words and sentences of the text, as on the purposes and goals that are being upheld and advocated".[88] It is worth noting that the principles and the procedural form of Islamic constitutional law could be found through the theory of the *maqasid al-shari'a*.

In relation to the position of religion vis-à-vis the state, another principle or criterion could be drawn from the Medina Charter.[89] One of the challenges for Islamic Constitutional law is the position of Islam (or *shari'a*) in the constitution. This could be examined on three levels: the position of Islam within Muslim community itself, the position of Islam in relation to other religions, and the relationship between Islam and the state.

In this context, the Constitution or Charter of Medina is a document reportedly drawn up by the Prophet Muhammad (d. 11/632), upon his migration from Mecca to Medina. The document establishes rights and obligations among the Ansar of Medina, the Muhajir who left Mecca with the Prophet, and the Jewish tribes of Medina as they embarked upon a new journey of coexistence and cooperation in the nascent Muslim polity founded in Medina. The text itself consists of a preamble and forty-seven clauses outlining various aspects of community organization, procedures for common defence, and the relationship between the Muslims and the Jewish inhabitants of Medina.

The Constitution of Medina declared all Muslim and Jewish tribes of Medina (apparently, there were no Christians) to be a single community. It also stipulated that non-Muslim minorities (Jews) had the same right of life protection (as Muslims); guaranteed peace and security for all Muslims based on equality and justice; guaranteed freedom of religion for both the Muslims and non-Muslim minorities (the Jews); and ensured equality between the rights of the Jews of Banu Najjar and those of the Jews of Banu Awf.[90]

Instead of strictly using the text, the spirit of the Constitution of Medina could be used as a principle or criterion of the modern Islamic constitutional law. Although there is not a single word in the document which referred to an Islamic state, the text states that "where a contention arises between two parties on a matter, the issue is to be referred to God and to Muhammad for a decision". This issue will be fully examined in Chapter 6 in order to clarify the debate between authoritarians and secularists on Islam being a religion and a state (*din wa dawla*).

CONCLUSION

I have shown that there is a group which believes that *shari'a* is incompatible with constitutionalism. This group is divided into two camps: authoritarian/ fundamentalist and secularist. There is also a second group which holds the view that *shari'a* can walk together with constitutionalism. This position rejects both the authoritarian and the secularist views on this subject. However, this group is also divided into two approaches: formal *shari'a* and substantive *shari'a*. It is essential to note that I support this second approach which holds the view on the compatibility of constitutionalism and *shari'a*.

While the formal *shari'a* attempts to use *shari'a* as a source or the primary source of law — which makes their position closer to authoritarian/ fundamentalist views — the substantive *shari'a* holds that *shari'a*, in this context, should be reinterpreted as consistent with democracy and constitutionalism. This substantive approach is based on the belief that the understanding of *shari'a* is not static and final. As has been argued earlier, it can be amended, reformed, modified or even altered, without neglecting its fundamental basis. This leads the substantive group into treating the principles, objectives or spirit of *shari'a* only as norms or values which inspires constitutions.

In the following chapters, through critical analysis of three main case studies — human rights, the rule of law, and religion vis-à-vis state — I will examine whether Islamic political parties are proposing the formal or the substantive *shari'a* when dealing with the Amendments to the 1945 Constitution.

Notes

1. Graham Hassal and Cheryl Saunders, Asia-Pacific Constitutional Systems (Cambridge: Cambridge University Press, 2002), p. 42. See also C. Perry Patterson, "The Evolution of Constitutionalism", *Minnesota Law Review* 32 (1948): 427–57.
2. For a full account, see International Crisis Group (ICG), "Iraq's Constitutional Challenge", *ICG Middle East Report*, No. 19, 13 November 2003; International Crisis Group (ICG), "Afghan's Flawed Constitutional Process", *ICG Asia Report*, No. 56, 12 June 2003.
3. See Ann Elizabeth Mayer, "Conundrums in Constitutionalism: Islamic Monarchies in an Era of Transition", *UCLA Journal of Islamic and Near Eastern Law* 1 (2002): 183.
4. Muhammad Asad, *The Principles of State and Government in Islam* (Kuala Lumpur: Islamic Book Trust, 1980); Abul A'la al-Maududi, *Political Theory of Islam* (Lahore: Islamic Publications, 1985).
5. Chibli Mallat, ed., *Islam and Public Law: Classical and Contemporary Studies* (London: Graham and Trotman, 1993), pp. 1–2.
6. Abdurrahman Taj, *al-Siyasa al-Shar'iya wa al-Fiqh al-Islami* (Cairo: Dar al-Ta'rif, 1953); Ahmad Syalabi, *al-Siyasa fi al-Fikr al-Islami* (Cairo: Nahdah al-Misriyah, 1983).
7. The common sources are al-Mawardi, *al-Ahkam al-Sutaniya* (Cairo: Mustafa Babi al-Halabi wa Auladuh, 1996); Ibn Khaldun, *Muqaddima* (Beirut: Dar al-Fikr, n.d).
8. In April 2000, a major international conference on Islam and Constitutionalism was held by the Islamic Legal Studies Program, Faculty of Law, Harvard University. The papers will be edited by Sohail Hashmi and Houchang Chehabi and published by Harvard University Press (forthcoming).
9. Louis Henkin, "Elements of Constitutionalism", Occasional Paper Series, Center for the Study of Human Rights, 1994. See also Francis D. Wormuth, *The Origins of Modern Constitutionalism* (New York: Harper and Brothers, 1949).
10. Dario Castiglione, "The Political Theory of the Constitution", in *Constitutionalism in Transformation*, edited by Richard Bellamy and Dario Castiglione (London: Blackwell Publishers, 1996), p. 5.
11. Alan S. Rosenbaum, ed., *Constitutionalism: The Philosophical Dimension* (Connecticut: Greenwood Press, 1988), p. 8 (Introduction); see also J. Lane,

Constitutions and Political Theory (Manchester: Manchester University Press, 1996), p. 25.

12. See the discussion in Muhammad Khalid Masud, *Shatibi's Philosophy of Islamic Law* (Pakistan: Islamic Research Institute, 1995), p. 17.

13. Ahmad Syalabi, *al-Hukuma wa al-Dawla fi al-Islam* (Cairo: Maktabah al-Nahdah al-Misriyah, 1958), p. 23.

14. See M. Abd al-Qadir Abu Faris, *al-Nizam al-Siyasi fi al-Islam* (Beirut: Dar al-Qur'an al-Karim, 1984), pp. 15–40.

15. Muhammad Asad, *The Principles of State and Government in Islam* (Kuala Lumpur: Islamic Book Trust, 1980).

16. For a full account, see Said Amir Arjomand, "Religion and Constitutionalism in Western History and in Modern Iran and Pakistan", in *The Political Dimensions of Religion*, edited by Said Amir Arjomand (Albany: State University of New York Press, 1993), pp. 69–99.

17. See Muhammad Salim al-'Awwa, *Fi al-Nizam al-Siyasi li al-Dawla al-Islamiyya* (Cairo: al-Maktab al-Misri al-Hadis, 1983).

18. Ayatollah Khomeini of Iran echoed this sentiment when he said: "This slogan of the separation of religion and politics and the demand that Islamic scholars not intervene in social and political affairs have been formulated and propagated by the imperialists; it is only the irreligious who repeat them. These slogans and claims have been advanced by the imperialists and their political agents in order to prevent religion from ordering the affairs of this world and shaping Muslim society, and at the same time to create a rift between the scholars of Islam, on the one hand, and the masses and those struggling for freedom and independence, on the other. They have thus been able to gain dominance over our people and plunder our resources, for such has always been their ultimate goal." — as quoted in Afshin Molavi, *Persian Pilgrimages: Journeys Across Iran* (New York: WW Norton, 2002), p. 166.

19. Ahmad Husain Ya'qub, *al-Nizam al-Siyasi fi al-Islam* (Iran: Mu'assasah Ansariyan, 1312 H), p. 250.

20. "... This day, I have perfected your religion for you, completed My Favour upon you, and have chosen for you Islam as your religion ..." (Qur'an 5:3).

21. Taqiyuddin al-Nabhani, *Nizam al-Islam*, available at http://www.hizb-ut-tahrir.org/arabic/kotobmtb/htm/01ndam.htm.

22. More information can be found in James T. McHugh, *Comparative Constitutional Traditions* (New York: Peter Lang, 2002), pp. 193–211.

23. Mayer, p. 206.

24. Ali 'Abd al-Raziq (1888–1966) was the most controversial Islamic political thinker in the twentieth century. His book *al-Islam wa Usul al-Hukm*, written in 1925, invited wide criticism in the Muslim world. He was then condemned and isolated by the *ulama* council of al-Azhar, and also dismissed from his position as judge and prohibited from assuming a position in the government. Raziq disagreed with many *ulama* who considered the establishment of *khilafa* as

obligatory for Muslims and, therefore, it would sinful if it were not carried out. He could not find any strong foundation to support this belief.

25. Bassam Tibi, *The Challenge of Fundamentalism: Political Islam and the New World Disorder* (Berkeley: University of California Press, 1998), p. 160.
26. For a full account, see Patricia Crone, *Medieval Islamic Political Thought* (Edinburgh: Edinburgh University Press, 2004), pp. 358–92.
27. Ann K. S. Lambton, *State and Government in Medieval Islam* (New York: Oxford University Press, 1991), pp. 203–208.
28. John L. Esposito and James P. Piscatori, "Democratization and Islam", *Middle East Journal* 45, no. 3 (1991): 428.
29. Qur'an 2:282 says: "if the two be not men, then one man and two women, such witnesses as you approve of, that if one of the two women errs the other will remind her ..."
30. Full text of Constitution of the Republic of Turkey can be read in http://www.mfa.gov.tr/grupc/ca/cag/I142.htm.
31. See Article 2 of the 1982 Constitution.
32. Article 75.
33. Article 101.
34. Article 24.
35. Charles Kurzman, "Liberal Islam: Prospects and Challenges", *Journal Middle East Review of International Affairs* 3, no. 3. Available at http://www.biu.ac.il/SOC/besa/meria/journal/1999/issue3/jvol3no3in.html.
36. See, for example, Kevin Boyle and Adel Omar Sherif, eds., *Human Rights and Democracy: The Role of the Supreme Constitutional Court of Egypt* (London: Kluwer Law International, 1996).
37. Clark Benner Lombardi, "Islamic Law as a Source of Constitutional Law in Egypt: The Constitutionalization of the Sharia in a Modern Arab State", *Columbia Journal of Transnational Law* 37 (1998): 81.
38. See Abdulaziz Abdulhussein Sachedina, *The Just Ruler (al-Sultan al-Adil) in Shiite Islam: The Comprehensive Authority of the Jurist in Imamite Jurisprudence* (New York: Oxford University Press, 1988).
39. For a full account, see Asghar Schirazi, *The Constitution of Iran: Politics and the State in the Islamic Republic* (London and New York: I.B. Tauris), 1997.
40. Ann Elizabeth Mayer, "The Fundamentalist Impact on Law, Politics, and Constitutions in Iran, Pakistan and Sudan", in *Fundamentalisms and the State*, edited by Martin E. Marty and R. Scott Appleby (Chicago: The University of Chicago Press, 1993), pp. 118–19.
41. More information can be obtained from Chibli Mallat, *The Renewal of Islamic Law* (Cambridge: Cambridge University Press, 1993), Chs. 2 and 3.
42. See Abdullahi Ahmed An-Naim, *Toward an Islamic Reformation: Civil Liberties, Human Rights, and International Law* (Syracuse, NY: Syracuse University Press, 1996); see Carolyn Fluehr-Lobban, ed., *Against Islamic Extremism: The Writings of Muhammad Sa'id al-Ashmawy* (Gainesville: University Press of Florida, 1998);

see also William E. Shepard, "Muhammad Said al-Ashmawi and the Application of Sharia in Egypt", *International Journal of Middle East Studies* 28, no. 1 (1996): 39.

43. Bernard Weiss, *The Spirit of Islamic Law* (Athens: University of Georgia Press, 1998), p. 116.

44. Khaled Abou El Fadl, "Constitutionalism and the Islamic Sunni Legacy", *UCLA Journal of Islamic and Near Eastern Law* 1 (2002): 67.

45. For instance, Amina Wadud al-Muhsin, a Professor at Virginia Commonwealth University, offers a hermeneutical approach to understand the Qur'an on women. See her article, "Qur'an and Woman", in *Liberal Islam: A Source Book*, edited by Charles Kurzman (Oxford: Oxford University Press, 1998), pp. 127–38; For the interpretation and historical context of the Prophet's statement — "Those who entrust their affairs to a woman will never know prosperity" — see Fatima Mernissi, "A Feminist Interpretation of Women's Rights in Islam", in *Liberal Islam*, pp. 112–26.

46. Mohammad Hashim Kamali, *Principles of Islamic Jurisprudence* (Cambridge: The Islamic Text Society, 1991), p. 366.

47. Ibid., p. 367; Hans Wehr, *A Dictionary of Modern Written Arabic* (London: Macdonald and Evans, 1974), pp. 142–43.

48. Sayf al-Din al-Amidi, *al-Ihkam fi Usul al-Ahkam*, Vol. 4, (Cairo: Dar al-Kutub al-Khidiwiya, 1914), p. 218; Kamali, *Principles of Islamic Jurisprudence*; see also Muhammad Taqi al-Hakim, *al-Usul al-'Ammah li al-Fiqh al-Muqarin* (Beirut: Dar al-Andalas, 1963), pp. 561–62.

49. Abu Hamid Muhammad al-Ghazali, *al-Mustasfa min 'Ilm al-Usul*, Vol. 4, (Medina: al-Jami'ah al-Islamiyah, n.d.), p. 4; see also Taha Jabir al-Alwani, "The Crisis of Thought and Ijtihad", *American Journal of Islamic Social Sciences* 10, no. 2 (1993): 237.

50. Muhammad Ma'ruf al-Dawalibi uses these classifications in his book *al-Madkhal ila 'Ilm al-Usul al-Fiqh* (Damascus: Matba'ah Jami'ah Damsyq, 1959), p. 389. Muhammad Salam Madkur mentioned Dawalibi's book when discussing this issue (see *Manahij al-Ijtihad fi al-Islam* (Kuwait: Matba'ah al-'Asriyah al-Kuwait, 1974), p. 396) and, shortly afterwards, Wahbah al-Zuhaili also referred to this book in 1977 (see *al-Wasit fi Usul al-Fiqh al-Islami* (Beirut: Matba'ah Dar al-Kitab, 1977), p. 484). However, Muhammad Taqi al-Hakim criticizes these categorizations and proposes only two classifications, namely, *al-ijtihad al-'aqli* and *al-ijtihad al-shar'i*. (See Muhammad Taqi al-Hakim, *al-Usul al-'Ammah*).

51. Joseph Schacht, *An Introduction to Islamic Law* (Oxford: Clarendon Press, 1998), p. 75.

52. Wael Hallaq, "Was the Gate of Ijtihad Closed?", *International Journal of Middle East Studies* 16 (1984): 3.

53. Wael Hallaq, "On the Origins of the Controversy about the Existence of Mujathids and the Gate of Ijtihad", *Studia Islamica* 63 (1986): 129.

54. Wael Hallaq, "From *Fatawa* to *Furu*': Growth and Change in Islamic Substantive Law", *Islamic Law and Society* 1, no. 1 (1994): 29.

55. Wahbah al-Zuhaili explains that a *mujtahid* is classified according to five levels. First, *al-mujtahid al-mustaqil* is the *alim* who carries out *ijtihad* by employing his own methodology and arriving at his own conclusions on Islamic law. Abu Hanifah (d. 150 AH/767 CE), Malik (d. 179 AH/795 CE), al-Shafi'i (d. 204 AH/820 CE), and Ahmad bin Hanbal (d. 241 AH/855 CE) were claimed to have qualifications at the level of *al-mujtahid al-mustaqil*. Secondly, *al-mujtahid al-mutlaq gair al-mustaqil* has qualifications to perform *ijtihad*, but follows the methodology of the Imam of his *madhab*. It is possible that, although he follows the Imam's methodology, the results of his *ijtihad* will differ from that of his Imam. However, the main point to stress is that he does not devise his own method. His position is lower in ranking than *al-mujtahid al-mustaqil*. Several well-known names in this classification are: Abu Yusuf (d. 182 AH/798 CE), Zufar (d. 158 AH/775 CE) from the Hanafi school, Ibn al-Qasim (d. 206 AH/823 CE) from the Maliki school, Muzani (d. 264 AH/878 CE) from the Shafi'i school, Ibn Taimiyah (d. 728 AH/1328 CE) from the Hanbali school and Ibn Hazm (d. 456 AH/1965 CE) from the Zahiri school. Thirdly, *al-mujtahid al-muqayyad* or *mujtahid al-takhrij* (another term is *mujtahid fi al-madhab*) is a person who follows the school of the Imam, but performs *ijtihad* by analysing the elements or the arguments of the school in order to defend the position or explain the opinion of his *madhab* about *fiqh*. It is possible for this person to perform *ijtihad* in cases where the Imam of the *madhab* did not pronounce on the issue. Al-Tahawi (d. 321 AH/933 CE) of Hanafi school, Ibn Abi Zaid of Maliki school and Abi Ishaq al-Shirazi (d. 476 AH/1093 CE) of Shafi'i school are claimed as possessing qualifications at this level of *mujtahid*. Fourthly, *mujtahid al-tarjih* refers to a person who performs *ijtihad* by choosing one from a number of opinions presented by *mujtahids*. The task of the *mujtahid al-tarjih* is to examine and analyse which is the best among several opinions. The last category is *mujtahid al-futya* (*mujtahid al-fatwa*), the person who issues a fatwa. See Wahbah al-Zuhaili, *Usul al-Fiqh al-Islami*, Vol. 2 (Beirut: Dar al-Fikr, 1986), pp. 1079–181.

56. al-Zuhaili, ibid. See also Shaista P. Ali-Karamali and Fiona Dunne, "The Ijtihad Controversy", *Arab Law Quarterly* 9 (1994): 238; M. Hobink, *Two Halves of the Same Truth: Schacht, Hallaq, and the Gate of Ijtihad* (Amsterdam: Middle East Research Associates, 1994); Frank E. Vogel, 'The Closing of the Door of Ijtihad and the Application of the Law", paper delivered at the American Oriental Society Conference, Cambridge, Massachusetts, 13 March 1992; Ibrahim Hosen, "Taqlid dan Ijtihad: Beberapa Pengertian Dasar", in *Kontekstualisasi Doktrin Islam Dalam Sejarah*, edited by Budhy Munawar-Rachman (Jakarta: Paramadina, 1995).

57. According to some scholars, *kalalah* refers to those who die leaving neither issue nor father nor grandfather. According to others, it refers to those who die

without issue (regardless of whether they are succeeded by father or grandfather). More information can be found in David S. Powers, *Studies in Qur'an and Hadith: The Formation of the Islamic law of Inheritance* (Berkeley: University of California Press, 1986).

58. Abu 'Abd Allah Muhammad b. Isma'il b. Ibrahim b. al-Mugirah b. Bukhari, Sahih Bukhari, book *al-Hajj* (Beirut: Dar al-Qalam, 1987), no. 1,469.

59. Abu 'Abd Allah Malik, al-Muwatta', book *al-Hajj* (Beirut: al-Shirkah al-'Alamiyah, 1993), no. 671.

60. Fazlur Rahman, *Islamic Methodology in History* (Lahore: 1965), pp. 180–81.

61. Ahmad Hasan, *The Early Development of Islamic Jurisprudence* (Islamabad: Islamic Research Institute, 1970), p. 120.

62. The decision of Umar bin Khattab to suspend *hadd* penalty (penalty prescribed by the Qur'an and Sunna) of amputation of hand during famine is an example of *istihsan* (juristic preference). Here the law was suspended as an exceptional measure in an exceptional situation. *Istihsan* is considered as a method of seeking facility and ease in legal injunctions and is in accord with the Qur'an (2:185). This suggests that Companions of the Prophet were not merely literalist. On the contrary, their rulings were often based on their understanding of the spirit and purpose of the *shari'a*.

63. More information can be found in Musdah Mulia, *Negara Islam: Pemikiran Politik Husain Haikal* (Jakarta: Paramadina, 2001).

64. Mawardi, *al-Ahkam al-Sutaniya*, pp. 80–92.

65. Abd al-Wahhab Khallaf, *al-Siyasa al-Shar'iya* (Cairo: Salafiyah, 1350 H), p. 25.

66. Ibid., pp. 41–51.

67. The doctrine of *ijma'*, or consensus, was introduced in the second century AH (eighth century) in order to standardize legal theory and practice and to overcome individual and regional differences of opinion. Though conceived as a "consensus of scholars", in actual practice *ijma'* was a more fundamental operative factor. From the third century AH, *ijma'* has amounted to a principle of rigidity in thinking; points on which consensus was reached in practice were considered closed and further substantial questioning of them prohibited. Accepted interpretations of the Qur'an and the actual content of the Sunna all rest finally on the *ijma'*. *Ijma'*, according to one definition, should be attended by all Mujtahids only. The problem is, if one refers to all books of Islamic legal theory, there is no definition of *ijma'* which is accepted by all *Mujathids*. There is no consensus (*mujma' 'alaih*) in defining *ijma'* itself. See Ali Abd al-Raziq, *al-Ijma' fi al-Shari'a al-Islamiya* (Beirut: Dar al-Fikr al-'Arabi, 1948), p. 6.

68. Fazlur Rahman, "The Principle of Shura and the Role of the Ummah in Islam", in *State, Politics, and Islam*, edited by Mumtaz Ahmad (Indianapolis: American Trust Publications, 1986), pp. 90–91 and 95.

69. Louay M. Safi, "The Islamic State: A Conceptual Framework", *American Journal of Islamic Social Sciences* (1991): 233.

70. Ermin Sinanovic, "The Majority Principle in Islamic Legal and Political Thought", *Islam and Christian-Muslim Relations* 15, no. 2 (2004): 237–56.

71. Mahmud al-Tahhan, *Taysir Mustalah al-Hadith* (Cairo: Dar al-Turas al-'Arabi, 1981), p. 19.

72. Muhammad Taqi al-Hakim, *al-Usul al-'Ammah*, p. 195.

73. As quoted in Abd al-Halim Uwes, *al-Fiqh al-Islami baina al-Tatawwur wa al-Tsabat* (Medina: Syirkah al-Madinah al-Munawwarah, n.d), p. 159.

74. See Nathan J. Brown, *Constitutions in a Non-Constitutional World: Arab Basic Laws and the Prospects for Accountable Government* (Albany, NY: State University of New York Press, 2002), p. 162.

75. These two concepts will be discussed further in Chapter 5.

76. Azizah Y. al-Hibri, "Islamic Constitutionalism and the Concept of Democracy", in *Border Crossings: Toward a Comparative Political Theory*, edited by Fred Dallmayr (Maryland: Lexington Books, 1999), pp. 63–87.

77. Azizah Y. al-Hibri, "Islamic and American Constitutional Law: Borrowing Possibilities or a History of Borrowing?", *University of Pennsylvania Journal of Constitutional Law* 1 (1999): 492, 497.

78. El Fadl, "Constitutionalism and the Islamic Sunni Legacy"; see also Anver Emon, "Reflections on the 'Constitution of Medina': An Essay on Methodology and Ideology in Islamic Legal History", *UCLA Journal of Islamic and Near Eastern Law* 1 (2002): 103.

79. H. Patrick Glenn, *Legal Traditions of the World* (New York: Oxford University Press, 2000), p. 35.

80. Ibid., p. 325.

81. See also H. Patrick Glenn, "The Capture, Reconstruction and Marginalization of 'Custom' ", *American Journal of Comparative Law* 45 (1997): 613.

82. Many Muslim scholars are firm in their belief that *shari'a* addresses the fundamentals of human rights. For instance, they identify the most important human rights principles in Islam to be: dignity and brotherhood; equality among members of the community without distinction on the basis of race, colour, or class; respect for the honour, reputation, and family of each individual; the right of each individual to be presumed innocent until proven guilty and individual freedom. See Tahir Mahmood, ed., *Human Rights in Islamic Law* (New Delhi: Genuine Publications, 1993). This book compiles articles from leading Muslim scholars such as Abul A'la Maududi, M. I. Patwari, Majid Ali Khan, Sheikh Showkat Husain, and Parveen Shaukat Ali. I will examine this issue in Chapter 4.

83. El Fadl, "Constitutionalism and the Islamic Sunni Legacy".

84. Kamali, *Principles of Islamic Jurisprudence*, p. 403.

85. El Fadl, "Constitutionalism and the Islamic Sunni Legacy", p. 88; more discussion on this topic can be found in M. Sa'd b. Ahmad b. Mas'ud al-Alyubi, *Maqasid al-Shari'a al-Islamiya wa 'Alaqatuha bi Adillah al-Shar'iyya* (Riyadh: Dar al-hijrah

li al-Nasyr wa al-Tawzi', 1998). This work is based on his Ph.D. thesis at al-Jami'ah al-Islamiyah bi al-Madinah al-Munawarah, 1995.

86. Taqi al-Din Ibn Taimiyah, *Majmu' al-Fatawa*, Vol. 2 (Beirut: Mu'assasah al-Risalah, 1398 H), p. 134.

87. As quoted in Kamali, *Principles of Islamic Jurisprudence*, p. 407.

88. Ibid., p. 408.

89. Full text of the Charter can be found in http://islamic-world.net/islamic-state/macharter.htm.

90. See Anver Emon, "Reflections on the 'Constitution of Medina' ".

3

INDONESIA, *SHARI'A*, AND THE CONSTITUTION
An Overview

I have argued at length in the previous chapter that *shari'a* is compatible with constitutionalism. However, the question remains: how can *shari'a* play a role in a constitution? Should it become the primary source by inserting its elements into a constitution? Should it be present only in spirit or as an inspiration? In this chapter, I will show how the Indonesian people have responded to this matter.

The aim of this chapter is to provide the institutional and historical context for the subsequent chapters analysing the influence of *shari'a* in the three main case studies: human rights, the rule of law, and religion vis-à-vis the state. In order to achieve this goal, it is necessary to discuss the evolution of the struggle for the inclusion of *shari'a* into the Indonesian Constitution from the Independence era in 1945 until the Reform era in 1999–2002. The political systems and practices during 1945–2002 will also be examined.

In August 1945, at the last moment, seven words from the Preamble to the Constitution (known as the Jakarta Charter) were removed and thus excluded from the Constitution. The seven words involved a requirement for Muslims to observe *shari'a*. During the last half-century the Indonesian Islamic-based parties have been attempting periodically to have the seven words reinstated, but without success. Under the Soeharto government

(1966–1998), support for the Jakarta Charter was considered subversive and could be punished with years of imprisonment.

Prior to President Soeharto's resignation on 21 May 1998, Indonesians had lived under authoritarian regimes for about forty years. The lack of democratic principles in the 1945 Constitution, such as the separation of powers, checks and balances and guarantees of citizens' civil and political rights, was an important factor contributing to the rise of authoritarianism in Indonesia, after a brief experiment with parliamentary democracy in the 1950s. Constitutional reform is a critical aspect of Indonesia's transition, for the original form of the 1945 Constitution was an inadequate foundation for democracy. Constitutional reform was also one of the basic demands of the student movement, which led to President Soeharto's resignation in 1998, and Indonesian political elites have been struggling with the issue ever since.

Soeharto's departure has also opened up the opportunity for several Muslim groups and political parties to propose the introduction of *shari'a* into the Constitution. Although there were Islamic political parties that supported the seven famous words in 1999, in this chapter, I will show the shifting position of the two largest Islamic organizations, in 1955 and in 1999, on the issue of *shari'a* and Constitution, which led to a polarization by nationalist and Muslim blocs (and modernist-traditionalist blocs) in 1955 to formal and substantive *shari'a* groups in 1999. While both Muhammadiyah and Nahdlatul Ulama (NU) (with around sixty million members) supported the inclusion of *shari'a* into the Constitution in 1955 parliamentary debates, both rejected such proposals in 1999–2002.

The chapter will be divided into three parts. The first part will evaluate the debate on the Jakarta Charter in 1945 and in 1955. The second part will examine the issue of *shari'a* vis-à-vis state ideology under the New Order government. The last part will focus on the process, the debate and the results of the Amendment to the 1945 Constitution following the fall of the Soeharto government. In particular, it will highlight the efforts of several Islamic political parties to propose the inclusion of *shari'a* into the Constitution.

THE JAKARTA CHARTER AND THE 1945 CONSTITUTION

From the beginning of the Japanese occupation, the Japanese military government had to cooperate with the available nationalist leaders against the Dutch and later assign them as intermediaries to rule the country, and to participate in the costly ongoing war against the Allies. During the last phase of the occupation the Japanese military leaders had to give in to the growing demands of the independence movement.

It was also natural that the Japanese occupying power should try to use religion, in this case Islam, for its own wartime ends. M. A. Azis, as quoted by B. J. Boland, explains:

> The Japanese considered Islam as one of the most effective means to penetrate into the spiritual recesses of Indonesian life and to infuse the influence of their own ideas and ideals at the bottom of the society. For exactly the same reasons, Christianity was chosen in the Philippines as an important vehicle for ideological penetration.[1]

On 29 April 1945, the Japanese established the BPUPK (the Investigating Committee for the Preparation of Independence) to discuss the foundation of the state and the constitution for the future of Indonesia. The BPUPK consisted of sixty-two members, with Dr Radjiman Wedyodiningrat and R. P. Soeroso as its president and vice-president respectively. With an eye towards facilitating a stable and peaceful transition, the Japanese tried to ensure that the BPUK was composed of men from the older and more experienced generation of leaders associated with the different pre-war nationalist and Islamic movements.[2]

Ideologically, the BPUPK represented the two main groups of thought: the "secular" nationalists, and the Islamic nationalists.[3] This explains why one of the issues during the first session of the BPUPK (19 May – 1 June 1945) was the basic foundation (or ideology) of the state: whether Indonesia would be an Islamic state or a state which would separate religious affairs from state affairs. In this regard, Professor Soepomo, one of members of BPUPK, remarked:

> On the one hand (there) is the opinion of the religious experts [*ahli agama*], who are proposing to establish Indonesia as an Islamic state, and on the other hand (there) is another proposal, as has just been proposed by Mr Mohammad Hatta, that is, a national unitary state which will separate the state from religious affairs.[4]

In order to find a solution, a sub-committee consisting of nine members was formed. The nine members were: Soekarno, Mohammad Hatta, A. A. Maramis, Abikoesno Tjokrosedjoso, Abdul Kahar Muzakkir, H. Agus Salim, Ahmad Soebardjo, Abdul Wahid Hasjim and Muhammad Yamin. After serious discussions, this sub-committee eventually succeeded in reaching a *modus vivendi* between the Islamic group and the secular group. On the first day of the second session, which was held on 10 July 1945, Soekarno reported on the agreement reached by the nine members. According to him, the five principles known as Pancasila, upon which a free Indonesia would be based, appeared in the preamble of the Constitution.[5] This preamble was signed by the nine-member committee in Jakarta on 22 June 1945, and later came to be known as the Jakarta Charter (Piagam Jakarta).[6] The five principles were: the belief in God with the obligation to implement Islamic *shari'a* for its adherents; a just and civilized humanity; the unity of Indonesia; a democracy guided by wisdom arising from consultation and representation; and social justice for the whole Indonesian people.

The agreement above reflected a compromise between the two opposing groups. The draft of the Constitution did not state that Indonesia was to be an Islamic state. It went further, stating that either a Muslim or a non-Muslim could be appointed as the Indonesian president.[7] Based on the agreement above, the draft accommodated non-Muslim concerns, stating that Islamic law would be applied only to Muslims. Both Islamic and nationalist groups agreed to reach this "middle position": the state recognized Muslims as the majority by granting them the right to implement their own law, and at the same time, the draft did not amount to the creation of a *Negara Islam* or Islamic state. In the words of M. B. Hooker, "While the Charter specifically refers to *shari'a*, it is vague as to its exact scope and competence, leaving much room for debate over its jurisdiction."[8] However, politically speaking, the vagueness could be seen as a win-win solution for both parties.

The agreement remained unchanged until 18 August 1945, one day after the proclamation of Indonesian independence,[9] when the PPKI (the Preparatory Committee for Indonesian Independence) was formed. This committee, which consisted of twenty-seven members and was headed by Soekarno and Mohammad Hatta as Chairman and Vice-Chairman respectively, held a meeting on the same day it was formed. Within a short time (between 11.30 a.m. and 1.45 p.m.) the meeting brought about several important changes to the preamble, in which the formulation of Pancasila appeared, and to the body of the Constitution.

A change was made to the first principle by omitting the seven words: *dengan kewajiban menjalankan Syariat Islam bagi pemeluknya* (with the obligation to carry out Islamic *shari'a* for its adherents). Therefore, the first principle became: the Belief in One Supreme God. This change surprised the Islamic group. Questions arose as to the reason why the formulation of the Jakarta Charter, which had been achieved with difficulty, could be changed with such ease. It was said that a Japanese officer of the *Kaigun* (Japanese navy) came to Mohammad Hatta to tell him that a Christian representative from Eastern Indonesia objected to the clause of "*shari'a*". He was warned that should it be kept unchanged, he and his people (non-Muslims from Eastern Indonesia) would separate from the Republic of Indonesia. Hatta was influenced by this message and promised to bring the message to the meeting.[10]

Consequently, most of the Muslim leaders agreed to Hatta's demands that references to the Jakarta Charter be removed from the preamble, that the related clause in the section on religion be excised. These changes were accepted by the PPKI, and Soekarno and Hatta were elected as President and Vice-President, respectively.

However, there was no doubt that several Muslim leaders felt betrayed. They had been involved in a long struggle for independence but when the fruits of their struggle, namely the freedom of Indonesia, had been achieved, their aspirations were neglected. The omission of the seven words meant that the 1945 Constitution did not specifically guarantee Muslims the right to implement their own law (*shari'a*). Isa Anshary, a prominent Muslim leader, considered this event to be tantamount to dishonest politics.[11]

Others took the view that the omission of the seven words reflected the biggest sacrifice by Muslims for the unity of the nation, which was very crucial at that time. The sacrifice was so great that not even the word "Islam" and "Muslim" or "*syari'at*" were mentioned in the constitution.[12] Later in 1978, Alamsjah Ratu Perwiranegara (Minister for Religious Affairs) interpreted that moment as "the greatest gift and sacrifice of the humble Indonesian Muslims as a majority population for the sake of Indonesian national unity and integrity".[13]

Soekarno reminded Muslim leaders that they could try to amend the text at a later date through constitutional procedures. To his credit Soekarno was able to convince even the most ardent opponents of the Jakarta Charter to lend their support, and as a result the draft constitution was unanimously accepted. Soekarno also stressed that the 1945 Constitution was only a "temporary constitution", a "lightning constitution", or a "revolutionary constitution", which, in due course, could be perfected by elected representatives of the people. In Soekarno's own words:

> Gentlemen, all of you realise that the Constitution we decide today [18 August 1945] is a temporary constitution. If I may I would like to use the words "a lighting constitution". At a later time when the State is in a peaceful and calm situation we would certainly bring together the members of the People's Assembly to make a more complete and perfect constitution.[14]

In this regard, several Muslim leaders were convinced that when the general elections came the issue could be discussed. As a majority, they believed that their group would achieve the majority vote.[15]

There were some Muslim leaders, such as Ki Bagus Hadikusumo, who believed that, although the seven words were omitted, their goals and struggle were implicitly accepted. Hadikusomo asked Hatta what was meant by the phrase "Belief in One Supreme God". Hatta answered that it was nothing other than the *tawhid* of Islamic monotheism.[16]

However, Sidjabat, a Christian scholar, took the view that the first principle of Pancasila is a general and neutral concept of God that gives room for everyone who worships God without becoming indifferent in matters of religions.[17] Thus, the Indonesian term *Tuhan* is capable of encompassing Christian, Islamic, Buddhist, and Hindu concepts of God. The term is used for "God" in place of the identical Arabic word, *Allah*, with its stronger Islamic connotations.

B. J. Boland shares Sidjabat's view, above, pointing out that:

> (the) first principle of *Pantjasila* is neither a syncretic compromise … nor is it a concept with only one interpretation, so that adherents of one religion could prescribe to others what their belief in God and their worship should be like, in order to be in accordance with the basis of the state. This first principle must be understood as a multi-interpretable formula and must be appreciated as providing a real possibility for people to agree while disagreeing.[18]

The government of the new republic realized that certain concessions would have to be made. One of the most significant of these came in January 1946, with the establishment of an Indonesian Ministry of Religious Affairs.[19] The establishment of this ministry provided proof that the government had implemented the first *sila* (pillar) of the Pancasila: Indonesia is neither a secular state, nor an Islamic state. In later years, the official structure of the Ministry also came to include separate sections addressing the needs of Indonesia's various religious communities, although the Muslim section still dominates all others, and generally controls the Ministry itself. For instance, all Ministers of Religious Affairs, since its establishment in 1946, have been Muslims.

However, the missing words of the *Piagam Jakarta* have never disappeared from the debate on what the state of Indonesia is supposed to represent for Islam, the religion to which the vast majority of the population adhere. The seven words are so central, in fact, that some Muslim groups have persistently called for reinclusion of the *Piagam Jakarta* in the Constitution, ever since those words were dropped in 1945. The Muslim leaders were basically unable to accept that in a country where Muslims are the majority there can be anything other than Islam as the basis of unity.[20] Ahmad Hassan, for instance, questioned why the 90 per cent Muslim majority must be overlooked because of the 10 per cent non-Muslim minority.[21]

There were more radical attempts to make *shari'a* the basis of the Indonesian state. Kartosoewirjo declared the Islamic State of Indonesia

(*Negara Islam Indonesia*). Kartosoewirjo's movement, later known by the name of Darul Islam, developed into a full-blown rival to the Republic, which resisted the return of the Siliwangi division to West Java in 1949, and, after 1950, continued a guerrilla war against the Jakarta government. Kartosoewirjo's Islamic State had its own Constitution, explicitly based on *shari'a*, and a judiciary where *ulama* delivered Islamic justice. The Darul Islam remained a military and political embarrassment to the Jakarta government until Kartosoewirjo's capture, and the surrender of the other West Javanese leaders in 1962.[22]

Konstituante

Indonesia has been governed by three constitutions since independence: the 1945 Constitution, the 1949 Constitution and the Provisional Constitution of 1950. The 1945 Constitution came into force on 18 August 1945. On 27 December 1949, the colonial government was back, and succeeded in breaking up the Republic of Indonesia (RI), whereupon the new Republic of the United States of Indonesia (Republik Indonesia Serikat, or RIS) came into being. A new constitution, known as the 1949 Constitution, replaced the 1945 Constitution.[23]

The 1949 Constitution did not last long, however, because there were tremendous efforts made within the RIS during its first seven months to transform Indonesia from a union of states (a federation of states) into a unitary state. On 17 August 1950, the Provisional Constitution came into force with the reestablishment of the Republic of Indonesia. The new state did not bring back the 1945 Constitution.[24]

The drive to make Islam the basis of the state was revived in the Constituent Assembly (Konstituante), which was the result of the first national general election in 1954. The debates led to a situation in which no faction had a majority of the vote. The Provisional Constitution of 1950 was enforced until mid-1959, when a decree by President Soekarno replaced it with the old 1945 Constitution, which was originally intended to be a temporary measure before the formal constitution, devised by the popularly elected assembly, was established. I will examine this political situation briefly.

The defeat of the Darul Islam movement transferred the struggle over the religio-political identity of Indonesia to the political sphere. Masyumi (Majelis Syura Muslimin Indonesia, or Consultative Council of Indonesian Muslims) became the Islamic party which played a prominent role in the politics of Parliamentary Democracy between 1950 and 1957. Masyumi was backed by the Muhammadiyah and the NU Islamic associations. Although some 85 per cent of Indonesians described themselves as Muslims, many among them, especially in Java, followed the Nationalist Party, Partai Nasional Indonesia (PNI). From 1950 to 1955 the PNI and Masyumi quarrelled over the role of Islam and of the Communists — who formed another party, Partai Komunis Indonesia (PKI).

In 1952, the NU withdrew from Masyumi and became a separate political party. This situation raised once again the old divide between traditionalist and modernist Muslims.[25] The traditionalist/modernist schism divided Masyumi at its very core and produced a power struggle between Natsir's religious-socialist faction and the base Nahdlatul Ulama constituency that ultimately produced a mass defection of the traditionalists from Masyumi three years before the general elections.[26] In other words, NU's withdrawal reduced Masyumi's popular support considerably.

Mochtar Naim's study ascribes NU's decision to two factors — the structure of Masyumi and the dualistic character of Masyumi's membership.[27] Anwar Harjono mentions another factor, the position of the Minister for Religious Affairs. Whereas the NU proposed that the position be filled from among its *ulama*, the leaders of Masyumi preferred a person from the Muhammadiyah.[28]

A Congress of Ulama and Islamic Propagators (Kongres Alim-Ulama dan Muballigh Islam), which was attended by no less than 217 *ulama* from all over Indonesia, was then held in Medan from 11 to 15 April 1953. The Congress eventually issued a *fatwa* (Islamic legal opinion) and passed a number of resolutions relating to the State ideology which Muslims should support. The *fatwa* stated:

> It is incumbent upon every Indonesian citizen who embraces Islam, women as well as men, and who possesses the right to vote, to go to the polls and elect only the candidates who will fight for the realization of Islamic teaching and law in the State.[29]

The question as to whether the *fatwa* was effective or not can be answered by looking at the results of the first national election in 1955. The loss of the traditionalists' organizational networks among the *kyai* and *pesantren* of East and Central Java was a tremendous blow to Masyumi's campaign efforts in 1955. The PNI with 22.3 per cent won the largest share of votes; the Masyumi came in second with 20.9 per cent, closely followed by the NU with 18.4 per cent. The results of the general election led to the formation of the Konstituante. It also confirmed the ideological polarization between the Islamic and non-Islamic parties, known as *politik aliran*, producing balance between them as well.[30]

These Islamic and non-Islamic factions were divided into three groupings, each advocating a specific state philosophy. Firstly, there was the Pancasila bloc, which upheld the five principles of Pancasila to be the basis of the state. Secondly, there was the socio-economic bloc, which stood for a socialist economy and democracy as the basis of the state; and thirdly, there was the Islamic bloc, which advocated Islam as the basis of the state.[31]

On 1 June 1959, based on the Islamic faction's proposal, there was voting on whether or not the seven words from the Jakarta Charter were to be restored to the 1945 Constitution. The vote was as follows: 201 votes were cast for the amendment and 265 were cast against.[32] This means that the Islamic bloc lacked the support of a two-thirds majority to restore the Jakarta Charter. Instead of writing a new constitution or making any amendments, the government then proposed to return to the 1945 Constitution. Lacking the support of all Islamic factions, who were disappointed with the rejection of their proposal on the previous day, on 2 June 1959, the return to the 1945 Constitution was rejected by 203 votes.[33] This means that once again the required two-thirds majority (312 votes) could not be achieved.

Unfortunately, while the Konstituante went into recess, Soekarno, backed up by military leaders, dissolved the Konstituante through his Presidential Decree of 5 July 1959, arguing that it could not make any progress in its charter. The Decree abrogated the 1950 Constitution and enforced the 1945 Constitution. In an analysis of these events, Adnan Buyung Nasution suggests that Soekarno and the military leaders played a "game", by providing the evidence that the Konstituante nearly finished its task, when Soekarno's decision dissolved it.[34]

The demise of the Konstituante led Indonesia back to the 1945 Constitution, which still remains in force. This means that the Muslims' hope for later inclusion of their aspirations in a new constitution never materialized in the Soekarno era. Once again, the attempt to include *shari'a* in the Constitution had failed. Legally speaking, there was no legal basis for Soekarno to issue the Decree which dissolved the parliament (the Konstituante). However, politically speaking, the military and the Prime Minister, Djuanda, supported Soekarno's decision.

It is particularly interesting to note in the preamble to the President's Decree the affirmation that the Jakarta Charter "gives life" to, or "influences" (*menjiwai*) the 1945 Constitution and that it forms an inseparable unit with the Constitution. These considerations were designed to unite two conflicting streams of thought: that of the supporters of the Pancasila in the Jakarta

Charter, and that of the supporters of the Pancasila in the preamble to the 1945 Constitution.

With regard to the relationship between the Jakarta Charter and the preamble to the Constitution, in which the two different formulations of the Pancasila are presented, B. J. Boland notes:

> It is worth mentioning that on May 5th, the representative of the Catholic Party, B. Mang Reng Say, stressed that for his party the Djakarta Charter was nothing more than "one of the historical documents from Indonesian soil which have occurred in the course of the history of the Indonesian people moving toward the proclamation of their independence", so that the Djakarta Charter "may not and cannot be a source of law" but may only be considered as a precursor, a draft, for the preamble of the constitution. The same point of view was also expressed by J.C.T Simorangkir, the speaker from the *Parkindo* (*Partai Kristen Indonesia*: the Indonesian Christian Party) in his speech at the Assembly on 17 May 1959.[35]

What did Muslim scholars say on this issue? In his *Demokrasi Pancasila* Professor Hazairin of the Faculty of Law, University of Indonesia, argued for the infusion of an Islamic spirit into the state's formulation of Pancasila. In presenting his case, he went so far as to argue that the Indonesian phrase "Ketuhanan Yang Maha Esa" was not the mere product of a committee compromise involving Indonesian Christians, Hindus, and Chinese, but rather a translation of the Qur'anic phrase: "The One and only God".[36] Hazairin also maintained that the 1945 Constitution as a whole could not be separated from the "spirit" which first animated it. Although he was not in favour of the creation of a formally Islamic state, for Hazairin, this spirit was most succinctly expressed in the preamble as originally formulated (the Jakarta Charter).[37] Consequently, although the Charter was not one of the sources of Indonesian law, there should be no law nor government regulation which contradicts the spirit of the 1945 Constitution (i.e., the Jakarta Charter). The controversy on the meaning of the Charter, particularly among legal experts and religious scholars, remains.[38]

Having read all the minutes of the meetings during Konstituante sessions from 10 November 1956 until 2 June 1959, Adnan Buyung Nasution observes that:

> In the debate on the return to the 1945 Constitution, the Islamic political parties ultimately demanded only the re-instatement of the "seven wordings" of the Jakarta Charter that had been deleted from the 1945 Constitution on 18 August 1945. In doing so, they manifested an underestimation of the dangers inherent in the 1945 Constitution of development of dictatorial

powers, which many of their members had previously criticized vigorously. Thus, in the debate on the *Dasar Negara* and again in the debate on the return to the 1945 Constitution, the coalition of Islamic parties in fact neglected the concept of constitutional government. The parties opposing the Islamic state did not do so from the point of constitutionalism, but because they objected to a counter-ideology.[39]

In other words, the debate on the ideological foundation of the state was intended to determine the further provisions of the constitution. It was seen as the basic principle, inspiring all articles of the constitution and other organic laws. The great majority of the Konstituante commission clung to this as an item on the agenda requiring thorough discussion. The parties in the Konstituante still remained fixated on ideological concerns. It was unfortunate that the "deadlock" over the state ideologies prevented the Konstituante from creating a constitution which would be based upon constitutionalism. I will explain the characteristic of the 1945 Constitution vis-à-vis constitutionalism in the next section, when dealing with the Soeharto government.

With the defeat of the Muslim aspirations to create an Islamic state and to restore the Jakarta Charter, control of the state was taken over by President Soekarno and the Army. The return to the 1945 Constitution was easily interpreted by Soekarno as an excuse to introduce his "guided democracy" and concentrate most of the power in his hands. In 1960 the Soekarno regime banned the Masyumi Party. It was alleged that several of its leaders had joined the rebels and formed a counter government in 1958. Masyumi opposed Soekarno's cabinet, because it contained Communists, and also opposed a National Council to represent workers, peasants, youth and regional interest groups.

Meanwhile, the NU maintained close ties with Soekarno. According to Lapidus, "While Masjumi was broken because of its ideological demands, Nahdlatul Ulama was able to retain political and tactical stability."[40] Even the NU accepted Nasakom, a Soekarno programme which attempted to synthesize nationalism, religion and communism, whereas other *ulama* condemned it by arguing that religion and communism could not be synthesized in any way. NU leaders believed that they had little choice but to accept Nasakom in order to avoid, firstly, the possible threat of retaliation from Soekarno, and the army, if NU did not support Soekarno's programme, and, secondly, the potential threat of the Communist party (PKI).[41]

Thus far, I have explained in this section the debate, political compromise, and the struggle for the state ideology during 1945–65. I have not only described political factions between nationalist group and Muslim groups, but have also indicated the internal friction within Muslim groups, such as Masyumi and the NU. In the next section, I will discuss the issues highlighted above in the period of the Soeharto government, particularly the relationship between the Soeharto government (1966–98), the 1945 Constitution and Islam vis-à-vis the state.

SHARI'A AND THE NEW ORDER GOVERNMENT

In this section, the characteristics of the Soeharto government will be evaluated in relation to constitutionalism. It will also examine the fluctuating relationship between Muslim communities and the government. Although, at the end of his government, Soeharto took a closer relation with Muslim societies, it is safe to argue that throughout the period of the New Order government, constitutional debate on the Jakarta Charter was forbidden because of the deep-seated suspicions of the government concerning its disruptive potential.

Islam under Soeharto

The alleged attempted Communist coup of 1965 is a watershed in modern Indonesian history. It brought about the fall of Soekarno.[42] The New Order government, as opposed to the Old Order of Soekarno, formally began when, on the evening of 27 March 1968, General Soeharto, aged 46, was formally sworn in as President of Indonesia by a decision of the Provisional People's Consultative Assembly (MPRS). Soekarno's regime left several pieces of "homework" for the New Order to contend with, such as the economic crisis, the remnant members of the Communist Party (PKI), which was banned by General Soeharto in 1966, and the disintegration of the Indonesian Armed Forces (ABRI), particularly the split between the Angkatan Darat (army) and the Angkatan Udara (air force).[43] From the beginning, Soeharto opted to solve economic problems as a priority, rather than alter the political system. The Soeharto government continually adopted the line that it could not talk about democracy and discuss the political system, when the people did not have enough food. Put it differently, Soeharto's New Order government focused mainly on economic development, in order to provide steadily improving standards of living for Indonesians.

Both the political and the legal systems had to support the development strategy of the nation. Therefore, the principles of the rule of law or Negara Hukum were accepted, only as long as they supported development, and Soeharto's assessment of the national interest. Accordingly, the rule of law seems to have played a very minor role, if any, in the economic development of the nation.

A. H. Johns describes the New Order government as "a government with the avowed aim of restoring the nation's confidence in itself and ensuring stability, even if authoritarian methods were needed".[44] R. William Liddle argues that the political structure of the New Order can be described as a steeply ascending pyramid, in which the heights are thoroughly dominated by a single office, the presidency. According to Liddle, the President commanded the military, which was *primus inter pares* within the bureaucracy, and which in turn held sway over society.[45] In this sense, he was practically the only effective institution in the country.

In the early days of the New Order, Indonesian Muslims hoped that they would have a greater say in the running of the country than during Soekarno's regime. Throughout 1968 and 1969, the Islamic parties sponsored "Jakarta Charter Commemoration Day" programmes to be held annually on 22 June. Their leaders were involved in discussions about the ideological direction of the state, but from the very beginning they affirmed that they supported Pancasila as the state philosophy. They did not want to establish an Islamic state. Their only real aim was that Islamic law should be implemented, and hence they requested that the Jakarta Charter be given official status. It might be said that Muslims supported the New Order government because of this hope. They went further by attempting to get the Jakarta Charter legalized as the Preamble to the 1945 Constitution, during the session of the People's Consultative Assembly (Majelis Permusyawaratan Rakyat or MPR) in March 1968, but they were to be disappointed.[46]

The New Order government continued Soekarno's policy of displaying respect for Islam as a private religious practice, but was determined that Islam would not become a powerful political force. Therefore, in the early period of the New Order, Muslims continued to play only a marginal political role.[47] The New Order feared that since Muslims could not accept Pancasila as the ideology of the state at that time, they would continue to be inspired by their aspirations to turn Indonesia into an Islamic state. In other words, at the beginning of New Order era, as Donald K. Emmerson writes, the generals of the ABRI, who formed a powerful element in the New Order, many of them only superficial Muslims, saw in Islam's cultural strength a distinct political threat.[48]

There were at least two principal views on the Jakarta Charter expressed by Islamic groups during the Soeharto government. Firstly, the statement that the Jakarta Charter "inspires" the 1945 Constitution was accepted without attempting to further define or modify it; Secondly, the Charter should become the Preamble to the 1945 Constitution, and this would be seen as a symbolic victory for the recognition of *shari'a* by the state. This would require an amendment to the preamble.

The government accepted the first view, since it was based on the 1959 Presidential Decree. The government was worried by the last view. The military felt that Muslims did not want to accept Pancasila (the five principles of the Indonesian state ideology) and aspired to replace it with Islamic ideology. Any effort to link *shari'a* to the Constitution would be considered as subversive.[49] Many Muslim activists were sent to jail because they rejected the *asas tunggal* (sole foundation), which was the government's programme to have Pancasila adopted as the only ideological foundation of all social and religious organizations.[50]

Eventually, however, the NU accepted Pancasila as an ideology of state. In 1985, K. H. Ahmad Siddiq, *Ra'is 'Am* (the General Chairman of NU), published a book which stated that the NU accepted Pancasila as the final form of ideology for Indonesia.[51] The Congress of the NU also explained that: "The Pancasila, as the basis of the Republic of Indonesia and the state's philosophy, is not a religion; neither can it replace religion, nor be referred to as replacing religion."[52] Once again the NU showed the accommodating position to government policies which it had shown during the period of Soekarno's Guided Democracy. However, this does not mean that the NU did not rely on religious arguments to support its position. Instead, the basic reason for the acceptance of Pancasila as the sole foundation of the NU was that Pancasila contained basic values which are not contradictory to Islam.[53]

Although Muhammadiyah, the second largest Muslim organization, took the very careful step of adopting Pancasila as its foundation, it affirmed that Pancasila was not a problem for Muhammadiyah since its earlier leaders such as Ki Bagus Hadikusumo, Kahar Muzakkir, and Kasman Singodimedjo had helped to formulate and accepted Pancasila as the state's basic foundation on 18 August 1945. This argument would mean that Pancasila was not in contradiction with Islam and could be adopted into the statutes of the organization.[54] The effect of the recognition of Pancasila as the sole foundation (*asas tunggal*) by the NU and the Muhammadiyah was that the government and the military began to regard an Islamic threat more sanguinely. Since then, from the late 1980s to the end of the New Order, the Government and the Muslims had entered a "honeymoon" period.[55]

This "positive" development continued when the government passed Law No. 7 of 1989, which pertains to Islamic courts in Indonesia.[56] Before

1989, the decision of a Religious Court needed the fiat of a District Court.[57] However, based on Law No. 7 of 1989, the position and the decisions of Religious Courts became equal to those of other courts. Religious Courts are under the supervision of the Ministry of Religious Affairs, whereas General Courts fall under the jurisdiction of the Ministry of Justice. Law No. 7 of 1989 defines "religious justice" as the justice system for people following Islam.[58] Therefore, the Religious Courts are for Muslims only, since only they observe Islamic law. However, the authority of Religious Courts is limited to specific areas: marriage, divorce, inheritance, *waqf* (pious endowment), and *hibah* (gift).[59]

Shortly afterwards, the Government sponsored the formation of ICMI (the Association of Indonesian Muslim Intellectuals). When Soeharto went to Mecca for the pilgrimage, Indonesian Muslims began to feel reassured. Soeharto subsequently changed his name: Haji Muhammad Soeharto. If we use Geertz's classification, many Indonesian Muslims believed that Soeharto was no longer *abangan*, and began to recognize him as *santri*.[60] He also lead the *takbir akbar* at the end of Ramadan in 1997.

Before the period of the "honeymoon", any government involvement in Islamic affairs was interpreted negatively as government intervention. The effect was that many government officials adopted Islamic attributes, and the Government involved itself in some Islamic issues in a much more positive way. For example, Muslim women were allowed to wear the *jilbab* (veil) at school and at government offices; the Government supported the building of new mosques and prayer houses; many Ministers went to the mosque for the Friday service and to celebrate the Ramadan rituals, and so on.[61]

Not only did relations between Islam and the New Order government improve during the "honeymoon" period, but also the relationship between Islam and the ABRI (Indonesian military) became much closer. According to Marcus Mietzner, in this period ABRI officers became more Islamic. There was a gradual shift in the military top brass, from a Christian and *abangan*-dominated leadership, to one with a *santri* background.[62]

Robert W. Hefner believes, however, that in the case of modern Indonesia, Geertz's categorization of *santri*, *abangan* and *priyayi* is no longer relevant. He wrote in 1995 that there is only "Islamization" or "Santrinization" in Indonesia right now. According to him, Indonesia's public culture today is far more Islamic than it was in the 1950s, and public piety is much greater. As he points out:

> cultural Islam has changed Indonesia's political culture, creating a Muslim middle class with greater initiative and influence than at any time in the New Order era. As Islamization brings more and more people to piety, it is

inevitable and, in fact, important that Muslims and non-Muslims reconsider the role of religion in public life.[63]

Whose Islam in Indonesia prevailed under the New Order government? The answer is fairly clear. The *ulama*, the military and the government were three elements which must be considered. The government, backed by the military, exercised an overarching role in Indonesia. This high level of influence was a result of three factors. Firstly, President Soeharto, a major general when he rose to power, used his personal knowledge of, and influence in, the military to make it the backbone of the New Order. Secondly, two-thirds of the Army's personnel comprise the "territorial system", units stationed at all levels of the state administrative system, from the capital down to the village level. This system was used to monitor and coerce the civilian bureaucracy. It remains largely intact to this day, although some of its more intrusive functions have been abandoned. Thirdly, the "dual function" (*dwi fungsi*) ideology justified not only a traditional defence role, but also a political and social role, for the Indonesian military.

If someone wanted to be the leader of an Islamic organization, that person had to seek the government's permission. The military also strategically placed representatives in Islamic organizations. For example, the secretary (1995–2000) of the Council of Indonesian Ulama (MUI), Nazri Adlani, is a general of the ABRI. The government and the ABRI allowed any Islamic movement, as long as it did not attempt, nor aspire, to replace Pancasila with Islam as the ideology of the state. This suggests that the fear of an Islamic threat continued to exist. It should be noted that the Minister for Religious Affairs (1993–98), Tarmizi Taher, was an admiral of the ABRI with two stars, which suggests that the military was taking nothing for granted.

It is interesting to note Tarmizi Taher's sanguine published view on Islam:

> Islamic resurgence in Indonesia is not to be suspected, since Indonesian Muslims themselves have firmly accepted Pancasila as the state ideology and as the sole basis for political as well as social organizations. Meanwhile, Indonesian Muslims will never consider whether Pancasila is final, or a springboard for another destination, since Pancasila is able to facilitate their demands. They will never be afraid that Pancasila puts their religion to one side. Three and half years ago, we ratified Bill No. 8, 1985. We also already have a code on education and also on religious jurisprudence. All of these codes conform to the values and spirit of Islam.[64]

Despite Tarmizi Taher stating that Islamic resurgence in Indonesia was not to be suspected, according to Karel Steenbrink, the government remained very wary of importing Middle Eastern frustration and fundamentalism into

Indonesia. Students who journeyed to the Middle East on private funds were closely scrutinized after their return home. It was different with students who studied Islamic Studies at Western universities. During the 1980s and 1990s an average of 200 Western graduates in Islamic Studies were planned for each Indonesian Five Year Plan.[65] The New Order government openly patronized students who wanted to undertake Islamic Studies at Western universities, not only for the benefit of those students, but also for its own benefit. It seems that the government believed that Muslim scholars from Western universities would not import the idea of fundamentalism upon their return. The government's fear of an Islamic threat may have diminished, but it was taking nothing for granted.

The 1945 Constitution and Soeharto

In this section, I will explain how and why Soeharto took the policy not to change nor amend the 1945 Constitution. Not only would such policy stop the debate on Islam vis-à-vis the state, but would also support his authoritarian government. During the Soeharto era, Indonesia had a government but it was not a constitutional government.

Soeharto controlled the legal machinery and the destiny of a nation. Under his government, the Indonesian legal system was marred by flaws. Electoral bodies suffered from the absence of independent and transparent elections. In almost all affairs, effective checks and balances were lacking. Even the formally installed rules, regulations, and laws, were not effective, and weakly enforced in almost all sectors and at all levels of organizations. Informal institutions and the prevailing social norms also suffered from the same predicament. When a very high-profile political or business matter was at stake, the ultimate decision generally was understood to have come from the very top person. Often, that would be Soeharto himself, or a member of his inner circle. In this sense, he was practically the only effective institution in the country.[66]

With regard to the 1945 Constitution vis-a-vis constitutionalism, President Soeharto had "unlimited" powers. Two factors contributed to the powers of the presidency in Indonesia during the New Order government.[67] Firstly, the 1945 Constitution provided for a very strong chief executive. Nine of thirteen articles in the Constitution, dealing with the presidency, provide powers to the President (key executive, legislative, judicial, foreign policy and security powers). Limitations and checks and balances on the presidency are not the main concerns of the 1945 Constitution. It is understood that President Soeharto did not want to change nor make amendments to the 1945 Constitution during his presidency partly for this reason.[68]

In order to maintain its power, the New Order government prevented any political and constitutional change by the *de facto* abolition of any procedural possibility to alter the 1945 Constitution. This in effect prevented any attempt to restore the Jakarta Charter as the preamble, or to insert the seven words into Article 29 of the 1945 Constitution.[69] The People's Consultative Assembly (MPR) issued its Decree No. 1/MPR/1983, determining that: (i) the MPR should permanently maintain the 1945 Constitution; (ii) before the MPR uses Article 37 of the 1945 Constitution on the procedure for constitutional change, a referendum must be held to gain the people's consent. This Decree contradicted Article 37 of the 1945 Constitution, which does not mention any referendum:

> 1. In order to alter the Constitution, at least two-thirds of the total members of the Majelis Permusyawaratan Rakyat must be in attendance.
> 2. A decision shall be taken with the agreement of at least two-thirds of the total number of members who are in attendance.

Secondly, in accordance with Indonesia's 1945 Constitution, the President and Vice-President are elected by the country's highest legislative body, the Peoples' Consultative Assembly (MPR). This 1,000-member body consisted of the 500 members of parliament and another 500 representatives of different functional groups and of Indonesia's twenty-seven provinces. The appointment of these 500 delegates, together with that of the hundred appointed members of the military faction of Parliament, was in the hands of the President. In practice, Soeharto controlled the appointment of 60 per cent of the delegates in the assembly which elected him. As a result, every fifth year until 1998, the MPR unanimously re-elected Soeharto to the presidency.

Soeharto allowed only three political parties/interest groups: Partai Persatuan Pembangunan (PPP), Golongan Karya (Golkar), and Partai Demokrasi Indonesia (PDI).[70] In the Soeharto era, Golkar (Soeharto's party) won more than 60 per cent of the vote in each of six heavily stage-managed elections between 1971 and 1997.[71] For instance, the results of the May 1997 election were that Golkar gained votes and seats, moving from 68 per cent of the votes in 1992 to 74.5 per cent in 1997, and winning 325 out of the 425 seats being contested (the number of seats at stake rose from 400 in 1992 to 425 in 1997, owing to the reduction in the number of seats allocated to the Armed Forces, from 100 to 75, out of the total of 500 seats in the People's Representative Assembly (Dewan Perwakilan Rakyat, or DPR).

The reservation of seats for the military in the legislative branch is inherently undemocratic for the reason, among others, that military representatives are not elected. Moreover, the military's participation in

Parliament creates serious conceptual difficulties and potential conflicts of interest. By participating in politics in this way, the military seems to become, in effect, another faction or interest group, rather than an institution which acts on behalf of the entire country, given the role expected of the military, so that it would seem untenable for the military to act in Parliament as an opposition.

Why did Golkar win? The Soeharto government did not allow the establishment of an independent supervisory committee for the election. Consequently, it was difficult to have genuine elections during the Soeharto era. The vote-counting process was completely dominated by the government apparatus, while the other two political parties were completely excluded. The Indonesian military (ABRI) and the government bureaucracy were not neutral. Directly or not, they supported Golkar. This could be seen in the existence of the so-called three channels (*tiga jalur*): A (ABRI), B (the bureaucracy), G (Golkar). The channels had the responsibility to secure the New Order's political and economic policy.[72]

The legal system simply did not work in the sense that Soeharto controlled its operation. The Government drafted bills and "influenced" the Parliament to accept them. All the Parliament's substantive discussions took place outside the official meetings. Only when substantive agreement had already been attained would the members of parliament meet in public. This was a concept of "consultation for consent" (*musyawarah untuk mufakat*) introduced by the Soeharto government. Voting, as a mechanism to reach a decision, was avoided. Members of parliament who dared to speak out would be recalled by their parties. The Government then issued Government Regulations, at its discretion, to interpret laws. With regard to the dependence and the subordinated position of both the judiciary and the legislature, no one could challenge such interpretations or discretions.

From the above discussion, it can safely be stated that during the Soeharto government, the 1945 Constitution, which gave wide scope to official discretion, has been used for justifying all sorts of arbitrary government acts. It is for this reason that constitutional reform became one of the demands for reform by the student movement in 1998. The struggle and demands for reform will be examined below.

STRUGGLE FOR REFORM

It is beyond the scope of this chapter to explain all the factors which led to the Amendment to the 1945 Constitution. Therefore, I will examine only several factors and conditions that relate to the overall argument of this book. On the day following Soeharto's re-election for another five-year term by the MPR on 10 March 1998, student protests began to spill out of the campuses.[73] They demanded the total eradication of corruption, collusion and nepotism, and since Soeharto was seen as part of the problem, students also asked him to step down. The first serious clashes between university students and security forces took place in the Central Javanese town of Solo and in the East Javanese capital, Surabaya. On 14 March 1998, Soeharto announced his new cabinet, which included his daughter, Mbak Tutut, and his close friend, Bob Hasan. The new cabinet was immediately condemned by students and other critics as a "crony cabinet".

In April 1998, clashes between security forces and students occurred in many big cities, such as Medan, Jambi, Mataram, Bandung, Yogyakarta, and in East Kalimantan. On 1 May, Interior Minister Hartono informed the press that Soeharto had stated that political reform must wait until after 2003, the year of the next scheduled MPR session.

While Soeharto was in Cairo for a summit conference on 12 May 1998, four university students were shot dead after a peaceful protest outside Jakarta's Trisakti University. On the following day, the four Trisakti students were buried. Professor Amien Rais of Gadjah Mada University and Chair of Muhammadiyah (the second largest Muslim organization) told the crowd that the military had to choose between defending "a certain family" or the people of Indonesia.[74] Meanwhile, rioting broke out in Jakarta, centred on the districts surrounding the Trisakti campus.

The following day, 14 May 1998, was the worst day of rioting in Jakarta. Jakarta looked like a death city. By the end of the day, in Jakarta and neighbouring cities, two hospitals, two sub-district offices, thirteen markets, forty shopping malls, eleven police stations, more than sixty bank offices, 383 private offices, twenty-four restaurants, twelve hotels, more than one thousand private homes and thousands of shops had gone up in flames, or had been seriously damaged.[75] The police and military could not do much to control the situation. In fact, soldiers were very visibly present in the streets. Some symbols of the Indonesian development under Soeharto were destroyed. On the next day, rioting began to abate in Jakarta and elsewhere. It was reported that many Chinese women were raped during the riots.[76]

However, when Soeharto returned from Cairo, he stated that he was not willing to resign. Instead, he was willing to reshuffle the cabinet. Responding to that statement, Amien Rais announced that Soeharto should step down within the week. The ruling élite began to crumble as Mien Sugandhi, head of the Golkar organization MKGR, called on the President to resign.

Although the word "reform" dominated the demonstrations, in free speech rostrums there were at least seven popular demands. They were:

(1) reform of the 1945 Constitution;
(2) repeal of five notorious laws on politics;
(3) abolition of the army's involvement in politics;
(4) reduction of the prices of basic foodstuff;
(5) the elimination of corruption, collusion and nepotism;
(6) the resignation of Soeharto; and
(7) the establishment of a court to try Soeharto, his followers and other perpetrators of human rights abuses.[77]

However, the main target was Soeharto. Without his resignation, the other six demands could not possibly be addressed. In other words, substantive reform could not be pursued within the system while Soeharto remained in charge. This explains why Soeharto's offers to initiate reform were rejected. Soeharto responded to the demands by calling for calm and stressing that he would not seek re-election and by announcing that a general election, based on a new law, was to be held as soon as possible. Students no longer put any trust in him.

In the words of Amien Rais:

> My thesis is simple: it is not possible for us to hope for a change in the style of leadership, state management, central or regional government administration, if there is no replacement of the president. So, it's not possible to change the system without changing the president. As I have repeatedly said, it's precisely the "person" (*sang figur*) who influences the system. And the "person" perpetuates the system to maintain the *status quo* for all time. It is an illusion if people hope that, with his advanced age, Soeharto can carry out fundamental or drastic reform.[78]

Pressure was increased by unremitting student demonstrations, and the constant stream of delegations visiting Parliament. Critics finally made Harmoko and the other chairpersons of Parliament realize that the institutions they headed represented the people and that the time for foot-dragging had passed; they had to do something immediately. On 19 May, Harmoko, Chair of the Parliament, reiterated to a rowdy press conference that the Parliament wanted the President to resign as soon as possible.[79] At the same time, the number of students demonstrating at the DPR increased, and large demonstrations continued elsewhere around the country. People asked the MPR to hold a special session to impeach the President.

General Wiranto responded to Harmoko's statement above: "Today's statement by parliamentary leaders was a statement of individual opinions, even though it was presented by a group."[80] According to Wiranto, for Harmoko's statement to have a sound legal basis, all members of parliament would first need to be consulted through a regular session of Parliament. Legally speaking, Wiranto was right. There needed to be a lengthy process before the Parliament, as an institution, could ask the President to step down.[81] Because Parliament was not in session, a formal resolution ratified by the full membership could not be produced. This was a legal procedural constraint. However, politically speaking, Wiranto's statement could be read as indicating that the military remained loyal to Soeharto. This was a clear message from the Commander of the Armed Forces.[82]

On the evening of 20 May 1998, fourteen ministers in the economic, financial and industry fields decided to send their resignation letters to Soeharto.[83] Prior to this, Harmoko announced that the President had to resign by 23 May, or the DPR would initiate a Special Session of the MPR, to unseat him. Soeharto then issued a Presidential Decree which empowered General Wiranto to take emergency measures. However, Wiranto hesitated to follow the order for two main reasons. Firstly, Soeharto whispered to him, "It is up to you whether you follow the decree or not."[84] Secondly, he was aware that by following the order, he would be declaring martial law, and clashes between the security forces and the people would take place. The situation would become worse. Therefore, he decided not to follow the order.[85]

Three former Vice-Presidents (Umar Wirahadikusumah, Soedharmono and Try Sutrisno) visited Soeharto and they suggested that Soeharto resign for the sake of the nation. Afterwards, Vice-President Habibie himself met the President. Habibie advised Soeharto to retire, but to do so on his own terms, rather than being pushed to do so by others. Soeharto also invited forty-five persons to cooperate with him in the new Cabinet, but forty-two refused. Nor could he find politicians prepared to join his new cabinet. It was the final blow. Unable to compose a cabinet, Soeharto surrendered.

Finally, on 21 May 1998, Soeharto read his resignation speech and, based on the 1945 Constitution, Vice-President, B. J. Habibie[86] was sworn in as his replacement. General Wiranto, of the Indonesian military, announced that the military would protect the former President and his family. This announcement indicated that while Soeharto might have lost power, he retained loyal supporters, particularly in the military and bureaucracy.

SHARI'A AND CONSTITUTION IN THE REFORM ERA

This section focuses on three issues: the emergence of Islamic political parties in the post-Soeharto era; the process, results and criticisms of constitutional reform; and an overall evaluation of the debate on *shari'a* and the Amendment to the 1945 Constitution.

Islamic Political Parties

The resignation of Soeharto has opened a new era for the Indonesian people. As part of its institutional and instrumental reforms, Habibie's government produced more than fifty statutes. For instance, it repealed Law No. 1 of 1985 on General Elections; Law No. 2 of 1985 on the Structure and Status of the MPR and the DPR, and Law No. 3 of 1985 on Political Parties and Golkar. Three election laws were passed on 1 February 1999 by the Parliament.[87] In general, the laws are significant advances and show the commitment of the administration and major opposition figures in creating a new system, in which free and fair elections are possible.[88] All major parties and political leaders appeared willing to participate in the elections under these new ground rules. The three laws cover the requirements for forming political parties, the election system, and the composition of the national and local representative bodies.[89]

Unlike Soeharto, Habibie allowed a multi-party system. The most significant parties were the PDI-P (Indonesian Democracy Party–Struggle) following former President Soekarno's nationalist precepts and led by his daughter Megawati Soekarnoputri; the PKB (National Awakening Party), in which long-standing religious leader Abdurrahman Wahid was the most prominent figure, primarily representing the traditionalist Islam of Central and East Java; and the PAN (National Mandate Party), led by prominent reform campaigner Amien Rais, which attempted to appeal to both the modernist Islamic tradition and an urban, liberal vote.

Apart from the PPP (Partai Persatuan Pembangunan), which was established in the Soeharto era, other Islamic political parties were formed during the reform era: Partai Umat Islam (PUI, or Islamic People's Party), Partai Kebangkitan Umat (PKU, or Islamic People's Awakening Party), Partai Syarikat Islam Indonesia 1905 (PSII 1905, or 1905 Indonesia Muslim Association Party), Partai Politik Islam Indonesia Masyumi (PPIIM, or Masyumi Indonesian Muslim Political Party), Partai Bulan Bintang (PBB, or Crescent and Star Party), Partai Keadilan (PK, or Justice Party) and Partai Nahdlatul Umat (PNU, or Nahdlatul Umat Party).[90] The reform era is an opportunity for Islamic groups to express their political aspirations, including the aspiration for the inclusion of *shari'a* into the Constitution.

The PPP, PBB and PK have all declared Islam as their ideology, although Islamists are more prominent in the PBB and PK than in the PPP. PPP leaders now claim that they are committed to making Indonesia an Islamic state, although the party did not campaign on that platform in 1999. Many observers believe that PPP's Islamism is half-hearted, a political calculation intended to distinguish it from the other big five parties, all of which supported Pancasila as the state doctrine, in the 2004 election campaign.[91]

The PBB did campaign for an Islamic state in 1999. Many of its leaders have family connections with Masyumi leaders of the 1950s (the crescent and star was Masyumi's ballot symbol). Given its tiny vote, compared to Masyumi's 21 per cent in 1955, the PBB is considered by most observers to be a party of the past. Yusril Ihza Mahendra, Minister for Law in Megawati's Cabinet, serves as General Chairman of PBB.[92]

Finally, despite its even smaller size, the PK is the most sophisticated and promising of the Islamist parties. A few of its top leaders were trained in religious studies in the Middle East, but many more have advanced Western-style education, often in foreign universities. Though their basic approach to Islam is modernist, in that they read the Qur'an and Hadith directly without the mediation of medieval scholarship, many PK activists do not have roots in any of the pre-existing modernist organizations, such as Muhammadiyah or the DDII (Indonesian Islamic Proselytizing Council), the main refuge for Islamists in the Soeharto years. PK thus represents something new in Indonesian politics. Most of the party's voters are urban and are particularly concentrated in the neighborhoods around major universities, where many leaders are lecturers and researchers.[93]

PK campaigners in 1999 stressed not the Islamic state but opposition to official corruption, their professional qualifications to govern, and an egalitarian economic policy, balancing phased industrial development with self-sustaining agricultural growth. Their platform also proposed a sharper separation of executive, legislative, and judicial powers, with a Supreme Court no longer appointed by the president.[94]

On 7 June 1999, forty-eight parties competed in the election, with twenty-one winning at least one of the 462 contested seats in Parliament. The PDI-P party won 34 per cent of the vote and 153 seats in Parliament, whilst the Golkar party, which had run the country for thirty years, won only 22 per cent of the seats.[95] The result was that, in October 1999, for the first time, Indonesian citizens successfully changed their government through an open, transparent democratic process. The People's Consultative Assembly elected

Abdurrahman Wahid (popularly known as Gus Dur) as President ahead of Megawati, although her party won the election (but not the majority of seats) since several Muslim leaders from different political parties (the group known as the Central Axis) united to prevent Megawati from gaining the presidency during the People's Consultative Assembly meeting of October 1999. This suggests that the existence of Islamic political parties is too important to ignore, particularly when they are united or share similar views. In order to prevent social chaos in several provinces, arising from Megawati's defeat, Gus Dur's party nominated Megawati as Vice-President.

Unfortunately, Gus Dur neglected to sustain the support of the coalition force which had made it possible for him to become the President in the first place. He lost the support of the PPP, the third-largest party, when he induced Hamzah Haz, Chairperson of that party, to resign from the cabinet on 26 November 1999, after insinuating that Haz was involved in graft. Gus Dur also fired General Wiranto, the former chief of the Indonesian military, from the Cabinet. As if this was not enough, he then angered the two largest parties, PDI-P and Golkar, by dismissing Laksamana Sukardi (PDI-P member) and Jusuf Kalla (from Golkar) after accusing the two ministers of graft. At that time, Gus Dur's presidency was in some trouble. He had lost supporters from the Muslim political parties, the Indonesian military, Golkar, and the PDI-P. It was only a matter of time for the Parliament to unseat him.

President Wahid was then alleged to have misappropriated a US$2 million gift from the Sultan of Brunei. The money was given by Sultan Hasanal Bolkiah for humanitarian aid in Aceh, and the gift was handled informally, with no record kept of its disbursement. It was claimed that the money was a "personal gift" from the Sultan to the President for the people of Aceh. The Attorney-General's office found, in early June 2001, that legally there was no evidence to support claims that the President had been involved in any wrongdoing in relation to this matter. However, politically, this case became one of the reasons why the MPR moved to impeach the President, on 23 July 2001, leading to the replacement of President Wahid by his Vice-President, Megawati Soekarnoputri.

CONSTITUTIONAL REFORM

Indonesian reform is expected to meet popular demands in the post-Soeharto era, such as a less powerful presidency, a multi-party system, a more powerful Parliament, and a reduction in, or eradication of, parliamentary seats for the military in the DPR.[96] There are differing opinions regarding the necessary first steps in the reform of Indonesian law. Some scholars suggest a reform of the Mahkamah Agung (Supreme Court) by replacing the Chief Justice and other judges.[97] Some take the view that the 1945 Constitution should be reformed, either by amendment, or by introducing a new constitution.[98] There is another school of thought maintaining that law reform should be initiated by repealing old laws, which are the product of Dutch colonial times. Others believe that law enforcement should be the priority, instead of producing new laws.[99]

Despite such views, it could be argued that reform of the 1945 Constitution has been one of the most important aspects of the transition to democracy in Indonesia, which began in 1998. Despite the weaknesses in the 1945 Constitution as the basis for democracy, it was explicitly or implicitly accepted by most major political forces as the framework for the transition in Indonesia, beginning in 1998. Subsequently, however, many of the most important political parties came to believe that the Constitution must be amended to address weaknesses in the country's political structure.

The first set of changes was passed during the October 1999 General Session of the MPR, so that the new democratically elected president would be bound by them.[100] These changes affected nine of the Constitution's thirty-seven articles. The MPR decided to follow the American practice of constitutional amendment, in which the full original text is accompanied by the changes to these nine articles, which, as a whole, are referred to as the first amendment. The first amendment focuses on strengthening the position of the legislative and judicial branches vis-à-vis the executive branch. It also reaffirms the decree passed at the MPR Special Session in November 1998, which limited the president and vice-president to two five-year terms. Nonetheless, the first amendment merely scratched the surface of the serious problems within the 1945 Constitution.

In October 1999, August 2000, November 2001, and August 2002, the MPR passed the first, second, third and fourth amendments, respectively. The MPR is the sole body empowered by the 1945 Constitution to amend it. The MPR consists of 695 members, 500 of whom are national legislators (DPR members); the remainder consisting of 130 regional delegates elected by provincial assemblies, and 65 representatives of social organizations, chosen by the Electoral Commission.

Constitutional reform was an important part of the democratic transition in Indonesia for at least two reasons. First, the amendments have altered the basis of the political game. The four amendments affect the fundamental rules. Among other changes, the amendments have:

(i)   established the presidential democratic principles of separation of powers, and checks and balances;
(ii) substantially revised the constitutional framework for executive-legislative relations;
(iii) reinforced the principle of civilian supremacy over the military;
(iv) devolved potentially significant powers to sub-national authorities;
(v)   established a second chamber of the national legislature to represent regional interests;
(vi) inserted sweeping guarantees of citizens' civil and political rights into the Constitution; and
(vii) established a Constitutional Court.

These amendments have fundamentally altered the rules under which the state relates to its citizens, the three branches of government deal with one another, civilians and the military interact, and the national, provincial, district and village authorities relate to each other. Such fundamental changes, even prior to their full implementation, have already begun to alter the behaviour of political actors.

Second, there were also efforts to include among the amendments the legal basis for the implementation of *shari'a*. From the perspectives of democracy, this process is important, since it accommodated different and conflicting views in a constitutional way. As has been mentioned earlier, some Muslim leaders felt betrayed when the Jakarta Charter, which had been formulated through an agreement between the nine members of the Preparatory Committee for Indonesian Independence, was changed on 18 August 1945. Owing to the military's pressure and the issuance of Soekarno's Decree, which abolished the Konstituante in 1959, Islamic political parties had to face the political reality that the inclusion of their aspirations to restore the Jakarta Charter had not materialized. Again, due to the military's pressure, the struggle for the Muslim parties in the 1968 MPR session to discuss the legal status of the Jakarta Charter was unsuccessful. In the Soeharto era, no political parties dared to talk about the Jakarta Charter.

In the reform era, when freedom of opinion is guaranteed, the proposal and the discussion on *shari'a* and the state in the Parliament is no longer restricted. Proposals to amend the Constitution, including inserting the famous seven words, would not be considered tantamount to treason. The agreement or the rejection of any proposal would be based on, and guaranteed by, the constitutional procedure; not based on mass demonstrations, military force nor presidential decree.

The Political and Legal Processes of Constitutional Reform

The MPR authorized a subcommittee of its members, known as the Working Body (Badan Pekerja), to draft and debate further constitutional reforms and report to its next plenary session, which took place in August 2000. This eighty-six-member body, in turn, established a forty-four-member subcommittee, Ad Hoc Committee I (Panitia Ad Hoc I, or PAH I), to be the primary forum for this work. All political forces in the MPR were represented in these bodies. These forces came to an early consensus in November 1999 on three major points:

(1) to leave the Constitution's preamble untouched, thereby retaining Pancasila as the state ideology;
(2) to maintain the basic structure of the state as unitary, thereby thwarting an emerging debate on federalism; and
(3) to maintain the basic structure of the government as purely presidential, thereby preventing a debate on the re-establishment of parliamentary government.[101]

Apart from these macro-level issues, all other parts of the Constitution were up for debate.

By retaining Pancasila as the state ideology, the MPR has assured the military that it would avoid a debate over an Islamic state. However, this did not stop Islamic political parties proposing to insert the seven famous words into Article 29, not into the preamble. The issue would not be the establishment of an Islamic state but the implementation of *shari'a*. This is a different issue but a closely related one. At the same time, Islamic political parties could still propose the amendment of other Articles based on their understanding of *shari'a*. In other words, as long as the preamble to the 1945 Constitution, which consists of the Pancasila, is untouched, other proposals to amend the constitution would be welcome.

Between November 1999 and May 2000, PAH I conducted witness hearings, provincial consultation meetings, and international study missions. After the legislature reconvened in May 2000, PAH I conducted a detailed article-by-article review of the 1945 Constitution, which it completed at the end of June. The PAH I proposals included revisions of the sixteen articles of the existing 1945 Constitution and the draft text for five new articles.[102]

At the MPR annual session in August 2000, the amended text was approved for five new articles of the Constitution: on regional authorities, the national legislature, citizens and residents, defence and security, and national symbols. In addition, two new articles, on human rights and on the national territory, were approved. These amendments, collectively called the second amendment, and the contents of several of the MPR decrees passed at the 2000 annual session, addressed four important issues in Indonesian politics, each of which contained important changes to the Indonesian political system:

(1) civil-military relations,
(2) the separation of powers, and checks and balances,
(3) decentralization of power to the regions, and
(4) a bill of rights.[103]

Although the second amendment began to address some of the fundamental weaknesses of the 1945 Constitution, many issues remained on the table. The MPR decided, in August 2000, to give itself a two-year timetable, until the annual session of August 2002, to make further decisions on constitutional amendments. This was the latest annual session at which it was possible to pass major changes to the structure of state institutions, with enough lead time to put the technical arrangements in place to conduct regularly scheduled elections under the new arrangements in 2004.

Some of the primary issues that remained on the table included the relationship of religion and politics; the structure and powers of the national legislature (unicameral or bicameral); the method of election for the president and vice-president; and the establishment of an independent judiciary, with powers of judicial review and constitutional interpretation.[104]

The delays in addressing these issues contributed to the presidential crisis in 2001 and probably retarded the process of democratic consolidation. As mentioned earlier, President Abdurrahman Wahid, who replaced Habibie in October 1999, was impeached by the MPR, following his Presidential Decree to dismiss the MPR and the Golkar party.[105] One of the primary causes of the presidential crisis of 2001 was conflict between the President and legislators, over the weak status of the presidency. This weak status was a result of the rules of the game, contained in not only the original 1945 Constitution, but also the first and second amendments.

Another problem was that the Supreme Court lacked powers of constitutional interpretation and judicial review. Prior to the passage of the third amendment in November 2001, the article on the judiciary was one of the most inadequate parts of the 1945 Constitution. It only said that there are to be a Supreme Court and other judicial bodies whose make-up and powers would be regulated by law.[106] The third amendment made significant progress in resolving many of these issues. It reiterated the power of the Supreme Court to conduct judicial reviews of legal determinations below the level of laws in the hierarchy. It transferred authority over the judicial review of laws from the MPR to the new Constitutional Court. The third amendment also indirectly granted the Constitutional Court the power of constitutional interpretation, by stipulating that the court can "resolve conflicts of authority between state institutions whose powers are established by the Constitution".[107] Finally, the Constitutional Court is also required to make a legal decision on the validity of the DPR's articles of impeachment, under the new impeachment rules contained in the third amendment.[108]

Soon after the August 2000 annual session, PAH I formed a thirty-member "Team of Experts" (Tim Ahli) to assist it in its work. During the first half of 2001, much of the time and energy of PAH I was spent studying and debating various proposed amendments with members of this team. In mid-2001, PAH I became preoccupied with helping to prepare for the Special Session in July, which removed President Abdurrahman Wahid and installed President Megawati.

The MPR's attention then turned to preparing for its next annual session, in November 2001, postponed from August owing to the special session. This session achieved agreement on many of the remaining issues, but decisions continued to be postponed, on several crucial items, until 2002. Most importantly, the third amendment, passed at this session, clarified the presidential nature of the system and continued the process of establishing greater separation of powers, and checks and balances, between the three branches of government. The results were:

(1) it stripped the MPR of its status of having formally unlimited powers;
(2) it inserted a chapter on elections as the basis for legitimate political power;
(3) it established the principle of direct, popular election of the president and vice-president;
(4) it clarified the grounds and procedures for presidential impeachment;
(5) it underscored that the president cannot dissolve the legislature;
(6) it established a second chamber of the national legislature, to represent regional interests;
(7) it strengthened fiscal oversight institutions; and
(8) it created a constitutional court and a judicial commission.

However, agreement could not be reached on several important issues. One of these was the make-up of the MPR. Under one proposal, the MPR would consist strictly of the two chambers of the national legislature. Under the other proposal, in addition to these two chambers, the MPR would also continue to include unelected members representing the military, police and social organizations. The second unresolved issue was the procedures for the second round of the presidential elections. The third amendment states that a ticket which wins a simple majority of the national popular vote, as well as at least 20 per cent of the vote in at least half the provinces, is considered the winning one. If no ticket crosses these thresholds, however, then there must be a second round. Under one proposal, the second round would also be a popular vote between the top two tickets from the first round. Under the other proposal, in the second round the winning ticket would be chosen by the MPR from the top two vote-getters in the first round. Other important unresolved issues included the relationship of religion and the state, and the independence of the central bank.[109]

In August 2002, the MPR convened for another annual session and succeeded, after extended debate, in meeting its self-imposed deadline for completing this round of amendments. Under the amendment to the 1945 Constitution, the MPR is a fully elected body based on the 2004 General Elections, consisting strictly of the two houses of the national legislature. The second round of presidential elections, if necessary, will also be by popular vote. The outcome of the debate on the central bank was less propitious: its independence (or lack thereof) will be regulated by law rather than the Constitution. The MPR also approved retaining the original language of Article 29, on religion, thereby rejecting efforts to establish a constitutional basis for the implementation of *shari'a*. I will deal with this issue later.

Criticisms

The overall results of the constitutional reform have been highly criticized. First, the process of amending the 1945 Constitution was seen as pragmatic and politically oriented. The main reason is that the MPR acts as a constitutional convention. The MPR did not want to establish an independent constitutional convention. In taking this position, contrasts were drawn with the new constitutions adopted in recent years by Thailand, the Philippines and South Africa, all of which have established this method.[110]

A career politician attending a constitutional convention may choose simply to advance his future political prospects. The constitutional amendment by MPR members would easily result in a patchwork, since it could be affected by party interests. Accordingly, the people should become the best judges about what is and what is not in their own interest. The people should elect persons noted for their integrity as well as their honesty and judgement — qualities not always found in those who choose politics for a career.

By limiting citizen input to the process, the MPR may also unintentionally have limited the popular legitimacy accorded to the amendments. There are many books and even drafts of the constitution produced by scholars, research institutions and political parties. However, this public participation could not influence the formal debate within the MPR unless they were invited as part of the Team of Experts at Badan Pekerja meetings.[111]

Another drawback is that in 1999–2004 the MPR itself was not a fully democratically established body. Although the majority of the members of the MPR (1999–2004) were elected through open and fair general elections, on 7 June 1999, which were held based on electoral reforms, according to R. William Liddle, the electoral system was not substantially changed. "The main argument is that those members of the DPR and the MPR were still chosen by the national party leaders of their respective parties."[112] This suggests that members of the DPR and the MPR are accountable to their party leaders; not to the people. Representation is nothing without accountability. An accountable political system holds both the government and the elected members of parliament responsible to their constituents to the highest degree possible. To the extent that the democratic legitimacy of the MPR has been called into question, the constitution it has produced may suffer a legitimacy deficit as well.[113]

The MPR solicited citizen input on only a limited basis, preferring to reserve to itself the final decision on amendments.[114] The MPR conducted public hearings across the country, and its plenary sessions were open to the public, but it rejected all calls for a popular referendum on amendments and, until 2002, refused to consider establishing a Constitutional Commission (Komisi Konstitusi). The MPR has retained control of the formation of this commission, has postponed its formation until 2003, and has limited its mandate to "studying" the constitutional amendments that have already been approved.[115]

However, this idea meant very different things to different participants in the debate. At one extreme, the NGO coalition envisaged the Commission as an independent body without membership from the legislature, which would present its report to the MPR on an accept or reject basis. At the other extreme, the detailed concept put forward in debate by PDI-P was essentially an enlargement of external, particularly regional, assistance to the existing constitutional review process taking place under the direction of the Badan Pekerja of MPR. Others rejected it altogether.[116]

This commission will report to the MPR, while the NGO proposal was for an independent body. Several members of the MPR whom I interviewed remind the Commission that amending the Constitution will require a petition by one-third of the members of the MPR and will require the support of over half its total membership with two-thirds of the members present. Therefore, it will not be easy for the Commission to persuade the MPR to agree with its recommendation.[117]

Moreover, 106 members of the Parliament took the view that the MPR has committed constitutional suicide. The amended Article 1(2) in 2001 abolished the status of the MPR as the sole embodiment of popular sovereignty. Popular sovereignty was now to be determined "according to the Constitution", implying that sovereignty could be subdivided between a number of institutions.[118] This could be interpreted to mean that the MPR could not complete the fourth amendment (2002), since it does not have the legitimacy to do so. Fourteen members of the PDI-P, such as Amin Aryoso, Sadjarwo Sukardiman, Bambang Pranoto, and Imam Mundjiat, went further, by suggesting that the MPR return to the original 1945 Constitution, and abandon the first, second and third amendments.[119] Such interpretation and suggestions were rejected by the PKB and Golkar, since it would lead to a constitutional crisis.[120] The association of retired Indonesian military members (Pepabri) has openly expressed opposition to the constitutional amendments. Their argument is that the process of the constitutional amendment has deviated from its original course, and must therefore be stopped.[121]

Secondly, it argues that, by making partial changes, especially regarding executive-legislative relations, the first and second amendments created as many problems as they solved. The Indonesian Institute of Sciences or LIPI took the position that not only was the process pragmatic and politically oriented, but also the language is used in the amendments is far from normative-legal language, its structure is inconsistent and, more importantly, its paradigm is unclear.[122] For instance, the original Constitution contained numerous vague and incomplete clauses which, in an authoritarian context, allowed Presidents Soekarno and Soeharto to establish dominant presidencies. One prominent theme in the first two amendments was, therefore, to bolster the position of the legislature, and weaken the presidency, in order to strengthen the new democracy by instituting greater checks and balances.

However, as Blair King points out:

> The problem — in the absence of amendments to other articles regarding the presidency — is that the balance of power seesawed to the opposite extreme. In a democratic context of political pluralism and competition, the

executive branch became severely crippled by its dependence on legislative support, resulting in political paralysis and instability.[123]

The third amendment reversed this trend and strengthened the presidency, primarily by establishing the principle of direct election of the president and vice-president and by tightening the rules and procedures for presidential impeachment. Furthermore, accordingly, despite the changes in the first three amendments that weaken presidential power, the Indonesian president remains comparatively powerful.

The criticisms above are related to the process and method of amending the 1945 Constitution. The third criticism will focus on some aspects of the content of the amendment. For example, the approval of the DPR must be sought for the appointment of ambassadors, the governor of the Indonesian bank, the chief of the national police and the chief of the Indonesian military. It seems that the presidency will not be effective since the president cannot appoint or dismiss any of his/her key office holders without the approval of the Parliament. This also means that any candidate for key offices should persuade members of parliament to endorse her/his candidacy. This would invite political (and economic) bargaining.

Moreover, according to the Amendment of the 1945 Constitution (Article 20.5), the Law shall come into force one month after the Parliament passed it regardless whether the President signs the Law or not. This also could lead to constitutional crisis. For instance, President Megawati did not sign the Law on National Education since her political party was not happy with the process of drafting and the content of the bill. However, the law has come into force. How can one expect the president to follow the law that she/he did not want to sign?

In addition, Article 28I(1) states that "the right not to be prosecuted under retrospective laws are basic human rights that may not be interfered with under any circumstances at all." This has invited controversy since it did not allow for past human rights offences to be prosecuted in the new human rights court. It was feared that the lack of a retroactive clause might fail to satisfy the international community's demands that those responsible for gross violations in East Timor should be prosecuted.[124]

Suspicion was intensified as it was exposed that the military had actively lobbied for the insertion of this clause. The clause, in fact, had not been discussed in the PAH I before the annual session. However, the addition of its clause was decided by political manoeuvring of the military against other MPR members during the annual session. Neither did Committee A of the MPR deliberate about it. Thus, it is a procedurally questionable amendment as well.

Without retroactive prosecution of crimes against humanity, it would be extremely difficult to convict those responsible for human rights violations in East Timor and elsewhere, and to show the international community that Indonesia was making a serious effort to hold those responsible for gross violations accountable.

The MPR neglected the fact that actually some human rights can be completely suspended in times of a serious and widespread emergency affecting the very life and existence of the whole country. Such suspension in times of public emergency is called derogation. States can create limitations on the exercise of such human rights, so long as they are reasonably based on one of these grounds, have been created by proper legal procedure, and are accessible, clear, and understandable to the public.[125]

Shari'a and the Constitutional Reform

What about the discourse of *shari'a* vis-à-vis constitutional reform? It is essential to acknowledge that whilst the modernist (represented by the Masyumi) and traditionalist groups (represented by the NU Party) shared the same views in 1950s, that the Jakarta Charter should be restored, making their views contrary to those of the nationalist group, such polarization in 1999–2002 was no longer extant.

If we accept the classic categorization of Geertz,[126] in the 1955 constitutional debate, the relationship between Islam and politics polarized the Muslim community into *santri* and *abangan* socio-religious groupings. While the *santri* were inclined to direct their political orientation towards Islamic political parties, the *abangan* were more apt at expressing their political associations within the Nationalist (PNI) or Communist (PKI) parties. Therefore, it is safe to argue that the debate in 1955 was a reflection of the polarization between *santri* and *abangan*.

In the 1955 parliamentary elections, two *santri* political parties, Masyumi and NU, representing 40 per cent of the electorate, favoured replacing Pancasila with Islam as the foundation of the Indonesian state. Muhammadiyah, then and now the pre-eminent modernist organization, provided the core leadership of Masyumi.

However, during constitutional reform in 1999–2002, both Muhammadiyah and NU, as an autonomous social and educational organization, and through their sponsorship of the PAN and PKB parties respectively, strongly oppose the state enforcement of *shari'a*, as conceived by other Islamic political parties (PPP and PBBB). The NU, still under the guidance of former President Abdurrahman Wahid, is committed to a policy of religious pluralism and opposes the identification of the state with Islam. The Muhammadiyah's chairman, Ahmad Syafii Ma'arif, has said, "implementing the Jakarta Charter will only add more burden to the country, which is now on the brink of collapse".[127] At the same time, there are some elements of the modernist group in the PBB and the traditionalist group in the PPP which support the inclusion of *shari'a* into the Constitution. As can be seen, nowadays the *santri* group have differing opinions and positions.

Therefore, I offer a suggestion of a new polarization within Muslim groups during 1999–2002: *formal* versus *substantive shari'a* groups. The formal *shari'a* holds the view that all constitutional issues should be based on *shari'a* practised by the Prophet and the companions, in Medina fifteen centuries ago. They refer to the Qur'an, the tradition of the Prophet and the Medina Constitution. Adherents of Islam constitute around 87 per cent of the country's population. For the formal *shari'a* group, this fact alone should function as a constitutional legitimizer for making *shari'a* an integral part of the Constitution. There should be no single word in the Constitution which is in contradiction with *shari'a*. The Constitution should, in point of fact, be based on *shari'a*.

In contrast, the substantive *shari'a* support group holds that *shari'a* should be reinterpreted in line with democracy and constitutionalism, in order to choose or to create the best suitable options. They do not oppose *shari'a* — no Muslim will do so. Instead, they are against the idea that the state should enforce *shari'a*. They do not refute the concept that the spirit of *shari'a* might contribute to the amendment of the 1945 Constitution. They take the middle position, between secularism and fundamentalism.

In this regard, the PAN and PKB, supported by Muhammadiyah and the NU respectively, could be classified as the substantive *shari'a* group, while the PPP and the PBB could be classified as the formal *shari'a* group. This is a strong indication that, unlike in the 1955 debate, not all Islamic parties now adhere to a single ideological orientation. They seem to have different, often contradictory, political agendas. Of the big seven political parties in 1999, the PBB, which won 2 per cent of the ballot, campaigned in favour of state enforcement of *shari'a*. If the PBB votes are combined with those for the PPP, the pro-formal *shari'a* group total vote rises to 12 per cent (71 seats), a 28 per cent decline since 1955.

How can one explain this decline? One of the possible answers is that, as has been highlighted, both Muhammadiyah and the NU stated officially that they do not support the formal *shari'a* group.

Mujani and Liddle explain further:

> The second explanation claims that Sukarno's and Suharto's repression of political Islam between 1955 and 1999 — and the response of Muslim

politicians and intellectuals to that repression — produced a sea change in Muslim political culture. A few turned to violence, but the government crushed them. Many more, notably the Masyumi ideologue Mohammad Natsir and his followers, maintained their pro-*shari'a* position but retreated into the world of education while awaiting a more favorable political climate. After the fall of Suharto, this group reemerged as PBB, winning only 2 per cent of the 1999 vote. The largest group, however, consisted of young Muslims leaving the schools and universities from the 1970s onward who wanted to make their peace with the secular state. They were led on the modernist side by the religious thinker Nurcholish Madjid and on the traditionalist side by the activist Abdurrahman Wahid. They and their descendants today hold many key positions in government and civil society. They control Golkar, PKB, and PAN, and are responsible for those parties' opposition to state enforcement of the *shari'a*.[128]

Another distinct feature is that while Muslim groups paid attention to the restoration of the Jakarta Charter in 1955, all political parties shared similar views against changing or amending the preamble to the 1945 Constitution during the 1999–2002 debate. Therefore, the recent issue was to what extent *shari'a* can contribute to, or play a role in, the body of the Constitution (not in the preamble). As will be explained through the discussion in the following chapters, the formal *shari'a* groups took the view that *shari'a* should play a role mainly by inserting the famous seven words into Article 29, while the substantive *shari'a* group took the position that *shari'a* should be used as spiritual inspiration. Thus it was not necessary to put *shari'a*, in a literal and textual way, into Article 29 nor any other Articles in the Constitution.

What about the Muslim perception on the state enforcement of *shari'a*? National opinion surveys conducted in 2002 by the PPIM (Center for the Study of Islam and Society) at the State Islamic University in Jakarta appear to show that the majority of Indonesian Muslims favour the Islamic state. Seventy-one per cent of respondents in 2002 agreed "that the state should require all Muslim men and women to abide by the *shari'a*". Sixty-seven per cent in 2002 agreed that "Islamic government ... under the leadership of Islamic authorities (*ulama*) is best for a country like ours". However, this is balanced by low percentages in favour of the state's enforcement of fasting (12.9 per cent) and of five daily prayers (9.9 per cent).[129]

There are indications in the PPIM results that the popular understanding of *shari'a* is looser, more abstract, than that by the formal *shari'a* group. Many Indonesian Muslims may favour the *shari'a*, without agreeing to its more controversial provisions. This suggests that the meaning of *shari'a* is varied among Indonesian Muslims. For example, only 33 per cent in 2002 agree "that the law of cutting off the hand of a Muslim thief, as stated in the Qur'an, must be implemented by the government of this country". This reflects ambiguity of Muslim respondents: they conform on the general idea of adopting *shari'a* but they dispute over how it should be implemented. The survey has also shown that the support base of formal *shari'a* is not the majority one and this is confirmed by the fact that the PBB and PPP gained only 12 per cent of the seats in Parliament.[130]

CONCLUSION

The original 1945 Constitution was an inappropriate foundation on which to erect the superstructure of a democracy. The constitutional supremacy of the MPR did not allow for the checks and balances which typify healthy presidential systems. This was reinforced by the lack of explicit protections for basic human rights in the Constitution. In addition to these philosophical considerations, four decades of authoritarianism, anchored by the 1945 Constitution, served as the proof of the pudding for many Indonesians. Since its reinstatement by President Soekarno on 5 July 1959, the 1945 Constitution has facilitated the establishment of two authoritarian regimes — Guided Democracy under Soekarno and the New Order under President Soeharto, which together lasted for almost four decades. The challenge, as the transition to democracy began in 1998, was what to do about the Constitution. I have outlined briefly in this chapter both the results and the criticisms of the constitutional reform.

I have demonstrated that for more than half a century Indonesia has been unable to conduct an uninterrupted dialogue, concerning the position of *shari'a* in the Constitution. In 1945 and 1955, efforts were hampered by the pressure of time and political manoeuvrings by Soekarno and the military. Under Soeharto, debate was forbidden, since his government was afraid of its disruptive potential. The moment for free dialogue and debate, through constitutional mechanisms, came after Soeharto's resignation. I have discussed the emergence of Islamic political parties in the post-Soeharto era. Some of these parties proposed the reinsertion of the famous seven words into the Amendments to the 1945 Constitution, while others took a substantive approach by using *shari'a* only as an inspiration or "spirit" for debate.

The above discussion will assist our discussion in dealing with the main case studies. In the next chapters, I will examine the role of *shari'a* in the amendment to the 1945 Constitution concerning human rights provisions, the rule of law, and the relationship between the state and religion.

Notes

1. M. A. Azis, "Japan's Colonialism and Indonesia", as quoted by B. J. Boland, *The Struggle of Islam in Modern Indonesia* (The Hague, 1982), p. 9; By comparison, see Shigeru Sato, *War, Nationalism and Peasants: Java under the Japanese Occupation 1942–1945* (Australia: Allen & Unwin, 1994), and Kobayashi Yasuko, "*Kyai* and Japanese Military", *Studia Islamika* 4, no. 3 (1997): 65–98, which discusses the relationship between the Indonesian *ulama* and Japanese military.
2. M. C. Ricklefs, *A History of Modern Indonesia, C. 1300 to the Present* (London: Macmillan, 1981), p. 209.
3. See Endang Saefuddin Anshari, "The Jakarta Charter of June 1945: A History of the Gentleman's Agreement between the Islamic and the Secular Nationalists in Modern Indonesia" (M.A. thesis, McGill University, 1976), p. 14.
4. Soepomo's statement above is quoted from H. Muhammad Yamin, *Naskah Persiapan Undang-Undang Dasar 1945*, Vol. 1 (Jakarta: Yayasan Prapanca, 1959), p. 250.
5. Yamin, ibid, pp. 153–54.
6. The full text of the Jakarta Charter (English version) can be read in Adnan Buyung Nasution, *The Aspiration for Constitutional Government in Indonesia: A Socio-legal Study of the Indonesian Konstituante 1956–1959* (Jakarta: Pustaka Sinar Harapan, 1992), Appendix 2, p. 436.
7. Wahid Hasyim of Nahdlatul Ulama (NU) actually proposed that the adherence to Islam as one of the qualifications to be eligible for the President or the Vice-President of Indonesia. Hasyim also suggested that "the religion of the state is Islam". These proposals were rejected. Soekarno, for instance, sought to assure that since Muslims are the majority, the President would obviously be a Muslim without necessarily mentioning this in the Constitution. See Yamin, *Naskah Persiapan*, pp. 261–63.
8. M. B. Hooker, "The State and *Shari'a* in Indonesia", in *Shari'a and Politics in Modern Indonesia*, edited by Arskal Salim and Azyumardi Azra (Singapore: Institute of Southeast Asian Studies, 2003), p. 38.
9. Before the promise of the Japanese government to grant independence for Indonesia was materialized, Japan surrendered unconditionally to the Allies in 1945, which meant that the Japanese military personnel had to maintain the status quo until the Allied forces, including the Dutch, took over. During this power vacuum, the national leaders of Indonesia took the risky initiative of proclaiming its independence on 17 August 1945. The next day, Soekarno and Hatta, the co-signers of the Independence Proclamation, became respectively the country's first President and Vice-President. On that same day, the members of the preparatory committee promulgated the Constitution. See Adam Malik, *Riwajat dan Perdjuangan Sekitar Proklamasi Kemerdekaan Indonesia 17 Agustus 1945* (Jakarta: Penerbit Widjaya, 1956), pp. 30–40.
10. B. J. Boland, *The Struggle of Islam in Modern Indonesia* (The Hague: Martinus Nijhoff, 1982), p. 45.

11. Anshari, "The Jakarta Charter", p. 42.
12. See Mohammad Natsir, "Pengorbanan Umat Islam Sangat Besar", interview, *Panji Masyarakat*, 11 June 1987, p. 28.
13. See *Pelita* (Indonesian daily newspaper), 12 June 1978.
14. As quoted in Yamin, *Naskah Persiapan*, p. 410.
15. Boland, *Struggle of Islam*, p. 37.
16. Natsir, "Pengorbanan Umat Islam".
17. W. B. Sidjabat, *Religious Tolerance and the Christian Faith* (Jakarta: Badan Penerbit Kristen, 1965), p. 74.
18. Boland, *Struggle of Islam*, p. 39.
19. Deliar Noer, *Administration of Islam in Indonesia* (Itacha, NY: Cornell Modern Indonesia Project Southeast Asia Program Cornell University, 1978), pp. 8–9; Hooker, "State and *Shari'a*", p. 36.
20. Ricklefs, *History of Modern Indonesia*, p. 190.
21. Howard M. Federspiel, *Persatuan Islam: Islamic Reform in Twentieth Century Indonesia* (Ithaca, NY: Cornell University, 1970), pp. 87–89.
22. See George Kahin, *Nationalism and Revolution in Indonesia* (Ithaca, NY: Cornell University Press, 1952), pp. 326–31. More information on Kartosuwirjo could be read in Kees van Dijk, *Rebellion under the Banner of Islam: The Darul Islam in Indonesia* (The Hague: Martinus Nijhoff, 1981); Al Chaidar, *Pemikiran Politik Proklamator Negara Islam Indonesia S.M. Kartosoewirjo: Fakta dan Sejarah Darul Islam* (Jakarta: Darul Falah, 1999).
23. See C. S. T. Kansil, Christine Kansil, and Engeline Palendeng, *Konstitusi-Konstitusi Indonesia Tahun 1945–2000* (Jakarta: Pustaka Sinar Harapan, 2001), especially Ch. 1.
24. Anhar Gonggong, *Menengok Sejarah Konstitusi Indonesia* (Yogyakarta: Ombak & Media Presindo, 2002), pp. 19–33.
25. Generally, it can be said that there are two groups of Indonesian Muslims: the traditionalists and the modernists. The traditionalists are mainly concerned with pure religion, *din* or *ibadah*. Islam is, for them, mostly *fiqh* (Islamic jurisprudence). They recognize *taqlid* (the obligation to follow the *ulama's* opinion without reserve), and they reject the validity of *ijtihad* (independent legal reasoning). In other words, they tend to restrict the role of *ijtihad* in preference to, and out of deference for, the established opinions of the masters of the schools of Islamic jurisprudence. The traditionalist Muslim is represented by the NU. At the moment, NU is the biggest Islamic organization numbering 30 million supporters. More information can be found in Greg Barton and Greg Fealy, eds., *Nahdlatul Ulama: Traditionalist Islam and Modernity in Indonesia* (Monash: Monash Asia Institute, 1996); see also Nadirsyah Hosen, "Collective *Ijtihad* and Nahdlatul Ulama", *New Zealand Journal of Asian Studies* 6, no. 1 (2004): 5–26.

    The modernists are concerned with the nature of Islam in general. To them Islam is compatible with the demands of time and circumstance. They recognize the Qur'an and Hadith as the basic sources of their ideas and thought. Furthermore, they maintain that "the gate of *ijtihad*" is still open and they reject the idea of *taqlid*. Muhammadiyah is the organization which represents modernist Muslims. It has 28 million supporters in Indonesia, and has built many schools, universities and hospitals. Moreover, it reinterprets Islam within the modern context. More information can be found in M. Sirajuddin Syamsuddin, "Religion and Politics in Islam: The Case of Muhammadiyah in Indonesia's New Order" (Ph.D. thesis, University of California Los Angeles, 1991); see also Nadirsyah Hosen, "Revelation in a Modern Nation State: Muhammadiyah and Islamic Legal Reasoning in Indonesia", *Australian Journal of Asian Law* 4, no. 3 (2002): 232–58.

26. See Harold Crouch, "Masjumi", in *The Oxford Encyclopedia of the Modern Islamic World*, Vol. II, edited by John L. Esposito (New York: Oxford University Press, 1995), p. 62.

27. Mochtar Naim, "The Nahdlatul Ulama Party (1952–1955): An Inquiry into the Origin of its Electoral Success" (M.A. thesis, McGill University, Montreal, 1960), p. 204.

28. Anwar Harjono, *Perjalanan Politik Bangsa* (Jakarta: Gema Insani Press, 1997), pp. 114–21; see also Ahmad Syafii Ma'arif, *Islam dan Masalah Kenegaraan* (Jakarta: LP3S, 1996), p. 119. Ma'arif's work was originally a Ph.D. thesis at the University of Chicago in 1982.

29. Naim, "Nahdlatul Ulama Party", p. 56; on the relationship between *fatwa* and politics, see Nadirsyah Hosen, "Fatwa and Politics in Indonesia", in *Shari'a and Politics in Modern Indonesia*, edited by Salim and Azra, pp. 168–80.

30. In *Indonesian Political Thinking, 1945–1965*, a classic book he co-edited with Lance Castles, Herbert Feith defined *aliran* in terms of "streams of political thinking". A dominant party was found in each stream. These parties were supported by various social groups, representing the youth, labour, women, students, intellectuals, artisans, and so on. See Herbert Feith, "Introduction", in *Indonesian Political Thinking, 1945–1965*, edited by Herbert Feith and Lance Castles (Ithaca, NY: Cornell University Press, 1970).

31. See Nasution, *Aspiration for Constitutional Government*, p. 32.

32. Ibid, p. 397.

33. Ibid, p. 398.

34. Ibid, p. 405.

35. Boland, *Struggle of Islam*, p. 95.

36. Qur'an 112:1 and 2:163.

37. See Hazairin, *Demokrasi Pancasila* (Jakarta: Tintamas, 1970), pp. 58–60. See also Sukiati Sugiono, "Islamic Legal Reform in Twentieth Century Indonesia: A Study of Hazairin's Thought" (M.A. thesis, McGill University, 1999).

38. More information can be found in Ismail Sunny, "Hukum Islam dalam Hukum Nasional", *Hukum dan Pembangunan* XVII/4 (August 1987): 351–57.

39. Nasution, *Aspiration for Constitutional Government*, p. 420.

40. Ira M. Lapidus, *A History of Islamic Societies* (Cambridge: Cambridge University Press, 1993), p. 771.

41. See Suzaina Abdul Kadir, "Traditional Islamic Society and the State in Indonesia: The Nahdlatul Ulama, Political Accommodation and the Preservation of Autonomy" (Ph.D. dissertation, University of Wisconsin-Madison, 1999), pp. 148–52; see also M. Ali Haidar, *Nahdatul Ulama dan Islam di Indonesia: Pendekatan Fikih dalam Politik* (Jakarta: Gramedia Pustaka Utama, 1994).

42. A. H. Johns, "Indonesia: Islam and Cultural Pluralism", in *Islam in Asia: Religion, Politics and Society*, edited by John L. Esposito (Oxford: Oxford University Press, 1989), p. 215.

43. For the background of the New Order, see Justus M. van der Kroef, *Indonesia After Soekarno* (Vancouver: University of British Columbia Press, 1971). For further discussion of ABRI, see Ulf Sundhaussen, "The Military: Structure, Procedures, and Effects on Indonesian Society", in *Political Power and Communications in Indonesia*, edited by Karl D. Jackson and Lucian W. Pye (Berkeley: University of California Press, 1978), pp. 45–81.

44. Johns, "Indonesia: Islam and Cultural Pluralism".

45. R. William Liddle, *Leadership and Culture in Indonesian Politics* (Sydney: Allen & Unwin, 1996), p. 18.

46. See Allan A. Samson, "Conceptions of Politics, Power, and Ideology in Contemporary Indonesian Islam", in *Political Power and Communications in Indonesia*, edited by Jackson and Pye, p. 221.

47. For discussion on the response of Indonesian Muslims to the New Order, see Mohammad Kamal Hassan, "Contemporary Muslim Religio-Political Thought in Indonesia: The Response to New Order Modernization" (Ph.D. dissertation, Columbia University, 1975).

48. Donald K. Emmerson, "Islam in Modern Indonesia: Political Impasse, Cultural Opportunity", in *Change and the Muslim World*, edited by Philip H. Stoddard (Syracuse: Syracuse University Press, 1981), p. 159.

49. The 1963 Anti-subversion Law carried a maximum penalty of death, and made it a crime to engage in acts which could distort, undermine, or cause deviation from the state ideology or the broad outlines of state policy, or which could disseminate feelings of hostility, or arouse hostility, or cause disturbances or anxiety amongst the population. The excessive vagueness of this law made it possible to prosecute persons merely for peaceful expression of views contrary to those of the government. Indonesia's National Human Rights Commission (Komnas HAM) commented on the Anti-subversion law, "The Anti-subversion Law can be used to punish people whose ideas are different from those of the government. It allows prosecutors and judges to act as if they can read the accused's mind." See *Jakarta Post*, 9 April 1996. Habibie government repealed the 1963 Anti-subversion Law in April 1999 (Law No. 26 of 1999).

50. See TAPOL, *Indonesia: Muslims on Trial* (London: TAPOL, 1987). Strong criticism on the concept of Pancasila as the sole foundation is expressed, for

example, by Deliar Noer in his book *Islam, Pancasila dan Asas Tunggal* (Jakarta: Yayasan Perkhidmatan, 1983). More information on this matter can be found in Faisal Ismail, "Pancasila as the Sole Basis for All Political Parties and for All Mass Organizations: An Account of Muslims' Response" (Ph.D. dissertation, McGill University, 1995).

51. See Greg Barton, "Islam, Pancasila and the Middle Path of *Tawassuth*: The Thought of Achmad Siddiq", in *Nahdlatul Ulama, Traditional Islam and Modernity in Indonesia*, edited by Greg Barton and Greg Fealey (Clayton: Monash Asia Institute, 1996), pp. 100–28; see also Einar Martahan Sitompul, *NU dan Pancasila* (Jakarta: Pustaka Sinar Harapan, 1989), pp. 165–70.

52. See "Keputusan Hasil Musyawarah Nasional Alim Ulama NU No. II/MAUNU/ 1404/1983".

53. Ibid.

54. See Lukman Harun, *Muhammadiyah dan Pancasila* (Jakarta: Pustaka Panjimas, 1986).

55. See Abdul Azis Thaba, *Islam and Negara dalam Politik Orde Baru* (Jakarta: Gema Insani Press, 1996), p. 287.

56. More information on Law No. 7 of 1989 can be found in Mark Cammack, "Indonesia's 1989 Religious Judicature Act: Islamization of Indonesia or Indonesianization of Islam", in *Shari'a and Politics in Modern Indonesia*, edited by Salim and Azra, pp. 96–124.

57. E. Damian and R. N. Hornick, "Indonesia's Formal Legal System: An Introduction", *American Journal of Comparative Law* 20 (1972): 518.

58. See Law No. 7 of 1989, Chapter 1, Verse 1: "Religious court is a court for Muslims".

59. See Law No. 7 of 1989, Chapter III, Section 49. It is interesting to note that some scholars rejected the Bill on the grounds that not only the existence of a separate Islamic court which enforces Islamic law is unconstitutional and contradictory to Pancasila, but also the fear that it would reassert (*menghidupkan kembali*) the Jakarta Charter. See, for example, Franz Magnis-Suseno, "Seputar Rencana UU Peradilan Agama", *Kompas*, 16 June 1989.

60. Clifford Geertz divides Indonesian Islam into three groups:
    - The *abangan* is the first sub-variant within the general Javanese religious system.
    - The purer Islam is the sub-tradition he called *santri*.
    - The *priyayi* is the elite group which stressed neither the animistic element in the over all Javanese syncretism as did the *abangans*, nor the Islamic element, as did the *santris*, but the Hinduistic elements.

    [Clifford Geertz, *The Religion of Java* (Chicago: The University of Chicago Press, 1979), pp. 5–6.]

61. See Nies Mulder, *Inside Indonesian Society* (Bangkok: Editions Duang Kamol, 1994), p. 128; Martin van Bruinessen, "Islamic State or State Islam? Fifty Years of State-Islam Relations in Indonesia", in *Indonesien am Ende des 20. Jahrhunderts*, edited by Ingrid Wessel (Hamburg: Abera-Verlag, 1996), pp. 19–34.

62. Marcus Mietzner, "Godly Men in Green", *Inside Indonesia*, No. 53, January–March 1998, p. 8.
63. See Robert W. Hefner, "Modernity and the Challenge of Pluralism: Some Indonesian Lesson", *Studia Islamika* 2, no. 4 (1995): 37–38.
64. See Tarmizi Taher, *Aspiring for the Middle Path: Religious Harmony in Indonesia* (Jakarta: CENSIS-IAIN Jakarta, 1997), p. 151.
65. Karel Steenbrink, "Itinerant Scholars", *Inside Indonesia*, No. 52, October–December 1997, p. 11; see also Michael R. J. Vatikiotis, *Indonesian Politics under Suharto* (London: Routledge, 1994), p. 127.
66. In this sense, Syed Farid Alatas argues that the presence of armed resistance in the context of a weak state and elite factionalism lead to an authoritarian Indonesia. By contrast, he shows how the absence of armed resistance, the presence of an internally strong state and a high degree of elite cohesion led to a democratic Malaysia. He takes the view that Malaysia is indeed more democratic than Indonesia. Syed Farid Alatas, *Democracy and Authoritarianism in Indonesia and Malaysia: The Rise of the Post-Colonial State* (Houndmills: Macmillan, 1997).
67. In order to distinguish the different orientations, the Soeharto government is called the New Order government, whilst the Soekarno era is called the Old Order government. Soeharto formally took over the presidency from Soekarno in 1968, in the wake of an abortive coup attempt (1965) in which six top army generals were murdered. In the Soekarno era, Indonesia had a very unstable government, such that economic development was not possible. New Order government orientations were to maintain political stability and to develop economic growth.
68. See Marsillam Simanjuntak, *Pandangan Negara Integralistik: sumber, unsur dan riwayatnya dalam persiapan UUD 1945* (Jakarta: Pustaka Utama Grafiti, 1994).
69. Chapter XI — Religion.
    Article 29
    1. The State shall be based upon the belief in the One and Only God.
    2. The State guarantees all persons the freedom of worship, each according to his/her own religion or belief.
70. See Law No. 3 of 1975 on Political Parties and Golkar.
71. H. D. Haryo Sasongko, *Pemilu '99: Komedi atau Tragedi* (Jakarta: Pustaka Grafiksi, 1999), p. 28.
72. Valina Singka Subekti, "Electoral Law Reform as Prerequisite to Create Democratization in Indonesia", in *Crafting Indonesian Democracy*, edited by R. William Liddle (Bandung: Mizan, 2001), p. 113.
73. See Edward Aspinall and Gerry van Klinken, "Chronology of Crisis", in *The Last Days of President Soeharto*, edited by Aspinall, Faith, van Klinken (Clayton: Monash Asia Institute, 1999), pp. 159–66, and James Luhulima, ed., *Hari-hari Terpanjang: Menjelang Mundurnya Presiden Soeharto dan Beberapa Peristiwa Terakit* (Jakarta: Kompas, 2001).
74. *Kompas*, 13 May 1998.

75. Kees van Dijk, *A Country in Despair: Indonesia between 1997 and 2000* (Jakarta: KITLV Press, 2001), p. 192.

76. See *Tempo*, Special Edition, 19–25 May 2003.

77. Ray Rangkuti, personal communication, 4 June 2003. He was one of the student leaders during May 1998. Currently, Ray Rangkuti is Executive Director of KIPP (Komite Independen Pengawas Pemilu, or Independent Election Monitoring Committee). A sticker circulated in 1998 by the Student Executive Body (Badan Eksekutif Mahasiswa, or BEM) of Universitas Indonesia in Jakarta, one of Indonesia's premier state universities, proclaimed a six-point "vision of reform" to be achieved through non-violent means: (1) rescind the military's dual functions; (2) establish the rule of law (i.e., bring Soeharto and his cronies to justice); (3) amend the 1945 Constitution; (4) establish broad regional autonomy; (5) create a democratic culture; and (6) hold the New Order accountable.

78. See his interview in *Forum Keadilan* (weekly national magazine), 12 January 1999, p. 24.

79. Aspinall, Faith, and van Klinken, *Last Days of President Soeharto*, p. 165.

80. *Kompas*, 19 May 1998.

81. The Indonesian Constitution is presidential in character but it contains a strong parliamentary element. The president is responsible to the MPR and cannot be deposed by the DPR. However, the system is unusual in that the majority of the members of the MPR are also members of the DPR. While the latter cannot, in their capacity as members of the DPR, vote the president out of office, their votes, in their capacity as members of the MPR, would be decisive if an attempt were made to impeach him. Although Indonesians often use the term *impeachment*, the process does not involve a trial but an evaluation by the MPR that the president has violated the constitution or the "National Will" (*Haluan Negara*) embodied in MPR decrees and should, therefore, be dismissed. The impeachment process begins with the adoption by the DPR of a memorandum warning the president of the alleged violations. If, after three months, the president does not respond satisfactorily to the memorandum, a second memorandum can be sent. If, after a further month, there is still no satisfactory response, the DPR can request the MPR to hold a special session to request the president to explain the issues raised in the memorandum. If the MPR is satisfied that the president "truly violated the National Will", he/she can then be dismissed by the MPR.

82. Stefan Eklof in his book argued that Wiranto never asked Soeharto to resign. He remained loyal until the last minute Soeharto read his text of resignation. See his *Indonesian Politics in Crisis: The Long Fall of Soeharto, 1966–98* (Copenhagen: Nordic Institute for Asian Studies, 1999), 212.

83. Luhulima, *Hari-hari Terpanjang*, p. 55.

84. Aidul Fitriciada Azhari et al., *Dari Catatan Wiranto Jenderal Purnawirawan Bersaksi di Tengah Badai* (Jakarta: IDe Indonesia, 2003), p. 35.

85. Ibid.

86. Habibie was appointed Minister of State for Research and Technology in 1978, and maintained this job for five terms of office in Soeharto's cabinet, until March 1998. He was appointed Vice-President on 11 March 1998 and, following the fall of Soeharto, was appointed President on 21 May 1998. He served his country for 512 days in office. See A. Makmur Makka, *BJ Habibie: His Life and Career*, 5th Ed. (March 1999).

87. They are Law No. 1 of 1999 on Political Parties, Law No. 3 of 1999 on General Election, and Law No. 4 of 1999 on Composition of the National and Local Representative Bodies.

88. See Nadirsyah Hosen, "Indonesian Political Laws in Habibie Era: Between Political Struggle and Law Reform", *Nordic Journal of International Law* 72, no. 4 (2003): 483–518.

89. On 7 June 2000, Law No. 4 of 1999 was amended by Law No. 4 of 2000.

90. More information on political parties in Indonesia from 1945 until 1998 can be found in Elaine Paige Johnson, "Streams of Least Resistance: The Institutionalization of Political Parties and Democracy in Indonesia" (Ph.D. dissertation, University of Virginia, 2002).

91. Bahtiar Effendy, *Islam and the State in Indonesia* (Singapore: Institute of Southeast Asian Studies, 2003), p. 216.

92. See Zainal Abidin Amir, *Peta Islam Politik: Pasca-Soeharto* (Jakarta: LP3S, 2003), pp. 61–83.

93. Ali Said Damanik, *Fenomena Partai Keadilan: Transformasi 20 Tahun Gerakan Tarbiyah di Indonesia* (Jakarta: Teraju, 2002), p. 240.

94. Ibid., p, 270.

95. See Pax Benedanto, ed., *Pemilihan Umum 1999: Demokrasi atau Rebutan Kursi?* (Jakarta: LSPP, 1999).

96. See Judith Bird, "Indonesia in 1998: The pot boils over", *Asian Survey* 39 (1999): 29.

97. Daniel S. Lev, "Reformasi Hukum Dimulai dari Penggantian Hakim Agung", (interview), *Kompas*, 27 October 1999. The reasons, as the critics say, are that the Supreme Court is subordinated to the executive and suffers from pervasive corruption. Probably, it is one of the most corrupt institutions in the whole of Indonesia.

98. Dr Adnan Buyung Nasution, a prominent lawyer, suggested amendment, while Professor Harun Alrasid of the University of Indonesia argued that the 1945 Constitution should be replaced with a new one. See *Kompas*, 6 May 1999.

99. Dr Amir Santoso and Ghazali Abbas Adan (both were Members of Parliament) highlighted this issue when they were interviewed by *Kompas*. See *Kompas*, 24 January 1998.

100. *Kompas*, 29 September 1999.

101. Suharizal, *Reformasi Konstitusi 1998–2002: Pergulatan Konsep dan Pemikiran Amandemen UUD 1945* (Padang: Anggrek Law Firm, 2002), p. 80.

102. Ibid, p. 62.

103. Ibid, p. 137.

104. Ibid, p. 159.
105. Kevin O'Rourke, *Reformasi: The struggle for power in post-Soeharto Indonesia* (Sydney: Allen & Unwin, 2002), p. 402.
106. 1945 Constitution, Ch. IX.
107. 1945 Constitution, Article 24C(1).
108. 1945 Constitution, Articles 7A, 7B and 24C(2).
109. *Koran Tempo*, 8 November 2001.
110. Mohammad Fajrul Falaakh, "Komisi Konstitusi dan Peran Rakyat dalam Perubahan UUD 1945", *Analisis CSIS: Di Ambang Krisis Konstitusi?*, No. 2, 2002, pp. 189–90; see also compilation of articles on Komisi Konstitusi in *Konstitusi Baru Melalui Komisi Konstitusi Independen*, by Bambang Widjojanto et al. (Jakarta: Pustaka Sinar Harapan, 2002).
111. For a full account, see Harun Alrasid, *Naskah UUD 1945 Sesudah Tiga Kali Diubah oleh MPR* (Jakarta: UI Press, 2002); Didit Hariadi Estiko, ed., *Amandemen UUD 1945 dan Implikasinya terhadap Pembangunan Sistem Hukum Nasional* (Jakarta: Tim Hukum Pusat Pengkajian dan Pelayanan Informasi Sekretariat Jenderal DPR-RI, 2001); Suwarno Adiwijoyo, *Amandemen UUD 1945* (Jakarta: Intermasa, 2000); The Habibie Centre, *Naskah Akademis dan Draf Rancangan Naskah Undang-Undang Dasar Republik Indonesia* (Jakarta: The Habibie Centre, 2001); Anhar Gonggong, *Amandemen Konstitusi, Otonomi Daerah dan Federalisme: Solusi untuk Masa Depan* (Yogyakarta: Media Presindo, 2001); Hendarmin Ramadireksa, *Visi Politik Amandemen UUD 1945 Menuju Konstitusi yang Berkedaulatan Rakyat* (Jakarta: Yayasan Pancur Siwah, 2002).
112. R. William Liddle, "Indonesia's Democratic Transition: Playing by the Rules", in *The Architecture of Democracy*, edited by Andrew Reynolds (Oxford: Oxford University Press, 2002), p. 373; see also Hosen, "Indonesian Political Laws in Habibie Era".
113. See Bima Arya Sugiarto, "Sidang Tahunan MPR 2002: Menuju Institusionalisasi, Menyelamatkan Transisi", *Analisis CSIS: Di Ambang Krisis Konstitusi?*, pp. 174–76.
114. Bell has observed that this formula to amend the Constitution was problematic, since it did not need for the involvement of the government or presidential approval or for a referendum. Gary F. Bell, "Obstacles to Reform The 1945 Constitution: Constitutions Do Not Perform Miracles", *Van Zorge Report on Indonesia: Commentary and Analysis on Indonesian Politics and Economics*, Vol. III, No. 6 (2001): 7. See also Todung Mulya Lubis, "Constitutional Reforms", in *Governance in Indonesia: Challenges Facing the Megawati Presidency*, edited by Hadi Soesastro et al. (Singapore: Institute of Southeast Asian Studies, 2003); Jimly Asshiddiqie, "Telaah Akademis atas Perubahan UUD 1945", *Jurnal Demokrasi & HAM* 1, no. 4 (2001): 17.
115. See MPR Decree No. IV/MPR/2003.
116. Indra J. Piliang, "Konstitusi Elit versus Konstitusi Rakyat", *Analisis CSIS: Di Ambang Krisis Konstitusi?*, pp. 202–32.
117. Hamdan Zoelva of PBB, Lukman Hakim Saifuddin of PPP, TB Soemandjaja of

PK, Mujib Rakhmat of Golkar and Mutammimul Ula of PK, in my personal communications with them, shared this view and they had prepared to reject the Commission's recommendations, before the Commission finished its task. On 12 August 2004, in its final report, the MPR admitted that there was a misunderstanding of the task of the Komisi Konstitusi between members of Badan Pekerja MPR and members of the Komisi Konstitusi. According to the MPR, the Komisi went too far by proposing a new draft of the Constitution, even though the MPR only asked them to produce an academic explanation on the outcome of the Amendments to the 1945 Constitution. Therefore, members of MPR 1999–2004 did not want to use the works of the Komisi Konstitusi. See *Kompas*, 13 August 2004; *Media Indonesia*, 26 September 2004.

118. *Kompas*, 3 August 2002.
119. *Kompas*, 16 July 2002.
120. *Kompas*, 10 April 2002; see also *Asia Times*, 23 April 2002.
121. *Media Indonesia*, 26 August 2003.
122. *Media Indonesia*, 19 February 2002.
123. Blair A. King, "Empowering the Presidency: Interests and perceptions in Indonesia's constitutional reforms, 1999–2002" (Ph.D. thesis, Ohio State University, 2004), p. 31.
124. Law No. 26 of 2000 reflects compromise on this issue. It provides for special ad hoc human rights courts to try gross violations of human rights which had occurred before the new law came into force. However, as a safeguard, such courts can be established only to try specific cases, through a special procedure. The president may establish an ad hoc court by decree, only on the explicit recommendation of the DPR (Article 43). Provision is also made for the resolution of gross violations through a Truth and Reconciliation Commission, to be established by a later law (Article 47).
125. Three months after the end of World War II, at the culmination of six weeks of intensive negotiations in London, the United States, Great Britain, the Soviet Union and France signed an agreement creating the International Military Tribunal (IMT) for the Prosecution and Punishment of the Major War Criminals of the European Axis. The judges held that the Charter was not *ex post facto* law designed to punish Germans only. "The law is not static", said the Tribunal, "but by continued adaptation follows the needs of a changing world". Both the Charter and judgement of the IMT were unanimously affirmed by the first General Assembly of the United Nations. Its principles were thereby confirmed as valid expressions of binding international law. See Benjamin B. Ferencz, "From Nuremberg to Rome", May 1998, available at http://www.benferencz.org/bonnlec2.htm.
126. See Geertz, *Religion of Java*.
127. *Jakarta Post*, 6 September 2001.
128. Saiful Mujani and R. William Liddle, "Politics, Islam and Public Opinion", *Journal of Democracy* 15, no. 1 (2004): 113; See also R. William Liddle, "New

Patterns of Islamic Politics in Democratic Indonesia", in *Piety and Pragmatism: Trends in Indonesian Islamic Politics* (Washington: Woodrow Wilson International Center, Asia Special Report No. 10, 2003), p. 9.

129. Mujani and Liddle, ibid., p. 114.
130. Ibid.

4

HUMAN RIGHTS PROVISIONS

Human rights are, literally, the rights that one has simply by being a human being.[1] The maximum level, or common standard, of the protection of human rights can be seen in the text of the Universal Declaration of Human Rights (UDHR). The UDHR was proclaimed in a Resolution of the UN General Assembly on 10 December 1948. It lists numerous rights to which people everywhere are entitled.[2]

Many Muslim scholars are firm in their belief that *shari'a* addresses the fundamentals of human rights. For instance, they identify the most important human rights principles in Islam to be: dignity and brotherhood; equality among members of the community, without distinction on the basis of race, colour, or class; respect for the honour, reputation, and family of each individual; the right of each individual to be presumed innocent until and unless proven guilty, and individual freedom.[3] This position suggests that Islamic law does protect human rights, but according to its own set of values. These values are fixed in divine law and are considered to be superior to any law created by humans and established by international institutions. Those Muslim scholars use the concept of cultural relativism to legitimize their adherence to *shari'a* vis-à-vis human rights.

Some tensions occur concerning, for instance, the allegedly unequal treatment of women in the Muslim world and religious liberty, including the rights to change one's belief and to inter-religious marriage. This epitomizes the tension between human rights in Islam, as they exist in relation to obligations towards God, fellow humans and nature, and the human rights adopted by international human rights institutions, which are devoid of any religious coercion.

This tension led several Muslims from Egypt, Pakistan and Saudi Arabia to establish the 1981 Universal Islamic Declaration of Human Rights (UIDHR), issued by the Islamic Council for Europe. In 1990, the Cairo Declaration on Human Rights in Islam was adopted by the Organization of the Islamic Conference (OIC). While the Islamic Council for Europe is a non-governmental organization (NGO), whose statements are by no means binding, the OIC brings together representatives of all Islamic states. Hence the Cairo Declaration, albeit not legally binding, does carry some political authority. As will be discussed, these documents reflect a formal *shari'a* approach.

Meanwhile, other Muslim scholars advocate an emancipated understanding of *shari'a*, stressing its original meaning as a "path" or guide, rather than a detailed legal code.[4] They demand the recovery of *ijtihad* in order to do justice both to modern needs and to the original spirit of *shari'a*. For this substantive group, no inherent contradiction exists between the principles of the *shari'a* and human rights, as embodied in the existing international standards. While the UIDHR and the Cairo Declaration tend to "Islamize" human rights and, at the same time, to "justify" their rejection of international human rights norms, a substantive *shari'a* approach tends to "accept" the UDHR based on the spirit of *shari'a*.

In this chapter those conflicting approaches will be used to examine the provisions of human rights in the second amendment to the 1945 Indonesian Constitution. In other words, while the formal approach tries to use *shari'a* as a source of constitutional provisions on human rights protection, the substantive approach attempts to protect the citizen's right according to international human rights norms. Therefore, the main question posed in this chapter is: to what extent has *shari'a* played a role in the provision of human rights in the amendments to the 1945 Constitution?

To answer the question, the chapter has been divided into two parts. The first part examines human rights protection in the Indonesian constitution prior to the amendments to the 1945 Constitution. It analyses the absence of protection for the citizens' rights and provides reasons for constitutional reform in the area of human rights. The second part deals with human rights provisions in the second amendment. I will examine those provisions by taking into account opinions and views of both formal and substantive *shari'a* groups. As a comparison, I will look at Iranian and Egyptian Constitutions and the Saudi Arabian Basic Laws. Having discussed all the issues, I would argue that none of the Islamic political parties in Indonesia proposed the *shari'a* as their formal source of legislation when discussing the amendments and, therefore, in the case of human rights, they all agreed with the substantive *shari'a* approach.

HUMAN RIGHTS BEFORE THE AMENDMENTS

I have indicated in the previous chapter that the main weakness in the original text of the 1945 Constitution is its vague provisions, with many delegations of the implementation of legislation. The 1945 Constitution was a very short and simple constitution, consisting of thirty-seven articles, of which only six explicitly dealt with human rights (Articles 26–31).[5] Other rights were referred to implicitly, or put in the elucidation section of the Articles. Those rights which were mentioned in the Constitution, such as the freedom of speech, assembly and association, were to be established by law, which allowed for their restriction by law as well.[6] As the provisions regarding state institutions were also to be enacted in laws and as the President holds legislative authority, it is not difficult to predict the result: whoever holds the power will hold absolute power under the 1945 Constitution.

At least fifteen human rights principles are honoured in the 1945 Constitution:

1. right to self-determination (Preamble and Article 1);[7]
2. right to citizenship (Article 26);[8]
3. right to equality before the law (Article 27);[9]
4. right to work (Article 27);[10]
5. right to a decent life (Article 27);
6. right of association (Article 28);[11]
7. right to express an opinion (Article 28);[12]
8. right to practise a religion (Article 29);[13]
9. right of national defence (Article 30);
10. right to education (Article 31);[14]
11. right to social welfare (Article 33);[15]
12. right to social security (Article 34);[16]
13. right to an independent judiciary (elucidation of Article 24 and 25);
14. right to preserve cultural traditions (elucidation of Article 32); and
15. right to preserve local languages (elucidation of Article 31).

Todung Mulya Lubis has noted that: .

> The return to the 1945 Constitution indicated that human rights are *given* and are not inherently possessed by human beings, simply by virtue of their

being born. The human rights provision in the 1945 Constitution, as well as in the implementing legislation, explicitly state that *rights* will be further regulated.

The fact that the 1945 Constitution empowers the government to regulate the exercise of human rights signifies that human rights are recognized in principle, but that their implementation will be regulated. Therefore, it is not entirely wrong to argue that the 1945 Constitution acknowledges only human rights principles, not human rights implementation.[17]

Several "further regulations" were issued under Soeharto, not to promote human rights but to limit and restrict them. Human rights were also regulated by the manner in which the government chose to exercise its discretion to interpret the Constitution. For instance, the 1945 Constitution contains a general provision on the right to freedom of expression. However, laws passed by the Parliament,[18] and regulations issued by the Soeharto government were in contradiction of Article 28 of the 1945 Constitution.[19] Soeharto's Press Law was illustrative.

Law No. 21 of 1982 (the 1982 Press Law) incorporated and enacted revisions and amendments to the 1966 Press Law. Article 13 of the 1982 Press Law requires that press publications obtain a Press Publication Business Licence (SIUPP) from the Minister for Information.[20] In addition to granting SIUPPs, the Minister for Information could also revoke licences, pursuant to Article 33 of the Ministerial Regulation No. 1 of 1984 (1984 Ministerial Decree). The most famous examples of the implementation of Article 33 are the 1994 revocation of the licences of the publications *Tempo*, *Editor* and *Detik*. Alleged non-compliance with licensing requirements and perceived threats to national security prompted the closing of these publications. The Department of Information sent written correspondence to *Tempo*, *Editor* and *Detik*, notifying them of the revocation of their licences because of the contents of certain articles.[21] Under the Soeharto government, freedom of the press was restricted, based on the nation's perceived economic priorities and developmental needs.[22]

When Habibie took over the presidency in May 1998, he faced a lot of pressure, both at national and international levels, to improve human rights conditions in Indonesia. Many NGO activists and constitutional experts urged Indonesia to amend its Constitution to guarantee human rights protection, since the 1945 Constitution, as has been mentioned earlier, had no adequate provisions on human rights. At the international level, the demands for reform came from the World Bank, when it raised its concerns over the human rights situation in Indonesia and East Timor. In a letter to President Habibie, the World Bank stressed the need for reform "for the international financial community to be able to continue its full support". The World Bank urged Habibie to take significant steps.[23] In a major report released on 4 September 1998, the Human Rights Watch warned that if the current political opening up process in Indonesia was not followed by legal and institutional protections for basic rights, the entire reform effort could unravel.[24]

Those pressures forced Habibie to give strong support to the idea of the universality of human rights in his state address before the MPR (Majelis Permusyawaratan Rakyat, or People's Consultative Assembly) session of 15 August 1998, on the eighty-seventh day of his presidency. He stated, "we have firmly abandoned the uncertainty phase, which earlier always considered human rights as a Western cultural product."[25] He also said, "we are determined to make human rights principles the yardstick in our life as a nation and country. We will promote and safeguard human rights in accordance with our democratic and welfare-based approach."[26]

In order to deal with the protection of human rights, President Habibie issued Presidential Decree No. 129 of 1998 concerning the National Human Rights Plan. The Decree states that Indonesia, as a member of the international community, holds in high esteem the UDHR and the 1993 Vienna Human Rights Declaration and the Programme of Action. Article 1 of the Decree also states that the purpose of the National Action Plan is to increase the protection of human rights in Indonesia, by taking into account the values of indigenous and traditional communities, as well as national cultures and religions, based on Pancasila, and the 1945 Constitution.

The Indonesian National Plan of Action 1998–2003 consists of four main pillars: preparation for ratification of international human rights instruments; dissemination of information and education on human rights; implementation of priority issues on human rights; and implementation of the international human rights instruments that have been ratified by Indonesia.

The highest state institution, the People's Consultative Assembly, adopted Decree No. XVII/MPR/1998 on Human Rights in 1998. By this Decree, for the first time in Indonesian history, an Indonesian Charter on Human Rights was introduced.[27] Many of the clauses in this MPR Decree were drawn directly from the UDHR. For instance, Articles 19–21 of the 1998 MPR Charter of Human Rights protect citizens' rights to freedom of expression without interference and to seek, receive and impart information and ideas, through any media. In addition, the guarantee of the rights of assembly and association, if enforced, would end the president's ability to disband political parties. Presidents Soekarno and Soeharto banned certain political parties and forced others to merge, as effective weapons against their political opponents.

On 23 September 1999, a month before the presidential election, President Habibie signed Law No. 39 of 1999 on Human Rights. This law implemented MPR Decree XVII on Human Rights, which decree had been adopted by the MPR at its session in November 1998. Law No. 39 of 1999 sets out a long list of internationally recognized human rights, which Indonesia is obliged to protect. The law contains provisions on human rights and fundamental freedoms, the responsibilities and obligations of the government in the promotion and protection of human rights, and the plan to set up a Human Rights Court. Law No. 39 of 1999 also strengthens the powers of the National Commission on Human Rights (Komnas HAM), which had been established by presidential decision in 1993 to monitor and report on human rights abuses. Most importantly for its future investigative role, the new law gave the Commission the legal power to force the attendance of witnesses, including those against whom complaints have been made.[28]

However, those regulations are not adequate to protect human rights, since they could easily be replaced by whoever is in power. Laws and other regulations should be based on the Constitution, whereas, as has been mentioned earlier, too many of the key clauses of the 1945 Constitution end with an injunction for further specification in laws, opening the door to subsequent manipulation. The Constitution also lacks guarantees of basic civil and political rights. Therefore, it was essential to insert articles in the 1998 MPR Decree as part of the second amendment to the 1945 Constitution in 2000.

ANALYSIS OF HUMAN RIGHTS PROTECTION IN THE SECOND AMENDMENT

This section deals with human rights provisions in the second amendment to the 1945 Constitution. According to Tim Lindsey, Articles 28A–28J in Chapter XA are "lengthy and impressive, granting a full range of protections extending well beyond those guaranteed in most developed states".[29] In the same vein, Gary Bell takes the view that the inclusion of human rights provision in the second amendment to the 1945 Constitution, which adopts a long list of individual rights, "has brought a significant change in the orientation of Indonesian constitutional law".[30] Unlike these two leading scholars' works, I will examine such rights in the perspective of *shari'a*.

The analysis offered hereafter of Chapter XA of the second amendment will be based on, firstly, the Cairo Declaration, the UIDHR, the human rights provisions in Iranian and Egyptian Constitutions, and the Basic Laws of Saudi Arabia; secondly, formal and substantive *shari'a* views on human rights; thirdly, international human rights instruments. Although the second amendment delivered a range of rights, such as the right to have a family, the right to collective action, the right to education, the right to access to information,[31] it is beyond the scope of this book to examine all these issues. The discussion in this chapter focuses on equality, women's rights, freedom of religion, and freedom of opinion.

Equality

The principle of equality is a primary principle of human rights. Human rights are for everyone — as much for people living in poverty and social isolation as for the visible and articulate. By international law, the principle of non-discrimination prohibits discrimination in the enjoyment of human rights on any grounds, such as race, colour of the skin, gender, language, religion, politics or other opinion, national or social origins, property, birth or other status. The term "or other status" might include personal circumstances, occupation, lifestyle, sexual orientation or health status.

Equality requires that all persons within a society enjoy equal access to the available goods and services which are necessary to fulfil basic human needs. Equality before the law prohibits discrimination in law or in practice, in any field regulated and protected by public authorities. Thus, the principle of non-discrimination applies to all state policies and practices, including those concerning healthcare, education, access to services, travel regulations, entry requirements and immigration.

The second amendment forbids discrimination on the basis of gender, race, disability, language or social status. It stipulates equal rights and obligations for all citizens, both native and naturalized. Article 28I(2) stipulates that: "Each person has the right to be free from discriminatory treatment on any grounds and has the right to obtain protection from such discriminatory treatment." Article 28D(1) states that: "Each person has the right to the recognition, the security, the protection and the certainty of just laws and equal treatment before the law." This article guarantees the right to equal treatment "before the law" and to the protection of human rights and freedoms, without discrimination.

Under Article 28D(2), anyone, without discrimination, has the right to work and to receive just and appropriate rewards and treatment in their working relationships. Moreover, the members of the MPR retained Article 27 of the original 1945 Constitution. This Article clearly guarantees the right to equality by stating that: "All citizens have equal status before the law and in government and shall abide by the law and the government without any exception."

It is safe to say that every constitution and human rights treaty contains a clause which provides for equality. The formulae of the clauses may differ, but the central issues remain the same.[32] For instance, Article 1 of the UDHR states that "all human beings are born free and equal in dignity and rights. They are endowed with reason and conscience and should act towards one another in a spirit of brotherhood". The provisions of "equality before the law" and anti-discrimination in the second amendment are in line with international standards, established by Article 2 of the UDHR:

> Everyone is entitled to all the rights and freedoms set forth in this Declaration, without distinction of any kind, such as race, colour, sex, language, religion, political or other opinion, national or social origin, property, birth or other status. Furthermore, no distinction shall be made on the basis of the political, jurisdictional or international status, of the country or territory to which a person belongs, whether it be independent, trust, non-self-governing or under any other limitation of sovereignty.

The acceptance of equality provisions by all Islamic parties is supported by Islamic literature, from both formal and substantive *shari'a* approaches, the UIDHR, the Cairo Declaration, and constitutions in Muslim countries such as Egypt and Iran. I will deal with them one by one.

According to Parveen Shaukat Ali, the concept of equality is an integral part of Islamic legal philosophy. He claims that one of the greatest contributions of the Qur'anic doctrine was that it rehabilitated the slave to a niche of respectability as a human being. The white man was not above the black nor the black above the yellow. All men are equal before God.[33] Zafarullah Khan refers to the Qur'an (4:2) in order to support the equality inherent in Islamic views. This verse draws attentions to there being no room for any claim of superiority in respect of origin or descent.[34]

The opinions of Muslim scholars, above, confirm the equality provisions in the 1990 Cairo Declaration on Human Rights, which states that "all men are equal in terms of basic human dignity and basic obligations and responsibilities, without any discrimination on the grounds of race, colour, language, sex, religious belief, political affiliation, social status or other considerations" (Article 1). In addition, Article 19(a) of the Cairo Declaration provides that: "All individuals are equal before the law, without distinction between the ruler and the ruled."[35] This reflects the principle of human dignity indicated by the Qur'an (95:4). In the words of Maududi, a legal scholar from Pakistan, "the rights granted by kings or legislative assemblies can be withdrawn as easily as they are conferred, but no individual and no institution has the authority to withdraw the rights conferred by God".[36]

The 1981 UIDHR also contains equality provisions:

a. All persons are equal before the Law and are entitled to equal opportunities and the protection of the Law.
b. All persons shall be entitled to an equal wage for equal work.
c. No person shall be denied the opportunity to work nor be discriminated against in any manner nor exposed to greater physical risk by reason of religious belief, colour, race, origin, sex or language.[37]

In this regard, Article 8 of the Egyptian Constitution stipulates that "the State shall guarantee equality of opportunity to all citizens". In addition, Article 20 of the 1979 Iranian Constitution provides that all citizens enjoy human, political, economic, social, and cultural rights according to Islamic standards. As can be seen, equality provisions are accepted by the second amendment to the 1945 Constitution, the Iranian Constitution, the Egyptian Constitution, the UIDHR, the Cairo Declarations, and in Muslim scholars' views. It is safe to conclude that equality provisions in the 1945 Constitution are in line with both international human rights instruments and *shari'a*. However, discussion of more specific issues regarding the right to equality is needed, in order to see how equal those equality provisions are. I will focus on equal protection of the law for women and religious minorities, since the problem of equality in Islamic society is centred on, as pointed out by Esposito and Piscatori, "unequal status between Muslims and non-Muslims as well as between men and women".[38]

Women's Rights

The second amendment to the 1945 Constitution does not specifically mention women's rights. However, there is no single article that restricts or limits women's right.[39] Women's rights are mentioned in both the 1998 MPR Decree on Human Rights and Law No. 39 of 1999 on Human Rights. For instance, Article 39 of MPR Decree No. XVII/MPR/1998 mentions that women's rights are similar to men's rights. In addition, women's rights are to be considered as human rights, in Law No. 39 of 1999 (see Article 45). The law stipulates that a fair representation of women in public appointments in the executive and judiciary and in the electoral process must be ensured (see Article 46). Other rights include the right to obtain teaching and education, to vote and to be elected and rights covering property in marriage. Article 49 provides a right to be "appointed in work, posts and professions in accordance with the requirements and regulations". In addition, women have a right to "special protection in performing their duties, against matters which can threaten their safety and/or health, relating to the reproductive function". Those rights highlight the notion that Indonesia takes the view that women have the same rights as men.

It is worth considering that Egypt recognizes women's right but such recognition is based on *shari'a*. These two Articles explain that:

Article 10
The State shall guarantee the protection of motherhood and childhood, take care of children and youth and provide the suitable conditions for the development of their talents.

Article 11
The State shall guarantee the proper coordination between the duties of woman towards the family and her work in the society, considering her equal with man in the fields of political, social, cultural and economic life without violation of the rules of Islamic jurisprudence.

The same approach has been taken by Iran. While respecting women's rights, Iran states clearly that women's rights should be based on "Islamic criteria".

Article 21
The government must ensure the rights of women in all respects, in conformity with Islamic criteria, and accomplish the following goals:

1. create a favorable environment for the growth of woman's personality and the restoration of her rights, both the material and intellectual;
2. the protection of mothers, particularly during pregnancy and childbearing, and the protection of children without guardians;
3. establishing competent courts to protect and preserve the family;
4. the provision of special insurance for widows, and aged women and women without support;
5. the awarding of guardianship of children to worthy mothers, in order to protect the interests of the children, in the absence of a legal guardian.

As can be seen, Iran and Egypt mention "Islamic criteria" or "Islamic jurisprudence" when providing women's rights in their constitutions. The vagueness in the Islamic criteria limiting women's rights allows great leeway to the authorities in choosing what kind of discriminatory measures they will impose. Based on its "Islamic criteria", in Iran a woman cannot obtain a passport without the permission of a male relative or her husband. A woman's testimony in court is given only half the weight of a man's. Women must conform to strict dress codes and are segregated from men in most public places.[40] It is worth noting that such regulations do not exist in Indonesia.

Perhaps the most publicized tension between *shari'a* and international human rights norms concerns the allegedly unequal treatment of women. Muslims who denounce this inequality defend *shari'a* by attesting that women are given a "special rank" in the Islamic order. They argue that *shari'a* makes special provisions for women to provide them with the financial security and stability which they were historically unable to achieve on their own. They base their position on Qur'anic provisions (4:34) which state that: "Men have guardianship (*qawwam*) over women because of the advantage that they have over them [women] and because they [men] spend their property in supporting them [women]."

In civil matters, the testimony of Muslim women is accepted, but it takes two women to make a single witness. A Muslim male is always a fully competent witness under the formal *shari'a* approach.[41] Another example of discrimination against Muslim women is to be found in *shari'a* is regarding inheritance. The general rule is that a female is entitled to half the share of a male who has the same degree of relationship to the deceased.[42] For instance, Article 20(d) of the UIDHR states that "the woman may inherit from her husband, her parents, her children and other relatives according to the *shari'a*". According to *shari'a* family law — as understood according to the formal approach — a Muslim male may marry up to four wives and divorce any of them at will, without having to justify or explain his decision to any person or authority. In contrast, a Muslim woman is confined to one husband at a time and can obtain a divorce only through the courts on very strict grounds, or through the consent of the husband. As if that was not enough, under the formal *shari'a*, a husband can beat his wife "lightly" if he deems her to be "unruly".[43] The formal group also believes that women cannot become president. They cite the saying of the Prophet: "Those who entrust their affairs to a woman will never know prosperity."[44] They interpreted this as implying that it is forbidden for Muslims to elect a woman to be their leader.[45]

A substantive *shari'a* approach seeks to defend *shari'a* on all of these instances of discrimination against women by citing historical sociological and political justifications. They reinterpret the text differently and contextually.[46] For instance, in the case of a woman as a leader, the substantive Muslim scholars take the view that the Prophet pronounced this Hadith when he learned that the Persians had named a woman to rule them.

Therefore, this Hadith was related to the context of the selection of a Persian leader; not to Muslim matters. They also believed that it should be understood that women lacked the knowledge to be leaders at that time. Accordingly, it is quite irrelevant to bring the situation and arguments of the seventh century to any current political situation.[47]

The UIDHR made it clear that *shari'a* prevails over the 1948 UDHR. While the UDHR holds that international human rights law supersedes religious law, the basic premise of the UIDHR is that religious law is above international human rights law and that the ultimate legal reference for Muslim societies must be the Qur'an and Islamic law. There are some clear contradictions between the two declarations. For example, Article 20(b) on the rights of married women, states that women are entitled to

> receive the means necessary for maintaining a standard of living which is not inferior to that of her spouse, and, in the event of divorce, receive during the statutory period of waiting (*iddah*) means of maintenance commensurate with her husband's resources, for herself as well as for the children she nurses or keeps, irrespective of her own financial status, earnings, or property that she may hold in her own rights.

This contradicts the UDHR, which does not limit the woman's right to maintenance to a statutory period of waiting.

As can be seen, the problem arises when the Iranian and Egyptian Constitutions (and also the UIDHR) put women's rights under the *shari'a* schemes.[48] Ann Elizabeth Mayer points out that:

> On the basis of the standards in international human rights documents, one expects that documents on human rights will aim at protecting human rights, not provide rationales for restricting or denying rights. In contrast, as the examination of these Islamic human rights schemes shows, in the area of women's rights, they actually serve the function of justifying the taking away of rights.[49]

Therefore, in this context, it is essential to highlight the fact that the second amendment to the 1945 Constitution does not put women's rights under *shari'a*. This is a strong indication that, in this case, all Islamic political parties take a substantive *shari'a* approach by not limiting women's rights, in the name of *shari'a* nor Islamic criteria.

Religious Freedom

The second test, to see whether the equality provisions in the second amendment provide full protection of equality rights, is to examine religious liberties. Gary Bell explains that:

even though the Republic of Indonesia "is based on the belief in the One and Only God", freedom of religion is protected and Islam, the religion of the majority has no special constitutional status. The secular nature of the State can be seen again as an effort at unity: there is no minority religion in law if there is no recognition of the majority religion by the law. Religion becomes an individual matter and all Indonesians individuals are treated equally. One could therefore say that the way the constitution mentions religious freedom without mentioning Islam is meant to afford constitutional protection to religious minorities.[50]

However, in the context of this book, the standard protection of freedom of religion is as stated in Article 18 of the UDHR: "Everyone has the right to freedom of thought, conscience and religion; this right includes freedom to change religion or belief." Article 28E(1) of the 1945 Constitution recognizes the right to choose a religion, but does not include the right to change one's religion.

There are, at least, two explanations. Firstly, it seems that in Indonesia, the biggest Muslim country in the world, it was not appropriate to mention the right to change one's religion, since apostasy is condemned in *shari'a*. Apostasy from Islam, after willingly accepting it and subsequently declaring an open revolt against it in such a manner as to threaten the solidarity of the Muslim community, is a crime punishable by death. No one is compelled to accept Islam, but at the same time no one is permitted to play tricks with it, as some Jews did during the Prophet's time: "A party of the People of the Book say, 'Believe in what has been revealed to the Believers' at the beginning of the day and reject it at the end of it, in order that they may turn back (from Islam)" (Qur'an 3:72). The Prophet ordered, "whoever changes his religion, kill him".[51]

However, the substantive *shari'a* takes the view that actually the Qur'an does not judge the apostate (*murtad*) in this world, namely, by capital punishment. It judges him/her in the hereafter, as stated in the Qur'an 2:217 and 4:137. The former Chief Justice of Pakistan, S. A. Rahman, believes that there is no reference to the death penalty in any of the twenty instances of apostasy mentioned in the Qur'an.[52] In addition, the chain of transmission (*isnad*)[53] of this Hadith quoted above was from the Prophet via only one individual.[54]

Moreover, the context of the order from the Prophet to kill the apostate should be fully understood. Apostasy in Islam should be seen as equal to treason. At the time of the Prophet, when a Muslim repudiated his faith, he rebelled against that order and endangered the security and the stability of the society to which he belonged. Since apostasy in Islam is not merely a private or ecclesiastical affair as it is in Western society (by withdrawal of church membership, for example), the state must act. Apostasy is treason towards Muslim society (*ummah*) and the undermining of the Muslim state, for Islam is the buttress of society and the state itself. Apostasy erodes and shakes the foundations of the order of society, and because it is treason, the state must prosecute it.[55] Therefore, in the modern context, the death penalty is not an appropriate response to apostasy since apostasy should no longer be seen as treason.

It is worth noting that there is no punishment in Indonesian criminal law for those who change their religion (for example, from Islam to Christianity) since *hudud* (the Islamic Criminal Code) is not applicable in Indonesia. Although apostasy is not considered a crime, mentioning the right to apostasy is a different thing, and would invite anger from Muslim leaders. Many Muslim scholars see inter-religious marriage as one of the reasons why Muslims change their religion. They substantiated the perception by citing some inter-marriage couples that broke up because the Muslim spouse did not want to be Christians or in which both spouses became Christians.

On 7 January 1992, the Minister for Religious Affairs, Munawir Syadzali, stated that Indonesia needed a new formulation of official regulations, which would allow people of different religions to marry. He stated that, since Indonesia has a heterogeneous society, mixed marriages were inevitable. This idea was responded to negatively by all Islamic organizations. The Muhammadiyah, the second-largest Muslim organization, took the view that mixed marriages could not be justified in Islamic law, and Law No. 1 of 1974[56] had already regulated marriage clearly and strictly, so that a new regulation or law concerning marriage between partners of different religions was not needed. If anything should be amended, this amendment should be only in the form of a confirmation of, or information added to, this law.[57] The Majelis Ulama Indonesia (MUI, or The Council of Indonesian Ulama) had already issued a *fatwa* in 1980, stating that inter-religious marriages were not allowed, according to Islamic law.[58] Furthermore, the NU (Nahdlatul Ulama) issued a number of *fatawa* on this issue in 1962, 1968 and in 1989, confirming the view that inter-religious marriage was not permitted.[59]

The contentious matter of inter-religious marriage is illustrative of the tension between Muslims and Christians in Indonesia. The UDHR stipulates that:

Article 16(1)
Men and women of full age, without any limitation due to race, nationality or religion, have the right to marry and to found a family. They are entitled to equal rights as to marriage, during marriage and at its dissolution.

Therefore, forbidding inter-religious marriage would be in contradiction of international human rights instruments. It is in this context that Indonesia's Article 28B stipulates that "each person has the right to form a family, and to continue the family line through legitimate marriage". It rejects the use of the language of the UDHR in order to avoid controversy. What is the meaning of "legitimate marriage"? Law No. 1 of 1974 on Marriage mentions that marriage is valid when it is undertaken in accordance with the law of the appropriate religion and belief. Therefore the legality and validity of inter-religious marriage are not positively based on law. Again, this is an example of how Indonesia avoids controversy, by using religious considerations.

Secondly, it is no secret that Muslim leaders tend to allege that the conversion of many Indonesian Muslims to Christianity is a result of "Christianization".[60] Therefore, it is necessary to curb such Christianization, by not guaranteeing the right to change one's religion. This situation will be understood better if the social and political environments are considered. The fear of Christianization, real or imaginary, affecting Indonesian Muslims has haunted Muslim leaders and society since the colonial period. Tireless efforts by the relatively well-organized Dutch missionary organizations were successful in Christianizing segments of the Indonesian population, especially in the heathen hinterland and outer island tribes. Provided with facilities and privileges, generally speaking, these Christian converts have had better opportunities than their Muslim neighbours, who mostly resented Western education and development as collaboration with the despised colonizers[61] or were excluded from such benefits.

In the post-colonial period, well-educated Christian scholars maintained their influential position. The need for their expertise, as well as the hidden fear of a danger perceived to be posed by Muslim intellectuals, led the Soeharto government to employ many Christian technocrats in key positions. At the grassroots level, the open campaign of propagating Christian gospels and benefits was intensified. The combination of these various factors heightened the tensions, some of which even manifested into open conflict of inter-religious relationships.[62] It is in this environment that the exclusion of the right to change religion, as brought up in the second amendment, should be seen. All political parties, including Islamic parties, are satisfied with the language of Article 28E of the second amendment: "Every person shall be free to adhere to his/her respective religion and to worship according to his/her religion." This language neither forbids nor permits the exercise of any possible right to replace one's current religion or belief with another. This clause is closely related to Article 29(2) of the 1945 Constitution.[63] I shall return to this issue in Chapter 6.

In the international context, religious freedom is also a controversial topic. When the General Assembly of the United Nations had to decide on the UDHR in 1948, the Saudi Arabian ambassador strongly objected to religious liberty, particularly to the right to change one's religion, a right explicitly mentioned in Article 18 of the UDHR.[64] It is no surprise that the Basic Laws (*al-nizam al-asasi li al-hukm*) of Saudi Arabia states: "The state protects human rights in accordance with the Islamic *Shari'a*" (Article 26). Therefore, since apostasy is claimed to be condemned by the formal *shari'a*, Saudi Arabia's Basic Laws will not consider the right to change one's religion, except to become a Muslim.

In addition, no guarantee of freedom of religion is afforded by the Cairo Declaration. It is essential to note that, by the standards of international human rights norms, freedom of religion is a fundamental and non-derogable right. Instead of guaranteeing freedom of religion, it has been found that the Cairo Declaration restricts it:

Article 10
Islam is the religion of unspoiled nature. It is prohibited to exercise any form of compulsion on man, or to exploit his poverty or ignorance, in order to convert him to another religion, or to atheism.

The failure to provide for religious freedom has serious practical implications for Muslims, given the number of Muslim dissenters from officially imposed constructs of Islam and members of local minority sects who have been mistreated, charged with apostasy from Islam, or subjected to pressures or threats, to compel them to abjure non-conformist beliefs. Many individuals who have been labelled "apostates" have not been converts at all, but devout Muslims who question conservative interpretations of Islam, and call for a more modern and tolerant version of their faith.

The apostasy law has been used to target many liberal free-thinking Muslims. In a case in Egypt in 1995, Nasr Hamid Abu Zayd, a lecturer at the American University in Cairo, was labelled an apostate for writing an academic book, which Islamic scholars deemed to be offensive to Islam. Abu Zayd had used hermeneutics to interpret the Qur'an, and the lawyers argued that his findings placed him outside the bounds of Islam. The courts ruled that, as an apostate, he must be divorced from his wife, and upheld the ruling even after he appealed. No longer able to live together as a couple in Egypt, Abu Zayd and his wife left for Holland in 1996.[65]

Article 10 of the Cairo Declaration appears to be based loosely on Article 18(2) of the International Covenant on Civil and Political Rights (ICCPR), but involves a serious distortion of the principle set forth in Article 18(2), which provides: "No one shall be subject to coercion which would impair his freedom to have, or to adopt, a religion or belief of his choice." Thus, whereas the prohibited coercion in Article 18(2) is coercion which interferes with religious freedom, in Article 10 of the Cairo Declaration, "compulsion", along with exploitation, is prohibited only when it is employed to convert a Muslim to another faith or to atheism, not when it is used to make someone adopt Islam. In this context, it is worth considering that Article 28E(2) of the 1945 Constitution stipulates that "each person has the freedom to possess convictions and beliefs, and to express their thoughts and attitudes in accordance with their conscience". If Abu Zayd had lived in Indonesia after the second amendment era, he would have not been charged with apostasy.

The absence of a provision for freedom of religion may also be detrimental for non-Muslims. Islamic criteria are used in the Iranian Constitution, and at the same time, Zoroastrian, Jewish and Christian Iranians are the only recognized religious minorities.[66] However, they are barred from election to representative bodies (though a set number of parliamentary seats are reserved for them), cannot hold senior government or military positions, and face restrictions on employment, education, and property ownership.

As a result of the combination of human rights protection and the formal *shari'a* approach taken by the Constitution, non-Muslims in Iran have to endure the Islamic restrictions imposed on all Muslim Iranians, including the Islamic dress code, the separation of the sexes in public, the prohibition on many books and musical compositions, and the prohibition on alcoholic beverages and pork in public places. The forced Islamic headcover imposed on religious minorities faced objections from Christian and Zoroastrian women. They have to tolerate the indignities of being forced to post signs in their shop windows, indicating ownership by a non-Muslim, so that the Muslim customers might avoid coming into contact with the impurity emitting from the *najs* (impure) operator.[67]

Some 300,000 Baha'is — Iran's largest non-Muslim minority — enjoy virtually no rights under the law. They face official discrimination, a complete denial of property rights, a ban on university admission, employment restrictions, and prohibitions on practising and teaching their faith. Their marriages are not recognized by the government, which leaves women open to charges of prostitution, and their children are regarded as illegitimate, and thus without inheritance rights. Hundreds of Baha'is have been executed since 1979.[68]

In the case of Egypt, Scott Kent Brown II argues that Egypt cannot create a society truly tolerant of religious pluralism, without first eliminating all forms of religious discrimination from its own Constitution.[69] He refers to the experience of the Coptic Church in Egypt vis-à-vis freedom of religion. He notes several problem areas, including the delays over building permits for new churches and for preventing the deterioration of ancient churches. He also indicates that Christians are underrepresented in the government, and that institutional discrimination exists in business, the military and universities. Although Article 46 of the Egyptian Constitution stipulates that, "the State shall guarantee the freedom of belief, and the freedom of practice of religious rites", Brown argues that Article 46 is limited by Article 2, which states that "the Principles of the Islamic *Shari'a* are *the* principle source of legislation" (author's italics). According to him, it needs to be clarified that Article 2 will not be used to deprive any Egyptian citizen of religious human rights.[70] The fear of non-Muslims over their status under the *shari'a* can be understood by looking at the concept of *dhimmi* (non-Muslims under Muslim rule). I will deal with this in Chapter 6.

Freedom of Opinion

This section deals with freedom of opinion. The second amendment to the Indonesian Constitution firmly guarantees freedom of opinion. There are two articles dealing with the subject:

Article 28E
1. Each person has the freedom to possess convictions and beliefs, and to express his/her thoughts and attitudes in accordance with his/her conscience.
2. Each person has the freedom to associate, gather, and express his/her opinions.

Article 28F
Each person has the right to communicate and to obtain information in order to develop him/herself and his/her social environment, and the right to seek out, obtain, possess, store, process, and transmit information using any means available.

These provisions are based on the principle that freedom of opinion is a manifestation of the people's sovereignty. In other words, freedom of opinion is guaranteed as a basic right for citizens. One of the consequences is that the press is free from any form of prevention, prohibition and/or pressure, so that the public right to information is guaranteed. It goes further to state that the press is free from censorship and is not subject to publication and broadcasting bans.

In exercising its social control function, a government's policies may be criticized and people may engage in public debate on political and economic issues. Based on the provisions above, the press may provide wide access to the public to obtain information. Moreover, the provisions above have opened the door for the press to act as the Fourth Estate.

The Fourth Estate view was originally borrowed from the British, to suit a modern system of government. Whereas the three Estates in England had been the clergy, nobility, and the House of Commons,[71] the three Estates in American terminology became the executive, legislative, and judicial branches of government. This Fourth Estate role has not gone uncriticized by legal scholars and commentators, especially in its pure sense as the "fourth branch of government".[72]

However, the essence of the Fourth Estate concept is the independence from governmental influence, interference, and control, in order that unbiased, provocative commentary might be made. The Fourth Estate seems rooted in the "checking" value that is free speech. A free press and free assembly can serve in checking the abuse of power by public officials.[73] Because autonomy is a crucial element of the Fourth Estate, it could be argued that institutional autonomy is a necessity. This means that once the autonomy of the press is threatened, or otherwise compromised, its power is considerably reduced. Thus, the term Fourth Estate is used today to refer to the mass media as a powerful watchdog over democracy, revealing abuses of state authority and defending the democratic rights of citizens. This reflects the supposed significance of press freedom in a democratic society. It is in this context that the provision of freedom of opinion in the second amendment to the 1945 Constitution was significant. Such provisions are in line with international human rights instruments.

Whilst the press should perhaps be taken into account as the Fourth Estate of a system of democracy, the Cairo Declaration does not provide for freedom of the press, and *shari'a* is used in the Cairo Declaration to restrain freedom of opinion. Article 22(a) grants the right freely to express opinions, "in such manner as would not be contrary to the principles of the *shari'a*".

Article 22(b) of the Cairo Declaration provides that: "Everyone shall have the right to advocate what is right, and propagate what is good, and warn against what is wrong and evil according to the norms of Islamic *shari'a*." It seems that Article 22(b) echoes the doctrine of *amr ma'ruf nahi munkar* (enjoin the good and forbid the evil). It is derived from the Qur'an (3:104), "Let there become of you a group of people which shall call for righteousness, enjoin the good and forbid the wrong. Such men will surely triumph." This suggests that Article 22(b) can be interpreted as stating that no right would be provided to advocate what is wrong or evil according to *shari'a*. This may open the way for the limiting of opinion, which is expressed by utilizing all available channels, such as television, radio, newspapers, Internet, novels, comics, and books.

The words "contrary to the principles of the *shari'a*" is vague. It depends on different schools of thought and, more importantly, it is up to the government to determine or justify sweeping censorship, which could be based on the government's political interests, backed up by religious authorities, fearing that such opinions could convert or corrupt Muslims, or weaken their faith. The same approach has also been taken by Article 24 of the Iranian Constitution: "Publications and the press have freedom of expression except when it is detrimental to the fundamental principles of Islam, or the rights of the public". Freedom House reports that the Iranian government directly controls all television and radio broadcasting, and has recently begun jamming RFE/RL (Radio Free Europe/Radio Liberty) Persian service broadcasts, and selectively enforcing a ban on satellite dishes. In addition, since 2000, over eighty-five publications have been shut down by the judiciary, and dozens of journalists have been arrested, often held incommunicado for extended periods of time, and convicted in closed-door trials.[74]

Religious Values

The human rights provisions in the second amendment were the result of a long process that started during the MPR Session of 1998. In 2000, members of Ad Hoc Committee I (PAH I) conducted comparative studies in several countries, including Iran and Egypt. One of the aims of their visits was to understand human rights protection in those countries.[75] The members also consulted constitutional law and human rights experts. From the minutes of meetings during the 2000 MPR Session,[76] it is safe to state that all Islamic parties supported the human rights provisions in the second amendment.

According to Lukman Hakim Saifuddin of the Partai Persatuan Pembangunan (PPP), there was no hot debate during the 2000 MPR session on this issue.[77] He provides two reasons: firstly, human rights provisions in the second amendment are based on MPR Decree No. XVII/MPR/1998. Since the debate had occurred during the 1998 MPR special session, it was not necessary to repeat the debate in the 2000 MPR session. Secondly, all Islamic political parties agreed with the provisions, since they satisfied the "religious values" mentioned in Article 28J(2):

> In the enjoyment of their rights and freedoms, each person is obliged to submit to the limits determined by law, with the sole purpose of guaranteeing

recognition and respect for the rights of others and to fulfil the requirements of justice, and taking into consideration morality, religious values, security, and public order, in a democratic community.

Hamdan Zoelva of Partai Bulan Bintang (PBB) specifically interprets this as "no articles on human rights in the second amendment may contradict religious values".[78] That is why his party accepts the human rights provisions in Chapter X of the 1945 Constitution.

It is important to note that Article 36 of the 1998 MPR Decree on Human Rights does not mention "religious values" as a limitation. The reason is that, during the 1998 MPR session, based on the 1997 general election only one Islamic party was involved, whereas in 2000 there were more than three Islamic parties contributing to the debate. Instead of suggesting the word *shari'a* in human rights provisions — as in the case of Egyptian and Iranian Constitutions, the Saudi Arabian Basic Laws, the Cairo Declaration and the UIDHR — those Islamic parties proposed only the words "religious values".

It is safe to argue that the term "religious values" is closely related to the substantive *shari'a* approach; not the formal one. No Islamic parties in Indonesia see the *shari'a* as something which is above the Constitution. The phrase "religious values" is placed along with justice, morality, security, public order, and the concept of a democratic country. This shows that the practice of human rights may well take into account these elements, and the only limitation is the law itself. As a comparison, the Cairo Declaration, which takes the formal *shari'a* approach, stipulates that:

Article 24
All the rights and freedoms stipulated in this Declaration are subject to the Islamic *shari'a*.

Article 25
The Islamic *shari'a* is the only source of reference for the explanation or clarification of any of the articles of this Declaration.

Such provisions do not exist in the second amendment to the 1945 Constitution, nor were they proposed by any of the Islamic parties. Having discussed all the issues, this chapter reaches the conclusion that, in the case of human rights, the second amendment accommodates *shari'a* in a substantive way, and regards *shari'a* as only a "religious value". This also indicates a pluralistic and inclusive approach, since "religious values" can also be interpreted according to the other religions which exist in Indonesia. By employing this approach, no inherent contradiction exists between the substantive *shari'a* and human rights, as embodied in the existing international standards.

CONCLUSION

This chapter has examined the human rights provision in the second amendment to the 1945 Constitution from the perspective of *shari'a*. Several key issues such as equality, women's rights, freedom of religion, freedom of opinion, and religious values have been analysed. Whilst the tendency of other human rights documents in Islam, ranging from the Constitutions of Iran, Egypt and Basic Laws of Saudi Arabia to UIDHR and the Cairo Declaration, is to restrict human rights provision under the rules of *shari'a*, such restriction does not exist in the second amendment to the 1945 Constitution. In other words, I have demonstrated that *shari'a* is neither above nor outside the human rights provision in the 1945 Constitution. The principles of *shari'a* inspire human rights protection since they can "walk" together side by side.

There are at least three possible explanations. Firstly, all Islamic political parties in Indonesia refer to the situation in the Soeharto era, particularly when many Muslim activists were sent to jail without human rights protection. I have examined this briefly in Chapter 3. Therefore, it is in the interests of Islamic political parties to ensure that such abuse would not occur in the post-Soeharto era. This explains why they have given full support to the inclusion of human rights provisions in the Amendment to the 1945 Constitution.

Secondly, all Islamic political parties take the position that human rights are compatible with the substantive *shari'a* approach. To put it differently, they operate on the premise that Islam is in substance compatible with Western human rights legal norms if interpreted accordingly. To support this contention, they refer on the general level to the elasticity of Islam and to its capability to accommodate various interpretations equally favourable or hostile to human rights.

The acceptance of human rights provisions without any restriction to the formal understanding of *shari'a* suggests that the Indonesian Islamic political parties which were involved in the process of constitutional reform during 1999–2002 differ in their position from other Muslim groups who openly reject the concept of human rights as based on alien Western notions or as a conspiracy against Islam and from those who take pains to establish a specifically Islamic human rights scheme within an ideological framework devoid of a legal reform in Islam.

Thirdly, although the second amendment to the 1945 Constitution accepts human rights in their full substance, this does not mean that religions do not have a role at all in Indonesia. Religious values along with justice, morality, security, public order, and democracy, should be taken into account in implementing human rights provisions of the 1945 Constitution. It is worth noting that the phrase "religious values" does not refer only to Islam but to other religions as well. Moreover, the word "values" connotes spiritual or ethical norms rather than law or regulation. In the context of Islam, religious values can be interpreted as *shari'a* in its original meaning as a "path" or guide, rather than a detailed legal code.

Mashood A. Baderin shares a similar observation:

> The scope of international human rights can be positively enhanced in the Muslim world through moderate, dynamic, and constructive interpretations of the *Shari'a* rather than through hardline and static interpretations of it.[79]

The full acceptance of human rights provisions has shown that Indonesia has provided a model for other Islamic countries to acknowledge the compatibility of human rights and Islamic law. This position is closely related to the role of public religion in Indonesia, which differs from the position of Iran, Egypt and Saudi Arabia. Such role will be fully explained in the next two chapters.

Notes

1. More information on history and philosophy of human rights can be read in Costas Douzinas, *The End of Human Rights* (Oxford: Hart, 2000).
2. The document was drafted by John Humphrey, a Canadian professor in law, and Rene Cassin, a French Nobel Laureate. Three other people played a significant role in subsequent drafting of the document: Eleanor Roosevelt, Dr Charles Malik of Lebanon and Dr Peng-chun Chan of China. As can be seen, the last two persons were Asians.
3. See Tahir Mahmood, ed., *Human Rights in Islamic Law* (New Delhi: Genuine Publications, 1993). This book compiles articles from leading Muslim scholars such as Abul A'la Maududi, M. I. Patwari, Majid Ali Khan, Sheikh Showkat Husain, and Parveen Shaukat Ali.
4. For instance, Muhammad Sa'id Ashmawy takes the view on the evolution of the meaning of *shari'a* that, at the beginning, the meaning of *shari'a* in the Arabic language can be traced to the meanings of "the path" (*al-thariq*), "the method" (*al-manhaj*) or "the way" (*al-sabil*). He refers to the fact that the term *shari'a* means the path of Islam consisting of three streams: (1) worship (*al-ibadat*), (2) ethical code (*al-akhlaqiyat*), (3) social interactions (*al-mu`amalat*); and not in

the imputed meaning of "legal system" in an "Islamic state". This original meaning of *shari'a* was what was initially applied by the first generation of Muslims. Over time the meaning of *shari'a* was expanded to include the legal rules found in the Qur'an and finally the concept of *shari'a* came to include the whole body of legal rules developed in Islamic history, including all the interpretations and opinions of the legal scholars. See Muhammad Sa'id al-Ashmawi, *al-Shari'a al-Islamiya wa al-Qanun al-Misri* (Cairo: Makatbah Madbuli al-Shaghir, 1996), pp. 7 and 21.

5. When drafting the 1945 Constitution, there were arguments to include the human rights articles in the constitution as the Western countries do. For instance, Mohammad Yamin pointed out the importance of regulating the basic human rights in the constitution, citing the Declaration of Independence and the Bill of Rights in the United States of America as examples (Sekretariat Negara (1995: 177–79)). Mohammad Hatta also suggested preventing arbitrary human rights intervention by the government by guaranteeing freedom of expression, association, and assembly in the constitution (Sekretariat Negara Republik Indonesia, *Risalah Sidang BPUPKI-PPKI 28 Mei 1945–22 Agustus 1945* (Jakarta: Sekneg, 1995), pp. 262–63). However, it was Soekarno as well as Soepomo who opposed to them with "the Family Principle". "The constitution we are drafting is based on the doctrine of family principle, not based on the doctrine of individualism we have rejected. Declaring the freedom of assembly and association in the Constitution is systematic from the doctrine of individualism, so that if we declare the freedom of assembly and association in our constitution, we will challenge the rationality of the family principle doctrine. … In the system of family principle, the attitude of the citizen (*warga negara*) is not always asking 'what is my right?', but asking 'what is my duty as a member of the big family, that is, this Indonesian State'." As Soepomo described it, he strongly opposed the articles of basic human rights as the adoption of individualism (Ibid., pp. 275–76). Article 28 in the 1945 Constitution was a meeting ground between the two camps (Ibid., pp. 358–61).

6. Article 28 of the 1945 Constitution said that the "freedoms of association and assembly, of oral and written speech and of others shall be established by law".

7. The International Covenant on Civil and Political Rights (ICCPR), Article 1, and the International Covenant on Economic, Social and Cultural Rights (ICESCR), Article 1.

8. See The Universal Declaration of Human Rights (UDHR), Article 6.

9. UDHR, Article 7.

10. UDHR, Article 23.

11. UDHR, Article 20.

12. UDHR, Article 19.

13. UDHR, Article 18.

14. UDHR, Article 26.

15. UDHR, Articles 22 and 25.

16. UDHR, Article 22.
17. Todung Mulya Lubis, *In Search of Human Rights: Legal Political Dilemmas of Indonesia's New Order 1966–1990* (Jakarta: Gramedia Pustaka Utama, 1993), pp. 293–94.
18. Prior to the Amendments to the 1945 Constitution (1999–2002), the Parliament (DPR) considered Bills presented to it by government departments and agencies, but did not draft laws on its own, although it had the constitutional authority to do so.
19. The Supreme Court theoretically stands on equal footing with the executive and legislative branches, but it does not have the right of judicial review over laws passed by Parliament. The Supreme Court had never exercised its authority (held since 1985) to review ministerial decrees and regulations. In 1993, Chief Justice Purwoto Gandasubrata laid out procedures for limited judicial review. As a result of the Amendments to the 1945 Constitution in 2002, the Supreme Constitutional Court was established in August 2003 and has the right of judicial review over laws passed by the Parliament. For discussion of the political subordination of the Supreme Court, see Tim Lindsey, "Paradigms, Paradoxes and Possibilities: Towards Understandings of Indonesia's Legal System", in *Asian Laws Through Australian Eyes*, edited by Veronica Taylor (Sydney: Law Book Company, 1997), pp. 90–110.
20. In Article 13, sections (5) and (6) shall be added to read as follows:
    (5) Every press publication undertaken by a press enterprise shall require a "*Surat Izin Usaha Penerbitan Pers*" (Press Publication Enterprise Permit), hereinafter abbreviated "*SIUPP*" issued by the Government. Provisions regarding the SIUPP shall be arranged by the Government, after hearing considerations from the Press Council.
    (6) The advertising media constitute one of the important supporting elements in the development of a press enterprise. Provisions concerning the advertising media shall be arranged by the Government after hearing considerations from the Press Council.
21. See Julian Millie, "The Tempo Case: Indonesia's Press Laws, the Pengadilan Tata Usaha Negara and the Indonesian Negara Hukum", in *Indonesia: Law and Society*, edited by Timothy Lindsey (Sydney: The Federation Press, 1999), pp. 269–78.
22. As a comparison, freedom of the press in Singapore and Malaysia has been explained in Chua Lee Hoong, "Walking the Tightrope: Press Freedom and Professional Standards — Singapore" (pp. 142–55), Syed Arabi Idid and Sankaran Ramanathan, "Walking the Tightrope: Press Freedom and Professional Standards — Malaysia" (pp. 119–32), both are published in Asad Latif, ed., *Walking the Tightrope: Press Freedom and Professional Standards in Asia* (Singapore: Asian Media Information and Communication Centre, 1998); see also Scott L. Goodroad, "The Challenge of Free Speech: Asian Values v. Unfettered Free Speech, an Analysis of Singapore and Malaysia in the New Global Order", *Indiana International and Comparative Law Review* 9 (1998): 259.

23. See Dana L. Clark, "The World Bank and Human Rights: The Need for Greater Accountability", *Harvard Human Rights Journal* 15 (2002): 205.

24. Human Rights Watch, "Indonesia: Soeharto-Era Abuses Must Go", 1998, available at http://www.hrw.org/reports98/indonesia2/.

25. See *Kompas*, 16 August 1998; full text of the Address can be found at http://www.dfa-deplu.go.id/policy/statements/president/paripurna150898.htm.

26. See the comment on Habibie's statement in Doug Cassel, "Universal Rights and Asian Culture: Indonesia Converts", *Worldview Commentary*, No. 2, 19 August 1998.

27. Besides this, there was an effort to establish the Bill of Basic Human Rights in the early period of the Soeharto regime. The general session of the MPRS, in July, 1966 adopted "the MPRS Decision of Year 1966 No. 14 about the set-up of MPRS ad hoc committees to carry out the duties of the survey of state institutions, the execution of a plan to separate authorities among state institutions according to the 1945 Constitution system, the preparation of a draft of a revised and enlarged edition of the 1945 Constitutional Commentary, and the preparation of detailed human rights regulations". According to this decision, four ad hoc committees (Panitia Ad Hoc) were established to discuss the survey of state institutions, separation of powers, a revised and enlarged edition of the Constitutional Commentary, and a Bill of Human Rights. The committee finished drafting the Bill of Human Rights itself in 1967, awaiting deliberation at the General Session of the MPRS the next year. However, when Soeharto was installed as the Acting President in 1967 and as the President in 1968, Golkar and the armed forces, which supported Soeharto, withdrew their support on the Bill of Human Rights. Afterwards, Soeharto never took up the Bill of Human Rights for discussion (Lubis, *In Search of Human Rights*, pp. 6–7).

28. For a full account, see Nadirsyah Hosen, "Human Rights and Freedom of Press in the Post-Soeharto Era: A Critical Analysis", *Asia-Pacific Journal on Human Rights and the Law* 3, no. 2 (2002): 1–104; Hikmahanto Juwana, "Special Report: Assessing Indonesian's Human Right Practice in the Post-Soeharto Era", *Singapore Journal of International and Comparative Law* 7 (2003): 644–77.

29. Tim Lindsey, "Indonesia: Devaluing Asian Values, Rewriting Rule of Law", in *Asian Discourses of Rule of Law*, edited by Randall Peerenboom (London: RoutledgeCurzon, 2004), p. 301.

30. Gary F. Bell, "Minority Rights and Regionalism in Indonesia: Will Constitutional Recognition Lead to Disintegration and Discrimination?", *Singapore Journal of International and Comparative Law* 5 (2001): 784.

31. Recent commentaries on the 1945 Constitution include those by Bell, ibid,; and also Gary F. Bell, "Obstacles to Reform the 1945 Constitution: Constitutions Do Not Perform Miracles", *Van Zorge Report on Indonesia; Commentary and Analysis on Indonesian Politics and Economics* III, no. 6 (2001): 4–13; Tim Lindsey, "Indonesian Constitutional Reform: Mud Towards Democracy", *Singapore Journal of International and Comparative Law* 6 (2002): 244–301; Bivitri Susanti, "Constitution and Human Rights Provisions in Indonesia: An

Unfinished Task in the Transitional Process", in *Constitutions & Human Rights in a Global Age: An Asia-Pacific Perspective*, edited by Tessa Morris-Suzuki (Canberra: Australian National University, 2003), pp. 5–14.

32. Kenneth W. Simons, "Equality as a Comparative Right", *Boston University Law Review* 65 (1985): 387.

33. Parveen Shaukat Ali, "Equality as a Basic Human Rights in Islam", in *Human Rights in Islamic Law*, edited by Tahir Mahmood, pp. 118–52.

34. Muhammad Zafrullah Khan, *Islam and Human Rights* (Islamabad: Islam International Publication, 1999), pp. 61–62.

35. Full text can be read in http://www.isesco.org.ma/pub/Eng/humanrights/page7.htm.

36. Abul A'la al-Maududi, *Human Rights in Islam* (London: The Islamic Foundation, 1983), p. 4.

37. See Article III of the 1981 UIDHR, available at http://www.al-bab.com/arab/docs/international/hr1981.htm#III.

38. John L. Esposito and James P. Piscatori, "Democratization and Islam", *Middle East Journal* 45, no. 3 (1991): 428.

39. It is important to note that on 9 October 1998 Habibie issued Presidential Decree No. 181 of 1998 on the Establishment of a National Commission for the Elimination of Violence towards Women (Komnas Perempuan). This decree is consistent with the ratification of the UN Convention on the Elimination of All Forms of Discrimination against Women (13 October 1984) and the UN Convention against Torture and Other Cruel, Inhuman or Degrading Treatment or Punishment (23 October 1998). The background to the establishment of Komnas Perempuan was the incident involving the rape of ethnic Chinese women during riots on 14 and 15 May 1998. Father Sandyawan, leader of the Volunteer Team for Humanity, which was investigating the rapes, published a report on the sexual violence. The report indicated that there were 168 cases of sexual violence, with 130 rape cases reported in Jakarta. The Indonesian government admitted that the riots were deliberatly instigated. On 2 June 1999, the National Commission on Human Rights condemned the violence and suggested that it was an organized effort. On 23 July, the government appointed a joint fact-finding team, Tim Gabungan Pencari Fakta (TGPF), to investigate the violence. The team includes armed forces members, government agencies, and human rights advocates. However, on 26 August 1999, General Wiranto told police that no evidence was found in 103 cases of rape. Wiranto's announcement was condemned by human rights activists. More information can be found in the Human Rights Watch Report, "Indonesia: The Damaging Debate on Rapes of Ethnic Chinese Women", http://www.hrw.org/hrw/reports98/indonesia3.htm; R. Charlie Carpenter, "Surfacing Children: Limitations of Genocidal Rape Discourse", *Human Rights Quarterly* 22 (2000): 428–77; Gerry van Klinken, "The Chinese Rapes, Economic Depression and Indonesian Communalism", *Inside Indonesia*, digest 68, 31 August 1998; Rudiah

Primariantari, "Women, Violence, and Gang Rape in Indonesia", *Cardozo Journal of International and Comparative Law* 7 (1999): 245; See also Tempo, Special Edition, 25 May 2003.

40. See Freedom House Report, available at http://www.freedomhouse.org/research/freeworld/2003/countryratings/iran.htm. Freedom House was founded nearly sixty years ago by Eleanor Roosevelt, Wendell Willkie, and other Americans concerned about peace and democracy. It is non-profit and non-partisan.

41. Qur'an 2:282 says: "if the two be not men, then one man and two women, such witnesses as you approve of, that if one of the two women errs the other will remind her …"

42. Qur'an 4:11 says: "God charges you, concerning your children: to the male the like of the portion of two females, and if they be women above two, then for them two-thirds of what he leaves, but if she be one then to her a half; and to his parents to each one of the two the sixth of what he leaves, if he has children; but if he has no children, and his heirs are his parents, a third to his mother, or, if he has brothers, to his mother a sixth, after any bequest he may bequeath, or any debt. Your fathers and your sons — you know not which out of them is nearer in profit to you. So God apportions; surely God is All-knowing, All-wise." For full account see Zainab Chaudhry, "Myth of Misogyny: A Reanalysis of Women's Inheritance in Islamic Law", *Albany Law Review* 61 (1997): 511.

43. "Admonish those women whose rebelliousness you fear, and leave them alone in their beds, and [even] beat them [if necessary]. If they obey you, do not seek any way [to proceed] against them." (Qur'an 4:32). Modern jurists and writers have done their best to weaken this verse by interpreting "rebelliousness" as disobedience and adultery, where beating would be the last means a man can resort to, in order to keep the woman from committing that heinous deed. See Mahmud Syaltut, *Al-Islam Aqidah wa Shari'a* (Cairo: Dar al-Syuruq, 1988), p. 166.

44. For full discussion, see Nadirsyah Hosen, "Can a Woman Become the President of the World's Largest Muslim Country? Megawati — An Indonesian Political Victim", paper presented at Women in Asia Conference, Australian National University, Canberra, 23–26 September 2001.

45. During 1999 Campaign, several Islamic political parties, on the basis of this Hadith argued that Megawati Soekarnoputri could not be the President. I will discuss this issue further in Chapter 5.

46. Amina Wadud al-Muhsin, a professor at Virginia Commonwealth University, offers a hermeneutical approach to understand the Qur'an on women. See her article, "Qur'an and Woman", in *Liberal Islam: A Source Book, edited by Charles Kurzman* (Oxford: Oxford University Press, 1998), pp. 127–38.

47. For the interpretation and historical context of the Hadith above, see Fatima Mernissi, "A Feminist Interpretation of Women's Rights in Islam", in *Liberal Islam*, edited by Kurzman, pp. 112–26.

48. See also Bharathi Anandhi Venkatraman, "Islamic States and the United Nations Convention on the Elimination of All Forms of Discrimination Against Women:

Are the Shari'a and the Convention Compatible?" *American University Law Review* 44 (1995): 1949.

49. Ann Elizabeth Mayer, *Islam and Human Rights: Tradition and Politics* (Boulder: Westview Press, 1991), p. 136.
50. Bell, "Minority Rights and Regionalism in Indonesia", p. 792.
51. For a full account, see Mohamed S. El-Awa, *Punishment in Islamic Law: A Comparative Study* (Indianapolis: American Trust Publication, 1982).
52. S. A. Rahman, *Punishment of Apostasy in Islam* (Kazi Publications, 1986).
53. Hadith composed of two parts: the *matn* (text) and the *isnad* (chain of reporters). A text may seem to be logical and reasonable but it needs an authentic *isnad* with reliable reporters to be acceptable. During the lifetime of the Prophet and after his death, his Companions used to refer to him directly, when quoting his sayings. The next generation (*tabi'un*) followed suit; some of them quoted the Prophet through the Companions, while others would omit the intermediate authority. It was found that the missing link between the *tabi'un* and the Prophet might be one person, that is, a Companion, or two people, the extra person being an older Successor who heard the Hadith from the Companion. This is an example of how the need for the verification of each *isnad* arose. The other more important reason was the deliberate fabrication of Hadith by various sects. According to the number of reporters involved in each stage of *isnad*, at least two categories of Hadith can be identified. *Hadith Mutawatir* (Consecutive) is a Hadith that is reported by such a large number of people that they cannot all be expected to agree upon a lie. *Hadith Ahad* (isolated) is a Hadith which is narrated by people whose number does not reach that of the *mutawatir*. More information can be read in Mahmud al-Tahhan, *Taysir Mustalah al-Hadith* (Cairo: Dar al-Turas al-'Arabi, 1981).
54. Mahmoud Ayoub of Temple University criticizes several key Hadith used by legal scholars to address both the existence of the category of crime labelled apostasy, and its accompanying punishment of death. He concludes that no Qur'anic or Prophetic tradition forms a strong, valid basis for the assigning apostasy the death penalty. See Mahmoud Ayoub, "Religious Freedom and the Law of Apostasy in Islam", in *Islamochristiana*, No. 20, 1994 (N.p.: Pontificio Istituto di Studi Arabi d'Islamistica), pp. 79–85.
55. See Frank Griffel, "Toleration and Exclusion: al-Shafi'i and al-Ghazali on the Treatment of Apostates", *Bulletin of the School of Oriental and African Studies* 64 (2001): 3.
56. More information on Law No. 1 of 1974 can be obtained in Mark Cammack, L. Young and T. Heaton, "Legislating Social Change in an Islamic Society: Indonesia's Marriage Law", *American Journal of Comparative Law* 44 (1996): 45; Mark Cammack, "Islam, Nationalism, and the State in Suharto's Indonesia", *Wisconsin International Law Journal* 17 (1999): 27; Azyumardi Azra, "The Indonesian Marriage Law of 1974", in *Shari'a and Politics in Modern Indonesia*, edited by Arskal Salim and Azyumardi Azra (Singapore: Institute of Southeast Asian Studies, 2003), pp. 76–95.

57. See *Jakarta Post*, 8 January 1992, and *Kompas*, 8 January 1992.
58. Majelis Ulama Indonesia, *Himpunan Keputusan dan Fatwa* (Jakarta: Sekretariat MUI, Masjid Istiqlal Jakarta, 1995), pp. 91–92; See also Nadirsyah Hosen, "Behind the Scenes: Fatwas of Majelis Ulama Indonesia (1975–1998)", *Journal of Islamic Studies* 15, no. 2 (2004): 147–79.
59. See Nadirsyah Hosen, "Fatwa and Politics in Indonesia", in *Shari'a and Politics in Modern Indonesia*, edited by Salim and Azra, p. 173.
60. More information can be found in Alwi Abdurahman Shihab, "The Muhammadiyah Movement and Its Controversy with Christian Mission in Indonesia" (Ph.D. thesis, Temple University, 1995).
61. On this matter, see Karel Steenbrink, *Dutch Colonialism and Islam in Indonesia: Conflict and Contact 1596–1950* (Amsterdam: Rodopi B.V., 1993).
62. See Tarmizi Taher, *Aspiring for the Middle Path: Religious Harmony in Indonesia* (Jakarta: CENSIS, IAIN, 1997).
63. Article 29(2) of the 1945 Constitution: "The State guarantees all persons the freedom of worship, each according to his/her own belief".
64. Heiner Bielefeldt, "Muslim Voices in the Human Rights Debate", *Human Rights Quarterly* 17, no. 4 (1995): 602.
65. In 2001, an Islamist lawyer accused Nawal Saadawi, the noted Egyptian feminist activist, physician, and writer, of apostasy, and argued that she should be divorced from her husband. See Nancy Gallagher, "Apostasy, Feminism, and the Discourse of Human Rights", 2003, http://repositories.cdlib.org/uciaspubs/editedvolumes/4/1058.
66. *Article 13*

    Zoroastrian, Jewish, and Christian Iranians are the only recognized religious minorities, who, within the limits of the law, are free to perform their religious rites and ceremonies, and to act according to their own canon in matters of personal affairs and religious education.

    Article 14

    In accordance with the sacred verse "God does not forbid you to deal kindly and justly with those who have not fought against you because of your religion and who have not expelled you from your homes" [60:8], the government of the Islamic Republic of Iran and all Muslims are duty-bound to treat non-Muslims in conformity with ethical norms and the principles of Islamic justice and equity, and to respect their human rights. This principle applies to all who refrain from engaging in conspiracy or activity against Islam and the Islamic Republic of Iran.

    Article 26

    The formation of parties, societies, political or professional associations, as well as religious societies, whether Islamic or pertaining to one of the recognized religious minorities, is permitted, provided they do not violate the principles of independence, freedom, national unity, the criteria of Islam, nor the basis of the Islamic republic. No one may be prevented from participating in the aforementioned groups, nor be compelled to participate in them.
67. Eliz Sanasarian, *Religious Minorities in Iran* (New York: Cambridge University

Press, 2000), p. 90. See also Daniel Tsadik, "The Legal Status of Religious Minorities: Imam, Shari'a, Law and Iran's Constitutional Revolution", *Islamic Law and Society* 10, no. 3 (2003): 376.

68. See the Baha'is of Iran in *Bahai News*, http://www.sullivan-county.com/id3/ bahai_iran.htm; see also Freedom House Report, http://www.freedomhouse.org/ research/freeworld/2003/countryratings/iran.htm. The more than a hundred year presence of Baha'i in Egypt has also caused a number of legal problems for Muslim jurists and Egyptian courts. Both have dealt with the status of Baha'i in personal status, criminal and administrative law. See Johanna Pink, "A Post-Qur'anic Religion between Apostasy and Public Order: Egyptian Muftis and Courts on the Legal Status of the Baha'i Faith" *Islamic Law and Society* 10, no. 3 (2003): 409.

69. Scott Kent Brown II, "The Coptic Church in Egypt: A Comment on Protecting Religious Minorities from Nonstate Discrimination", *Brigham Young University Law Review 2000* (2000): 1049; See also Maurits Berger, "Public Policy and Islamic Law: The Modern Dhimm in Contemporary Egyptian Family Law", *Islamic Law and Society* 8, no. 1 (2001): 88.

70. Brown II, ibid, p. 1094.

71. David L. Lange describes the historical evolution of the term "Fourth Estate", in his article "The Speech and Press Clauses", *UCLA Law Review* 23 (1975): 77.

72. See Lucas A. Powe, Jr., *The Fourth Estate and the Constitution: Freedom of the Press in America* (California: University of California Press, 1991); Julianne Schultz, *Reviving the Fourth Estates: Democracy, Accountability and the Media* (Cambridge: Cambridge University Press, 1999). While Powe's work evaluates the Press in America, Schultz analyses the role of journalism in Australia and the scope of its democratic purpose. She examines key news stories and looks at the attitudes of Australian journalists themselves.

73. It is interesting to note that in the post-Soeharto era, several scholars and politicians in Indonesia also regard the press as the Fourth Estate. See "Jadi Pilar Demokrasi, Pers Tuntut Budaya Hukum", *Kompas*, 11 October 2002.

74. Freedom House, http://www.freedomhouse.org/research/ freeworld/2003/ countryratings/iran.htm.

75. See Sekretariat Jenderal MPR, *Risalah Rapat ke-6 Badan Pekerja MPR RI*, 23 May 2000 (Jakarta: Setjen MPR, 2000).

76. Ibid.

77. Lukman Hakim Saifuddin, personal communication, 10 December 2003.

78. Hamdan Zoelva, personal communication, 15 December 2003.

79. Mashood A. Baderin, *International Human Rights and Islamic Law* (Oxford: Oxford University Press, 2003), p. 219.

5

RULE OF LAW

The term "rule of law" has no fixed meaning. It originated in normative writings on law and government, principally by Western authors, and each tailored the term to fit his or her vision of the "ideal" or "just" state. As a consequence, one recent survey of how the concept has been used in Germany, France, the United Kingdom, and the United States concludes that it "belongs to the category of open-ended concepts which are subject to permanent debate".[1] The term is worth taking seriously because it suggests the possibilities and limitations of a law-based approach. Whatever may be its ultimate scope, the rule of law offers itself as a counter-proposition to arbitrary rule, or rule by caprice. It is a statement of the supremacy of law over personal rule, or expedient politics. As such, the rule of law acts to restrain the exercise of power, by imposing the need for accountability on those who employ power in the name of the public good.

The rule of law provides a foundation for legal respect for human dignity. It is rightly regarded as the central principle of constitutional governance.[2] Critically surveying the work of such theorists as Friedrich von Hayek,[3] Ronald Dworkin[4] and Roberto Unger,[5] Judith Shklar takes the view that the rule of law should be recognized as an essential element of constitutional government in general, and of representative democracy in particular. Its boundaries are set by enduring concerns over the fear of violence, the insecurities of arbitrary government and the discriminations of injustice.[6]

Meanwhile, as has been mentioned earlier, the topic of the rule of law vis-à-vis *shari'a* is a controversial topic. The image is that Islamic law allows the ruler (Caliph, King, Prime Minister, or President) to govern without accountability and transparency. This concurs with other images that *shari'a* does not provide procedural regulations to control the government; *shari'a* does not have a clear rule on how to elect the government and how to limit the powers of the government; and there is no judicial independence in the countries that enforce *shari'a*.

Historically, it is the ruler's discretion — not the rule of law — which plays a greater part in Islamic constitutional law. Islamic jurisprudence came to accept the idea of *siyasa shar'iyya*, which accords the terrestrial ruler a reservoir of discretionary power of command in the public interest. If deviations from the strict *shari'a* doctrine were required to protect the *maslahah al-ammah* (public interest)[7] in implementing the guiding principles behind *shari'a*, then such deviations were allowed.[8] This expansive doctrine of government discretion was justified in terms which reflected the privileged position of the Caliph as head of state of the Islamic nation. Since caliphs were presumed to possess keen piety and the ability to engage in *ijtihad* (independent legal reasoning), they were also presumed to be ideally qualified for their office and were to be allowed the discretion to take such steps as they in their wisdom saw fit.[9]

In the context of the rule of law, discretion can be described as the space between or within rules. In other words, discretion may be described in terms of situations where there is power to make choices between courses of action, or where the end is specified but a choice exists as to how it should be achieved. It is a recognition of the limited capacity of rules to deal with every conceivable situation and, at the same time, a recognition that purely rule-based government is an ideal which could never be attained in any country. In addition, discretion fills the gap left by legislators, as well as situations where two or more rules challenge each other. It also fills the gap where rules break down, or work unfavourably as in cases where the consequences of the application of the rule is incompatible with the stated purposes of the legislature. Above all, it is impossible for the law-maker to anticipate and provide for all possible cases which the particular rule may be required to cover. However, the discretion of law enforcement agencies should not be unlimited.

As has been outlined in Chapter 2, formal *shari'a* believes that sovereignty belongs to Allah, and therefore any ruler should be bound by *shari'a*, while other governments are based on whimsical despotism. A leader is a shadow of Allah on earth, meaning that he is Allah's agent on earth, with Allah as his source. The presence of a head of state is intended to secure the effectiveness of all the commands and laws of Allah. The tradition of the Prophet, works of classical jurists and the practice of Islamic government in medieval times provide a justification of the system of Islamic government.

By contrast, the substantive *shari'a* group strongly disagrees with the above views. Since Allah orders Muslims to consult with others before making decisions in their affairs, an Islamic government cannot be a theocratic one. If everything was to be decided by the heavens, there would be no need to consult anyone. What the Prophet left behind was an extremely primitive state-structure based more on local traditions. Therefore, *shari'a* does not determine any definite form of government, nor does it lay down details for it. It lays down only some foundational principles based on the substance of Islamic values. For this group, the absence of any definite form of government in Islam is considered as a blessing because it makes it possible for Islam to march with the progress of time and adjust itself to social change. It is in this context that this group accepts the idea of the rule of law.

This chapter will discuss the rule of law according to the amendment to the 1945 Constitution vis-à-vis *shari'a*. Which approach (formal or substantive) has influenced the discussion and the result of the new structure of Indonesian government will be the main point of discussion. I will consider Muslim jurists' works (classic and modern), the Constitutions of Iran and Egypt, and the Basic Laws of Saudi Arabia in my approach to the topic. Meanwhile, the MPR's minutes of meeting and interviews with members of the MPR will also be examined. Prior to analysing the rule of law under constitutional reform (1999–2002), I will evaluate the structure of the Indonesian state according to the original form of the 1945 Constitution in order to show the demands and the expectations of such reform. Having examined all the issues, I would argue in this chapter that a new structure of the Indonesian state could be seen as the product of political *ijtihad* by Muslims in Indonesia. It is safe to argue that such *ijtihad* is performed by considering the substantive *shari'a* approach; not the formal one.

THE RULE OF LAW BEFORE THE AMENDMENTS

At the heart of Indonesia's problems lies at least a thirty-two-year absence of the rule of law. The term *Negara Hukum* or *rechtsstaat* is used in Indonesia as an equivalent of the Western notion of the rule of law. According to Lindsey, the rule of law "is a highly charged notion that has played a central role in Indonesian political and legal thinking".[10] However, as Lindsey has correctly pointed out, "the use of common law traditions of 'rule of law' to understand

Negara Hukum is problematic" since no consensus has been reached on the exact meaning of *Negara Hukum* (Law State).[11]

It is also worth considering that the concept of *rechtsstaat*, which had been introduced into the German constitutional and political debate in the early nineteenth century, has also been interpreted in various ways. It has evolved over time in Europe to incorporate democracy and fundamental rights.[12] Some have tried to distinguish the rule of law from the *rechtsstaat*, by stressing that the former is a theoretical ideal while the latter is concerned with actual obedience to the law.[13]

The Civil Law *Rechtsstaat* is described, by Peerenboom[14] as a "thin" version of rule of law. A more apt label for this version might be "rule *by* law", for it entails no connotation of legal limitations. The idea of rule *by* law is that law is a means by which the state operates in the conduct of its affairs; "that whatever a government does, it should do through laws."[15] Tim Lindsey also states that rule by law or the thin version of the rule of law is "often linked to the 'Civil Law' *Rechtsstaat* idea".[16]

The literal meaning of *rechtsstaat* was stipulated in the elucidation of the 1945 Constitution.[17] However the elucidation did not explain the notion of *rechtsstaat*. It only stated: "Indonesia is a state based on law (*rechtsstaat*), not merely based on power (*machtsstaat*)." In other words, the spirit of the 1945 Constitution is that Indonesia is based on right rather than might. Lack of a clear definition of *rechtsstaat* invites the criticism that its meaning is subject to interpretation "which is frequently done subjectively by the government".[18]

Lubis explains this problem further:

> The Old Order government, for example, subscribed to a *rechtsstaat* cast in terms of the romantic vision of Soekarno's notion of unfinished revolution, enabling him to interfere in the judiciary. The New Order government, by contrast, interpret[ed] the *rechtsstaat* in a sense that support[ed] the goals of economic development, stability, security and order. Implicitly, the *rechtsstaat* [was] subordinated to those goals.[19]

Lubis's explanation provides evidence that both the Soekarno (1945–66) and the Soeharto (1966–98) governments used the notion of *Negara Hukum* as their rhetoric. Neither government created institutions and frameworks, nor did they establish basic infrastructure. Legal frameworks are necessary for creating a predictable and secure living and working environment for ordinary citizens, and for entrepreneurs and investors. A fair and effective legal framework requires that a set of rules be known in advance, that the rules be enforced, that the means to ensure the application of the rules exist, that any conflicts be resolved by binding decisions made by an independent and credible judiciary, and that procedures be available for changing the rules when they cease to serve the purpose for which they were intended. Those legal frameworks have long been absent in Indonesia.

There is a school of thought that believes that constitutional reform will convert Indonesia into a *Negara Hukum* (literally, a nation of law) which is based on the rule of law; not the law of the ruler.[20] All Indonesian jurists agree that Indonesia needs law reform as a basis for becoming a *Negara Hukum*, although they have different interpretations of law reform. David K. Linnan outlines these different approaches:

(a) a sociological *qua* political science approach, asserting that "elite" preferences have trumped formal governance structures including law;

(b) a psychological or cultural approach asserting that traditional Indonesian (or more properly Javanese) "feudalistic" attitudes must be changed before the rule of law can take hold; and

(c) an approach stressing basic problems of government organisation under Indonesia's 1945 Constitution (or UUD 1945) linked with bureaucratic competition in a public choice sense immobilising reform within government.[21]

Although the concepts of the rule of law, *rechtsstaat*, and *Negara Hukum* have different meanings,[22] this chapter takes the position that they share the common view that the government and the state apparatus should be subject to the law, that areas of discretionary power should be defined and limited, and that citizens should be able to turn to the courts to defend themselves against the state and its officials.[23] The rule of law entails equal protection of human rights of individuals and groups, as well as equal punishment under the law. It protects citizens against arbitrary state action. It ensures that all citizens are treated equally and are subject to the law rather than to the whims of the powerful. The law should also afford vulnerable groups protection against exploitation and abuse.

The notion of human rights (including equality before the law) has been discussed in the previous chapter. In this chapter, the discussion will be limited to the structure of the Indonesian state in the 1945 Constitution. It is essential that the rule of law must determine the offices to be filled by election, the procedures to elect those office-holders, and the definition of, and limits to, their powers, in order for the people to be willing to participate in, and to accept, the outcomes of the democratic regime. The rule of law in this context is also understood to include the rules of "separation of powers", in which mechanisms for checks and balances are guaranteed and the independence of the judiciary is secured. How did the 1945 Constitution respond to these issues?

The Structure of the State

In Article 1 of the 1945 Constitution, the form of government was determined to be a republic, rather than a monarchy. The president, as the head of state, held the executive power and organized the government (Article 4). This means that a kind of presidential system was employed, rather than a parliamentary system. However, the presidential system in Indonesia was not a simple presidential system, based on an assumption that the post of the president shall be guaranteed during his term of office and he shall not be forced to resign by the parliament.[24] In Indonesia, the president is not responsible for the legislative body, the House of Representatives (Dewan Perwakilan Rakyat, or DPR), and, accordingly, has no right to dissolve it.

The president, however, was elected by the "legislative" body, named the People's Consultative Assembly or MPR (Majelis Permusyawaratan Rakyat), which consisted of the DPR and other appointed members. On 7 June 1999, more than 125 million Indonesians went to the polls to elect 462 of the 500 members of a new national parliament, or People's Representative Council (DPR). The remaining 38 seats were appointed from the Indonesian Armed Forces (Angkatan Bersenjata Republik Indonesia, or ABRI). Elections were held simultaneously for the provincial assemblies (Dewan Perwakilan Rakyat Daerah I, or DPRD I) and the district assemblies (Dewan Perwakilan Rakyat Daerah II, or DPRD II). The 500 members of parliament joined with the 135 representatives chosen by the provincial assemblies (five from each of the country's 27 provinces) and 65 representatives of functional groups[25] to form the 700-member MPR. Thus, the president was responsible to the MPR (Article 6). In addition, the president did not have the right to dissolve the MPR. This means that the post of president was not guaranteed during his/her term of office, but, as the perceived need arose, he/she could be forced to resign.

The DPR is the principal legislative body of Indonesia. Members of the DPR are automatically members of the MPR. While the latter cannot, in their capacity as members of the DPR, vote the president out of office, their votes, in their capacity as members of the MPR, would be decisive if an attempt were made to impeach him. Although Indonesians often use the term "impeachment", the process did not involve a trial but an evaluation by the MPR that the President had violated the constitution or the "National Will" (Haluan Negara) embodied in MPR decrees and should, therefore, be dismissed. The impeachment process began with the adoption by the DPR of a memorandum warning the president of the alleged violations. If, after three months, the president did not respond satisfactorily to the memorandum, a second memorandum could be sent. If after a further month there were still no satisfactory response, the DPR then could request the MPR to hold a special session to request the president to explain the issues raised in the memorandum. If the MPR were satisfied that the president "truly violated the National Will", he/she then could be dismissed by the MPR.

The procedures described above were outlined in MPR Decree III/1978, Article 7; not in the 1945 Constitution.[26] This has made the Indonesian constitution presidential in character while still retaining a strong parliamentary element. The mix of presidential and parliamentary features established by the 1945 Constitution created an imbalance in executive-legislative relations. The DPR could ask the MPR to remove the president during mid-term for political reasons, yet the president could not dissolve the DPR and called for early elections.

For instance, opposition politicians in the DPR and MPR took advantage of these rules to attack President Abdurrahman Wahid during 2000 on "Bulog-Gate" and "Brunei Gate".[27] Since the majority of the members of the MPR were also members of the DPR, President Wahid alleged that in reality the DPR, not the MPR, deposed him, and that this was against the Constitution. Wahid then issued his Presidential Decree to dismiss the MPR and call new legislative elections. Although consistent with the parliamentary logic under which he was being removed, under the existing rules of political game in Indonesia these actions were illegal. Unlike Soekarno's Presidential Decree in 1959, Wahid's Decree was not supported by the military, thus leading to his removal from office.[28] An unclear relationship between the president, MPR and DPR, and the unclear mixed system with both presidential and parliamentary features contributed to this case.

Therefore, the MPR, as the highest organ of the state, was not the same type of institution as a parliament.[29] As stated in Article 1, Clause 2, of the 1945 Constitution, the MPR is the manifestation of all the people of Indonesia, fully exercising sovereignty in the name of the Indonesian people. The MPR as a political institution was literally the highest state organ, positioned above all other state organs, such as the president, the DPR, and the Supreme Court. The MPR was to hold a General Assembly at least once every five years (Article 2(2)) for the amendment of the constitution, decision-making on the National Will, or the Broad Outline of State Policy (Garis Besar Haluan Negara, or GBHN)[30] laid down for guidance of his policies during the president's term in office, and for the election of the President/

Vice-President (Articles 3, 6(2), and 37). Then, according to the GBHN decided by the MPR, five high state organs below the MPR — the president, the DPR, the Supreme Court, the Supreme Advisory Council (Dewan Pertimbangan Agung, or DPA), and the Financial Audit Board (Badan Pemeriksa Keuangan, or BPK) — exercised their respective functions. The MPR was thus the "embodiment" (*penjelmaan*) of the entire Indonesian nation.

As has been discussed in Chapter 3, political institutions in Indonesia did not assume a separation of the three state powers and checks-and-balances between the legislative, the executive, and the judiciary, in order to prevent misuse of state power. Professor Soepomo, a leading figure in the drafting process of the 1945 Constitution, as a chairperson of the Small Committee of Drafting the Constitution (Panitia Kecil Perancang Undang-Undang Dasar) under the Investigating Committee for the Preparation of Independence, explained that the reason why Indonesia should not adopt the separation of the three powers was "because in practice a law-making institution was handed over to governmental works, a court was handed over to governmental works, and the government was given authority making laws. Because of it, the separation of three powers (*Trias Politica*) in theory did not fit with reality."[31]

After rejecting individualism and liberal democracy as being the bases of the new democratic regime, the founding fathers adopted the "Big Family principle" (*kekeluargaan*) as a philosophical base for constructing original political institutions in Indonesia. The Constitution was expected to establish political institutions in which power was concentrated in the president, as the head of the big family, standing above all the people.[32] The clearest manifestation of this philosophical heritage was the status, composition and purpose of the People's Consultative Assembly, as described above, and the position, power and status of the president, as examined below.

Prior to the reform era, the 1945 Constitution was described as "executive-heavy", since the superiority of the executive over the legislative was written clearly into the Constitution. Regulations pertaining to the president in the Constitution amounted to nineteen points, thirteen articles. Chapter III, Articles 4–15 on "The State Administration Power"; Chapter V, Article 17 on "The Cabinet"; and Chapter VII, Article 22(1) on "the DPR" covered the various powers that were given to the president. For example, the president held the supreme right to command the army, the navy, and the air force (Article 10). The president could declare war (with the ratification of the DPR), conclude peace and sign treaties (Article 11) and declare a state of emergency (Article 12). The president held authority to appoint and accept diplomatic envoys (Article 13), and to grant amnesty (Article 14). The president, as the head of the Cabinet, also appointed state ministers (Article 17) and participated in daily administration.

The most important among the President's authorities, in terms of the concentration of power in his hands, was the right to legislate. Article 5(1) says that "the President holds the right to determine a law with the agreement of the DPR". This shows a formulation that the president and the DPR co-hold the right to legislate, which is different from a system in which the right to legislate belongs to the parliament only, one typically seen in modern constitutionalism. Thus, it does not reflect the idea of power control — that the executive is to be restricted by legislation and its activity are to be controlled by the legislature. Rather, the president and the DPR should cooperate and coordinate in proposing legislation. The president, as the head of the administration (Article 4(1)), might also "determine an ordinance to implement a law" (Article 5(2)) and "determine an ordinance in the place of a law in the time of emergency" (Article 22(1)). Thus, the president was given the right to legislate such matters as laws and ordinances.

On the other hand, the regulations about the DPR consisted of only nine points in five Articles. Furthermore, regulations about the courts consisted of only three points — Articles 24 and 25 in Chapter IX on "The Justice System". As Article 20(1) stipulated that "all laws have to get approval from the DPR", the right to legislate is defined in the Constitution. However, since the president was given the right of veto over a law passed by the DPR (Article 21(2)), the superiority of the DPR's legislative rights over the president was rather low. In contrast to the president's right to veto DPR-initiated laws, the DPR was not given any method by which to restrain the president's right of appointing personnel, treaty conclusion, and legislation. Thus, it was difficult for the legislature to control the executive in terms of law. The only regulation to establish the superiority of the legislature over the executive was the right to vote for the Budget (Article 23(1)) and the right to tax (Article 23(2)).

The chapter on the judiciary was one of the most inadequate parts of the 1945 Constitution. Article 24(1) determined only that "the right of Justice is exercised by the Supreme Court and … other organisations of justice" and that the organization, authorities, and methods of appointment of judges would be regulated by relevant laws. The elucidation of the 1945 Constitution said that "Indonesia is a state of law" (*negara yang berdasar atas hukum* [*rechtsstaat*]) and the judiciary is a power independent of the executive, while the details are not defined in the Constitution. As the provisions regarding state institutions are also to be enacted in laws and the president holds legislative authority, it is not difficult to predict the result: whoever holds power will wield absolute power, under the 1945 Constitution.

In particular, the Supreme Court lacked the power of constitutional interpretation and judicial review. Because the 1945 Constitution did not regulate judicial review, there was no method for the judiciary to check the executive and the legislative. In fact, MPR Decree III/1978, Article 11(4) limited the Supreme Court to reviewing only legal products below the level of laws in the hierarchy, leaving unresolved the issue of which body had the power of judicial review over laws.

So far I have examined the position, power and status of the president, the DPR, the MPR, and Supreme Court under the original form of the 1945 Constitution. The governing political institutions have drastically changed, through the amendments to the 1945 Constitution that were enacted during the period 1999–2002. It is time to move to the main discussion.

ANALYSIS OF THE NEW STRUCTURE OF THE INDONESIAN STATE

In this section, I will focus on the form of the Indonesian state, sovereignty and the powers, method of election, requirements, accountability, and relationship between the executive, the parliament and the judiciary. I will analyse these issues by examining the opinions of Muslim scholars, the Egyptian and Iranian Constitutions, and the Basic Laws of Saudi Arabia.

Form of Government

The question of whether *shari'a* has established a certain form of government remains controversial. Taqiyuddin al-Nabhani opines that the *khilafa* is the valid form of Islamic government.[33] His views are supported by classic Muslim thinkers such as al-Mawardi (974–1058) who took the view that the establishment of *al-Imama* (or *khilafa*)[34] is obligatory, since it is intended as the vicarate of the prophecy, in upholding the faith and managing the affairs of the world (*al-imama mawdu'ah li khilafa al-nubuwwa fi hirasat al-din wa siyasa al-dunya*).[35] This structure was in existence, and Muslims had never been without a Caliph, until Mustapha Kemal abolished the *khilafa* system in 1924.[36] Since then, the idea of a non-caliphate structure of government has been introduced by Western colonialism. This fact alone is sufficient as evidence that any other types or forms of government are concepts alien to Muslim tradition. For instance, Ahmad Husayn Ya'qub clearly states that *al-nizam al-siyasi al-Islami laysa nizaman dimuqratiyyan* (the system of political

Islam is not a system of democracy).[37] Since the Islamic state is the *khilafa*, it means that when a Caliph is present the Islamic state exists. Therefore, there is no genuine Islamic state today. Many Islamic movements such as *Hizbut Tahrir* attempt to re-establish the caliphate and, consequently, they refuse to "imitate" the Western concept of government.

The fall of the Ottoman Caliphate in 1924 led to the notion of nation-states in Muslim communities. There is no single world-government for all Muslim societies. Since then, the concept of nationalism, along with democracy, republics, and the rule of law have become political and legal discourses among several Muslim scholars. They began to ask: Is the Caliphate the only form of Islamic government? Did the practices of the Caliphate from Abu Bakar (the first Caliph) until those of the Ottomans have the same form? They went further, by returning to the primary sources of Islam (the Qur'an and the Sunna) in order to find out the structure of Islamic government.

Those scholars such as Muhammad Abduh,[38] Ali Abdur Raziq,[39] M. Husayn Haykal,[40] who took the substantive approach to *shari'a*, came to the conclusion that the universality of Islam lies not in its political structure, but in its faith and religious guidance. Both the Qur'an and the Sunna literature do not prefer a definite political system; both primary sources have laid down a set of principles, or ethical values and political morals, to be followed by Muslims in developing life within a state. Therefore, the claim that the *khilafa* is the only valid type of Islamic government is questionable.

The administration of *khilafa* from the first Caliph until the last one varied in practice. There were several caliphates or dynasties (Buyids, Saljuks, and Fatimid) at the same time in different locations; thus, the claim of there being a single Caliph for all Muslims is not entirely true. In fact, since the Umayyad era (661), the institution of the caliphate turned into a monarchy.[41] As has been discussed previously, Islamic legal tradition justifies the elements or the principles of constitutionalism, and consequently, the idea of upholding the rule of law is not an alien concept for Muslims.[42]

Abd al-Wahhab Khallaf goes even further by stating that the Islamic government is a constitutional, as opposed to a tyrannical, government (*al-hukuma al-islamiya dusturiya*).[43] In other words, based on his understanding of *shari'a*, government in Islam is not based on the charisma of the person. He also asserts that Islam guarantees individual rights (*huquq al-afrad*) and separates power into *al-sulta al-tashri'iya*, *al-sulta al-qadaʾiya*, *al-sulta al-tanfidhiya* — which could easily be classified as the legislative, judiciary, and executive powers, respectively.[44] Khallaf's views can be justified on the grounds that the Qur'an provided the basic principles for a constitutional democracy without providing the details of a specific system. Muslims were to interpret these basic principles in the light of their customs and the demands of their historical consciousness.

It is in this context that all Islamic political parties in Indonesia discuss the amendments to the 1945 Constitution. Not a single Islamic political party proposed the idea of the *khilafa* as the form of Indonesian government. They did not even propose that Indonesia became an Islamic state. According to the amendments, Indonesia remains a republic with a presidential system and three branches of government. Article 1(1) of the 1945 Constitution stipulates that "the State of Indonesia is a Unitary State which has the form of a Republic".[45] This suggests that Indonesian people accepts the idea of the nation state, which is structurally and fundamentally different from the caliphate system.

Sovereignty

The concept of sovereignty in Western political thinking was gradually developed. Sovereignty was initially attributed to the monarch, then to the state, and then to the people. The concept was formulated in Europe at the end of the sixteenth century. In the initial stages, sovereign power attached to individual people (the ruler). Hobbes in the mid-seventeenth century developed the notion of sovereignty by insisting that it should lie with the state. John Locke then proposed the idea that sovereignty should remain with the people. In the mid-eighteenth century, Rousseau took the view that sovereignty should be vested in the people. It should be unlimited and no law or constitution can bind it. Sovereignty has varied connotations, but it usually signifies the highest governmental authority and the ultimate communal source of absolute political or legal power.[46] In the context of *shari'a*, the question is: Does sovereignty belong to Allah or the people? This is another controversial topic.

According to the formal *shari'a* approach, sovereignty is vested in Allah, as expressed through *shari'a*. Allah is the source of all power and law (3:154; 12:40; 25:2; 67:1). It is Allah who knows what is good and what is bad for His servants. His say is final. Man is the vice-regent, the agent or the representative of Allah on earth (2:30; 6:165). Allah is the sovereign and man is His representative. Man should do as Allah commands him to do. The Islamic political system makes the ruler and the government responsible firstly to Allah.

This explains why, during the Caliphate era, there was no political nor legal mechanism for the accountability of caliphs. In theological terms, the Caliph would report his works to Allah and be questioned by Allah in the hereafter. Another consequence is that Allah is the legislator (*shari'*) and no one can change, replace or modify any law which Allah has laid down, even if the desire for such legislation, or for a change in it, is unanimous.[47] The caliphs were acting merely as instruments of the will of God. Moreover, Sayyid Quthb strongly objected to the notion of popular sovereignty. In his view the sovereignty of the people is an usurpation of God's sovereignty, or aggression against God's governance on earth, and a form of tyranny, for it subordinates the individual to the will of other individuals.[48] Quthb's view is supported by Muhammad Asad.[49]

In contrast, many modern Muslim thinkers, such as Namik Kemal,[50] Abdullahi Ahmed An-Na'im,[51] Muhammad B. al-Muti'i,[52] and Abd al-Qadir Audah,[53] propose the idea that the *ummah* (the totality of the Muslim population of the state) becomes the collective agent of the divine sovereign, rather than an individual person (caliph). It is the *ummah* which appoints its representatives to interpret God's law, and to discharge the duties of government, and holds them accountable to itself. The basis or justification for this views is the saying of the Prophet, "all Muslims will not agree on an error",[54] meaning that the consensus of the *ummah* is legitimate. This reminds us of *vox populi, vox Dei*. Louay M. Safi also notes that the "legitimacy of the state ... depends upon the extent to which state organization and power reflect the will of the *ummah* [the Muslim community], for as classical jurists have insisted, the legitimacy of state institutions is not derived from textual sources but is based primarily on the principle of *ijma'*".[55] According to this understanding, an Islamic constitution is a human product of legislation, based on the practices of consultation and consensus, and thus, virtually, no longer the result of a divine act. It is set and approved by the people.

Who then has sovereignty in Indonesia? Article 1(2) of the amended Constitution clearly now states that "sovereignty is in the hands of the people and is exercised in accordance with the Constitution". A different approach is taken by the Iranian government and the Kingdom of Saudi Arabia. "The Kingdom of Saudi Arabia is a sovereign Arab Islamic state with...God's Book and the Sunna of His Prophet (God's prayers and peace be upon him), are its constitution ..."(Article 1); and "Government in Saudi Arabia derives power from the Holy Koran and the Prophet's tradition" (Article 7). Under the terms of the Islamic revolution, the Iranian Constitution states that:

> **Article 1**
> The form of government of Iran is that of an Islamic Republic, endorsed by the people of Iran on the basis of their long-standing belief in the sovereignty of truth and Qur'anic justice...

Article 2
The Islamic Republic is a system based on belief in:
1. the One God (as stated in the phrase "There is no god except Allah"), His exclusive sovereignty and the right to legislate, and the necessity of submission to His commands....

Can we reconcile these two kinds of sovereignty? Ahmad Hasan has found another way to explain away the contradiction between the supremacy of God and popular sovereignty. He distinguishes two kinds of sovereignty: ultimate and immediate. The first refers to God, in a sense that no law enacted by the people shall contradict the obvious teachings of the Qur'an and the Sunna. The latter refers to the people (popular vice-regency) in a sense that it is the people who make the law. The immediate sovereign is, therefore, the community at large.[56]

Hamdan Zoelva of the PBB (Partai Bulan Bintang, or Crescent Star Party) provided similar arguments when answering my question on why his party accepts popular sovereignty. Although God is the supreme power, He needs people to implement and exercise His laws. Although sovereignty belongs to Allah, authority belongs to the people. The two should not be in mutual contradiction. The people have the authority to abrogate, amend, interpret or suspend *shari'a* depending on the circumstances, without neglecting its fundamental basis. Therefore, he does not see any contradiction of views between his party's vision on *shari'a* and popular sovereignty. He is not afraid that popular sovereignty will ruin God's law, since the majority of Indonesian people are Muslims and, therefore, it would be impossible to enact any law which is against the obvious teachings of Islam.[57]

It is sufficient to argue that, as a consequence of rejecting the caliphate form, the Indonesian people (including all Islamic political parties) therefore adopt popular sovereignty. It is worth considering that the issue of sovereignty never came up during constitutional debate at the MPR Session (1999–2002). Indonesian Muslims have departed from classical debate of *shari'a* vis-à-vis sovereignty.

Executive

In this section, I will focus on the pre-conditions to becoming the president, the method of election, accountability and impeachment and, lastly, the powers of the president. These issues will be discussed by comparison with those in *shari'a*. I would argue that Indonesia takes a substantive approach to *shari'a* on these issues.

Eligibility

According to Article 6(1) of the amendments to the 1945 Constitution, there are four pre-conditions to becoming the president. Firstly, candidates must have been Indonesian citizens since birth. Secondly, they also must never have taken, of their own accord, another citizenship. These two related conditions replace the original form: "The President shall be a native Indonesian citizen". The word "native" is vague and could be interpreted on racial grounds. Therefore, the amendments make it clearer that the word "native" means to be born in Indonesia.

Thirdly, candidates must never have committed treason. The last condition is that candidates must be spiritually and physically able to carry out the duties and obligations of the president and vice-president. In 2004, the last condition proved to be controversial. Having read the minutes of meetings of the MPR during the constitutional debate, one can sense that the background to this condition is the disabilities of President Wahid.[58] Two strokes at the beginning of 1998 had left him blind, physically frail and somewhat emotionally unstable, and several members of the MPR felt that Wahid could not serve the country well because of his disabilities. The controversy arose when in 2004 Wahid wanted to run in the presidential election. Wahid asked for a judicial review, on the grounds that he was suffering discrimination. Let the people choose who would become the president, he said, not the law. Both the Supreme Constitutional Court (Mahkamah Konstitusi) and the Supreme Court rejected his application for judicial review.[59]

The pre-conditions to becoming a leader have been discussed widely by Muslim political thinkers. Al-Mawardi, for instance, argued that there are seven conditions for eligibility for supreme leadership. He stressed that, among other things, a caliph should be of Arab nationality, of the notable Qurayshite descent. He also mentioned the need for sound hearing, vision and speech, physical fitness and freedom from handicaps to movement or agility of action.[60] Al-Ghazali went further by outlining ten conditions that have to be met: A candidate must be an adult, of healthy mind, free and not a slave, a male, of Quraysh descent, healthy of hearing and vision, have real power, possess guidance, possess knowledge and be observant of religious obligations.[61]

From these conditions, it is interesting to note that only two are mentioned in the Sunna: Quraysh descent and a male. Literally speaking, the other conditions are not found in the Qur'an and the Sunna. They are based on al-Ghazali's (or al-Mawardi's) own judgement. I will examine the two conditions briefly.

As has been noted in Chapter 4, there was a saying of the Prophet, "Those who entrust their affairs to a woman will never know prosperity." Based on this Hadith, al-Ghazali and Rasyid Rida (1865–1935) would not permit a woman to become the supreme leader.[62] However, as mentioned earlier, the substantive Muslim scholars take the view that the Prophet uttered this Hadith when he learned that the Persians had named a woman to rule them. Therefore, this Hadith was related to the context of the selection of a Persian leader; not to Muslim matters. They also believed that it should be understood that women were thought to have lacked the knowledge to be leaders at that time. Accordingly, it is quite irrelevant to bring the situation and arguments of the seventh century to any current political situation.

Remarkably, this is the only Hadith which says women should not be rulers. Fatima Mernissi, a contemporary Moroccan feminist writer, then goes further. She argues that the Hadith above was never uttered by the Prophet, and probably made up, for personal reasons, by Abu Bakrah (not to be confused with Abu Bakr, the first Caliph), who claimed to have heard the Hadith spoken by the Prophet. First, she determines from her research that Bakrah must have had an excellent memory because he recalled the Hadith about twenty-five years after the Prophet supposedly uttered it. At the same time the Fourth Caliph, Ali b. Abi Thalib retook Basrah after having defeated A'isyah, the Prophet's widow, at the Battle of the Camel. This leads Mernissi to wonder if Abu Bakrah made up the Hadith to give reason for not supporting A'isyah in the battle. Mernissi also attacks the morals of Abu Bakrah and finds out that he had been found to have given false testimony in a case to the Caliph Umar. So with the improbability of extraordinary memory and convictions for lying in other areas of his life, Mernissi gives reason to reject Abu Bakrah as a reliable source of "the Hadith" above.[63]

In her *Forgotten Queens of Islam*, Mernissi investigates Islamic women who have risen to power, how they accomplished the feat, and under what social constructs and limitations they operated. Many women who came to power, or had great influence over men in power, are discussed, along with their ascent and descent. Mernissi covers accounts of women from pre-Islamic times such as, Balqis, Queen of Sheba, to A'isyah and Benazir Bhutto. She argues that throughout the history of Islam, a small number of women have seized power in both political and military spheres, where their Western sisters were unable to do so. However, since the very thought of a woman ruler is so outrageous to Islamic historians, many of these women are simply ignored in historical accounts.[64]

In Indonesia, the debate over the eligibility of women to become president came about when Megawati Soekarnoputri ran in the 1999 presidential election. Based on its Islamic point of view, the PPP (Partai Persatuan Pembangunan) stated that it was forbidden for a woman to become the president.[65] Obviously, it referred to Megawati. However, when she replaced President Wahid in 2001, Hamzah Haz, Chairman of PPP, became the Vice-President. This explains why, during the constitutional debate on the third amendment, the PPP did not propose that a woman was ineligible for the post, although their fatwa not permitting a woman to be appointed as the president still exists.

Regarding the condition concerning Quraysh descent mentioned above, Ibn Khaldun (1332–1406) attempts to reinterpret the saying of the Prophet, "'the leader comes from the tribe of the Quraysh". According to Khaldun, the word "Quraysh" does not mean Quraysh itself, but it should be read as the characteristic of the Quraysh such as strong, smart and capable. Ibn Khaldun had to make a re-interpretation, because at his time Islam was widespread; not only in the Middle East region. He opposed the jurists who continued to maintain that the Qurayshite descent still formed a condition of the Caliphate, even if the candidate was incapable of meeting the obligations towards the Muslim community.[66]

There are approximately 200,000 Indonesians of Arabic descent, and many of them even claim descent from the Prophet. Indonesians of Arabic descent include Ali Alatas and Alwi Shihab who are both former Ministers for Foreign Affairs. Both Alatas and Shihab reached their position because of their capabilities; not because they are of Quraysh descent.[67] Therefore, it is worth noting that, although many Quraysh descendants also live in Indonesia, Islamic political parties did not feel that it was necessary to propose special rights for them or to acknowledge their existence in the Constitution. They are treated as ordinary citizens. Once again, it could safely be stated that Indonesian Muslims are in favour of providing substantive understanding of the two sayings of the prophet discussed above. In other words, the majority of Indonesian Muslims do not read the two Hadith in a literal or formal way.

The last important point is that, in Indonesia non-Muslims have the right to become the president and vice-president. This view is in opposition to Maududi's writing, which, for instance in his *First Principles of the Islamic State*, clearly states that the ruler should be a Muslim.[68] Abu Faris also shares similar views (*an yakuna ra'is al-dawla al-Islamiya musliman wa la yajuzu li al-kafir*).[69] Such an opinion is opposed by Ibn Taimiyah (1263–1329) who proposes the idea that a just head of state, even an unbeliever (*kafir*) is better than an unjust head of state, even if he is a Muslim. Consequently, according to him, Allah will support a just state although it is an infidel state, and that

Allah does not support an unjust state, though it be Islamic.[70] The spirit of Islamic government should be justice.

It seems that this view is supported by all Islamic political parties in Indonesia.[71] Given the fact that the majority of Indonesians are Muslims (more than 80 per cent), it is worth noting that not a single word in the amendments provides special rights for Muslims to becomes the president and vice-president. Therefore, constitutionally speaking, it is possible for a non-Muslim to be elected to the top position in Indonesia. Politically speaking, according to Abdurrahman Wahid, it is very natural for Muslims to choose a Muslim candidate as the president, but the most important thing is that every citizen (including non-Muslim citizens) has the right to be appointed. The situation in the United States is illustrative: according to the Constitution, there can be presidential candidates who are of colour, although the situation would be far from political reality.[72]

Presidential Tenure

The 1945 Constitution provides citizens with the right to change their government peacefully, and citizens exercise this right in practice through periodic, free and fair elections, held on the basis of universal suffrage. Prior to the amendments, the President of Indonesia served a five-year term and could be re-elected without limitation. Thus, Indonesia had Soekarno, who governed from 1945 to 1966, and Soeharto, who led the country for thirty-two years (1966–98). This was not a healthy democracy, and in fact both leaders were considered to be dictators. Therefore, the first constitutional target in enacting the first amendment was to limit the term of office to two five-year terms for both the president and the vice-president.

This limitation is clearly at variance with the formal *shari'a*. There is no limitation on the caliph's period in office. So, as long as he abides by the *shari'a*, implements its rules and is able to manage the state's affairs, he continues as a caliph until he passes away.[73] Actually, there is no single statement in the Qur'an and the Hadith on this issue. The supporters of the formal *shari'a* refer to Islamic history, particularly the era of the first four "rightly-guided Caliphs" (*khulafa al-rasyidin*), when such limitations did not exist. Abu Bakr governed for two years (632–34), Umar ran the country for ten years (634–44), Usman held power from 644 to 656, and Ali served the Muslim community from 656 to 661. Their power ended when they passed away. Based on this history, it is understood that the office of the caliphate was for life.

However, since the purported regulation is based on history (not on the obvious teachings of the Qur'an and the Hadith), the issue is debatable. *Ijtihad* (independent legal reasoning) can play a role here. As in the case of women's eligibility to become president, one may ask, "is it relevant to continue to employ the historical account of the seventh century to cope with new challenges and developments in the twenty-first century?" The Indonesian political parties seem to give a negative answer.[74] Their reasons are that if the leader stays in power for life or for too long, power corrupts him, which could lead to the collapse of the government, as in the case of Soekarno and Soeharto, and people become jealous of the leader, because they want to share the power. In this regard, one may see that all Islamic political parties did not refer to Islamic history, but instead referred directly to Indonesian own history, particularly in the Soeharto's period.

All four *khulafa al-rasyidin* stayed in power until death (Abu Bakr) or assassination (Umar, Usman, and Ali). Islamic history also tells us of the third caliph, Usman, who stayed too long in office and grew very old. There was a move to force him to resign, but the caliph refused to do so. In the end, he was killed, and Muslims entered a period of civil war. History continues with other caliphs ending their terms in one of the following ways: poisoned, forced to resign by military actions, or died peacefully in their old age.

In the United States, presidential tenure is limited two terms. This regulation is based on the twenty-second amendment passed in 1933. It is important to note that the Ottoman Caliphate was dissolved in 1924. Therefore, it is well understood that Muslim political thinkers did not propose the idea of a limit to the caliph's tenure when the caliphate existed. It is an idea which came up after the disappearance of the caliphate. However, it is not easy to understand why, even today, some Muslim countries and some Muslim thinkers still believe in unlimited terms for their leaders. Even if there is a constitutional mechanism which determines tenure, some leaders in some Muslim countries have held power for long periods. For instance, President Mohammed Hosni Mubarak has ruled Egypt since 14 October 1981. The President is nominated by the People's Assembly for a six-year term. As in Indonesia during Soeharto's time, Mubarak is able to gain popular support. The 1999 National referendum validated President Mubarak's nomination by the People's Assembly to a fourth term, in which he was re-elected unopposed. In Saudi Arabia, citizens do not have the right to change their Government. The King is also the Prime Minister, and the Crown Prince serves as Deputy Prime Minister.

Issues related to public affairs change from time to time. A leader who was qualified to deal with particular issues may not be qualified for new issues. New leaders who are more qualified will emerge from society, and society should give them a chance to deal with these challenges. Unlimited terms for leaders have a negative impact on the rule of law. I will elaborate on this further when discussing the accountability and the impeachment procedures, below, but prior to this discussion I would examine the method of election.

Method of Election

As pointed out by Schedler, elections should have four characteristics: they should be inclusive; be free (have classical civil, political and human rights that allow the free expression of choice); be correct (i.e., without electoral fraud); and be competitive, meaning that there must be the possibility to compete, if not necessarily the chance to win. In other words, inclusiveness, competition, freedom and correctness describe the defining procedural minima of democratic elections. The absence of any one of them would make for democracy becoming a mere façade, or having a distorted form.[75]

In the context of the rule of law, not only should the electoral system be designed through consensus and consultation, as mentioned above, but it also must ensure two things. Firstly, people should elect their representatives in a democratic way. People must know who will get their vote. They have the right to know who will represent them in parliament and/or government. Secondly, those who are elected must be accountable to the people who chose them. This is to ensure that the people will "monitor" their representatives.[76] In other words, along with consensus and consultation, accountability is also an essential element.

The rule of law suggests that elections may provide opportunities to rotate élites, to select leaders, and to express grievances and desires. Elections are said to compel élites to consider the wishes of the rest of the population, to provide opportunities for public dialogue, to confer legitimacy on governments, and to strengthen the sense of power and belonging of individuals.

The Indonesian system is basically presidential. In Articles 4–5 and 10–15, the 1945 Constitution grants the president the authority to act as both head of state and head of government, as in a pure presidential system. There is no position akin to a prime minister as in a pure parliamentary system. The president is not accountable directly to the DPR.[77] However, prior to 2004, the president was not elected directly by the citizenry, as is typical of pure presidential systems, but indirectly by the MPR.[78] An indirectly elected president lacks legitimacy and is often also easier to remove from office.

As has been mentioned, the experience of President Abdurrahman Wahid gives weight to this caveat. Based on the accountability and removal procedures associated with indirect election, he was removed by the MPR in July 2001 when he lost the political support of the vast majority of MPR members. This very real threat of removal means that the Indonesian president is not as free to make use of his or her extensive powers as a directly elected president with those same powers would be.

During its 2001 session, the MPR amended the 1945 Constitution to provide for direct presidential and vice-presidential elections. In 2002 the MPR approved the fourth amendment, which requires presidential and vice-presidential candidates to run together on a single ticket. It provides for a second round of direct voting if no one candidate gets a clear majority of votes cast, as well as at least 20 per cent of the vote in at least half of the provinces.[79]

Direct election will strengthen the presidency for two reasons. First, it will raise the democratic legitimacy of the presidency to be on a par with that of the DPR. Second, an amendment for direct election will have to be accompanied by changes in presidential impeachment procedures, which will most likely make it harder to remove the president in mid-term, than under the earlier procedures.

All Islamic political parties (PPP, PKB, PAN, PBB and PK) were consistent in their support of direct presidential elections.[80] They believe that a directly elected president is more powerful, owing to the democratic legitimacy thereby conferred on the office, and to the fact that directly elected presidents are often protected by more stringent impeachment procedures. PBB was the smallest parliamentary party numerically but was vocal and important in that it represented conservative modernist Muslims. PK drew on the same conservative constituency as PBB, but had formed a legislative alliance with the more moderate modernist PAN, somewhat muting its voice. PKB was the main political vehicle for traditionalist Muslims and was a solidly moderate party. PPP was a conglomeration of modernist and traditionalist Muslim wings.

This does not suggest that there was no hot debate on this matter. While direct elections by the people were introduced in the third amendment, there was a difference of opinion between the PDI-P, who wanted the second vote in the MPR, and the Islamic parties, who suggested the second direct vote by the people, whenever no candidate can obtain a majority vote in the first round of the election.[81] The opposing opinions were caused by a difference in strategy in the presidential election, between the PDI-P, who could deliver one-fourth of the total seats in the legislature, and the Islamic parties, who could not be united at party level. In the end, the Islamic parties' proposal was accepted.

However, in the context of the book, the question remains: Can direct election be justified under *shari'a*? The concept of *bay'at* could be one of the answers. Etymologically, the term expresses an act undertaken by the ruler and the ruled, resulting in mutual obligations.[82] Legally speaking, *bay'at* refers to "the election of a person to a post of command, in particular the election of a caliph".[83] However, the required number of electors for a valid procedure of *bay'at* has remained undefined, in both historical procedure and in juristic literature.[84]

The first Caliph, Abu Bakr, was elected without planning or preparation because the Prophet, according to the Sunni school, did not leave any message or testament as to who should succeed him as the leader of the Islamic community. In addition, al-Mawardi states that Abu Bakr was elected by five persons: Umar b. Khattab, Abu Ubayda al-Jarrah, Usayd b. Hudayr, Bisyr b. Sa'ad, and Salim, and the client (*mawla*) Abi Huzaifah.[85] Umar b. Khattab was elected by the former caliph directly. Furthermore, Usman b. Affan was chosen by an election committee (six persons) nominated by Umar. Lastly, Ali b. Abi Thalib was elected by only one person, Abbas, the uncle of the Prophet Mohammad.[86]

This means that there is no set standard for elections to be a caliph. Al-Mawardi, for instance, states that supreme leadership is established in two ways: selection by the electors (*bi ikhtiyar ahl al-'aqd wa al-hall*), or appointment by a predecessor (*bi 'ahd al-imam min qabl*).[87] However, he does not indicate the best method of choice, the one which should properly be followed. Al-Mawardi explains further:

> There is considerable disagreement among scholars on the number of electors necessary for the valid investment of the sovereign. Some have argued that he would be invested by no fewer than the generality or majority of the electors throughout the land, in order for his election to be unanimously approved and his authority universally accepted. This view is refuted by the vote of allegiance to Abu Bakr given by those who were present, without waiting for the arrival of those were absent. Another group has maintained that the minimum number of electors for a binding election is five, who may unanimously agree on a candidate or concur in the choice made by one of them... Scholars from Kufah have argued, however, that only three persons are needed, one of them taking office with the agreement of the other two, thus constituting one ruler and two witnesses, as in the

case of a marriage contract, which is validated by one guardian and two witnesses. Still others have asserted that the election of the sovereign would be binding if undertaken by a single person, for al-Abbas said to Ali, "Give me your hand so that I may pledge you my allegiance…" They also consider the election a kind of judgment, and a judgment made by a single individual is enforceable.[88]

It is worth considering that all those different opinions have the same aim: to legitimize the process of succession of the first four "rightly guided Caliphs" (*khulafa al-rasyidin*). Those opinions come after the time of the *khulafa al-rasyidin* era, not at the time of the caliphs. The classic *ulama* were only "theorizing" about the practice. As can be seen from the above quotation, some of them even went so far as to make an analogy to the marriage contract and the practice of relying on a single judge.

This suggests that *ijtihad*, once again, can play a role in this matter, and it is sufficient to argue that direct election, as proposed by Indonesian Islamic political parties, is one of the products of such *ijtihad*. One of the arguments to support this kind of election is that, although all the *khulafa al-rasyidin* were selected by different methods, there was one similarity: after they were elected by "certain" people, the next day, the Muslim community gave their agreement publicly. In other words, the *bay'at* of that limited circle was followed by the bay'at of the masses.[89]

By comparison, in Iran, the executive branch is headed by President Mohammad Khatami, who won a second four-year term in June 2001, with 77 per cent of the popular vote, in a multiparty election. In Egypt, the President is nominated by the People's Assembly, and the nomination must then be validated by a national, popular referendum. Lastly, Saudi Arabia uses the monarchical system, wherein rule passes to the sons of the founding King, Abd al-Aziz b. Abd al-Rahman al-Faysal Al Sa'ud, and to their children's children — perhaps on the grounds of appointment by a predecessor (*bi 'ahd al-imam min qabl*) as outlined by al-Mawardi.[90] As can be seen, even in the modern era, no standard method to decide succession exists in Muslim countries.

Accountability

There are at least three issues on accountability: to whom the executive shall be responsible, the form of responsibility, and the mechanism of impeaching the president.[91] The most important guarantee of governmental accountability is the right of the citizens to control the direction of governmental policy, and the identity of those who exercise governmental power, through the electoral process. I have discussed above the fact that Indonesia now follows a direct election system. Direct election is seen as more democratic and as fostering greater accountability of the president to the people, as well as reducing the possibility of vote-buying in the presidential election process. The 1999–2002 amendments, if fully implemented, would make the president and vice-president directly accountable to constituents.

Democratic governments are given the authority to make decisions through their electoral mandate. In other words, citizens choose government representatives. Regular elections allow opposition parties to compete and present alternative policies to the voting public. Citizens are then able to hold government officials accountable by having the periodic right, and opportunity, to vote them out of office.[92] In the context of the rule of law, a good election is a prerequisite for having a "checks and balances" mechanism between the people, the Parliament and the government.[93]

In addition, elections have domestic purposes. Elections delegitimize protests, riots, and public violence. They are the obvious and traditional way of ensuring accountability, and providing an institutional framework for the peaceful resolution of conflicts among competing political parties.[94] They also moderate some opposition supporters by convincing them that even though they may have lost this time, future elections might turn out differently.

The constitutional changes also restrict authority of the MPR to impeach the President. The procedure for impeaching the President is clearly stated in Article 7B of the Amendments to the 1945 Constitution. When the DPR proposes the impeachment of the president to the MPR, the Constitutional Court, a newly established institution under the amendments, evaluates its justification before the MPR begins to deliberate its proposal. The MPR can pass the proposal with a two-thirds majority of votes at the plenary session in which over three-quarters of the total number of MPR members participate. This revision improves unbalanced power relationship between the stronger legislature and the weaker executive, making it difficult for the former to dismiss the latter. On the other hand, in order to maintain legislative authority, Article 7C determines that the president cannot freeze and/or dissolve the DPR.

The sections above have examined the *shari'a* perspectives on sovereignty, presidential tenure, and method of elections. These issues can be viewed also in light of accountability. I will examine the role of Parliament in the next section. Therefore, in this section, I will focus on the issue of impeachment vis-à-vis *shari'a*. The main questions will be: is it possible to impeach the ruler under the Islamic governmental system? If so, what is the procedure to do so?

Regarding one of the implications of the basic premise that the power of a head of state comes from Allah, and not from the people, several Muslim scholars such as al-Farabi (870–950) and al-Ghazali (1058–111) did not discuss whether a head of state could be removed from office or not. Mawardi (975–1059) was the only Islamic political thinker of the Middle Ages who believed that a head of state could be replaced if it were obvious that he could no longer perform his duties, owing to moral or other problems.[95] Other Muslim thinkers cite the statement of Abu Bakr when the latter was elected as the first Caliph:

> Assist me when I act rightly; but if I go wrong, put me on the right path. Obey me as long as I remain loyal to Allah and His Prophet; but if I disobey Allah and His Prophet, then none is under the slightest obligation to accord obedience to me.[96]

Abu Bakr's statement confirmed the saying of the Prophet: "A Muslim has to listen and to obey (the order of his leader) whether he likes it or not, as long as those orders involve not one in disobedience (to Allah), but if an act of disobedience (to Allah) is imposed one should not listen to it nor obey it."[97] This is an indication that the first Caliph was aware that he was appointed, watched, and corrected by the people.

However, Abu Bakr himself did not explain how the Caliph's conformity with *shari'a* may be determined and how to hold the caliph accountable. This lack of a procedural mechanism continues in the Islamic governmental system. Mawardi's work also did not indicate the method of dethroning the head of state, and its implementation. In Islamic history, it is difficult to find a precedent in which a head of state was impeached in a legal way. Caliphs lost their position either because they were assassinated, poisoned, forced to resigned or died in a natural way.

In this sense, Ann Lambton has correctly pointed out that:

> Normally the subject owes a duty of complete and unquestioning obedience to the Imam. If, however, the Imam commands something that is contrary to God's law, then the duty of obedience lapses, and instead it is the duty of the subject to disobey — and resist — such a command. This principle is frequently cited by latter writers, but it never became an effective basis for "limited government" or "justified revolution" because first the jurists seldom discussed, and never answered, the question of how the lawfulness or sinfulness of a command was to be tested, and secondly no legal procedures or means were devised, or set up, to enforce the law against the ruler.[98]

This, once again, leads Muslims in contemporary world to perform *ijtihad* in order to fill the gap. From the substantive *shari'a* point of view, the procedure of impeachment outlined by the amendments to the 1945 Constitution, as has been described earlier, can be seen as an attempt by Islamic political parties (along with other parties) in Indonesia to exercise their legal and political reasoning.

Thus far I have examined the executive provisions in the amendments to the 1945 Constitution from the *shari'a* perspective. At least two trends can be identified here. Firstly, the amendments have modified the concept of the formal *shari'a*, as in the cases of the form of government, sovereignty, and conditions to become the head of state. Secondly, the amendments have filled the gap left by the formal *shari'a*, as in the cases of presidential tenure, method of elections and method of dethroning the head of state. What Indonesia, the world's largest Muslim country, did is important because under the formal *shari'a* the head of state can hold power for life, can be appointed by the previous leader, and the method of his dismissal is unclear. Indonesian Islamic political parties are not in favour of such "dictatorship".

Parliament

The legislature, or Parliament, is a fundamental component of a democratic government. The need for strong legislature is reflected in the very meaning of democracy: "rule by the people". In order for the people to rule, they require a mechanism to represent their wishes — to make (or influence) policies in their name and oversee the implementation of those policies. It is thought that legislatures serve these critical functions. A legislature reflects in its ranks a broad spectrum of a country's political opinion, and as such is the principal forum for debate on vital issues. A legislature, or parliament, can serve as a demonstration of pluralism, tolerance of diversity and dissent, as well as a place for compromise and consensus-building.[99]

In authoritarian systems, the legislature serves as a "rubber stamp" or a justification of a government's decisions. In other words, the power of parliament is subordinated, and this is clearly against the idea of the rule of law. The balance of power between the legislative and executive branches in a country can be changed through political and legal reform. If new legislatures are going to have a central role in a nation's governance, it is up to legislators themselves to build strong legislative institutions, by asserting themselves in the regular law-making or oversight functions, or through specific structural changes via constitutional amendment, legislation, or rules of procedure. In the context of the rule of law, it can be argued that the executive must act within the confines of laws passed by Parliament; otherwise its actions will be invalid.

In this section, I will focus on the functions, the elections and the positions of Parliament vis-à-vis the executive. Prior to these discussions, a brief observation on the Indonesian Parliament after the passage of the amendments will be highlighted. One of the most significant Amendments is the revised Article 2(1), which stipulates that the MPR is composed of DPR members and DPD (House of Regional Representatives) members, who are all elected in the general elections. This means that the MPR has no appointed members who are regional representatives, organizational representatives, and military representatives. All the members in the MPR are elected directly by the people. Institutionally, the MPR is not the *highest* state organ anymore, but one of the high state organs, along with other state organs.

Article 20A, a new provision of the 1945 Constitution, states that the DPR has the following functions and rights: the functions of making laws, examining the state budget, and checking the activities of administration; and the rights to interpellate (*hak interpelasi*), and investigate government affairs (*hak angket*). In addition, DPR members have the rights to submit questions, deliver proposals, express opinions, and present views with immunity (*hak imunitas*). These amendments are intended to strengthen the powers of the legislature and rectify the power bias of the Soeharto period in favour of the executive branch.

The establishment of the DPD is also regulated in Article 22C and Article 22D. With this provision, members of regional representatives, who were formerly appointed by the DPRD, are directly elected in each province, forming an independent legislative assembly. The DPD has the authority to discuss, supervise, and submit laws on regional autonomy or central-local relations. In addition, it possesses the right to submit considerations to the DPR on the state budget and draft laws relating to tax, education and religion. The members of the DPD may not exceed one-third of the numbers of the DPR. The next section will examine what *shari'a* says about a Parliament.

The Nature of Shura

One of the key concepts of Islamic governmental system is *shura*. It is a consultation process with the people (particularly with members of the shura council, namely *ahl al-hall wa al-aqd or ahl al-ikhtiyar*), in matters related to public affairs. Although there is a direct reference to the term *shura* in two verses of the Qur'an (3:159 and 42:38), it is an essentially contested concept. This happens because the Qur'an does not provide detailed provisions on the technical aspects of the shura.

In Islamic history, the second caliph, Umar b. Khattab, did not want to follow the method used by Abu Bakr when the latter appointed him. Umar appointed six people and asked them to select the next caliph. It seems that Umar was the first caliph to institutionalize the *shura*, although in its first form it had been left solely to the discretion of the caliph as to whom he should consult. This explains why in al-Mawardi's book the main task of *ahl al-ikhtiyar* is to appoint the caliph, and the *ahl al-ikhtiyar* or the *shura* council is appointed by the caliph.

Others interpret *shura* as advice, wherein the ruler merely asks religious leaders, tribal leaders or influential people for advice. Such an interpretation was practised by Mu'awiya, who governed in 661–80. The implication of this practice is that the ruler does not have any obligation to follow or implement the advice. Maududi, for instance, takes the view that the head of state is not obliged to follow the opinion of the *shura* council, which is supported by the majority of votes. He can also follow the opinion supported by a minority group, and he can even totally neglect the (majority or minority) opinion of the *shura* council.

Fazlur Rahman rejects this kind of *shura*, on the grounds that this totally alters the original foundation of the *shura*. The *shura* should be "mutual advice, through mutual discussions, on an equal footing."[100] A *shura* council has an equal position with the government. Therefore, the outcome of the *shura* should be legally binding on both the ruler and the community. Hasan al-Turabi provides a solid justification for this, when he recalls that:

> the Prophet used to consult his companions and take their views on almost every issue related to public affairs, and sometimes even related to his private life, though he was the Prophet of God and supported by divine revelation.[101]

According to Rahman, the phrase *"amruhum"* in the Qur'an (42:38) refers to the community as a whole, not an élite nor any specific group.[102] Rahman's interpretation is opposed to Maududi,[103] and Abd al-Wahab Khallaf[104] who express the view that those participating in *shura* must be a well-specified group of people (i.e., *ulama* or Muslim scholars).[105] One of the consequences is that it is the community which chooses its representatives (*ahl al-hall wa al-aqd* or *ahl al-ikhtiyar*), not the head of state. Given the practice of the *shura* in Islamic history, this will radically change the face of Islamic government. For instance, Saudi Arabia is a monarchy, without elected representative institutions or political parties. The Majlis al-Shura, or Consultative Council, consists of 120 appointed members.

How then can members of the *shura* council be elected? Once again, neither the Qur'an nor the classic works of Muslim scholars cover this topic. Once again, this provides wide room for *ijtihad* in the modern era. Even a fundamentalist thinker, like Sayyid Quthb, does not insist on a particular form of *shura*. According to Quthb, let the Muslim community decide its own methods to facilitate the *shura*, in relation to its environment, social circumstances and requirements.[106]

Therefore, it is up to Muslims to choose one electoral system, to determine the best system for casting and counting votes, with regard to the situation in the country concerned, such as its geography, ethnic composition, demography, political format, legal system and so on. There are two main electoral systems that can be selected or combined. The first electoral system is the proportional system (commonly known as the proportional representation system). This system is based on the principle of "one person one vote", and the concept that parties should be represented in an assembly or parliament in direct proportion to their overall voting results. Their percentage of seats should equal their percentage of votes gained. The second system is the district system (single constituency system or majority system), which means that the country is divided into constituencies, each approximately the same size. Voters select a single candidate by marking the candidate's name on the ballot paper. The candidate with the most votes wins the district seat (the "First-Past-the-Post" rule).[107] According to Gamil Mohammed El-Gindy, the flexibility of the *shura* makes it compatible with any of these electoral systems.[108]

Apart from appointing the caliph, other functions of *ahl al-ikhtiyar* have not yet been determined by classic Muslim scholars. So, what are the other functions? Has the Parliament the right to legislate? This has been a major question, since legislation in Islam is a crucial matter. The debate over popular sovereignty and God's sovereignty reappears. Quthb, for instance, takes the position that the *shura* does not fit with secular government, since the *shura* is divinely inspired, and its foundation lies in God's sovereignty.[109] The main consequence is that the Parliament cannot produce legislation or regulation in contradiction to *shari'a*.

However, what the words "contradiction" and "*shari'a*" mean remain a subject for debate, as illustrated in Chapter 2. It is in this context that two Islamic political parties (PPP and PBB) have proposed the reinsertion of the famous seven words in Article 29, as an obligation for state to guarantee the implementation of *shari'a*. This would provide a balance between the function of legislator and the aspiration of Indonesian Muslims. However, this proposal is rejected. Indonesia has not followed Egypt, which amended its Constitution so that "the Principles of the Islamic *shari'a* are *the* principal source of legislation". Other Indonesian Islamic political parties have the firm belief that such amendment is unnecessary, since the Constitution guarantees the right of citizens to observe their religion, and no regulation can be made against the obvious teaching of religions (including Islam). I will elaborate on the issue further in the next chapter.

Since popular sovereignty was adopted into the 1945 Constitution (and is accepted by all Islamic political parties), the legislative functions of the Indonesian Parliament are asserted to be, along with others: budgetary and supervisory functions. Are these functions in contradiction to *shari'a*? The answer is, "no". Even in Saudi Arabia, the Majlis al-Shura debates, rejects and amends government-proposed legislation, holds oversight hearings over government ministries, and has the power to initiate legislation.

The final issue is the structure of Parliament. Turabi expresses the view that the unicameral legislature model is the best option for an Islamic state. He provides the evidence that Muslims do not have two gods, and therefore do not like to have two legislative houses.[110] It would appear that Turabi's argument is made in the context of legislation under God's sovereignty, in which case it is impossible to have two kinds of legislators.

Turabi's argument seems odd, since in Egypt the bicameral system is used. It consists of the People's Assembly, or Majlis al-Sha'b (454 seats; 444 elected by popular vote, 10 appointed by the president; members serve five-year terms) and the Advisory Council or Majlis al-Shura, which functions in only a consultative role (264 seats; 176 elected by popular vote, 88 appointed by the president). In this sense, Mujib Rakhmat of Golkar expresses his view that the constitutional decision to adopt the DPR and DPD, as has been explained above, does not mean that Indonesia believes in two Gods. The chamber has never been interpreted as having the role of denying the principle of monotheism, as reflected in Pancasila (Indonesian state ideology), nor "stealing" the power of Allah as a *shari'* (the Creator of Islamic law).[111]

The choice between one and two chambers in Western democracy is not related to monotheism nor polytheism. Unicameral parliaments are justified on the grounds that an assembly based on direct popular election is a reflection of the popular will and, therefore, should not be hindered by a second chamber. Such arguments are rejected by the defenders of bicameral parliaments. They believe that the upper chamber provides checks and balances. It can play this role by defending individual and regional interests, and those of other groups, against a potentially oppressive majority in the lower house. Moreover, a second chamber guarantees a voice in parliament for distinct territories within the state.[112]

Therefore, the choice of one or two chambers is dependent upon the structure of, the environment surrounding, and the circumstances faced by Muslim communities. This is not opposed to the concept of the *shura* in Islamic tradition since, as has been stated, the Qur'an does not explain it in detail. To conclude, the shura might not equate with Parliament in a modern sense, but the concept of the *shura* can be modified and adapted to the contemporary era. I argue that Indonesian Islamic political parties' acceptance of the Amendments to the 1945 Constitution should be read in this context.

Judiciary

Thus far, I have examined the role of the executive and the Parliament. In this section, I will focus on the last topic: the judiciary. Special focus will be given to the issue of judicial independence. Judicial independence is critical on at least two grounds. Firstly, protection of human rights depends partly on a robust, fair, and independent judiciary, willing to hold all political and social actors accountable to legal and constitutional protections. Secondly, judicial independence facilitates political stability and fairness. What are the elements of judicial independence? The seventh United Nations Congress on the Prevention of Crime and the Treatment of Offenders, held at Milan from 26 August to 6 September 1985, adopted a number of rich principles that guarantee judicial independence. These are known as the Basic Principles on the Independence of the Judiciary. These principles were then endorsed by General Assembly Resolutions 40/32 of 29 November 1985 and 40/146 of 13 December 1985.[113]

The principles, endorsed by the UN General Assembly, fall into six categories. The first concerns general issues of judicial independence that must be guaranteed. The judiciary must also be given jurisdiction; it must receive the resources necessary to perform its tasks; its rulings must be implemented; and tribunals eschewing established procedures must not be used as a device to bypass the judiciary. The second category concerns freedom of expression and association.

The third group of principles endorsed by the UN General Assembly involves the qualifications, selection and training of judges. The principles do not require specific practices, but they bar discrimination and improper criteria in judicial appointments. The fourth group of principles covers the conditions and terms of service for judges. Here the principles require that such matters be governed by law, that judges serve either until retirement or until a legally fixed term expires, and that assignment of cases be based on internal administrative grounds. The fifth group of principles involves professional secrecy and immunity, barring judges from revealing, or being forced to reveal, confidential information; and requiring that they receive appropriate immunity from civil suits, connected with their professional duties. The sixth and final set of principles involves the disciplining, suspension and removal of judges, requiring appropriate processes, and insisting that judges may be disciplined only for good cause.[114]

In Indonesia, the articles on the judiciary are widely enriched by the amendments. Article 1(3) defines Indonesia as "a State of Law" (*Negara Hukum*). Articles on independence of the judicial and court organizations are amended to guarantee their power and independence (Article 24). A new clause defines the qualification of Supreme Court judges as well (Article 24A(2)). Articles 24A(3) and 24B regulate the newly established independent Judicial Commission (Komisi Yudisial). It has the role of proposing candidates to the DPR. The DPR then selects its preferred candidates from the Commission's list, and they are confirmed by the President. The Judicial Commission is also empowered to guard and enforce judicial ethics (Article 24B(1)).

More importantly, Article 24C provides for a new Constitutional Court (Mahkamah Konsitusi). The Constitutional Court has authority to conduct judicial review of legislation, decide on conflict of interest within state institutions relating to the constitutional powers of state institutions, regulate activities for the dissolution of political parties, and makes decisions on objections to the results of general elections. According to Lindsey, significantly the Court has some potential to renovate the relationship between the judiciary and the legislative branch by creating a new check on the practices of law-makers and the presidency.[115]

What Islamic law says on judicial independence will now be examined. Both normative and historical interpretation of the term in the classic and the modern era will be discussed, in order to show the link and connection between Islamic law discourse and the amendments to the 1945 Constitution.

Al-Sulta al-Qadā'iya

The topic of *qada* (judiciary) has been discussed widely in Islamic law literature. It is claimed that the independence of the judiciary is "a cardinal principle of Islam".[116] This claim is supported by a number of arguments. Firstly, Muhammad Idris al-Shafi'i takes the view that a judge must be a Muslim scholars (*mujtahid*), because of the mastery of the religious sciences and integrity of character required to perform *ijtihad*.[117] Khallaf shows similar views when he says: *fakana rijal al-qada' min al-mujtahidin* (persons who are in charge at the court are *mujtahid*).[118] In the context of judicial independence, such views are significant on the grounds that not only must judges possess the same knowledge as that of Muslim scholars (mujtahid), but also their decisions must be based on their independent judgement on religious problems.

Mawardi explains further:

> A Shafi'ite may appoint to a judgeship a follower of Abu Hanifah's doctrine, for a judge has the right to use personal opinion in his rulings, and does not have to follow the precedent of members of his own school in problems or judgments. If he is a Shafi'ite he does not have to implement the pronouncements of al-Shafi'i unless he is led to accept them by his own efforts. But if his endeavours lead him to adopt Abu Hanifah's views, then he should do so.[119]

The theory of *ijtihad* requires judges to be independent in the exercise of personal reasoning. Umar, the second caliph, is considered to have been the first person to guarantee judicial independence.[120] This leads to the second argument: the practices of the *khulafa al-rasyidin* who respected the judges' decisions. For instance, Kamali provides examples that Umar and Ali (the fourth caliph) appeared before judges as parties to litigation, and both made clear statements that the judge should not give them any special treatment.[121] Usman, the third caliph, appeared personally before the court to get back a suit of armour from a Jew. However, Usman's claim was dismissed, since the only witnesses who supported his claim were his slave and his son; both are not competent witnesses under Islamic law.[122]

The third argument supporting the claim to judicial independence in Islam is the existence of *wilaya al-mazalim* (the redress of wrongs). It is the embryo of the administrative tribunal, or constitutional court, in the modern sense. Mawardi has outlined ten areas which can be reported to this tribunal, including oppression and maltreatment of the public by government officials, and the implementation of sentences when judges are too weak to enforce them, owing to the sentenced person's power or social standing.[123]

All three arguments above prove that the *qada* (judiciary) played a vital role in the administration of the state and the life of the community and also in the transmission of Islamic traditions. However, this claim should be examined critically. From early times, there was reluctance on the part of the pious to accept office from the caliph, for fear of jeopardizing their integrity. For instance, Yazid ibn Amr, Governor of Iraq, proposed that Abu Hanifah, the Imam of the Hanafi school, become a judge for the law court of Kufah. Abu Hanifah refused the appointment. Following his refusal, at the command of Yazid, he was given a whipping, one hundred and ten blows to the head. His face and head swelled. Abu Hanifah was not alone; other pious scholars like Zufar (Abu Hanifah's disciple), Abd Allah b. Faruq (a scholar-jurist at Qairawan), Aban b. Isa b. Dinnar (a Muslim scholar in Spain) refused to serve as judges, owing to executive interference in the judiciary.[124]

Irit Abramski-Blig observes that during the Umayyad and early Abbasid periods, judges were assigned non-judicial functions as tax collector, tribal administrator, governor or chief of police. He cites that under Mu'awiyah regime, Fadala b. Ubayd al-Ansari was in charge of *qada* and military raiding, and Abida b. Qays al-Salmani served both as judge and part of the military staff.[125] This suggests that the independence of the judiciary in the early Islamic periods was dependent on the personal attitude of both caliph and judge, since the *qada* was not as yet institutionalized and formalized as a clearly religious-judicial post, separate from governmental-administrative works. This explains why the topic of the independence of the judiciary in Islamic history is a controversial one. One can point to a certain period of time, or to certain persons, to prove the independence or the subordination of the judiciary in Islam.[126] This is understandable since the notion of judicial independence is a modern one, and it is difficult to judge old period with more recent experience.

Another problem is the conflict between theory, or doctrine, and practice. While the doctrine of *ijtihad* suggests the independence of legal reasoning as a basis of a judge's decision, in practice, *ijtihad* has been restricted to certain forms and cases, or, to some extent, has even been abandoned completely. I have examined this issue in Chapter 2. This problem also reaches the modern era, where all modern constitutions guarantee judicial independence, but not all countries implement them.[127] For the purpose of this book, it is enough to demonstrate that, theoretically, the character of judicial independence is recognized and valued in the Islamic legal tradition. "There is nothing in Islam", as Khallaf has observed, "against the independence of the judiciary".[128]

It is in this context that one should read the provisions for judicial independence in the Indonesian Constitution, the establishment of which all Islamic political parties support. As a comparison, in Saudi Arabia for instance, the Basic Law provides for an independent judiciary. In Egypt, the Constitution provides for the independence and immunity of judges and forbids interference by other authorities in the exercise of their judicial function. Judges are appointed for life, with mandatory retirement at age sixty-four. In Iran, according to Article 164 of its Constitution, a judge cannot be removed, whether temporarily or permanently, from the post he occupies, except by trial and proof of his guilt, or in consequence of a violation justifying his dismissal. All these four Muslim countries are in favour of judicial independence, at least as written in their constitutions.

CONCLUSION

This chapter has examined provisions relating to the executive, the parliament and the judiciary in the 1945 Constitution. This has been done in order to see the influence of and the response to *shari'a* to the issues of establishing and promoting the rule of law in the Indonesian context. There are at least five main findings from the discussion.

Firstly, not a single Islamic political party proposed the idea of the *khilafa* as the form for Indonesian governance. The very fact that Indonesia is the largest Muslim country in the world does not lead them even to propose that Indonesia become an Islamic state, like Egypt, Iran or Saudi Arabia. According to the amendments, Indonesia remains a republic, with a presidential system and three branches of government.

Secondly, Islamic political parties have accepted that sovereignty belongs to the people. I have shown the justification for this position from the substantive *shari'a* approach. Without necessarily ignoring the role of God, the *ummah* (the totality of the Muslim population of the state) becomes the collective agent of the Divine Sovereign, rather than an individual person (caliph). As a consequence of rejecting the caliphate form, the Indonesian people (including all Islamic political parties) adopted popular sovereignty. In fact, the issue of sovereignty was never raised during constitutional debate at the MPR Session (1999–2002). It has been accepted without any controversy. It is safe to argue that Indonesian Muslims have modified the views of the formal *shari'a*, as in the cases of the form of government, sovereignty, and pre-conditions for becoming the head of state.

Thirdly, not a single word in the amendments provides special rights for Muslims to become the president or vice-president. Therefore, it would be constitutional if a non-Muslim were elected to the top position in Indonesia. The Constitution does not forbid a woman becoming president. While there is no limitation on the caliph's period in office, the Indonesian Constitution limits the term to two five-year terms for both the president and vice-president. The amendments also adopt direct election for the presidency, while the exercise of the flexibility of the *shura* and *bay'at* makes them compatible with any of the electoral systems. Moreover, the amendment regulates the procedure to impeach the president. The adoption of this new provision is a clear departure from the formal *shari'a* tradition.

As has been demonstrated, these cases justify the notion that the Indonesian people are not only willing to accept the substantive *shari'a* approach, but also to value the rule of law. More importantly, the amendments have filled the gap left by the formal *shari'a*, as in the cases of presidential tenure, method of elections, and method of dethroning the head of state, by providing new regulations.

Fourthly, since popular sovereignty is adopted into the 1945 Constitution (and is accepted by all Islamic political parties), the legislative functions of the Indonesian parliament are asserted, along with other functions, such as budgetary and supervisory functions. These are to ensure that the checks and balances systems work. Once again, the Indonesian Constitution fills the void left by Islamic history, owing to the fact that *ahl al-hall wa al-aqd* had only one main function: to elect the caliph. The substantive *shari'a* approach encourages the extension of the functions and power of *ahl al-hall wa al-aqd*.

Fifthly, in order to fulfil one of the requirements of *Negara Hukum*, the Indonesian Constitution establishes judicial independence. Although Islamic history reveals many different stories on whether or not caliphs respected and valued the judicial independence, it follows from the amendments that all Islamic political parties in Indonesia take the position that judicial independence is a tool for establishing constitutional government, and there is no provision in the Qur'an that responds negatively to the independence of the judiciary.

Following the resignation of President Soeharto, the establishment of a *Negara Hukum* through the amendments to the 1945 Constitution becomes significant. The thirty-two years of the Soeharto government proved that, without the rule of law, constitutional government will become an item on a wish list. The contributions of Islamic political parties to the process of the Amendments, by adopting a substantive *shari'a* approach, should be seen as their *ijtihad*. Not only does this suggest that the rule of law is compatible with the *shari'a*, it also reflects the ability to deal with a modern constitution without abandoning the principles and the objectives of *shari'a*.

Notes

1. Rainer Grote, "Rule of Law, Rechtsstaat and *Etat de Droit*", in *Constitutionalism, Universalism and Democracy: A Comparative Analysis,* edited by Christian Starck (Baden-Baden: Nomos Verlagsgesellschaft, 1999), p. 271. See also David Clark, "The Many Meanings of the Rule of Law", in *Law, Capitalism and Power in Asia,* edited by Kanishka Jayasuriya (London: Routledge, 1999), pp. 28–44.
2. Yet there are tensions between democracy and the rule of law. Whereas democracy revolves around infusing the law with the will of the majority, the appeal of the

rule of law is an appeal to its supremacy over the wills of persons, however measured or aggregated. For more information on this complex issue, see Ian Saphiro, *The Rule of Law* (New York: New York University Press, 1994), especially Part I, pp. 13–100. Another important issue is that the donor community (international financial institutions, or IFIs) is imposing neoliberal models of governance on the developing world. Ohnesorge labels the model as "the neoliberal rule of law of the 1990s" (John K. M. Ohnesorge, "On Rule of Law Rhetoric, Economic Development, and Northeast Asia" (English version of "Etat de droit (rule of law) et developpement economique"), *Critique Internationale* 18 (2003): 46–56, available at http://www.law.wisc.edu/facstaff/download.asp?ID=73; See also John K. M. Ohnesorge, "The Rule of Law, Economic Development, and the Developmental States of Northeast Asia", in *Law and Development in East and Southeast Asia,* edited by Christoph Antons (London: RoutledgeCurzon, 2003), pp. 91–127).

The label above is often seen as synonymous with the phrase "Washington Consensus", coined by Williamson in 1990 (John Williamson, "What Should the World Bank Think about the Washington Consensus?", *World Bank Research Observer* 15, no. 2 (2000): 251–64) which focuses on privatization, deregulation, and trade liberation. This emphasis on Western-style commercial law contains assumptions about the importance of establishing the rule of law in developing countries in the face of the pressures exerted by global economic and capital markets. It assumes that the injection of Western law, imitation of Western legal institutions, and building upon Western legal expertise into the developing country's legal culture would facilitate a rapid economic growth in the developing countries. Accordingly, massive law reforms based upon Western type legal models have been suggested and implemented in developing nations for the purpose of ensuring quick development therein.

The main criticism is that the donors' concept of the rule of law is *ideological* and based on the currently dominant Anglo-American/liberal/pluralist socio-political doctrine. From this perspective, the rule of law promoted by IFIs is seen as a form of economic, legal, cultural and political hegemony. Critics assert that one of the most significant reasons for the failure of IFI programmes is the naive belief that the Western legal system, particularly the American model, can be easily transplanted to recipient countries. It is important to note that this book does not examine the rule of law in the context of the IFIs agenda (law-economics and neoliberal ideology) above. This book examines the rule of law from the perspective of constitutional issues.

3. The Diceyian tradition of Lockean conservatism has been continued by Friedrich Hayek in the contemporary debate over the rule of law. For Hayek, the rule of law stands in unequivocal opposition to state redistribution and planning; it is the essential and most important condition of individual freedom. It is not simply a constitutional principle of "legality", but comprises a substantive vision of the correct and just relations between individuals and society. See

Friedrich von Hayek, *The Political Ideal of the Rule of Law* (Cairo: National Bank of Egypt, 1955).

4. The work of Ronald Dworkin, temporarily at least, dominates the animated contemporary debate over the judicial role under the rule of law. Adjudication is claimed to satisfy the rule of law by meeting the democratic demand for judicial objectivity and the popular need for political equity. Dworkin argues that, if judges are to fulfil their democratic responsibilities under the rule of law, they must make political decisions, albeit not personal or partisan ones. For Dworkin, judges are political actors whose power is limited by a legal system's history and its liberal character. See R. Dworkin, "Political Judges and the Rule of Law", *A Matter of Principle* (Cambridge: Harvard University Press, 1985), p. 31.

5. The negative mirror image of the Dicey-Hayek model of the rule of law can be found among the writings of the radical legal critics of liberalism, most notably Roberto Unger. For Unger, the rule of law is the entire legal order of the liberal state. It was in force until the coming of the welfare state, and its purpose and character were as Hayek describes them. However, instead of functioning to protect a spontaneous order of any kind, it served to mask hierarchies and exploitation, and the destruction of the pre-capitalist communities. Unger thinks that this system has failed and indeed never could have lasted. Indeed, it was never "real". See Roberto M. Unger, *Law in Modern Society* (New York: Free Press, 1976), pp. 52–57 and 238–42. To see a general picture of this criticism, see R. A. Belliotti, "The Rule of Law and the Critical Legal Studies Movement", *University of Western Ontario Law Review* 24, no. 1 (1986): 67–78.

6. Judith N. Shklar, "Political Theory and the Rule of Law", in *The Rule of Law: Ideal or Ideology*, edited by Allan C. Hutchinson and Patrick Monahan (Vancouver: Carswell, 1987), pp. 2–16.

7. More information on the concept of public interest in Islam can be found in Husain Hamid Hasan, *Nazariyah al-Maslahah fi al-Fiqh al-Islami* (Cairo: Dar al-Nahdah al-'Arabiyah, 1971).

8. Abdurrahman Taj, *al-Siyasa al-Shar'iya wa al-Fiqh al-Islami* (Cairo: Dar al-Ta'rif, 1953), pp. 10–11.

9. Taqiyuddin al-Nabhani, Nizam al-Islam, available at http://www.hizb-ut-tahrir.org/arabic/kotobmtb/htm/01ndam.htm.

10. Timothy Lindsey, "From Rule of Law to Law of the Rulers: To Reformation?", in *Indonesia: Law and Society*, edited by Timothy Lindsey (Sydney: The Federation Press, 1999), p. 13

11. Timothy Lindsey, "Indonesia: Devaluing Asian Values, Rewriting Rule of Law", in *Asian Discourses of Rule of Law: Theories and Implementation of Rule of Law in Twelve Asian Countries, France, and the U.S.,* edited by Randall Peerenboom (London: RoutledgeCurzon, 2004), p. 299.

12. It is interesting to note that the *rechtsstaat* can be classified into a "formal" and

"material" ideas of *rechtsstaat*. The focus of the formal *rechtsstaat* is to create a legal structure that follows the law, rather than giving the structure any specific content or values, which such laws would have to implement. Consequently, the limit of the power of the state is simply in the form (legal or otherwise) in which its decisions have been taken. Meanwhile, a material meaning of the *rechtsstaat* legal model is related to a model of construction of a legal system in which such ideas/values as human and economic rights, recognized at an international law level, are to be implemented by the law, regardless of whether they are formally recognized by the national legal system of the country being assisted (see Mauro Zamboni, "'Rechtsstaat': Just What is Being Exported by Swedish Development Organisations?", *Law, Social Justice & Global Development Journal (LGD)* 2 (2001), available at http://elj.warwick.ac.uk/global/issue/2001-2/zamboni.html).

13. See Grote, "Rule of Law", p. 270; Michel Troper, "The Limits of Rule of Law: The Rechtsstaat and the Problem of Obedience to the Law", Rule of Law Lecture Series, The Centre for Comparative Constitutional Studies, University of Melbourne, 10 April 2001; Mary Gaudron, "Reply to Professor Michel Troper 'The Limits of the Rule of Law' ", Rule of Law Lecture Series, The Centre for Comparative Constitutional Studies, University of Melbourne, 10 April 2001; David K. Linnan, "Indonesian Law Reform, or Once More Unto the Breach: A Brief Institutional History", *Australian Journal of Asian Law* 1 (1999): 27.

14. Randall Peerenboom, "Varieties of Rule of Law: An Introduction and Provisional Conclusion", in *Asian Discourses of Rule of Law*, edited by Peerenboom, pp. 1–55. According to Peerenboom, the "thick" (substantive) concept of the rule of law consists of the basic elements of the formal rule of law, and then goes further by adding on content requirements in various combinations "... such as particular economic arrangements (free market capitalism, central planning, 'Asian developmental state' or other varieties of capitalism), forms of government (democratic, socialist, soft authoritarian) or conceptions of human rights (libertarian, classical liberal, social welfare liberal, communitarian, 'Asian values,' etc.)". While Peerenboom has classified the rule of law into the "thick" and the "thin", Paul Craig has used the term "formal" and "substantive". See Paul Craig, "Formal and Substantive Conceptions of the Rule of Law", *Public Law* (1997): 467.

15. Noel B. Reynolds, "Grounding the Rule of Law", *Ratio Juris* 2 (1989): 1, 3.

16. Tim Lindsey, "Legal Infrastructure and Governance Reform in Post-Crisis Asia: The Case of Indonesia", *Asian Pacific Economic Literature* 18 (2004): 1, 17.

17. The elucidation of the 1945 Constitution was abolished by the MPR in 2002.

18. Todung Mulya Lubis, "The *Rechtsstaat* and Human Rights", in *Indonesia: Law and Society*, edited by Lindsey, p. 172.

19. Ibid.

20. Information regarding the practice of the rule of law in the Soeharto government

can be read in Hans Thoolen, ed., *Indonesia and the Rule of Law: Twenty Years of "New Order" Government* (London: Frances Pinter, 1987).

21. Linnan, "Indonesian Law Reform", p. 2.

22. See Lindsey, "From Rule of Law to Law of the Rulers", p. 13; See also Gottfried Dietze, *Two Concepts of the Rule of Law* (Indianapolis: Liberty Fund, 1973).

23. Stern distinguishes the following elements of the *rechtsstaat* principles: The constitutional state, liberty and equality, the separation and control of government authority, legality, judicial protection, a system of reparation and the prohibition of the excessive use of government authority. See Francois Venter, *Constitutional Comparison: Japan, Germany, Canada and South Africa as Constitutional States* (Cape Town: Juta and Co., 2000), p. 49. Regarding the concepts of the rule of law and its German equivalent, *rechtsstaat*, I will not draw any distinction between them. It is sometimes argued that the Anglo-American idea of rule of law is different from the idea of *rechtsstaat*, owing to the common-law tradition in English-speaking countries. In the context of the book, the difference is exaggerated. The two concepts *basically* refer to the same thing, and people of different languages have no trouble understanding each other.

24. The United States is an example of the classic presidential model which separates the legislative and executive into two distinct branches with their own independent electoral mandates. It is therefore possible (and not uncommon) to find situation of "divided government", where the members of the legislature and its officers belong to a party different to that of the president. The legislature in this system can remove the president, but only by invoking a rarely used impeachment process which typically requires a super-majority vote by the legislature. Impeachment proceedings usually require that the president be found to have acted improperly, whereas a vote of no confidence in the Westminster parliamentary system is a function of political support (or lack thereof). A president appoints and dismisses members of his or her cabinet. Presidential cabinet members, like their parliamentary counterparts, wield significant power over their respective agencies. Unlike parliamentary ministers, however, they tend to be "advisors and subordinates" to the president, rather than potential successors. In the presidential systems of South Korea, Nigeria, the Philippines, and the United States, the legislature plays a role in executive appointment. Legislative authority varies, from the power of outright rejection, to an advisory role (for example, the U.S. Senate's "advice and consent" on presidential appointments). Legislatures in some presidential systems (primarily in Latin America) possess the power to censure cabinet members, a process which leads occasionally to their dismissal by the president. For additional information, see Arend Lijphart, ed., *Parliamentary Versus Presidential Government* (New York: Oxford University Press, 1992); David Close, ed., *Legislatures in the New Democracies in Latin America* (London: Lynne Rienner Publishers, 1995); Michael Laver and Kenneth A. Shepsle, eds., *Cabinet Ministers and Parliamentary Government* (Cambridge: Cambridge University Press, 1994).

25. "Functional groups representation" is a concept under which people are represented not as individuals but as members of a group deemed to have a common interest, for example, based on profession/occupation, religion, ethnicity, gender or other identified position or role in society.

26. See Gary F. Bell, "Constitutions Do Not Perform Miracles", *Van Zorge Report on Indonesia*, Vol. III, No. 6 (2 April 2001): 11.

27. Early in Wahid's administration, he inquired regarding the availability of monies from the State Logistics Agency (Badan Urusan Logistik, or Bulog) employees' pension fund for funding humanitarian activities in strife-torn Aceh. When he was told such a transfer would require a presidential decree, he claimed to have abandoned the option. Subsequently, the deputy chair of Bulog, Sapuan, took advantage of the request to embezzle 35 billion rupiah (US$4 million) from the pension fund, apparently claiming it was on behalf of the president. The other case arose because President Abdurrahman failed to get the money he was looking for from Bulog. He subsequently received a US$2 million donation from the Sultan of Brunei for humanitarian activities in Aceh and failed to report the donation to the DPR as part of government revenue. He claimed to have accepted the gift as a private individual and channelled the money to Aceh through several NGOs run by his friends and relatives, supposedly obviating the need for including it in official revenue reports. In September 2000, the DPR established a Special Committee to investigate these cases and four months later concluded, in the Bulog case, that there was "suspicion" that the President was "directly involved" and, in the Brunei case, that the President should have reported the donation to the DPR, as part of official state revenues. However, in neither case was evidence ever presented that the President had broken any laws or personally profited from the funds.

28. Kevin O'Rourke, *Reformasi: The Struggle for Power in Post-Soeharto Indonesia* (Sydney: Allen and Unwin, 2002), p. 402.

29. A full two-thirds of the MPR was the DPR itself. Thus the MPR did not at all function as an upper chamber as in many bicameral legislatures, i.e., as a gathering place of more experienced politicians with cooler heads than those which sometimes prevail in the lower chamber. In this way, the upper chamber provides another useful check within a larger system characterized by the separation of powers and multiple checks and balances. Instead, the MPR was simply an extension of the DPR, in which the same political conflicts were played out in a body with much more extensive powers. I have explained this in detail in Chapter 3.

30. The GBHN was a set of policy guidelines drafted by the MPR, passed as a decree, and presented to the newly elected president as the policy agenda for his or her five years in office. Establishing the GBHN was one of the three functions of the MPR explicitly mentioned in the 1945 Constitution (besides establishing and amending the Constitution and the (now deleted) election of the president and vice-president). The GBHN was one of the primary yardsticks

by which the MPR evaluates the performance of the President at its annual, general and special sessions. As an MPR decree, the GBHN was thus legally binding; as a set of policy guidelines, it was a political yardstick.

31. Sekretariat Negara Republik Indonesia, *Risalah Sidang BPUPKI-PPKI 28 Mei 1945–22 Agustus 1945* (Jakarta: Sekneg RI, 1995), pp. 221–22.

32. For a full account, see Marsilam Simanjuntak, *Pandangan Negara Integralistik: Sumber, Unsur dan Riwayatnya dalam Persiapan UUD 1945* (Jakarta: Pustaka Utama Grafiti, 1994). In addition, David Bourchier argued that "integralism" (*kekeluargaan*), the philosophy behind the 1945 Constitution, owes a considerable intellectual debt to a stream of European organicist theory developed mainly by German philosophers, including Adam Muller and von Savigny — transmitted to Indonesia through the influence of the legal scholars of Leiden University in the 1920s and 1930s — in strong opposition to positivism. See David Bourchier, "Lineages of Organicist Political Thought in Indonesia" (Ph.D. thesis, Monash University, 1996).

33. See Taqiyuddin al-Nabhani, *Nizam al-Islam.*

34. He did not distinguish the technical meanings of *al-imama* and *al-khilafa*. Both terms have the same general meaning.

35. Abu Hasan al-Mawardi, *al-Ahkam al-Sultaniyya* (Beirut: Dar al-Fikr, n.d), p. 5.

36. On the historical view of the abolition of the caliphate in 1924, see Hamid Enayat, *Modern Islamic Political Thought* (London: Macmillan, 1982), pp. 52–68.

37. Ahmad Husayn Ya'qub, *al-Nizam al-Siyasi fi al-Islam: Ra'y al-sunna, ra'y al-shi'a, hukm al-shar'* (Iran: Mu'assasah Ansariyan, 1312 A.H.), p. 250.

38. Abduh believes that "political organization is not a matter determined by Islamic doctrine but is rather determined from time to time according to circumstances, by general consultation within the community". See Malcolm H. Kerr, *Islamic Reform: The Political and Legal Theories of Muhammad 'Abduh and Rashid Rida*, (Berkeley: University of California Press, 1966), p. 148.

39. Raziq believes that the caliphate was the product of history, an institution of human, rather than divine, origin, a temporary convenience, and therefore a purely political office with no religious meaning or function. The rules which the Prophet did lay down concerned only such things as prayer and fasting; and they were in fact rules appropriate for his particular culture, for people in a simple state with a natural government. See Hamid Enayat, *Modern Islamic Political Thought.*, pp. 62–68.

40. According to Haykal, there is no standard system of government in Islam. The Islamic community is free to follow any governing system which ensures equality among its citizens (both in rights and responsibilities) and in the sight of the law, and manages affairs of state based on consultation, by adhering to Islam's moral and ethical values. See Musdah Mulia, *Negara Islam: Pemikiran Politik Husain Haikal* (Jakarta: Paramadina, 2001).

41. For a full account, see Antony Black, *The History of Islamic Political Thought:*

From the Prophet to the Present (Edinburgh: Edinburgh University Press, 2001), pp. 18–31.

42. See numerous articles in Eugene Cotran and Adel Omar Sherif, eds., *Democracy, the Rule of law and Islam* (London: Kluwer Law International, 1999).

43. Abd al-Wahhab Khallaf, *Al-Siyasa al-Shar'iyya* (Cairo: Salafiyah, 1350 A.H.), p. 25.

44. Ibid., pp. 57–58.

45. By comparison, Iran and Egypt also have the form of both a republic and a unitary state, not a federal one, while Saudi Arabia is a monarchy without elected representative institutions, or political parties.

46. For a full account, see Hideaki Shinoda, *Re-examining Sovereignty: From Classical Theory to the Global Age* (New York: St. Martin's Press, 2000).

47. Abul A'la Maududi, *First Principles of the Islamic State* (Lahore: Islamic Publications, 1983), p. 25.

48. Quthb's view can be read in his *Ma'alim fi al-Tariq* (Cairo: Dar al-Syuruq, 1987). This book becomes the standard reference for members of Ikhwan al-Muslimin in Egypt and over the world. For a full account, see M. Amien Rais, "The Moslem Brotherhood in Egypt: Its Rise, Demise, and Resurgence" (Ph.D. dissertation, University of Chicago, 1984).

49. Muhammad Asad, *The Principles of State and Government in Islam* (Kuala Lumpur: Islamic Book Trust, 1980), pp. 37–38.

50. Niyazi Berkes, *The Development of Secularism in Turkey* (Montreal: McGill University Press, 1964), p. 210.

51. Abdullahi Ahmed an-Na'im, *Toward an Islamic Reformation* (New York: Syracuse University Press, 1990), p. 83.

52. Muhammad al-Muti'i, *Haqiqah al-Islam wa Usul al-Hukm* (Cairo: Maktabat al-Nahda al-Hadisa, 1344 A.H.).

53. See Abd al-Qadir Audah, *al-Islam wa Awda'tuna al-Siyasiyah* (Beirut: Mu'assasat al-Risalah, 1980).

54. See, Abu 'Abd Allah Muhammad b. Yazid b. Majah, *Sunan Ibn Majah* (n.p.: Dar al-Turas al-Arabi, 1975), HN: 3,940.

55. Louay M. Safi, "The Islamic State: A Conceptual Framework", *American Journal of Islamic Social Sciences* (1991): 233.

56. Ahmad Hasan, "The Political Role of Ijma'", *Islamic Studies* 8 (1969): 136.

57. Hamdan Zoelva, personal communication, Jakarta, 15 December 2003.

58. See Sekretariat Jenderal MPR, *Risalah Sidang Panitia Ad-Hoc I, Badan Pekerja MPR-RI* (Jakarta: MPR, 2000).

59. See Denny Indarayana, "Menguji Kesehatan Capres", *Kompas,* 19 April 2004; Dono Widiatmoko, "Kriteria Sehat Calon Presiden", *Kompas,* 19 April 2004.

60. Mawardi, *al-Ahkam al-Sultaniyya*, p. 6.

61. Munawir Syadzali, *Islam and Governmental System: Teachings, History, and Reflections* (Jakarta: INIS, 1991), p. 55. Abu Hamid al-Ghazali (450/1058 – 505/1111) is arguably one of the most influential thinkers in the history of

Islamic thought and modern scholarship has awarded him a greater share of attention than any other medieval Muslim figure. It is worth noting that al-Ghazali mentions ten caliphal qualifications above in his book *Fada'ih al-Batiniyya wa Fada'il al-Mustazhiriyyah* (known as *Kitab Mustazhiri*) which is available at http://www.ghazali.org/works/fadiah.pdf (in Arabic) and at http://www.ghazali.org/books/mz-4.pdf (in English). In this work, al-Ghazali attempted to refute the doctrines of the Ismailis or *Batiniyyah* (one sect of Shi'a). More information on this debate can be read in Farouk Mitha, *Al-Ghazali and the Ismailis: A Debate on Reason and Authority in Medieval Islam*, Ismaili Heritage Series, p. 5. (London: I. B. Tauris in association with the Institute of Ismaili Studies, 2001). Al-Ghazali's other book on this subject is *al-Tibr al-Masbuk fi Nasihat al-Muluk* which is available at http://www.al-eman.com/Islamlib/viewchp.asp?BID=167&CID=2#s10. It is a manual of advice composed for rulers, ministers and governors on how they should govern their realms. However, these works are not read widely among Indonesian Muslim students. They are more familiar with al-Ghazali's *Ihya Ulum al-Din* which is widely regarded as the greatest work of Muslim spirituality.

62. Enayat, *Modern Islamic Political Thought*, p. 93.
63. Fatima Mernissi, *Women and Islam: An Historical and Theological Enquiry* (Basil: Blackwell, 1991), pp. 50–53; see also Mernissi, *Islam and Democracy: Fear of the Modern World* (London: Virago Press, 1993).
64. See Fatima Mernissi, *The Forgotten Queens of Islam* (Minneapolis: University of Minnesota Press, 1993).
65. See "Muslim leader moves to block Megawati", BBC News, available at http://news.bbc.co.uk/1/hi/world/asia-pacific/373658.stm, 20 June 1999.
66. Ibn Khaldun, *Muqaddimah* (Mecca: Dar al-Bazi, 1978), pp. 194–96; see also Muhammad Mahmoud Rabi', *The Political Theory of Ibn Khaldun* (Leiden: E.J. Brill, 1967), pp. 122–24.
67. Ali Alatas was a long-time career diplomat, while Alwi Shihab was awarded two Ph.D. degrees from the University of 'Ain Shams (Cairo) and Temple University (USA).
68. Maududi, *First Principles of the Islamic State*, p. 60.
69. Muhammad Abdul Qadir Abu Faris, *al-Nizam al-Siyasi fi al-Islam* (Beirut: Dar al-Qur'an al-Karim, 1984), p. 179.
70. See Ibn Taimiyah, *Enjoining Right and Forbidding Wrong*, available online at http://www.ymofmd.com/books/erfw/. See also Syadzali, *Islam and Governmental System*, pp. 62–63.
71. The PPP's views can be read in *Risalah PAH I BP MPR 2000*, Rapat Ke-3, 6 December 2000, pp. 23–25 and Rapat Ke-4, 7 December 2000, p. 5; The PBB's views can be read in *Risalah PAH I BP MPR 2000*, Rapat ke-3, 6 December 2000, pp. 27–32.
72. Wahid's views on this matter can be read in Masykuri Abdillah, *Responses of

Indonesian Muslim Intellectuals to the Concept of Democracy (1966–1993) (Hamburg: Abera Verlag, 1997), p. 104.

73. Nabhani, *Nizam al-Islam*.
74. Personal communications with Hamdan Zoelva of PBB Party (15 December 2003), TB. Soemandjadja of the PK (7 December 2003), and Lukman Hakim Saifuddin of the PPP (10 November 2003).
75. See Andreas P. Schedler, "Taking Electoral Promises Seriously: Reflections on the Substance of Procedural Democracy", paper prepared for presentation at the XVIth World Congress of the International Political Science Association (IPSA), Berlin, 21–25 August 1994.
76. See Arend Lijphart, *Electoral System and Party Systems: A Study of Twenty-Seven Democracies 1945–1990* (Oxford and New York: Oxford University Press, 1994).
77. MPR Decree III/1978, Article 8(5).
78. 1945 Constitution, Article 6(2).
79. President Habibie is given credit by some for rekindling the discourse on constitutional amendment, with his proposal in May 1999 for direct presidential elections (Slamet Effendy Yusuf and Umar Basalim, *Reformasi Konstitusi Indonesia: Perubahan Pertama UUD-1945* (Jakarta: Pustaka Indonesia Satu, 2000), p. 49, fn. 4).
80. "Semangat PAH I BP MPR Pemilihan Presiden Langsung", *Kompas*, 11 September 2001; "Beda Prinsip di Putaran Kedua Pemilihan", *Kompas*, 13 June 2002.
81. "PDI-P Isyaratkan Tolak Pemilihan Langsung", *Media Indonesia*, 30 June 2002.
82. Fathi Osman, "The Contract for the Appointment of the Head of an Islamic State", in *State, Politics, and Islam*, edited by Mumtaz Ahmad (Indianapolis: American Trust Publications, 1986), p. 57.
83. E. Tyan, "Bay'a", in *The Encyclopaedia of Islam*, Vol. I, edited by B. Lewis, Ch. Pellat and J. Schacht (Leiden: E.J. Brill, 1965), pp. 1, 1113.
84. More information can be found in Ahmad Fuad Abd al-Jawad, *al-Bay'ah 'inda Mufakkiri Ahl al-Sunna wa al-'Aqd al-Ijtima'i fi al-Fikr al-Siyasi al-Hadith: Dirasah Muqaranah fi al-Falsafah al-Siyasiya* (Cairo: Dar Quba', 1998).
85. Mawardi, *al-Ahkam al-Sultaniyya*, p. 6.
86. It is worth noting that in Shi'a tradition, they believe that the leader after the Prophet's death must be from the family of the Prophet. In this sense, they believe that Ali b. Abi Thalib, cousin of the Prophet, was designated by the Prophet to lead Muslims. Unlike the majority of Muslims who recognize Abu Bakr as the first caliph, they recognize Ali as their first Imam. Moreover, the process of succession in Shi'a was through testament from the previous leader; not by election. The central evidence of Ali's legitimacy as successor to the Prophet is the event of Ghadir Khumm when the Prophet, as they claimed, chose Ali to the "general guardianship" *(walayat ammah)* of the people and made Ali, like himself, their "guardian" *(wali)*. It is also claimed that the next

Imams are chosen by this method. In Sunni tradition, Ali himself is elected as the fourth caliph.

Shi'a did not undergo any divisions during the imamate of the first three Imams: Ali, Hasan, and Husayn. But after the martyrdom of Husayn, Shi'a was divided. Among them are the Zaydi and the Isma'ili which continue to exist until now. To this day communities of these branches are active in various parts of the world such as the Yemen, India, and Syria. The majority group (known as Twelve-Imam Shi'ism or Ja'fari) lives in Iran. After the last Imam by Divine Command went into occultation — and he will reappear for the second time by the end of this world — Shi'a under Iranian Constitution selects its religious leader by elections. According to Article 109 of Iranian Constitution, the task of appointing the religious leader shall be vested with the experts elected by the people. The experts will review and consult among themselves concerning all the scholars possessing the qualifications specified in Articles 5 and 109. In the event they find one of them better versed in Islamic regulations, the subjects of the *fiqh*, or in political and social issues, or possessing general popularity or special prominence for any of the qualifications mentioned in Article 109, they shall elect him as the leader. Otherwise, in the absence of such a superiority, they shall elect and declare one of them as the leader. The religious leader thus elected by the Assembly of Experts shall assume all the powers of the *wilayat al-amr* and all the responsibilities arising therefrom. The leader is equal with the rest of the people of the country in the eyes of law. Information on Shi'a is available at http://al-islam.org/index.php; see also Abdulaziz Abdulhussein Sachedina, *The Just Ruler (al-Sultan al-Adil) in Shiite Islam: The Comprehensive Authority of the Jurist in Imamite Jurisprudence* (New York: Oxford University Press, 1988).

87. Ibid.

88. Mawardi, *al-Ahkam al-Sultaniyya*, pp. 6–7; see also Abu Faris, *al-Nizam al-Siyasi fi al-Islam*, pp. 231–34.

89. Fathi Osman, "The Contract for the Appointment", p. 58.

90. Mu'awiya, the founder of the Umayyad Dynasty, established the hereditary principle in 676 (four years before his death) by securing *bay'at* for his son, Yazid, and having him confirmed as the next caliph during Mu'awiyah's own time. This precedent was subsequently followed throughout the Umayyad and Abbasid dynasties. See Patricia Crone, *Medieval Islamic Political Thought* (Edinburgh: Edinburgh University Press, 2004), pp. 44.

91. Charles D. Kenney, "Reflections on Horizontal Accountability: Democratic Legitimacy, Majority Parties and Democratic Stability in Latin America", paper for the conference on Institutions, Accountability, and Democratic Governance in Latin America, Kellogg Institute for International Studies, University of Notre Dame, 8–9 May 2000.

92. Bernard Manin, *The Principles of Representative Government* (Cambridge: Cambridge University Press, 1997), p. 124.

93. See International Commission of Jurists, *The Dynamic Aspects of the Rule of Law in the Modern Age*, Report on the Proceedings of the South-East Asian and Pacific Conference of Jurists, Bangkok-Thailand, 15–19 February 1965, p. 44.

94. Muna Ndulo, "Globalisation and Empire: the Democratization Process and Structural Adjustment in Africa", *Indiana Journal of Global Legal Studies* 10 (2003): 350.

95. Mawardi, *al-Ahkam al-Sultaniyya*, pp. 17–20.

96. Maududi, *First Principles of the Islamic State*, p. 57; and Fathi Osman, "The Contract for the Appointment", p. 54.

97. Abu al-Husain al-Qusyari al-Naisaburi, *Sahih Muslim*, book *al-Imara*, HN: 3,423.

98. Ann K. S. Lambton, *State and Government in Medieval Islam* (New York: Oxford University Press, 1991), pp. 63–64.

99. Ron Gould, Christine Jackson, and Loren Wells, *Strengthening Democracy: A Parliamentary Perspective* (Aldershot: Dartmouth, 1995), p. 41.

100. Fazlur Rahman, "The Principle of Shura and the Role of the Ummah in Islam", in *State, Politics, and Islam*, edited by Mumtaz Ahmad (Indianapolis: American Trust Publications, 1986), pp. 90–91.

101. Mishal Fahm al-Sulami, *The West and Islam* (London: RoutledgeCurzon, 2003), p. 123.

102. Rahman, "Principle of Shura", p. 95.

103. Maududi believes that only the *ulama* can legislate on matters not covered by the Holy Texts. Maududi, *First Principles of the Islamic State*, pp. 30–31.

104. Khallaf proposes that they should consist of Muslim scholars *(al-mujtahidun wa ahl al-futya)*. Khallaf, *Al-Siyasa al-Shar'iyya*, p. 42.

105. See Fazlur Rahman, "A Recent Controversy Over the Interpretation of Shura", *History of Religions* 20 (1981): 291–301.

106. See Sayed Khatab, "The Concept of Jahiliyyah in the Thought of Sayyid Quthb" (Ph.D. thesis, University of Melbourne, September 2002), p. 245.

107. For a full account, see David M. Farrell, *Comparing Electoral Systems* (London: Prentice Hall/Harvester Wheatsheaf, 1997).

108. Gamil Mohammed El-Gindy, "The Shura and Human Rights in Islamic Law: The Relevance of Democracy", in *The Rule of Law in the Middle East and the Islamic World*, edited by Eugene Cotran and Mai Yamani (London: I.B. Tauris, 2000), p. 166; see also Ibrahim Hosen, "Fiqh Siyasah dalam Tradisi Pemikiran Islam Klasik", *Jurnal Ulumul Qur'an* 2, no. 4 (1993): 58–66.

109. Khatab, "Concept of Jahiliyyah", p. 246.

110. Al-Sulami, *The West and Islam*, p. 141.

111. Mujib Rakhmat, personal communication, 13 October 2003. Rakhmat is an *al-hafiz* (a person who can memorize all the verses of the Qur'an).

112. Rod Hague and Martin Harrop, *Comparative Government and Politics* (Hampshire: Palgrave, 2001), p. 220.

113. See "Basic Principles on the Independence of the Judiciary", adopted by the

seventh UN Congress on the Prevention of Crime and the Treatment of Offenders, held at Milan from 26 August to 6 September 1985, and endorsed by General Assembly Resolutions 40/32 of 29 November 1985 and 40/146 of 13 December 1985. It is worth considering that the General Assembly did not attempt to devise a single system for all countries. Instead, it proclaimed twenty general principles which should apply, regardless of the prevailing legal and political order. The document recognizes that there continues to be a gap between theoretical principles and actual practice and expresses the wish that the twenty principles would serve to "assist Member States in their task of securing and promoting the independence of the judiciary, should be taken into account and respected by Governments, within the framework of their national legislation and practice, and be brought to the attention of judges, lawyers, members of the executive and the legislature, and the public in general."

114. Ibid.
115. Lindsey, "Indonesia: Devaluing Asian Values, Rewriting Rule of Law", p. 307.
116. Shad Saleem Faruqi, "Constitutional Law, the Rule of Law and Systems of Governance in Islam", paper presented in Islamic Law and the West: Can Secular Laws and Syari'ah Co-Exist?, Asian Law Centre, University of Melbourne, 19 September 2002, available at http://www.law.unimelb.edu.au/ alc/assets/ faruqi%20paper.pdf.
117. Ibn Rusyd, *Bidayah al-Mujtahid*, Vol. 2 (Beirut: Dar al-Fikr, 1995), p. 377.
118. Khallaf, *Al-Siyasa al-Shar'iyya*, p. 47.
119. Mawardi, *al-Ahkam al-Sultaniyya*, p. 67.
120. Muhammad al-Zuhayli, *Tarikh al-Qada' fi al-Islam* (Beirut: Dar al-Fikr al-Mu'asir, 1995), p. 91.
121. Mohammad Hashim Kamali, "Appellate Review and Judicial Independence in Islamic Law", in *Islam and Public Law*, edited by Chibli Mallat (London: CIMEL, 1993), p. 53.
122. C. G. Weeramantry, *Islamic Jurisprudence* (Basingstoke: Macmillan, 1988), p. 80.
123. Mawardi, *al-Ahkam al-Sultaniyya*, pp. 80–92.
124. More information on the refusal of appointment of judges in the early centuries of Islam can be found in Noel J. Coulson, "Doctrine and Practice in Islamic Law", *Bulletin of the School of Oriental and African Studies* 18, no. 2 (1956): 211–26. However, it should be noted that Abu Yusuf (d. 798 A.D.), the chief disciple of Imam Abu Hanifah, was the Chief Justice (*qadi al-qudat*) under the Harun al-Rasyid regime. See Al-Haj Mahomed Ullah Ibn S. Jung, *The Administration of Justice of Muslim Law* (Delhi: Idarah-I Adabiyat-I Delhi, 1977).
125. Irit Abramski-Blig, "The Judiciary (Qadis) as a Governmental-Administrative Tool in Early Islam", in *The Formation of Islamic Law*, edited by Wael Hallaq (Burlington: Ashgate, 2004).
126. For instance, one of the unstated conditions of becoming a judge in Nasrid

kingdom of Granada (629/1232 to 897/1492) was loyalty to the sultans. The political elite used removal from office as a mechanism for control of the judiciary. See M. Isabel Calero Secall, "Rulers and Qadis: Their Relationship During the Nasrid Kingdom", *Islamic Law and Society* 7, no. 2 (2000): 235. However, in Cordoba (5th/11th century), unlike other officials, the Qadis jurisdictional authority could be terminated only by dismissal; it could not be temporarily interrupted by the interference of the ruler in a particular case. See Christian Muller, "Judging with God's Law on Earth: Judicial Powers of the Qadi al-Jama'a of Cordoba in the Fifth/Eleventh Century", *Islamic Law and Society* 7, no. 2 (2000) 159.

127. The intersection of law, courts and politics is demonstrated in Herbert Jacob et al., *Courts, Law, and Politics in Comparative Perspective* (New Haven: Yale University Press, 1996).

128. Khallaf, *Al-Siyasa al-Shar'iyya*, p. 48.

6

ARTICLE 29 ON RELIGION

At the outset of this book, I have shown the historical debate on the famous seven words in the 1945 Constitution, which involved a requirement in 1945 for Muslims to observe *shari'a*, and which led to the proposal to establish an Islamic state in the 1950s. During the 1999–2002 constitutional reform, the issue was again raised by several Islamic political parties. Unlike in the periods of the Soekarno and Soeharto governments, in the reform era all political parties, members of parliament and the government examined the issue in a constitutional and democratic way, without issuing either presidential decrees to unilaterally stop the discussion or using military force to influence the process.

Another significant feature, and this could be argued as one of the main factors in keeping the military away from using its power, was the shifting of the issue from the idea of Islam becoming the foundation of the state (*Dasar Negara*) to the implementation of *shari'a* in Article 29. In other words, while the previous debate examined the preamble to the Constitution, which could change the state ideology of the Indonesian republic, the contemporary debate was more concerned with the special rights of Muslims and the obligation for the government to implement *shari'a*.

As has been discussed in Chapter 5, none of the Indonesian Islamic political parties wanted to adopt a caliphate system. They acknowledged the nation-state system. They did not even propose to establish an Islamic state based on nation-states like those in Iran, Egypt or Saudi Arabia. However, some of them made it clear that they wanted a constitutional guarantee that their rights to observe *shari'a* would be fully implemented. In this case, the amendment to Article 29 was perceived as essential. In order to understand this proposal, many issues will be examined in this chapter. Among them are the position of public religion in a plural society, the choice between Islamic law and an Islamic state, and the issues of *dar al-Islam*, as compared to *dar al-Harb*.

These discussions will be a reflection of the struggle between secularism, which is considered by some as normal, progressive and enlightened, and the religious approach, which is seen as backward and reactionary. To what extent is it legitimate to use religion as a basis for political decisions on public policy? There is a view that such use of religion ultimately results in violations of the separation of church (or faith) and state as a basis of a secular state, and thus other people's religious liberty. Other religious believers, however, argue that it is wrong to exclude religion from public debates, and that such a policy effectively constitutes discrimination against religion and religious believers.

In Islamic terms, the distinction between an Islamic state and a non-Islamic state, with all its legal consequences, has been discussed by many classic and modern Islamic thinkers. Such opinions are based on their conceptions of *jihad*, and their understanding of the world order during their times. In this chapter, I will demonstrate both the substantive approach to *shari'a* and the formal approach on these issues.

The later part of the chapter will bring together all these theoretical issues to examine the debate on Article 29 during the 1999–2002 MPR sessions. Firstly, the discussion will focus on constitutional debate which took place *inside* the MPR. I will rely on the minutes of meeting and the results of interview with several leading figures. Secondly, I will also analyse the text of Article 29, both in its original form and the alternative proposed for its amendment. The final part of this chapter will compare the proposal to include *shari'a* in the Indonesian Constitution with the inclusion of *shari'a* in the Constitution of Egypt.

Having examined all the main issues, the chapter will argue that the failure of some Islamic political parties to reinsert a provision that enforces Islamic law was due to their formal approach to *shari'a*. This failure once again provides solid evidence that Indonesia, as a plural society, is in favour of substantive *shari'a*; not the formal one.

PUBLIC RELIGION IN CONSTITUTIONAL DEBATE

There are at least three different interpretations of the notion of religion and state. The first view sees the unity of state and religion. Secondly, there is a view that the state should not establish, nor fund, religious activities. A commonly advocated position is that the government should be a secular institution; that is, no state religion, no legislation that outlaws nor favours one religion over another, and no religiously motivated regulations on the eligibility of the nation's politicians. A secular state has no power over the nation's religious institutions, and the nation's religious institutions have no political powers over the members of the government.

This is a strict separation of church (or religious institutions) and state, which rests on the assumption that the independent and autonomous institutions of church and state should rigorously be kept separated. This requires the government not to involve itself in the affairs of religious institutions, by keeping religious beliefs out of the motivations of public policies, preventing interference from religious authorities into state affairs, and disapproving of political leaders expressing religious preferences in the course of their duties. According to this view, when the power, prestige and financial support of government are placed behind a particular religious belief, there will be indirect coercive pressure upon religious minorities to conform to the prevailing officially approved religion. Therefore, to ensure freedom of religion such separation is necessary.[1]

According to Ira Lapidus, such views ignore the situation in various parts of Europe. Lapidus explains that:

> It [this view] ignores the numerous examples of state control of religion, the phenomenon of established churches (such as the Anglican church in England), and the concordats in Italy. It ignores the integral connection between religious and political nationalism in such countries as Ireland or Poland. It ignores the close identity between religious affiliation and nationality in Holland and Spain. Finally, it ignores the connection between religion and activist political movements, such as the liberation churches in Latin America.[2]

Therefore, there is a third interpretation of secularism, which sees that separation of church and state is a notion related to, but separate from, freedom of religion. There are many countries with an official religion, such as the United Kingdom or Belgium, where freedom of religion is also guaranteed. This school of thought holds that religion is a fundamental and essential part of many moral and ethical values, and that the removal of public displays of religion from government is a form of religious discrimination, in that it prohibits people from exercising their religious views in the forum of government.

Instead of insisting on "the wall of separation", this view seeks mutual cooperation to acknowledge and preserve the harmonious existence of religion and state, without necessarily being in favour of their intermixing. In other words, the state should recognize and respect the cultural and religious heritage of its citizens by developing a policy of benevolent neutrality towards religious groups. This type of neutrality requires the government to treat various religious groups with a policy of impartiality. In this sense, not only is the relationship between religion and state in the private domain, but also religion can play its role in the public area.

According to sociologist Jose Casanova, the privatization of religion is "mandated ideologically by liberal categories of thought which permeate not only political ideologies and constitutional theories but the entire structure of modern Western thought".[3] This has made the religious movements become united "by a common enemy — Western secular nationalism — and a common hope for the revival of religion in the public sphere".[4] The question is: has religion so completely lost its social role that it operates as nothing more than personal belief?

Casanova looks at five cases from two religious traditions (Catholicism and Protestantism) in four countries (Spain, Poland, Brazil and the United States). In Spain and Poland, Casanova analyses the positive role of the Catholic church in the transition from authoritarian to democratic regimes. In Brazil, the case of Liberation Theology is examined as an instance of the church's commitment to human rights, and the defence of society and its autonomy from the incursions of the state. The final cases deal with evangelical Protestantism and Catholicism in the United States. Here too, analysis centres on the politicized nature of religion, its intervention in public debates (around military power, economic justice, abortion), and its role in participating in and also in restructuring the public sphere of what Casanova terms civil society.

These cases challenge post-war assumptions about the role of modernity and secularization, that contemporary religion in those societies rooted in the Christian tradition is a marginal or, at most, a private matter. Casanova argues a strong case for the "repoliticization" and "deprivatization" of religion, at the close of the twentieth century.[5] This deprivatization is not restricted to Western society and Christianity.[6] Instead, its horizons are widened to include other religious traditions as well, such as Islam, Judaism and Hinduism.

Casanova is not alone. The rejection of the thesis of secularization — as religious decline — is increasing.[7] Peter Berger, for instance, admits his "big mistake which [he] shared with almost everyone who worked in this area in the 1950s and 1960s, [that is] to believe that modernity necessarily leads to a decline in religion".[8] This means that treating religion as purely a private matter, as a prequisite of modernity, should be called into question.

Instead of suggesting a "separation", Casanova takes the view of secularization as differentiation. Religion must be differentiated from other spheres of public life, such as the state.[9] David Hollenbach explains this position further:

> The differentiation of religion and various dimensions of public life has a different connotation than does "separation" … Religious influence in public and even political life can occur, however, even where state and church are institutionally distinct. Thus, there is a third alternative to "integralism" [church-state unity] on one hand and the privatization of religion on the other. In this third alternative, religious communities can have an impact on public life, while at the same time, free exercise and non-establishment of religion are fully protected.[10]

In his other work, Hollenbach argues that religious beliefs and traditions may have their influence on law and state policy in an indirect way. This occurs through the activity of self-governing citizens, informal discussion, voting, political campaign, and lobbying.[11] Thus, the role of religion in public life does not imply that all political institutions are under the control of religion. It is not theocratic nor linked to any particular belief. General belief in God can be upheld by the state, but not the beliefs of any one specific religion. Religion is seen as value, virtue, common good, inspiration and moral obligation. In this third alternative, differentiation of religion from the domain of state power does not rule out all religious influence in public life, nor in politics, broadly conceived. This can happen because the main role for public religion is to strengthen civil society vis-à-vis the state.[12]

In this regard, Saiful Mujani also argues that people who are religious, and active in religious activities, become democratic, and contribute to democratic development as well. For instance, in the context of Indonesia, participation in religious organizations like Nahdlatul Ulama or Muhammadiyah leads the community to be more open towards the complexities of social life. Since democracy requires political engagement and political participation, it can be argued that the involvement of religious organizations in public life in various other non-religious civil society activities (such as *arisan* [social gatherings with door-prizes], voluntary activities in the village or ward, sports, cultural clubs, co-operatives, labour unions and professional organizations) is important as social capital of democracy.[13] In short, having conducted two national mass surveys in 2001 and 2002, he argues that religious people tend to be supportive of democracy.[14]

In Indonesia, Pancasila (the five pillars that eventually became the state foundation: Belief in one God, Humanitarianism, National Unity, Representative Democracy, and Social Justice) in this regard basically compromises between secularism, where no single religion predominates in the state, and religiosity, where religion (especially Islam) became one of the important pillars of the state. An Islam-inspired agenda is welcome, to the extent that it corresponds with, and does not contradict, Pancasila. In other words, it is a common belief that Indonesia is neither a secular nor an Islamic state. Both terms have negative images in Indonesian society, and therefore the use of the terms "secular" and "Islamic state" has been avoided in legal and political areas. Under the 1945 Constitution, Indonesia has been designed to stand in the middle position, or — borrowing Hollenboch's term — follow "the third alternative".[15] The Pancasila-based state, which begins with the principle of "One Godhead", not only allows but also encourages religion to inspire Indonesian public life in humanitarianism, national unity, representative democracy, and social justice.

However, it is misleading to say that there has been no attempt at advocating Islam as the state ideology throughout the history of the Republic. In fact, some Muslim groups were unhappy to stand in the middle position, as has been discussed in Chapter 3. They demanded that the Constitution should have a clear position: the logical consequences of a Muslim-majority state was to have Islam as the state foundation. The presence of an Islamic state, then, was perceived as an efficient tool to bring all Indonesian Muslims' faith to a higher state. In a current position, such a function would be less effective.

Having learned from history that any attempt to change Indonesia into an Islamic state is doomed to failure, in the light of the reform era, owing to Soeharto's resignation after a thirty-two-year presidency, several Islamic groups proposed inserting a clause in the 1945 Constitution that would guarantee the implementation of *shari'a*. This suggests that they did not want to establish an Islamic state; but demanded *only* the application of their own law to themselves.

However some questions remain: what, for instance, do they mean by *shari'a*? Since one of the aims of constitutionalism is to protect minority rights, their asking for constitutional protection for the implementation of their law and belief is questionable. Have they felt, as a majority group, that their rights and freedoms are less than protected in the 1945 Constitution; or is it right to see their proposal as only a "bridge" for greater demands (the establishment of an Islamic state)? What is the difference between having Islamic law fully implemented, and establishing an Islamic state? I will examine these issues, firstly by looking at constitutional provisions on religion, followed by a brief explanation on the five official religions in Indonesia. Afterwards, analysis of the concept of an Islamic state in Islamic literature will be useful in order to understand the proposal to implement *shari'a*.

RELIGION IN THE 1945 CONSTITUTION

Article 29 of the Indonesian Constitution under the title of "Religion" provides to "all persons the right to worship according to his or her own religion or belief", and states that "the State is based upon belief in one supreme God". Believing in one supreme God becomes the state religion. By not referring to any particular belief, this Article deals with religious pluralism, autonomy and freedom of religion. There are a number of reasons why Indonesia is neither a secular state nor an Islamic state on the basis of this constitutional provision.

Firstly, unlike the Indian and Turkish Constitutions, the 1945 Indonesian Constitution does not state that the nation is a secular one. In its preamble, the Indian Constitution states that "We, the people of India, having solemnly resolved to constitute India into a sovereign socialist secular democratic republic, …" [Constitution of India, Forty-second Amendment Act, 1976, s. 2]. In Turkey, the preamble stipulates that, "as required by the principle of secularism, there shall be no interference whatsoever by sacred religious feelings in state affairs and politics".[16] Not only do both India and Turkey not recognize nor establish state religions, but also their constitutions state clearly that they are secular states, although it is well known that Hindus and Muslims form the majority in India and Turkey, respectively.

Secondly, unlike the Constitutions in Iran, Egypt and (Basic Laws of) Saudi Arabia, no single word in the Indonesian Constitution refers to Islam as the state ideology. As has been examined in previous chapters, the Constitution does not give Islam special rights and provisions. It is worth considering that, unlike the Egyptian Constitution, the 1945 Indonesian Constitution does not regard Islamic law as the primary source of law. It can safely be stated that, from this point of view, Indonesia is not an Islamic state.

Thirdly, while Article 29 of the 1945 Constitution provides freedom of religion, there is no provision that states that the state shall not interfere in religious affairs; nor that religion shall not interfere in the affairs of the state. The lack of such a provision leads T. B. Simatupang, a Protestant scholar, to interpret this as meaning that "the Pancasila-state is responsible not only for ensuring religious freedom, but also for promoting the role of religions in society".[17] It is in this sense that the Department of Religious Affairs was founded in 1946. It supervises religious education, Muslim marriages, the Islamic courts (which deal with divorce and inheritance matters only) and the *haj* (pilgrimage). It also has separate directorates for the other religions: Catholicism, Protestantism, Hinduism and Buddhism.

The above functions make the Indonesian Department of Religious Affairs fundamentally different from the Department of Religious Affairs in Turkey. Under Article 136 of the Turkish Constitution, "The Department of Religious Affairs, which is within the general administration, shall exercise its duties as prescribed in its particular law, in accordance with the principles of secularism, removed from all political views and ideas, and aiming at national solidarity and integrity."

Five Official Religions

It has been stated earlier that belief in one supreme God is a "state religion" in Indonesia. However, it does not mean that Indonesia follows syncretism, which mixes all religions into one belief. It does mean that Indonesia recognizes any religion that believes in one God. The language used in this Article 29 postulates a universal value. The problem comes when Presidential Decree No. 1 of 1965 (which was adopted later in Law No. 5 of 1969) interprets the clause to cover only five faiths: Islam, Catholicism, Protestantism, Buddhism and Hinduism. Religious organizations other than those of the five recognized faiths are able to register with the government, but only with the State Ministry for Culture and Tourism and only as social organizations. Since then, it has become a popular practice for the state to recognize only these five religions as a set of official state religions.[18]

The latest data available from 2000, account for 201,241,999 Indonesians; the Indonesian Central Bureau of Statistics (BPS) estimated that the census missed 4.6 million persons. The BPS report indicated that 88.22 per cent of the population label themselves as Muslim, 5.87 per cent as Protestant, 3.05 per cent as Catholic, 1.81 per cent as Hindu, 0.84 per cent as Buddhist, and 0.2 per cent as "Other", including traditional indigenous religions, other Christian groups and Judaism.[19] Animism and other types of traditional belief systems, generically termed "Aliran Kepercayaan", are still practised by sizeable populations in Java, Kalimantan, and Papua. Many of those who practice Kepercayaan describe it as more of a meditation-based spiritual path than a religion. The law requires adult citizens to carry a national ID card (KTP), and this card lists the citizen's religious affiliation. Animists, Confucianists and followers of the indigenous religion of the Dayak people in Indonesia find it difficult or impossible to obtain a KTP that accurately reflected their faiths, and consequently, many are identified incorrectly as adhering to one of the five religions. They are "forced" to identify themselves with one of the state-recognized religions.[20]

Since the Government recognizes only five major religions, persons of other faiths frequently experience official discrimination, often in the context of civil registration of marriages and births, or the issuance of identity cards. Those who choose not to register their marriages or births of children risk future difficulties. For example, many children without a birth certificate cannot enrol in schools or may not qualify for scholarships. Individuals without birth certificates will not qualify for government jobs.

The second problem is related to equal treatment for the five state-recognized religions. Although the 1945 Constitution guarantees people freedom to exercise their beliefs, the Constitution does not prevent the Parliament from passing laws that favour one of the five state-recognized religions. In comparison with the United States, its first amendment has been interpreted as requiring a secular state since it states that: "Congress shall make no law respecting an establishment of religion." Since Indonesia does not follow the American model, it is possible that Islam as the religion of the majority receives "special" treatment. There are some indications of this possibility: there are some laws which regulate Muslim affairs, such as the law on religious courts, *zakat* (alms), *waqf* (religious endowment), and *haj* (pilgrimage), whereas other religions do not have such special regulations.[21] Moreover, the Department of Religious Affairs practically becomes a Muslim department and no non-Muslim has ever been appointed as the Minister for Religious Affairs.

The government requires official religions to comply with the Ministry of Religious Affairs and other ministerial directives, such as the Regulation on Building Houses of Worship (Joint-Ministerial Decree No. 1 of 1969), the Guidelines for the Propagation of Religion (Ministerial Decision No. 70 of 1978), Overseas Aid to Religious Institutions in Indonesia (Ministerial Decision No. 20 of 1978), and Proselytising Guidelines (No. 77 of 1978). All these regulations are allegedly aimed at supporting and protecting Muslim affairs. For instance, many members of minority faiths complain that the government has imposed unequal treatment regarding the building of houses of worship. It is more difficult for non-Muslims to acquire a building licence.[22]

On the other hand, some Muslim groups take the view that their right to practise their own belief, as stipulated in Article 29(2), has not been fully exercised. They believed that the full implementation of *shari'a* is part of their freedom of religion. Since it has not been achieved yet, owing to the political and legal problems outlined in Chapter 3, they have proposed the adoption of the famous seven words, which involved a requirement for Muslims to observe *shari'a*. During the last half-century, Indonesian Islamic-based parties have been attempting periodically to have the seven words reinstated, but without success.

The third problem is that the government has been involved in determining which school of teachings of a particular religion can be accepted in Indonesia. However, Article 29 of the 1945 Constitution does not "provide any criteria for deciding whether a certain religion is based on Belief in One God or which authority would make such decision".[23] Quite often the government acts as a "judge", or as some say as "God", by having the right to decide which faiths and beliefs are classified as illegitimate sects. In order to secure this role, the government establishes the Bureau for Supervision of Religious Movements (Pakem) under the Ministry of Religious Affairs, and staffed it with people from the Attorney-General's office. The Ahmadiyah group, for instance, has been declared as an illegitimate form of Islam. Among Buddhist adherents, there are two major social organizations — the Indonesian Great Sangha Conference (KASI) and the Indonesian Buddhist Council (WALUBI). However, relations between WALUBI and KASI are strained, with KASI members feeling that the Government has unfairly thrown its support behind WALUBI. Smaller Christian groups include the Jehovah's Witnesses, who claim an active membership of approximately 17,100, not including children. The existence of the Jehovah's Witnesses is not officially recognized in Indonesia. These instances suggest that discrimination occurs not only among religions, but also among sects within a particular religion.

In this subsection, I have evaluated the position of religion under the 1945 Constitution. The discussion has gone further by examining some problems related to state-recognized religions and inter-relationship between and within them. Such problems have opened the door to political compromise or confrontation between different groups with their own ideas of religious freedom. I have also pointed out that the main problem is the reduction of the value of the universal statement of Article 29 on the belief in one God, by the government's interpretation of this Article. Another problem is related to the desire of some Muslim groups to promote a greater role for Islamic law. The discussion below will focus mainly on the second problem. Against this background I will discuss the political process and the debate on Article 29 during the MPR session, followed by an analysis of the proposal to include *shari'a* in Article 29 of the 1945 Constitution.

POLITICAL CONTEXT

Chapter 3 has examined the fact that, for more than half a century, Indonesia has been unable to conduct an uninterrupted dialogue concerning the position of *shari'a* in the Constitution. In 1945 and 1955, efforts were hampered by the pressure of time, and the political manoeuvrings by Soekarno and the military. Under Soeharto, debate was forbidden since his government was afraid of its disruptive potential. There was a worry that such discussion on Article 29 in the post-Soeharto era would persuade some elites, particularly the military and the government, to use an unconstitutional way to end the debate, as had happened in the past. However, it is essential to note that the debate during 1999–2002, as part of constitutional process, went smoothly. There was no voting, no presidential decree to dismiss the Parliament, no military force and no imprisonment for Muslim leaders.

However, it is misleading to say that there was no hot debate. In fact, debate and discussion on Article 29 took place inside and outside Parliament during the 1999–2002 constitutional reform period. It was clearly a sensitive issue, which invited comment from diverse voices in Indonesian society. For instance, the Islam Defence Front (FPI) mobilized thousands of its supporters outside the Parliament building. They demanded the 1945 stipulation on Islamic law be included in any constitutional amendment.[24] In addition, the First Indonesian Mujahidin Congress of November 2000 called for the inclusion of the Jakarta Charter in the Constitution and for *shari'a* to be applied as state law.[25] Some went even further. The periodical *Tempo* reported on student cells in the Bogor Agricultural Institute (IPB) and the Bandung Institute of Technology (ITB). These two leading Indonesian state universities had sworn oaths of allegiance to the Proclamation of the Islamic State of Indonesia, which was declared in 1948 by Kartosurwiryo, the leader of the Darul Islam rebellion. These student cells declared the Soekarno-Hatta declaration of an independent republic in August 1945 as null and void.[26]

Within Parliament, political parties PPP and PBB lodged their formal proposal to amend Article 29 by reinserting *shari'a* into the Constitution. Both parties had small number of seats in the Parliament. If the PBB votes are combined with those for the PPP, the pro-formal *shari'a* group total vote rises to 12 per cent (71 seats). The two biggest Islamic organizations in Indonesia, Nahdlatul Ulama (NU) and Muhammadiyah (then part of the Masyumi Party), which pushed for an Islamic state in 1955, have departed from their 1955 position as they no longer share the agenda of formally adopting *shari'a* into the Constitution.

Hasyim Muzadi of NU argues that fighting for *shari'a* to be enforced in Indonesia is not realistic. He urges the need to develop universal values for the people's prosperity instead of pushing the idea for *shari'a*.[27] According to Syafi'i Ma'arif of Muhammadiyah, the Laskar Jihad (Jihad Warriors) in Solo felt disappointed with the Muhammadiyah for not supporting the restoration of the Jakarta Charter in Article 29. Some Muslim hardliners allege that the NU and Muhammadiyah are no longer Islamic, or are no longer articulating Muslim aspirations. Ma'arif was reported to have said: "I believe that many people within our (NU and Muhammadiyah) community will condemn our stance, but I have warned them that we must be committed to promoting unity, which our founding fathers declared when establishing this nation."[28]

Both NU and Muhammadiyah leaders assert that even without formal acceptance of *shari'a* in the Constitution, Muslims' demands can be met by the state. In the words of Anies Rasyid Baswedan, "the focus is no longer on how to bring Islam into the foundation of the State, but how to bring Islamic coloration into policies produced by the State."[29] This departure shows that the two Islamic organizations have used the substantive *shari'a* approach. In Parliament, the PKB with 51 seats and PAN with 35 seats, which have close connections with the NU and Muhammadiyah, respectively, rejected the proposal to include *shari'a* in Article 29.

With a combined total of only 71 seats, it was understood that the PPP and PBB did not want members of the MPR to vote on their proposal. In committee meetings, other political parties and appointed police, military and functional representatives who together held a majority of seats in the MPR, rejected proposals to amend the Constitution to include *shari'a* and, therefore, the measure never came to a formal vote. Yusril Ihza Mahendra, General Chairman of the PBB, argued that the truth (i.e., *shari'a*) cannot be subject to voting.[30] Lukman Hakim Saifuddin also stated that they were aware that their struggle would not succeed at that time, but they would reopen the debate in the future. That is the reason behind their decline for a formal vote as it could hamper their efforts to bring up the proposal of the amendment in future.[31]

According to Mutammimul Ula of the PK, it would take fifty to seventy years to reopen the debate. He refers to the very fact that it had taken more than fifty years (1945–2000) to initiate the discussion on Article 29 in a constitutional way. Ula also asserts that unless Islamic political parties gain two-thirds of the parliamentary seats, as a requisite to changing the Constitution, the issue would never be brought up again. According to Ula, Islamic political parties could win majority support only in the next fifty to seventy years.[32] In the words of Hamdan Zoelva, "our party has proposed to include *shari'a* in Article 29. We have to stop our struggle due to limited support from other members of the MPR, but the idea is still there, and we will never withdraw our proposal. In terms of constitutional debate, this is not the end of our struggle."[33]

When we met in December 2003, Zoelva also promised to use the issue of Article 29 as the PBB's political campaign during the 2004 general election. As has been mentioned earlier, in 1955 the supporters of the Jakarta Charter obtained 40 per cent of the seats. However, in 1999, the proponents of the inclusion of *shari'a* in the 1945 Constitution won only 12 per cent, a 28 per cent decline since 1955. The results of the recent 2004 general election show that the PPP has won 8.2 per cent of the votes and PBB only 2.6 per cent.[34] This means that both parties have 10.8 per cent (see Table 6.1), a slight decrease from 12 per cent in 1999. This result shows that almost 90 per cent

TABLE 6.1
Indonesia 2004 National Legislative Election Results

Party (in order of seats won)	National Vote (%)	DPR Seats
Golkar	21.6	128
Indonesian Democracy Party-Struggle (PDI-P)	18.5	109
Development Unity Party (PPP)	8.2	58
Democrat Party (PD)	7.5	57
National Awakening Party (PKB)	10.6	52
National Mandate Party (PAN)	6.4	52
Prosperous Justice Party (PKS)	7.3	45
Reform Star Party (PBR)	2.4	13
Prosperous Peace Party (PDS)	2.1	12
Star and Crescent Party (PBB)	2.6	11
Nationhood Democracy Unity Party (PPDK)	1.2	5
Concern for the Nation Functional Party (PKPB)	2.1	2
Pioneer Party	0.8	2
Indonesian Unity and Justice Party (PKPI)	1.3	1
Freedom Bull National Party (PNBK)	1.1	1
Marhaenisme Indonesian National Party (PNIM)	0.8	1
Indonesian Democratic Upholder Party (PPDI)	0.8	1
Pancasila Patriot Party	0.9	0
Indonesian NU Unity Party (PPNUI)	0.8	0
Freedom Party	0.7	0
United Indonesia Party (PSI)	0.6	0
New Indonesia Alliance Party (PPIB)	0.6	0
Regional Unity Party (PPD)	0.6	0
Democratic Socialist Labor Party (PBSD)	0.6	0

of Indonesian people are not in favour of the PBB's and PPP's campaigns to implement *shari'a* at the state level.

ARTICLE 29 IN QUESTION

Chapter 3 examined the fact that during the Soeharto regime, the Government prohibited all advocacy of an Islamic state. With the loosening of restrictions on freedom of speech and religion, following the fall of Soeharto in May 1998, proponents of the Jakarta Charter resumed their advocacy efforts. This section will focus on constitutional debate regarding Article 29 during the MPR session. Firstly, I will discuss the arguments put forth by several Islamic political parties, which proposed the amendment of Article 29. Then, the counter-arguments against the amendment of Article 29 will be discussed.

There were four opinions prevalent in this issue. There was a group that proposed the reinsertion of the famous seven words; another group suggested modifying Article 29 by mentioning not only Islam but also all religions; others tended to believe that all five pillars in Pancasila should be added to Article 29, not only the first pillar; and, finally, the majority members of parliament took the view that Article 29 should remain unamended.

Arguments to Amend Article 29

The main argument for reinserting the famous seven words (see Table 6.2, alternative 2) was that since Muslims have accepted a Pancasila state — and this could be seen as "the greatest gift and sacrifice of the humble Indonesian

TABLE 6.2
List of Alternatives for Article 29

Alternative 1	The state is based on Belief in One Almighty God.
Alternative 2	The state is based on Belief in One Almighty God with the obligation upon the followers of Islam to carry out Islamic law.
Alternative 3	The state is based on Belief in One Almighty God with the obligation upon the followers of each religion to carry out its religious teachings.
Alternative 4	The state is based on Belief in One Almighty God, Just and Civilised Humanitarianism, the Unity of Indonesia, Democracy Guided by the Wisdom of Representative Deliberation, and Social Justice for all Indonesians.

Muslims as a majority population for the sake of Indonesian national unity and integrity"[35] — Muslims should ask for "compensation"; and that the Constitution guarantees the implementation of Islamic law as part of their freedom to exercise religion. This means that the PPP and PBB, which proposed introducing *shari'a*, were not asking for Indonesia to establish an Islamic state. What they wanted was only the implementation of Islamic law for Muslims.[36]

This proposal invites several important questions: First, after Islamic law has been fully implemented, what is the difference in features between an Islamic state and the Pancasila state? Second, a number of questions relating to Islamic law also appear: what do they mean by "*shari'a*"? Does it mean the inclusion of *hudud*? Will Islamic law become one of the sources of Indonesian law, which would change the Indonesian legal system dramatically? Third, it is also important to note that without the existence of the famous seven words, the government has accommodated Muslim aspirations, for instance, by issuing several laws and regulations on Muslim affairs. If they want another regulation or statute in order to support their practising of Islam as a way of life, Muslims or Muslim parties can propose such bills through Parliament, as has been done on several occasions. Why is it necessary to amend Article 29 when Islam can be practised freely? I will examine these issues in detail in the next sections.

Implementing Islamic Law, or Establishing an Islamic State

By presenting the argument that Islamic political parties do not want to establish an Islamic state and ask only for the right to practise Islamic law, the positions of both the PPP and PBB led to the assumption that *shari'a* is not the important ingredient of an Islamic state. This assumption will be examined by analysing Islamic literature. I assert that the assumption is false since Islamic literature shows that, for the proponents of an Islamic state, the test of whether the state can be called Islamic or not is whether *shari'a* is fully enforced or another body of law is in operation. This issue is far more complex than that suggested by the Islamic political parties.

As stated in Chapter 2, the definition of what constitutes an Islamic state is debatable. In Asghar Ali Engineer's words, "There is no fixed concept of an Islamic state."[37] To put it differently, Muslim scholars have not reached an agreement regarding the concept of what is an Islamic state and what is a non-Islamic state. However, for proponents of an Islamic state, it is important to divide the world into at least two divisions: the territory of Islam (*dar al-Islam*) and the territory of unbelievers (*dar al-Kufr*), known also as the territory of war (*dar al-Harb*).[38]

What then are the main elements that distinguish the differences between the two worlds? Abu Yusuf (d. 182 AH/798 AD) took the view that if *shari'a* is enforced, the territory becomes *dar al-Islam*.[39] Muhammad al-Shaybani (d. 189 AH/805 AD) also stated that once a *dar al-Islam* replaced Islamic law with foreign law, it could no longer be considered an Islamic state.[40] These opinions are based on the fact that Islamic law is an essential part of Islamic faith. Accordingly, Islam encompasses all domains, including law and the state, and that the state and the religious community are one and the same.

Habib Rizieq Shihab, the leader of Front Pembela Islam (FPI, or Islamic Defence Front) has stated clearly that "if *shari'a* is enforced, then Indonesia will become an Islamic state automatically, whether you want to call it the 'Islamic Republic of Indonesia' or maintain the title 'Republic of Indonesia', is not a problem."[41] Accordingly, submission to the rule of Islam necessitates the existence of the Islamic state. If that is the case, then enforcing *shari'a* in a formal way, as proposed by some Islamic political parties during constitutional debate in 1999–2002, could be suspected of being a "bridge" in the planned establishment of an Islamic state.

In the context of enforcing Islamic law, *shari'a* can be split into five levels: personal status (marriage, divorce); economic matters (banking); proscribing practices seen as unIslamic (alcohol consumption, gambling, inappropriate dress); criminal law; and as a guide for government matters.[42] Was the proposal to amend Article 29 by reinserting the implementation of *shari'a* related to all of these levels?

Muslims tend to agree on certain basic premises about the nature of *shari'a*. They agree that *shari'a* is the sum total of God's normative categorizations of human acts. God has placed every conceivable act into one of five ethico-legal categories: obligatory (*wajib*), recommended (*mandub*), permissible (*mubah*), reprehensible (*makruh*), and forbidden (*haram*). Muslims must strive to determine what acts fit into what categories and to live their life accordingly. However, as has been discussed in Chapter 2, these basic points of agreement quickly give way to innumerable disagreements. Islamic scholars disagree as to the appropriate way to analyse the Qur'an and the traditions of the Prophet in order to discover the rules of *shari'a*. They thus group themselves into competing schools, defined by their different methods of deriving rules from the dictates of the Qur'an and the example of the Prophet. Because they use different ways of deriving and expanding God's law, the competing schools ultimately ended up with different rules and regulations. Each champions its own rules as the true rules of *shari'a*. Therefore, the question is: What do proponents of this proposal mean by *shari'a*?

Which *Shari'a*?

In contradiction to the five legal spheres explained above, Lukman Hakim Saifuddin of the PPP explains that there are three levels of *shari'a*. Firstly, *shari'a* as universal values in relation to justice, humanity and equality. *Shari'a* in this meaning should be implemented for all people. Secondly, *shari'a* as special regulations for all Muslims, such as pilgrimage and charity. Non-Muslims will not be the subject of these regulation. Thirdly, *shari'a* that is interpreted and practised differently by various schools of thought (*madhahib*). He mentions the wearing of the veil (*jilbab* or *tudung*) and implementing hudud as examples of the third level, which is subject to controversy even among Muslims themselves.

According to him, like other parties, the PPP is always striving for the first meaning of *shari'a* (i.e., universal values). He also asserts that the PPP will not ask for the implementation of *shari'a* at the third level since not all Muslims agree with it. The proposal to amend Article 29 is aimed at guaranteeing the implementation of *shari'a* up to the second level.

However, when asked if it is correct that even without reinserting the famous seven words, Indonesian Muslims have enjoyed special regulations on Islamic law, Saifuddin admitted this was correct. However, he quickly stated that "this [constitutional debate] is our momentum to reopen the matters which were prohibited [to be discussed] by Soeharto. We do not want to miss this opportunity since our supporters want to see us delivering their aspirations, and who knows, if Allah wills it, we would succeed [in amending the article]."[43] In asking the question, I was referring to the fact that Indonesia already has a *shari'a* judicial system, based on Law No. 7 of 1989, operating through a network of Religious Courts (Pengadilan Agama), which has jurisdiction in marriage, divorce, inheritance and *waqf* (religious endowment). This answer shows that, for politicians, there is always an opportunity to show their commitment to supporters.

Hamdan Zoelva of the PBB gives more clarification. According to him, although several regulations on Islamic matters have been implemented, particularly during the later period of the Soeharto government and also during the Habibie government, there is no guarantee that the next government and Parliament would not abandon such regulations. Statutes can easily be replaced by other statutes. This explains why a constitutional guarantee is necessary.[44]

When I asked Zoelva if "is it right that Article 29(2) already guarantees that everyone is free to exercise his/her own faith?", he replied, "It is not enough! What we need is a clear provision that there is an obligation for the state to give Muslims their right to observe Islamic law."[45] This statement would invite questions on rights to observe other religious law. When the right to freedom of religion or belief is mentioned, the first thing that comes to mind is the right of individuals to act in accordance with conscientious beliefs, to worship freely, and to be able to enjoy life in society without discrimination on the basis of such beliefs. However, if the Constitution discriminates one religion over others, it will invite problem of inequality.

Equality

Equality may mean identical treatment for everyone. The simplest version of this concept forbids laws from excluding anyone, or drawing any distinctions between people. Therefore, the Constitution should protect minority groups and individuals. It goes further that the Constitution should not be interpreted by majoritarian institutions, such as the legislature. Since judges at the Constitutional Court (Mahkamah Konstitusi) are not elected and are not accountable through the elections, they are best able at interpreting the Constitution in a way that will protect minorities. Accordingly, the principles of equality and protecting minority rights will be tainted if Article 29 is amended by mentioning Islamic law.[46] What about other religions?

It is in this context that the PKB,[47] PAN and PKS proposed this alternative to Article 29: "The state is based on Belief in One Almighty God with the obligation upon the followers of each religion to carry out its religious teachings" (alternative 3 in Table 6.2). These parties believe that this version will satisfy all groups. T. B. Soemandjaja of the PK (Justice Party), for example, highlighted that this proposal would suit the plural society of Indonesia.[48] According to Hidayat Nur Wahid, President of the PK, instead of proposing the reintroduction of the famous seven words of the Jakarta Charter, his party refers to the Medina Charter, which was created by the Prophet along with the Jewish community.[49]

The Medina Charter declared all Muslim and Jewish tribes of Medina to be one community. At the same time, each tribe retained its identity, customs and internal relations. Among the rights protected was the right to freedom of religion.[50] Another reason to refer back to the Medina Charter rather than to the Jakarta Charter is provided by Mutammimul Ula, one of the leaders of the PK. He stated firmly that his small party was trying to avoid the sentiment or feeling of the Jakarta Charter owing to its connection to the historical and political context of the past. In essence, he said, like the Jakarta Charter, the Medina Charter also enforces Islamic law, since the charter stipulated that: "In case of any dispute or controversy, which may result in trouble, the matter must be referred to Allah and Muhammad." He then admitted that by proposing the Medina Charter his party was able to avoid a dilemma. On the one hand, the national political atmosphere did not support the inclusion of the Jakarta Charter, and on the other hand, the PK constituents support the enforcing of Islamic law through the amendment of Article 29.[51]

If other political elites and military did not want to use words from the Jakarta Charter, then why did the PPP and PBB not try to find other words? I posed this question to Saifuddin. His reply was: "the famous seven words represent a symbolic defeat of the Muslim struggle in Indonesian history to enforce Islamic law. And it is also important to borrow the famous seven words of the Jakarta Charter, since the Presidential Decree of 5 July 1959 stipulates that the Jakarta Charter inspires the 1945 Constitution."[52] In order to ensure "victory" of the history, it seems that Saifuddin's party (PPP) wanted to step forward from treating Jakarta Charter as an "inspiration" to put the Jakarta Charter in the body of the Constitution (i.e., Article 29).

Zoelva provides other interesting arguments. He takes the view that his party did not want to adopt the varient, "The state is based on Belief in One Almighty God with the obligation upon the followers of each religion to carry out its religious teachings" (alternative 3 in Table 6.2), since his party believes that only Islam has a holy law. Other religions do not have special laws; they only provide ethics and theology. He added further, "this is the reason why other religions will also reject Alternative 3, since they are aware that this alternative is a sneaky way. We do not want to use ambiguous language. We want the famous seven words back into the 1945 Constitution."[53]

Zoelva's statement may be questioned on at least four grounds. Firstly, it is not entirely true that other religions do not have their own sacred laws. For instance, the juridical law of the Roman Catholic Church is Canon Law, which is the body of laws and regulations made by, or adopted by, ecclesiastical authority.[54] Canon Law is not a moral code. It is the administrative, civil, jurisdictional, procedural and penal law of the Catholic Church. In addition, Patrick Glenn also showed that the Hindu religion has its own legal tradition. Hindu law is a body of rules, customs and usages guiding the beliefs and ways of life of the Hindus. There are two schools of thought about Hindu law, namely Dayabhaga and Mitaksara. The Dayabhaga, a treatise on the inheritance and succession, based mainly on the Yajnavalkya-smrti, is believed to have been written sometime after the eleventh to thirteenth centuries by Jimutavahana. On the other hand, the Mitaksara, written by Vajnanesvara (eleventh century), seems to be an elaborate commentary on the Yajnavalkya-smrti. On matters relating to inheritance and succession, the Dayabhaga was used extensively as an authority in Bengal.[55]

Secondly, the rejection by other political parties of Alternative 3 is owing to the fact that it is redundant. Article 29(2) has already guaranteed freedom of religion, and therefore there would be a repetition once alternative 3 of Article 29(1) was adopted. It is for the same reason that alternative 4, which borrowed all of the pillars of Pancasila, was rejected. From both technical and legal viewpoints, such repetition should be avoided. Thirdly, another reason for the rejection of alternative 3 by other parties is to avoid losing in the voting game, since too many alternatives would break up the votes, and it would be possible that the proposal to insert the seven words of the Jakarta Charter would succeed. Therefore, they chose to keep the original Article 29, and reject *any* alternative to modify it.[56]

Fourthly, Christian scholars reject alternative 3, since they do not want the state to be involved in religious affairs. Their faith cannot, and should not, be regulated by the Constitution, as this would lead to the politicization of religion. T. B. Simatupang, a Protestant scholar, stated clearly that "there is nothing in the Pancasila that is in contradiction with the Christian faith."[57] On the relationship between the Church and the state in Indonesia, Eka Darmaputera, another Protestant scholar, takes the view that "*ada pemisahan tapi tidak ada keterpisahan*" (there is separation but not division).[58] Therefore, he believes that:

> Once religion allows itself to be co-opted by a certain political power, it will instantly lose its transcendental character. And the society will lose the opportunity to enjoy the very characteristic contribution only religion could give, i.e. its transcending-critical engagement. At the same time, when politics allows itself to become merely a tool of certain religious interests, it will also immediately lose its most noble function, namely to protect the well-being of all its citizens, without discrimination. Both the politicization of religion and the religionization of politics are actually suicidal, for all the parties concerned.[59]

However, Darmaputera does not suggest strict separation of religion and the state. He believes that there is always a religious character to the state and a political dimension to religion. Every person is simultaneously a religious and a political creature. To put it differently, although religion and the state should not be united in institutional terms, religion is inseparable from politics in terms of the involvement of society (including the Church) in public affairs. In this sense, Darmaputera asserts that the Pancasila state is the only viable alternative if Indonesia is to maintain its unity and pluralistic character.[60] In other words, Darmaputera rejects the proposal to establish an Islamic state. To him, Indonesia is a multi-religious state.

Frans Magnis Suseno, an Indonesian Catholic scholar, has similar views. He rejects a secular state as well as a religious state. He explains that:

> Though there are differences between Islam and Christianity, in terms of religious tasks towards people's life, basically, as far as I see, they both agree that religious life could not be restricted to mosque or church buildings, nor limited to Fridays or Sundays, but should also be extended to all aspects of man's life. Christians are also Christians when they get involved in economics, and Muslims would not leave their faith when they participate in politics.[61]

In short, the Pancasila-based state is a place where no religion in Indonesia wins, and no one loses. It is a win-win solution for all religions. On one hand, it is a state where religious life is supported and advanced and, thus, it is not secular. On the other hand, religion is not directed at other faiths coercively and, thus, it is not a religious state either. He claims that Pancasila values not only do not oppose but indeed harmonize with the Christian faith.[62] This does not imply that the Church's participation in Indonesia would lead to the establishment of a Catholic or a Protestant country.[63]

Non-Muslims as Second-Class Citizens

The fear of non-Muslims over their status under *shari'a* can be understood by looking at the concept of *dhimmi* (non-Muslims under Muslim rule). Non-Muslims tend to stress the inequality of non-Muslim residents as citizens of secondary rank under the term *dhimmi*, whereas Muslims emphasize the tolerance of Islam. Muslims, for instance, point out to the fact that Islamic law allows non-Muslim communities living under Islamic rule to be entitled to legislative and judicial autonomy, with regard to their religious and personal-status affairs. Al-Shaybani explains that the Christians as *dhimmi* have all the freedom to trade in wine and pork in their towns freely, even though such practice is considered immoral and illegal among Muslims. However, *dhimmi* were prohibited from doing the same in towns and villages controlled by Muslims.[64] Al-Mawardi recognizes the right of *dhimmi* to hold public office, including the office of judge and minister.[65]

To put it differently, *dhimmi*, who included monotheists such as Jews and Christians but not pagans, were allowed to practise their religions and follow their own community laws, as long as they accepted a politically subordinate, tributary status. Karen Armstrong points out: "In the Islamic empire, Jews,

Christians and Zoroastrians enjoyed religious freedom. This reflected the teachings of the Qur'an which is a pluralistic scripture, affirmative of other traditions. Muslims are commanded by God to respect the People of the Book, and reminded that they share the same belief and the same God."[66]

However, under Islamic rule, non-Muslims cannot be appointed as caliph nor president. Under formal *shari'a* approach, it seems that the value of non-Muslims' leadership skills and other qualities is seen as less than that of Muslims, by the suggestion being made that a person's righteousness can create a basis for unequal treatment. The *dhimmi* are freed of military obligation and *zakat*, but have to pay *jizyah* (tax) to guarantee their loyalty towards the country and the Islamic government protecting their security.

Nowadays, many liberal Muslims, such as Fahmi Huwaydi who adopt a substantive *shari'a* approach, suggest that a differentiation based on faith only applies when standing individually before God, and forms no basis for any civil inequities. They rejected the *dhimmi* classification of non-Muslims as a historically bound concept.[67] Modern states have been established by the joint struggle of both Muslims and non-Muslims. The imposition of *jizyah* has therefore become irrelevant and impractical. In fact, Islam makes no difference between Muslims and non-Muslims, as stipulated in the Qur'an.[68]

If Indonesia enforces *shari'a*, non-Muslims are afraid that the concept of *dhimmi* would be applied to them. Although Muslims claim that such fear is unjustified, it is essential to note that by modern standards of citizenship and rights, this *dhimmi* minority status would now be a form of second-class citizenship. It is against the notion of equality before the law.

State Law

I asked Zoelva whether the legal consequences of modifying Article 29, on the basis of his party's proposal, would lead to *shari'a* being one of the sources or, indeed, the primary source of law, as is the case in Egypt. While admitting his lack of knowledge as to what applies in Egypt, he asserts that there would be a shifting of position from the current position, that "any law should not contradict with Islamic teachings" to the new position, and that "Islamic law becomes one of the sources of any law in Indonesia".[69] This new feature would change the face of Indonesian law significantly.

According to MPR Decree No. III/MPR/2000, on Sources of Law and the Hierarchical Order of Legislative Rules, sources of Indonesian law are:

a. 1945 Constitution;
b. MPR Decree;

c. Law (Undang-Undang);
d. Government Regulation in Lieu of a Law (Perpu);
e. Government Regulation;
f. Presidential Decree; and
g. Regional Regulation.

As can be seen from the above list, there is no special place for Islamic law to become the primary source nor even a source of law. Zoelva did not reject the possibility that the list would be modified by mentioning *shari'a*, if Article 29 was amended. Perhaps not only would there be a judicial review to examine the existing laws that do not refer to *shari'a* or those in contradiction with it, such as criminal law and *hudud*, but more laws and regulations pertaining to Muslims' daily affairs could be introduced.

Before speculating further on what would happen if Article 29 were amended, the experience of Egypt should be taken into account. In 1980, the Egyptian Government decided to amend the Egyptian Constitution in order to make *shari'a* "the principle source of Egyptian legislation". The wording of Article 2 of the Constitution was thus changed from *"mabadi' al-shari'a al-Islamiyya masdar ra'isi li al-tashr"* (the principles of the Islamic *shari'a* are *a* principal source of legislation) to the more forceful statement, *"mabadi' al-shari'a al-Islamiyya al-masdar al-ra'isi li al-tashr"* (the principles of the Islamic *shari'a* are *the* principal source of legislation). The Supreme Constitutional Court of Egypt has interpreted this clause to mean that all future legislation respects a number of broad principles, which it identifies as the "universals" or "fundamental principles" of *shari'a*. These principles, the Court says, are mentioned in the sacred texts of Islam and have always been accepted as essential premises of Islamic law, although they have been applied differently in different places to come up with Islamic laws appropriate to their particular time and place.[70]

Legislation must not contradict the general spirit of *shari'a*. One of the most important fundamental principles of the law is the principle that no law should create hardship (*mashaqqa*) for people.[71] The implication of the Court's interpretation is that: any law that respects all of the broad, universal and fundamental principles of *shari'a* is acceptable as Islamic law. One may argue that despite the formal approach taken by the 1980 amendment, the Supreme Constitutional Court (SCC) interprets Article 2 in a substantive way.[72]

This ambiguous position seems to explain that the Court does not have much choice in terms of both political and legal tensions. The Egyptian Government must prevent fundamentalist groups taking Article 2 as their legal basis for "Shari'a-ization" of Egypt.[73] On the other hand, as Lombardi has pointed out, the SCC must come up with a way to recognize the higher principles of Islamic law that are suitable for the accommodation of "modern notions of human rights and modern economic institutions".[74]

In this sense, there is also some speculation that the proposal from the PPP and the PBB to reinsert the seven words from the Jakarta Charter would turn *shari'a* into state law. In this regard, Khaled Abou El-Fadl makes an important statement:

> the law of the state, regardless of its origins or basis, belongs to the state. Under this conception, no religious laws can or may be enforced by the state. All laws articulated and applied in a state are thoroughly human and should be treated as such. These laws are a part of Shari'ah law only to the extent that any set of human legal opinions can be said to be a part of Shari'ah. A code, even if inspired by Shari'ah, is not Shari'ah.[75]

As can be seen, there are two interesting views here: the SCC of Egypt asserts that any law that respects all the broad, universal and fundamental principles of *shari'a* is acceptable, and treated as Islamic law, whilst El-Fadl argues that a law which is inspired by *shari'a* should not be claimed as being part of *shari'a*. These two views reflect two sides of the same coin. For liberal Muslims, any law that confirms the universal aspect of *shari'a* is as Islamic as *shari'a* itself, and therefore, there is no need to Islamicize such laws. For non-Muslims, any law that is enforced by the state cannot be treated as Islamic law, even when such law is inspired by *shari'a*.

The first view is based on the theory of public utility.[76] It extrapolates from the principles a putative social goal. This theory is now manifested in the expansive doctrine of government discretion. From about the eleventh century, Islamic jurisprudence came to accept the idea of *al-siyasa al-shar'iyya*, which accords the terrestrial ruler a reservoir of discretionary power of command, in the public interest. If deviations from the strict *shari'a* doctrine were required to protect the public interest in implementing the guiding principles behind the *shari'a*, then such deviations were allowed.[77]

The theory of public utility in the Islamic legal system is based on the notion of *maqasid al-shari'a* (the objectives of Islamic Law).[78] Securing benefit and preventing harm in this life and in the Hereafter is the intent of *shari'a*. This consideration is an extremely important factor for jurists in contemporary Islamic world. Under this theory, the flexibility of Islamic law is secured. For instance, according to this approach, *daruriyyat* (essentials or necessities), changes of condition, and *maslahah al-ammah* (public interest) allow the adoption of measures that are normally and textually disallowed.[79]

The second view, which is supported by El-Fadl, is based on the rejection of theocratic concept. El-Fadl believes that Islam is compatible with democracy. He explains that:

> According to this paradigm, democracy is an appropriate system for Islam, because it both expresses the special worth of human beings — the status of vice-regency — and at the same time deprives the state of any pretense of divinity, by locating ultimate authority in the hands of the people, rather than the *ulama*.[80]

It seems that he is afraid that the claim, wherein any law which is not against the fundamental principle of *shari'a* will be seen as Islamic law, will lead to the divinity of such laws. To him, state law is processed and enforced through state mechanisms and, therefore, belongs to the state and cannot be claimed as belonging to the divine law, despite the fact that any state law should consider values (including Islamic ones) in society. El-Fadl's argument seems to confirm the idea of public religion at the civil society level; not the state level, as proposed, for instance, by Casanova.[81] This distinction is useful in terms of employing the middle position of secularism and the unity of Faith-State. Religion plays its role in public life in society.

Civil society is the sum of political, economic, social and cultural institutions, which act, each within its own field independently of the state, to achieve a variety of purposes. These include political purposes, such as participating in decision-making at national level, an example of which is the activity in which political parties engage. Civil society is based on voluntary participation, whereas the state is based on coercion. Society consists of a wide variety of orders, such as the family, the economy, religion, and non-governmental organizations (NGOs). All these elements have interests in influencing and contributing to any law or bill, drafted and discussed in parliamentary meetings, which will affect them either as individuals or as parts of society. Civil society is believed to contribute to democratic consolidation as it assists in bridging the gap between democratic government and citizen.

In this context, Robert Hefner has coined the term "civil pluralist" Muslims.[82] He explains that:

> Civil pluralist Muslims deny the necessity of a formally established Islamic state, emphasize that it is the spirit and not the letter of Islamic law (*shariah*) to which Muslims must attend, stresses the need for programmes to elevate the status of women, and insists that the Muslim world's most urgent task is to develop moral tools to respond to the challenge of modern pluralism.[83]

The proposal to include *shari'a* in the Constitution would put religion's role at state level. I will examine this issue by looking at the famous seven words. If the phrase is adopted, who has the obligation to observe *shari'a*: the state, or Muslim society? If the legal consequence of adopting the phrase is to put an obligation on the state to implement *shari'a*, then the phrase will be seen as breaking the "third" position discussed earlier, that Indonesia is neither a secular nor a religious state.

Whose Obligation?

Apart from the problem of having *shari'a* as a source of law, there is also the problem with the word "obligation" (*kewajiban*) from the phrase "*dengan kewajiban menjalankan syariat Islam bagi pemeluknya*" (with the obligation to carry out Islamic *shari'a* for its adherents). What does this word "*kewajiban*" mean? The obligation for Muslims to practise Islamic teachings comes from God, not from the state. It is essential to note that, whether the phrase is included in the Constitution or not, Muslims are obliged by God to follow His rules. Constitutionally speaking, by adopting this phrase, the state must ensure that every Muslims practises his/her religion. If Muslims do not practise it, the state may punish them. Again, one should note that the state is based on coercion, while civil society is based on voluntary participation. For instance, can the state punish those who do not fast in Ramadan or do not perform the five daily prayers?

Zoelva explains that it is true that the obligation comes from God, not from the state. However, according to him, there are some areas in *shari'a* that need the involvement of the state. Under the current form of Article 29, such involvement is voluntary. The seven words above would place the state under a "constitutional obligation" to facilitate Muslims practising their faith. This suggests that the word "obligation" refers to the government.[84]

If that is the case, I argue that the phrase "*dengan kewajiban menjalankan syariat Islam bagi pemeluknya*" is vague. Zoelva's explanation is not convincing since the phrase does not state clearly that it is the state that has an obligation to implement Islamic law. In the words of M. B. Hooker, "While the [Jakarta] Charter specifically refers to *shari'a*, it is vague as to its exact scope and competence, leaving much room for debate over its jurisdiction."[85] In addition, the government has already facilitated Muslims (and other religions) in the practice of their beliefs, by establishing the Ministry of Religious Affairs. Each year the government facilitates Muslims in performing the pilgrimage to Mecca. The government has also established the Religious Courts, and some Muslim holidays are celebrated as national holidays (the

Ascension of the Prophet, Idul Fitri, Idul Adha, the Muslim New Year, and the Prophet's Birthday). These facilities are given under the current version of Article 29.

CONCLUSION

I have shown in this chapter that the dispute over the meaning of the phrase *"dengan kewajiban menjalankan syariat Islam bagi pemeluknya"* centred on three crucial interpretive questions: *shari'a*, the obligation, and the legal consequences of the Islamization of the sources of Indonesian law. Apart from the meaning of the phrase, I have also examined some objections to the proposal to include *shari'a* in Article 29, such that the full implementation of formal *shari'a* will lead to the establishment of an Islamic state, which will possibly lead to inequality among Indonesian citizens. I have also examined other alternatives to modify Article 29 and reasons for their rejection.

It is unfortunate that the PPP and PBB did not learn from the Egyptian experience. It would be more reasonable if these two Islamic parties, using the formal approach to *shari'a*, proposed to modify Article 29 by stating that *shari'a* is one of the sources of Indonesian law. They did not have to propose *shari'a* as the primary source. It is sufficient to suggest *shari'a* as one of the sources, along with other sources. They might argue that Dutch law, *adat* law, and Islamic law are the three components of Indonesian national law. Although there would still be no guarantee that this proposal would be accepted by other parties, at least in terms of comparative constitutional law, the Egyptian model, prior to the 1980 Amendment, could be worthy of consideration. In this sense, from the formal *shari'a* approach point of view, the aim and the target of modifying Article 29 would be much clearer: to recognize *shari'a* as one of the sources of law.

To clarify, I am not suggesting that Indonesia should adopt Article 2 of the Egyptian Constitution (either before or after the 1980 amendment) as a replacement for Article 29 of the 1945 Constitution. I have only shown that there is an alternative for the PPP and PBB instead of insisting on the use of the phrase from the Jakarta Charter, to propose the inclusion of *shari'a* in the Constitution.

I take the view that one of the main reasons for the PPP and PBB to push for the adoption of the famous seven words was the historical symbolic meaning of this phrase. I have earlier quoted Saifuddin's statement, which confirms this view. It should be remembered that many Muslim leaders in 1945 were not happy with the last-minute removal of these seven words. This historical context stayed on for so long in the memory of Muslims activists as to make their position inflexible, as articulated by the PPP and PBB during 1999–2002. They were not ready to find other alternative words or sentences. It seems that they wanted to achieve two main targets simultaneously: implementation of *shari'a*, and "revenge" for their 1945 defeat. I have demonstrated in this chapter the rigidity of the PPP and PBB in insisting on using the phrase from the Jakarta Charter. This has made them ignore the vagueness of the phrase and uncritically accept the famous seven words.

The historical context of Article 29 also led both the PPP and PBB to depart from the substantive *shari'a* approach and adopt the formal *shari'a* approach. As has been discussed in other chapters, Islamic political parties, including the PPP and PBB, have used the substantive approach when discussing human rights protection and the rule of law. However, whilst other Islamic parties have used a consistently substantive approach, the PBB and PPP moved to examine Article 29 using the formal concept of *shari'a*. Such a formal approach was rejected.

It is also worth noting that by not modifying Article 29 of the 1945 Constitution, the Indonesian Parliament rejects secularization, which would see the privatization or the decline of religion. Indonesia still stands in — borrowing Hollenbach's term — the third alternative, in which "religious communities can have an impact on public life",[86] while at the same time, the role of religion in public life does not imply that all political institutions are under the control of religion, as in a theocratic system. Under Article 29 of the 1945 Constitution, religion can play its public role at society level. This once again proves that Indonesia is neither a secular nor an Islamic state.

Notes

1. The amount of literature on this issue is staggering. For instances, see Robin Gill, "The Future of Religious Participation and Belief in Britain and Beyond", in *The Blackwell Companion to Sociology of Religion*, edited by Richard K. Fenn (Oxford, U.K.; Malden, MA: Blackwell Publishers, 2001); Darren E. Sherkat and Christopher G. Ellison, "Recent Developments and Controversies in the Sociology of Religion", *Annual Review of Sociology* 25 (1999): 363; Dwight B. Billings and Shaunna L. Scott, "Religion and Political Legitimacy", *Annual Review of Sociology* 20 (1994): 173; Steve Bruce, *Religion and Modernization: Sociologists and Historians Debate the Secularization Thesis* (Oxford: Clarendon Press, 1992).
2. Ira Lapidus, "State and Religion in Islamic Societies", *Past and Present* 151 (1996): 3.
3. Jose Casanova, *Public Religions in the Modern World* (Chicago: University of Chicago Press, 1994), p. 215.

4. Mark Juergensmeyer, *The New Cold War? Religious Nationalism Confronts the Secular State* (Berkeley and Los Angeles: University of California Press, 1993), p. 4. More discussion can be found in Hugh Heclo and Wilfred M. McClay, eds., *Religion Returns to the Public Square: Faith and Policy in America* (Washington, D.C.: Woodrow Wilson Center Press; Baltimore, MD: Johns Hopkins University Press, 2003).
5. Casanova, *Public Religions*, pp. 69–207.
6. Ibid., p. 10.
7. It is interesting to note Rodney Stark's choice of title "Secularization, R.I.P. — Rest in Peace", published in *Sociology of Religion* 60, no. 3 (1999): 249–73, available at http://www.findarticles.com/p/articles/mi_m0SOR/is_3_60/ai_57533381/pg_10 At the end of the article, Stark writes: "After nearly three centuries of utterly failed prophesies and misrepresentations of both present and past, it seems time to carry the secularization doctrine to the graveyard of failed theories, and there to whisper 'requiescat in pace'."
8. Peter Berger, "Protestantism and the Quest for Certainty", *Christian Century* 115, no. 23 (1998): 782. Berger also stated that "I think what I and most other sociologists of religion wrote in the 1960s about secularization was a mistake. Our underlying argument was that secularization and modernity go hand in hand. With more modernization comes more secularization. It wasn't a crazy theory. There was some evidence for it. But I think it's basically wrong. Most of the world today is certainly not secular. It's very religious." (Peter Berger, "Epistemiological Modesty: An Interview with Peter Berger", *Christian Century* 114 (1997): 974; see also Peter Berger, "Secularism in Retreat", *The National Interest*, Winter 1996/1997, pp. 3–12).
9. Casanova, *Public Religions*, p. 15.
10. David Hollenbach, "Politically Active Churches: Some Empirical Prolegomena to a Normative Approach", in *Religion and Contemporary Liberalism*, edited by Paul J. Weithman (Notre Dame: University of Notre Dame Press, 1997), p. 301.
11. David Hollenbach, "Contexts of the Political Role of Religion: Civil Society and Culture", *San Diego Law Review* 30, no. 4 (1993): 878.
12. Casanova, *Public Religions*, p. 219.
13. Robert W. Hefner states that:

> In many respects, what is happening in the Muslim world resembles what the German sociologist Jurgen Habermas described some years ago as the emergence of the "public sphere" in the West. Habermas's study of eighteenth-century European society emphasized that public arenas, like coffee houses, literary clubs, journals, and "moral weeklies," helped to create an open and egalitarian culture of participation. Habermas suggests that this development provided vital precedent for the next century's struggles for democratic representation ... Like Alexis de Tocqueville's observations on democracy in America, however, Habermas's analysis has the virtue of emphasizing that democratic life

depends not just on government but on resources and habits in society at large.

(Robert W. Hefner, *Civil Islam: Muslims and Democratization in Indonesia* (Princeton, NJ: Princeton University Press, 2000), p. 11)

14. Saiful Mujani, "Religious Democrats: Democratic Culture and Muslim Political Participation in Post-Suharto Indonesia" (Ph.D. thesis, Ohio State University, 2004).

15. By comparison, in the United Kingdom there are two state-approved churches; the Presbyterian Church in Scotland and the Anglican Church in England. The former is a national church, guaranteed by law to be separate from the state, while the latter is a state-established church. Neither Wales nor Northern Ireland have established churches. The King or Queen must promise to uphold the rights of the Presbyterian Church in Scotland and the Anglican Church in England. He or she is the Supreme Governor of the Anglican Church but an ordinary member of the Presbyterian Church. Neither church receives direct funding from taxation. Public schools must provide religious instruction and regular religious ceremonies, with the choice of religion left up to the local voters. Senior bishops have a right to sit in the House of Lords, the upper chamber of the British legislature (http://www.state.gov/g/drl/rls/irf/2002/13989.htm).

16. According to Rainer Hermann, in recent years Islam has become more visible in Turkish public space. For over half a century the Kemalist establishment had succeeded in keeping Islam out of politics and public discourse. In the 1980s and 1990s, however, a new political Islam challenged the Kemalist principles of the Republic more than ever before. In 1996 the Islamist veteran, Erbakan, became for one year the first Islamist Prime Minister of Turkey, and in 2000 the Justice and Development Party (AKP), a party with Islamist roots, won a landslide victory in the elections. The AKP presents itself, however, as a party of the conservative mainstream. See Rainer Hermann, "Political Islam in Secular Turkey", *Islam and Christian-Muslim Relations* 14, no. 3 (2003): 265–76.

17. As quoted in Robert Lumban Tobing, "Christian Social Ethics in the Thoughts of TB Simatupang: The Role of Indonesian Christian in Social Change" (Ph.D. thesis, University of Denver, 1996), p. 166.

18. Ahmad Baso, "UU NO.1/PNPS/1965 dan Soal 'Agama Resmi' Itu: Sebuah Tatapan untuk JPS", paper for Rakernas "Perencanaan Strategis Jaringan", Pokja-pokja Jamaah Persaudaraan Sejati di Puncak, Ciloto, 28–31 July 2004.

19. See Biro Pusat Statistik (BPS), 2000, available at http://www.bps.go.id/sector/population/pop2000.htm.

20. See, for instance, Jennifer Connolly, "Becoming Christian and Dayak: A Study of Christian Conversion among Dayaks in East Kalimantan, Indonesia" (Ph.D. thesis, New School University, 2004). This study explores the social impact and cultural meaning of Christian conversion among Dayaks. The research revealed that conversion is a complex process motivated not only by social and political

expediency, but also by the desire to gain access to a new supernatural realm, some groups' cultural receptivity to Christian messages, and personal ties and circumstances.

21. A recent example comes from Law No. 18 of 2001, which granted Aceh special autonomy and included authority for Aceh to establish a system of *shari'a* as an adjunct to, not a replacement for, national civil and criminal law. Before it could take effect, the law required the provincial legislature to approve local regulations (*qanun*) incorporating *shari'a* precepts into the legal code. Law No. 18 of 2001 states that the *shari'a* courts would be "free from outside influence by any side". Article 25(3) states that the authority of the court will apply only to Muslims. Article 26(2) names the national Supreme Court as the court of appeal for Aceh's *shari'a* courts. During 2002, the provincial legislature approved five *qanun*. Local regulation No. 10 of 2002 grants authority to *shari'a* courts "to examine, decide and resolve cases related to family, civil and criminal law", Local regulation No. 11 of 2002 requires the preservation of Aceh's Islamic culture, the observance of Islamic holidays, and the wearing of "Islamic dress" by Muslims. Local Regulations Nos. 12 of 2002, 13 of 2002, and 14 of 2002 prohibit Muslims from drinking alcoholic beverages, gambling, or being in "close proximity" with "off-limits" persons of the opposite sex. In March 2003, Presidential Decree No. 11 of 2003 formally established *shari'a* courts in Aceh by renaming the existing religious courts and retaining their infrastructure, jurisdiction, and staff. On Islamic law in Aceh, see Arskal Salim, "'Shari'a From Below' in Aceh (1930s–1960s): Islamic Identity and the Right to Self-Determination with Comparative Reference to the Moro Islamic Liberation Front (MILF)", *Indonesia and the Malay World* 32, no. 92 (2004): 80; Michelle Ann Miller, "The Nanggroe Aceh Darussalam Law: A Serious Response to Acehnese Separatism?", *Asian Ethnicity* 5, no. 3 (2004): 333.

22. See "Indonesia", International Religious Freedom Report 2004, released by the Bureau of Democracy, Human Rights, and Labor, 15 September 2004.

23. Hyung-Jun Kim, "The Changing Interpretation of Religious Freedom in Indonesia", *Journal of Southeast Asian Studies* 29, no. 2 (1998): 357.

24. See "UUD Bukan Kitab Suci" [The Constitution is not the Holy Book], *Sabili*, No. 23, 16 May 2002.

25. Documents of Kongres Mujahidin (Yogyakarta, 5–7 August 2000) is available at http://www.geocities.com/kongresmujahidin/.

26. See *Tempo Interaktif*, 28 February 2000.

27. *Jakarta Post*, 30 December 2002.

28. *Jakarta Post*, 25 July 2002. Abdurrahman Wahid also "does not aspire to an Islamic state for Indonesia, and therefore rejects any 'formalization' of religion within the state", (see Mujiburrahman, "Islam and Politics in Indonesia: The Political Thought of Abdurrahman Wahid", *Islam and Christian–Muslim Relations* 10, no. 3 (1999): 344). Amien Rais reaffirmed that the Islamic state is not the appropriate model for Indonesia, given the country's diversity (*Tempo Interaktif*, 11 January 1999).

29. Anies Rasyid Baswedan, "Political Islam in Indonesia: Present and Future Trajectory", forthcoming article in *Asian Survey*. The article is based on a paper presented at the conference on Political Islam in Southeast Asia at the Paul H. Nitze School of Advanced International Studies, Johns Hopkins University, 25 March 2003.

30. *Kompas*, 25 July 2002.

31. Lukman Hakim Saifuddin, personal communication, 10 December 2003.

32. Mutammimul Ula, personal communication, 5 September 2003.

33. Hamdan Zoelva, personal communication, 15 December 2003.

34. For a full account on the 2004 general election, see National Democratic Institute for International Affairs (NDI), "Advancing Democracy In Indonesia: The Second Democratic Legislative Elections Since the Transition", June 2004, available at http://www.accessdemocracy.org/library/1728_id_legelections_063004.pdf.

35. See statement by Alamsjah Ratuperwiranegara, Minister for Religion Affairs, in *Pelita* (Indonesian daily newspaper), 12 June 1978.

36. See "Pendapat Akhir Fraksi Persatuan Pembangunan MPR RI", Sidang Tahunan MPR, Jakarta, 15 August 2000, in Sekretariat Jenderal MPR, *Risalah Sidang Tahunan MPR Tanggal 7 Sampai Dengan Tanggal 18 Agustus 2000*, Buku Ketiga Jilid 9 (Jakarta: Setjen MPR, 2000), pp. 477–79.

37. Asghar Ali Engineer, *The Islamic State* (New York: Advent Books, 1980), p. 199.

38. In one of the leading modernist expositions of Islam international law, Mohammad Talaat al-Ghunaimi dismisses the *dar al-Islam/dar al-Harb* distinction as an idea introduced by certain medieval legal thinkers in response to their own historical circumstances, but having no basis in Islamic ethics. (See Mohammad Talaat al-Ghunaimi, *The Muslim Conception of International Law and the Western Approach* (The Hague: Martinus Nijhoff, 1968), p. 184). Further countering this classification, Taha Jabir al-Alwani points out that even in the past, scholars were unanimous in their view that the entire Earth was the land of Allah and did not divide it into such spheres. Instead, some scholars like Imam al Razi considered the Earth to consist of *dar al-Ijabah*, which replaces the term *dar al-Islam*, and *dar al-Da'wah*, which replaces the term *dar al-Harb*. *Dar al-Da'wah* means a land for dialogue and inter-faith communication, a land where people are not classified, but all human being are considered as one family. This family is divided into two parts. One is identified as *Ummat al-Ijabah*, instead of *Ummat al-Muslim*, and other as *Ummat al-Da'wah*, instead of *Kuffar* or *Harbiyun*. This part of Islamic heritage and legacy represents Islam more accurately than the other part, because the whole Earth has been created by Allah as humanity's home. See Taha Jabir al Alwani, "Globalization: Centralization not Globalism", *American Journal of Islamic Social Sciences* 15, no. 3 (1998): vii.

39. al-Mawardi, *al-Ahkam al-Sultaniya* (Cairo: Mustafa Babi al-Halabi wa Auladuh, 1996), p. 138.

40. For a full account, see Majid Khadduri, *The Islamic Law of Nations: Shaybani's Siyar* (Maryland: Johns Hopkins Press, 1966).

41. Habib Rizieq Shihab, "Jika Syariat Islam Jalan, Maka Jadi Negara Islam", interview in *Tashwirul Afkar,* Vol. 12, 2002, p. 104. The FPI arose almost at the same time as the fall of the Old Order regime and the birth of the reformation movement. It has carried out many actions of defence in the interests of Islam and its people. The troops of FPI in a number of cities (Jakarta, Tangerang, Solo) have conducted many movements aimed at "preventing evil" in the form of "sweeping" [raiding] places of iniquity, prostitution, gambling, alcohol and drugs.

42. Daniel Price, *Islamic Political Culture, Democracy, and Human Rights: A Comparative Study* (Westport: Connecticut, Praeger, 1999), p. 145.

43. Saifuddin, personal communication, 10 December 2003.

44. Zoelva, personal communication, 15 December 2003.

45. Ibid.

46. For instance, Gregorius Seto Harianto of the PDKB faction has stated that the inclusion of Islamic law in the Constitution will discriminate against other religions. See "Piagam Jakarta Terganjal Lagi", *Suara Hidayatullah,* September 2000.

47. However, it should be noted that the final position of the PKB is not to amend Article 29. Saifullah Ma'sum, personal communication, 29 November 2003.

48. T. B. Soemandjaja, personal communication, 30 November 2003.

49. Hidayat Nur Wahid, "Mewujudkan Konstitusi yang Adil dan Demokratis (Kasus Amandemen Pasal 29 Ayat 1 UUD 1945)", paper available at official website of Partai Keadilan at http://www.keadilan.or.id. I also telephoned him to confirm this position (1 December 2003).

50. Full text of the Medina Charter can be found in http://msanews.mynet.net/books/lessons/ constitution.html.

51. Ula, personal communication, 5 September 2003.

52. Saifuddin, personal communication, 10 December 2003.

53. Zoelva, personal communication, 15 December 2003.

54. Full text of the Code of Canon Law can be read at http://www.vatican.va/archive/cdc/index.htm.

55. H. Patrick Glenn, *Legal Traditions of the World* (New York: Oxford University Press, 2000), pp. 251–78.

56. See Sekretariat Jenderal MPR, *Risalah Rapat Panitia Ad Hoc I Badan Pekerja MPR RI ke-21 s.d 30 Tanggal 28 Maret 2002 s.d 19 Juni 2002* (Jakarta: Setjen MPR, 2002).

57. T. B. Simatupang, "Sebagai Penutup: Sepuluh Dalil", in *Iman Kristen dan Pancasila* (Jakarta: BPK Gunung Mulia, 1985), p. 206.

58. Eka Darmaputera, "Aspek-aspek Etis Teologis Hubungan Gereja-Negara", in *Hubungan Gereja dan Negara dan Hak Asasi Manusia,* edited by Weinata Sairin and J. M. Pattiasina (Jakarta: BPK Gunung Mulia, 1996), pp. 19–20.

59. Eka Darmaputera, "Prinsip-prinsip Hubungan Agama-Negara", in *Pergulatan Kehadiran Kristen di Indonesia: Teks-teks Terpilih Eka Darmaputera,* by Trisno Sutanto et al. (Jakarta: BPK Gunung Mulia, 2001), p. 367.

60. For a full account, see Eka Darmaputera, *Pancasila and The Search for Identity and Modernity in Indonesian Society: A Cultural and Ethical Analysis* (Leiden: E.J. Brill, 1988).
61. Frans Magnis Suseno, "Beberapa Dilema Etis antara Agama dan Negara", in *Kuasa dan Moral* (Jakarta: Gramedia, 2000), p. 104.
62. Ibid., pp. 110–15.
63. More information can be read in Th. Sumartana et al., *Agama dan Negara Perspektif Islam Katolik, Hindu, Buddha, Konghucu, Protestan* (Yogyakarta: Interfidei, 2002), which is a compilation of articles from prominent scholars in Indonesia on the relationship between state and religion. In general, they supported the notion that Indonesia is neither a secular nor a religious state.
64. Majid Khadduri, *Islamic Law of Nations.*
65. Mawardi, *al-Ahkam al-Sultaniya*, p. 59.
66. Karen Armstrong. "The Curse of the Infidel", *The Guardian*, 20 June 2002.
67. See Fahmi Huwaydi, *Muwatinun la dhimmiyun* (Cairo: Dar al-Syuruq, 1985).
68. Qur'an, 2:126.
69. Zoelva, personal communication, 15 December 2003.
70. See Clark Benner Lombardi, "State Law as Islamic Law in Modern Egypt: The Amendment of Article 2 of the Egyptian Constitution and the Article 2 of Jurisprudence of the Supreme Constitutional Court of Egypt" (Ph.D. thesis, Columbia University, 2001).
71. Clark Benner Lombardi, "Islamic Law as a Source of Constitutional Law in Egypt: The Constitutionalization of the Sharia in a Modern Arab State", *Columbia Journal of Transnational Law* 37 (1998): 82.
72. See Bernard Botiveau, *al-Shari'a al-Islamiya wa al-Qanun fi al-Mujtami'at al-'Arabiyah*, translated from *Loi Islamique Et Droit Dans les Sociétés Arabes* (Cairo: Sina li al-Nashr, 1997), pp. 238–41.
73. See Tamir Moustafa, "Law versus the State: The Judicialization of Politics in Egypt", *Law and Social Inquiry* 28 (2003): 833–69.
74. Lombardi, "Islamic Law as a Source of Constitutional Law in Egypt", p. 121.
75. Khaled Abou El Fadl, "Islam and the Challenge of Democracy: Can Individual Rights and Popular Sovereignty Take Root in Faith?", *Boston Review*, April/May 2003, available at http://bostonreview.net/BR28.2/abou.html.
76. See Ihsan Abdul Bagby, "Utility in Classical Islamic Law: The Concept of *Maslahah* in *Usul al-Fiqh*" (Ph.D. thesis, University of Michigan, 1986).
77. Abdul Wahab Khallaf, *al-Siyasa al-Shar'iyya* (Cairo: Salafiyah, 1350 H), p. 5.
78. Most jurists classify *maslahah* into three categories each of which must be protected: (1) the daruriyyat (essentials), (2) the *hajiyyat* (complements), and (3) *tahsiniyyat* (embellishment). Each divine ruling aims at one of these three. The *daruriyyat* are those interests upon which life depends and the disregard of which results in disruption and chaos. The *daruriyyat* consist of five essential interests: the preservation of *din* (religion), *nafs* (life), *aql* (intellect), *nasl* (progeny), and *mal* (property). In order for any law to be valid and applicable, it must not

violate any of these five essentials and the ultimate intent of the law. The *hajiyyat* are those interests the disregard of which result in hardship but not in the destruction or ruin of the community. The *hajiyyat* are complementary to the *daruriyyat*. Lastly, the *tahsiniyyat* are those interests whose realization leads to improvement and the attainment of that which is desirable. An example of such is cleanliness in personal appearance. Without these *tahsiniyyat*, or embellishments, life would be less beautiful and less refined. For more details see Husain Hamid Hasan, *Nazariyyah al-Masalahah fi al-Fiqh al-Islam* (Cairo: Dar al-Nahdah al-'Arabiyyah, 1971); Muhammad Sa'd b. Ahmad b. Mas'ud al-Alyubi, *Maqasid al-shari'a al-Islamiya wa 'Alaqatuha bi Adillah al-Shar'iyya,* (Riyadh: Dar al-Hijrah li al-Nashr wa al-Tawzi', 1998).

79. One should not confuse *maslahah al-ammah* with *maslahah al-mursalah*. The latter is one of the methods in Islamic legal theory, supported by Hanafi, Hanbali and Maliki theorists, though rejected by the Shafi'i and Zahiri schools. Al-Ghazali illustrates *maslahah al-mursalah* with this example: "If unbelievers shield themselves with a group of Muslim captives, to attack this shield means killing innocent Muslims — a case which is not supported by textual evidence. If the Muslim attack is withheld, the unbelievers will advance and conquer the territory of Islam. In this case it is permissible to argue that even if Muslims do not attack, the lives of the Muslim captives are not safe. The unbelievers, once they conquer the territory, will root out all Muslims. If such is the case, then it is necessary to save the whole of the Muslim community rather than to save a part of it". Abu Hamid Muhammad al-Ghazali, *al-Mustasfa min 'Ilm al-Usul,* Vol. 1 (Medina: al-Jami'ah al-Islamiyah, n.d.), pp. 294–95.

80. El-Fadl, "Islam and the Challenge of Democracy".

81. Casanova, *Public Religions*, p. 61.

82. Robert W. Hefner, "Islam, State and Civil Society: ICMI and the Struggle for the Indonesian Middle Class", *Indonesia* 56 (1993): 1–35. In his most recent book, he writes:

> Civil pluralist Islam is an emergent tradition and comes in a variety of forms. Most versions begin, however, by denying the wisdom of a monolithic "Islamic" state and instead affirming democracy, voluntarism, and a balance of countervailing powers in a state and society. In embracing the ideals of civil society, this democratic Islam insists that formal democracy cannot prevail unless government power is checked by strong civic associations. At the same time, it is said, civic associations and democratic culture cannot thrive unless they are protected by a state which respects society, by upholding its commitment to the rule of law.
>
> (See Hefner, *Civil Islam,* p. 12]

83. Robert W. Hefner, "Secularization and Citizenship in Muslim Indonesia", in *Religion, Modernity, and Postmodernity*, edited by Paul Heelas (Oxford: Blackwell Publishers, 1998), p. 148.

84. Zoelva, personal communication, 15 December 2003; see also "Pendapat Akhir Fraksi Partai Bulan Bintang MPR", Sidang Tahunan MPR 2000, reprinted in *Amandemen UUD 1945 Tentang Piagam Jakarta*, edited by Ramlan Mardjoned and Lukman Fatullah (Jakarta: DDII, 2000), pp. 3–26.
85. M. B. Hooker, "The State and *Shari'a* in Indonesia", in *Shari'a and Politics in Modern Indonesia*, edited by Arskal Salim and Azyumardi Azra (Singapore: Institute of Southeast Asian Studies, 2003), p. 38.
86. David Hollenbach, "Politically Active Churches", p. 301.

7

CONCLUSION

This book has traced the process and the outcome of constitutional reform from the perspective of *shari'a*, which took place in Indonesia from 1999 to 2002 as part of the democratic transition. In particular, I have focused on three main issues: human rights provisions, the rule of law, and the position of religion in the amendments to the 1945 Constitution.

This concluding chapter serves two purposes. First, it summarizes the findings of each of the earlier chapters. This summary is designed to clearly identify answers to the questions posed in Chapter 1 and to emphasize the contribution that this book has made to the scholarly literature. The second purpose of this chapter is to look ahead at the prospects for the establishment of *shari'a* in Indonesia. In particular, I will consider how the debate, process and outcome of constitutional reform during 1999–2002 might influence the current and future situation.

SUMMARY OF FINDINGS

This book has asked the crucial question implicit in the amendments to the 1945 Constitution: can Islam and democratic constitutionalism be fused without compromising on human rights, the rule of law and religious liberty? The study reveals one possible picture of how Islam and constitutionalism can co-exist in the same vision, not without risk of tension, but with the possibility of success.

At the outset of this book, I have shown that there is a group that believes that *shari'a* is incompatible with constitutionalism. This group is divided into two camps: authoritarian/fundamentalist and secularist. On the other hand, there is a second group that holds the view that *shari'a* can walk together with constitutionalism. This position rejects both the views of authoritarians and the secularists on this subject. It is essential to note that I support this second group which holds the view that constitutionalism and *shari'a* are compatible.

However, this second group is also divided into two approaches: *formal shari'a* and *substantive shari'a*. The formal *shari'a* attempts to use *shari'a* as a source or the primary source of law — which makes their position closer to the authoritarian/fundamentalist views. This suggests that human rights protection, checks and balances mechanisms, independence of the judiciary and separation of powers are accepted in their constitutional theory as long as these elements of constitutionalism are in line with their formal interpretation of *shari'a*.

The substantive *shari'a* holds that *shari'a*, in this context, should be reinterpreted in line with democracy and constitutionalism. This substantive approach is based on the belief that the understanding of *shari'a* is not static and final. As has been argued earlier, it can be amended, reformed, modified or even altered, without neglecting its fundamental basis. The substantive approach treats the principles, objectives or spirit of *shari'a* only as norms or values which inspire constitutions.

Those who follow the formal approach might question whether the substantive group's arguments for constitutionalism are accepted in Islamic tradition. As has been mentioned, the substantive approach stresses the importance of substance of belief rather than its outer form. The question is how far the substantive group can go into substance or content and ignore the formal part of *shari'a*? And how can this group convince Muslims that their interpretation on the content of *shari'a* is still (considered) Islamic? To the formal group, the substantive group deviates too far from Islamic tradition, and they suspect that the substantive group's position is influenced by secularism.

On the other hand, the substantive circle tends to see *shari'a* as an ethical basis to arrange the social life, without being involved further in its formalization. They share a view of Islam that emphasizes justice, human dignity and equality, the rule of law, the role of the people in selecting leaders, popular sovereignty, the obligation of consultative government, and the value of pluralism. They believe that their opinions and thoughts can be justified under the term "*ijtihad*", and they also take the position that it is necessary to "maintain that which is old and good, and embrace that which is new and better" (*al-muhafazah ala al-qadim al-salih wa al-akhz bi al-jadid al-aslah*).

In this sense, they do not neglect the foundation of *shari'a* and at the same time they do not hesitate to modify, amend or alter the works of classical authors and Muslim scholars who have interpreted the Qur'an and the Hadith according to their time, situation and condition. Although the formal *shari'a* recognizes the compatibility of Islam and constitutionalism, one may question whether such an approach is adequate to bring Muslims into a democratic era when they still depend not only on the idea and the practice of Islamic state dating more than a thousand years, but also on the authority of classical Muslim scholars. In other words, they need to develop new interpretations of the original sources while studying the interpretations of the past, both to learn from their insights and to understand them as products of their historical environment. To put it differently, Islam is, like all the great religions, a reservoir of values, symbols and ideas from which it is possible to derive a contemporary political and social code: the answer as to why this or that interpretation is put upon Islam resides therefore, not in the religion and its texts itself, but in the contemporary needs of those articulating Islamic politics.[1]

Behind all these lies a basic question: can a state be at once truly democratic and in some sense Islamic in character? In other Muslim countries, the alternative to trying democracy has been autocracy, whether secular dictatorship or religious monarchy. Indonesia before 1998 shared similar experiences. It is worth considering that the original 1945 Constitution was an inappropriate foundation on which to erect the superstructure of a democracy. Since its reinstatement by President Soekarno, on 5 July 1959, the 1945 Constitution has facilitated the establishment of two authoritarian regimes, "Guided Democracy" under Soekarno, and the "New Order" under President Soeharto, which together lasted almost four decades.

I have demonstrated in Chapter 3 that for more than half a century Indonesia has been unable to conduct an uninterrupted dialogue, concerning the position of *shari'a* in the Constitution. In 1945 and 1955, efforts were hampered by the pressure of time and political manoeuvrings by Soekarno and the military. Under Soeharto, debate was forbidden, since his government was afraid of its disruptive potential. The moment for free dialogue and debate, through constitutional mechanisms, came after Soeharto's resignation on May 1998. The challenge, as the transition to democracy began in 1998, was what to do about the Constitution. In this sense, the main question is: to what extent did *shari'a* contribute to constitutional reform in Indonesia in 1999–2002?

The overall empirical finding is that the formal *shari'a* approach has failed to influence the process of constitutional reform not only in the issue of religion vis-à-vis the state (Article 29 of the 1945 Constitution), but also in the issue of human rights and the rule of law. *Shari'a* has contributed to constitutional reform in Indonesia (1999–2002) through substantive *shari'a*. There are, at least, three main reasons for this claim.

Firstly, I have examined human rights provision in the second amendment to the 1945 Constitution from the perspective of *shari'a*. Several key issues such as equality, women's rights, freedom of religion, freedom of opinion, and religious values have been examined. While the tendency of other human rights documents in the Islamic world, ranging from the Constitutions of Iran and Egypt and the Basic Laws of Saudi Arabia to the Universal Islamic Declaration of Human Rights (UIDHR) and the Cairo Declaration, has been to restrict human rights provision under the rules of the formal *shari'a*, such restriction does not exist in the second amendment to the 1945 Constitution. In other words, I have demonstrated that *shari'a* is neither above nor outside the human rights provision in the 1945 Constitution.

The principles of *shari'a* inspire human rights protection since they can walk together side by side. To put it differently, the substantive approach operates on the premise that Islam is in substance compatible with Western human rights legal norms if interpreted accordingly. To support this contention, this approach refers, on the general level, to the elasticity of Islam and to its capability to accommodate various interpretations equally favourable or hostile to human rights. It is safe to state that the full acceptance of human rights provisions has shown that Indonesia has provided a model for other Islamic countries to acknowledge the compatibility of human rights and Islamic law. In this sense, Mashood A. Baderin shares a similar view:

> The scope of international human rights can be positively enhanced in the Muslim world through moderate, dynamic, and constructive interpretations of the *Sharî'ah* rather than through hardline and static interpretations of it.[2]

Secondly, provisions relating to the executive, the Parliament and the judiciary in the 1945 Constitution have been examined. Such provisions are examined in order to see the influence and the response of *shari'a* on the issues of establishing and promoting the rule of law in the Indonesian context. The very fact that Indonesia is the largest Muslim country in the world does not lead Islamic political parties to propose that Indonesia become an Islamic state like Egypt, Iran or Saudi Arabia. According to the amendments, Indonesia remains a republic, with a presidential system and the three branches of government.

Indonesian Islamic political parties have accepted that sovereignty belongs to the people. I have shown the justification for this position from the substantive *shari'a* approach. Without necessarily ignoring the role of God, the *ummat* (the totality of the Muslim population of the state) becomes the collective agent of the Divine Sovereign, rather than an individual person (caliph). More importantly, the amendments have filled the gap left by the formal *shari'a*, as in the cases of presidential tenure, method of elections, and method of dethroning the head of state, by providing new regulations.

As has been discussed in Chapter 5, not a single word in the amendments provides special rights for Muslims to become the president or vice-president. The Constitution does not forbid a woman from becoming the president. While there is no limitation on the caliph's period in office, the Indonesian Constitution limits the term to two five-year terms for both the president and vice-president. It is also worth noting that the amendments adopt direct election for the presidency, while the exercise of the flexibility of the *shura* and *bay'at* makes them compatible with any of the electoral systems. The amendment regulates the structures of political accountability. This new provision is important. As Nathan J. Brown points out, the problem with Islamic constitutionalism could be seen to lie in the lack of attention to the structures of political accountability.[3] It is safe to argue that the amendments to the 1945 Constitution have met this requirement.

In addition, the Indonesian Constitution fills the void left by Islamic history, owing to the fact that *ahl al-hall wa al-aqd* had only one main function: to elect the caliph. The substantive *shari'a* approach encourages the extension of the functions and power of *ahl al-hall wa al-aqd*. The legislative functions of the Indonesian Parliament are asserted, along with budgetary and supervisory functions. These are to ensure that the checks and balances systems work. The adoption of this new provision is a clear departure from the formal *shari'a* tradition. It also follows from the Amendments that all Islamic political parties in Indonesia take the position that judicial independence is a tool for establishing constitutional government.

Thirdly, while other Islamic parties have used a consistently substantive approach, the PBB (Partai Bulan Bintang, or Crescent and Star Party) and PPP (Partai Persatuan Pembangunan, or United Development Party) moved to examine Article 29 using the formal concept of *shari'a*. How does one explain this inconsistency? It should be remembered that, as has been discussed in Chapter 3, many Muslim leaders in 1945 were not happy with the last-minute removal of the seven words "*dengan kewajiban menjalankan syariat Islam bagi pemeluknya*" (with the obligation to carry out Islamic *shari'a* for its adherents). This historical context stayed on for so long in the memory of Muslims activists as to make their position inflexible, as articulated by the PPP and PBB during 1999–2002. However, such a formal approach was rejected by the MPR (People's Consultative Assembly). The two most important religious organizations in the country, Muhammadiyah and Nahdlatul Ulama (NU), also rejected the insertion of the seven words from the Jakarta Charter during the amendment process.[4]

It is also worth noting that, by not modifying Article 29 of the 1945 Constitution, the Indonesian Parliament rejects the secularization that would see the privatization, or the decline, of religion. At the same time, the state has already facilitated Muslims (and some other religions) in the practice of their beliefs. I have argued in Chapter 6 that the Pancasila state is the only viable alternative if Indonesia wants to maintain its unity and pluralistic character, in which "religious communities can have an impact on public life".[5] At the same time, the role of religion in public life does not imply that all political institutions are under the control of religion as in a theocratic system. Under Article 29 of the 1945 Constitution, religion can play its public role at society level. This suggests that Indonesia still stands in the middle position that it is neither a secular nor an Islamic state. It is essential to note that this position is compatible with the substantive *shari'a* approach.

It is also essential to note that the contributions of Islamic political parties in Indonesia to the process and the outcome of the amendments, by adopting a substantive *shari'a* approach, should be seen as their *ijtihad*. It reflects the ability to deal with a modern constitution without abandoning the principles and the objectives of *shari'a*. In the Muslim world, this model is important since the Indonesian experience has demonstrated that *shari'a* does provide a basis for constitutionalism. This suggests that it is possible to reconcile Islam with democratic constitutionalism.

The substantive approach of *shari'a* that has been used in Indonesia has shown that the Muslim world can, and should, reform its constitutions without "assistance" or "direction" from Western or U.S. foreign policy. This study has demonstrated that Islamic constitutionalism comes from within Islamic teaching and the Islamic community itself. It is a home-grown product.

By providing a detailed examination of selected areas of constitutional amendments during Indonesia's transition from authoritarian to democratic constitutionalism, this book has attempted to make a valuable contribution to the literature on *fiqh siyasa* or Islamic constitutionalism, Indonesian constitutional law, and law reform in the post-Soeharto era.

REFLECTIONS

In my examination of constitutional reform in the post-Soeharto era, I have highlighted the struggle between two broad camps: the formal and the substantive *shari'a*. What then are the prospects for the establishment of *shari'a* in Indonesia in the future? It is important to note that while in the 1955 general election, the supporters of the Jakarta Charter obtained 40 per cent of the seats, in 1999 the proponents of the inclusion of *shari'a* into the 1945 Constitution won only 12 per cent, a decline of 28 percentage points. The results of the recent 2004 general election show that the PPP has won 8.2 per cent of the votes and PBB only 2.6 per cent.[6] This means that both parties have 10.8 per cent, a slight decrease from 12 per cent in 1999. This result shows that almost 90 per cent of Indonesians are not in favour of the PBB and PPP's campaigns to implement formal *shari'a* at the state level. In addition, Hamzah Haz, the chairperson of PPP and then incumbent vice-president, obtained only 3.06 per cent of the vote when he was running for the presidency in the 2004 direct elections.

Another supporter of the inclusion of formal *shari'a* in Article 29 of the Constitution is PBB. Instead of voting for Hamzah Haz in the presidential election, this party surprisingly supported Susilo Bambang Yudhoyono, a retired four-star general. Although Yudhoyono emerged as the winner, it would be misleading to say that PBB's support is the main factor of such achievements. It remains unclear why the PBB voted for a candidate who would not support the formal *shari'a* approach.[7] Perhaps this can be seen as an inconsistency of these supporters of formal *shari'a* group in promoting their political vision. Another possible speculation is that PBB's struggle to establish the formal *shari'a* is half-hearted. Many of its leaders have family connections with Masyumi leaders of the 1950s. It is worth considering that the Masyumi party supported the Jakarta Charter in 1955.[8] This suggests that the PBB can be considered as a party of the past. On the other hand, Masyumi's younger generations, represented by Yusril Ihza Mahendra, the current General Chairman of PBB party, take a more pragmatic approach in order to survive in the political battle.

The results of the 2004 general elections also show that the PBB will not be permitted to compete in the 2009 general election since it could not satisfy the required electoral threshold of 3 per cent.[9] A party falling under the threshold would be rendered a "lame duck" for five years in the current People's Representative Assembly (Dewan Perwakilan Rakyat, or DPR), since it would be disqualified from competing in the next election. In such circumstances, it is very unlikely that they would represent their constituents in an effective way.

It could be argued that unless Islamic political parties that supported the formal approach of *shari'a* gain two-thirds of the parliamentary seats in 2009, as is required to amend the Constitution, the issue of the famous seven words in Article 29 would never arise. In this sense, one Islamic party that has the potential to obtain a significant portion of the votes would be PKS (Partai Keadilan Sejahtera, or Prosperous Justice Party). The PKS had made steady efforts to expand its support base through community social programmes. PKS succeeded in organizing a demonstration of one million people against the Iraq war in Jakarta in March 2003. The party also manages to create its clean image amid the current corruption and money politics in Indonesia. The PKS more than quintupled its votes between 1999 and 2004 by going door-to-door with a simple, clear message of fostering a clean government and fighting corruption. Unlike the PPP and PBB, during the 2004 general election it did not campaign for the inclusion of *shari'a* into the Constitution or for the implementation of *shari'a* in a legal, formal and technical sense. It spread a message that the party is not an Islamic fundamentalist party. Its leader, Hidayat Nur Wahid, has been elected as the speaker of the MPR in 2004. However, given its platform as a missionary party (*partai dakwah*),[10] there is speculation that the PKS would shift its position and support the formal *shari'a* once they can get a majority vote in the next election. Right now, it is too soon to tell.

What is the next agenda of formal *shari'a* in the Indonesian Parliament? It seems that their position would be to ensure that *no law should contradict Islamic teachings*. Under current constitutional terms, it is not possible to treat Islamic law as one of the formal sources of any law in Indonesia. In other words, their position in the context of the implementation of formal Islamic law would be passive, not active. However, it should be highlighted once again that what the formal group meant by "no law should contradict Islamic teachings" is open for public debate, inside and outside the Parliament building.

At the other end of spectrum, the full acceptance of Article 29 of the 1945 Constitution suggests that we are not only watching the existence of substantive *shari'a* group in Indonesia, but also substantive religious communities which seek mutual cooperation to acknowledge and preserve the harmonious existence of religion and state, without necessarily being in favour of their intermixing. Tensions between the two sides (religious values and democratic constitutionalism), if any, are to be resolved by Constitutional Court — as part of democratic mechanisms outlined by the amendments to the 1945 Constitution.

In this sense, it is interesting to note that Jimly Asshiddiqie, the Chief Justice of the Constitutional Court (Mahkamah Konstitusi), is not only a professor of constitutional law, but is also a prominent Muslim scholar. He has served as the vice-secretary of Majelis Ulama Indonesia (MUI, or Council of Indonesian Ulama) and Ikatan Cendekiawan Muslim se-Indonesia (ICMI, or Association of Indonesian Muslim Intellectuals) for ten years. He had studied in Islamic boarding schools. His LL.M. thesis was on Islamic criminal law, and his Ph.D. thesis was on the discourse of popular (not divine) sovereignty in the Constitution. His personal background might be seen as one of the clear indications of the compatibility of Islamic law with the Constitution in Indonesia.

It is worth considering that the outcome of the 1999–2002 constitutional reform serves as the common denominator (*kalimat sawa'*) for the Indonesian people to support human rights, the rule of law and religious liberty. However, Gary Bell has correctly pointed out that "constitutions do not perform miracles".[11] This suggests that it would be misleading to assume that the amendments to the 1945 Constitution would automatically bring Indonesian people out of economic, political and legal crisis. In other words, the first challenge faced by the Indonesian people is to ensure that the amendments do not turn out to have little more value than the wallpaper in the houses of the politicians and generals who have ignored them.

The second challenge is to socialize the outcome of this constitutional reform to Indonesian society at all levels. As examined in Chapter 3, this is important since the MPR solicited citizen input only on a limited basis, preferring to reserve to itself the final decision on amendments. The MPR rejected all calls for a popular referendum on amendments. The public involvement would contribute to building national solidarity and helping construct or solidify a national identity, themselves worthy goals. More importantly, public involvement should increase the development of constitutionalism, and public acceptance and respect for the Constitution through the process that is transparent and as public as possible. In this sense, since the public participation in the process of Indonesian constitutional reform has been limited, it is now necessary to fill that gap by educating the public about the meaning and principles of constitutionalism, the rule of law, human rights protection, and religious liberty outlined in the amendments to the 1945 Constitution.

Lastly, beyond the three case studies examined in this book, the amendments to the 1945 Constitution also include other interesting provisions on such matters as the role of the central bank (Articles 23A–D), national economy (Article 33), decentralization of power to the regions (Articles 18, 18A and 18B), national defence and security (Article 30), state audit board (Articles 23E–G), and national education (Article 31). Since these provisions are not covered by this book, they will need to be examined more fully — either in the perspective of *shari'a* or constitutional law — in future studies.

Having examined all the issues above, I recommend that the substantive *shari'a* approach that has been performed by most Islamic political parties in Indonesia during the 1999–2002 constitutional reform should be taken into account by other Muslim countries. Under this approach, the flexibility of Islamic law is secured, and the citizens' constitutional rights are guaranteed.

The recent 2004 elections in Indonesia is illustrative. Indonesian people have exercised their constitutional rights to rotate elites, to select leaders, to express grievances and desires, in free and fair elections. In the context of the Muslim world, certainly this rare experience is a significant way to show that the compatibility of *shari'a* and constitutionalism does not lead to a political chaos or to inflict harm (*mafsadah*) upon society. Instead, it protects *maslahah al-ammah* (public interest) — as the main objective of *shari'a*.

Notes

1. Fred Halliday, "The Politics of Islamic Fundamentalism: Iran, Tunisia and the Challenge to the Secular State", in *Islam, Globalization and Postmodernity*, edited by A.S. Ahmed and H. Donnan (London: Routledge, 1994), p. 96.
2. Mashood A. Baderin, *International Human Rights and Islamic Law* (Oxford: Oxford University Press, 2003), p. 219.
3. See Nathan J. Brown, *Constitutions in a Non-Constitutional World: Arab Basic Laws and the Prospects for Accountable Government* (Albany, NY: State University of New York Press, 2002), p. 162.
4. See Bahtiar Effendy, *Islam and the State in Indonesia* (Singapore: Institute of Southeast Asian Studies, 2003). This book is based on Effendy's Ph.D. thesis in the Department of Political Science, Ohio State University (1997). Although most of the chapters focus on the relationship between the state and Islam during Soeharto era, this book devotes the last chapter to the discussion on the situation in the post-Soeharto era. The last chapter was presented at a seminar on "Sharia and Democracy: The Southeast Asian Experience", organized by Center for Contemporary Islamic Studies and Konrad-Adenauer Stiftung, Singapore, 13–14 March 2004.
5. David Hollenbach, "Politically Active Churches: Some Empirical Prolegomena to a Normative Approach", in *Religion and Contemporary Liberalism*, edited by

Paul J. Weithman (Notre Dame: University of Notre Dame Press, 1997), p. 301.

6. For a full account on the 2004 general election, see National Democratic Institute for International Affairs (NDI), "Advancing Democracy in Indonesia: The Second Democratic Legislative Elections since the Transition", June 2004, available at http://www.accessdemocracy.org/library/ 1728_id_legelections_063004.pdf.

7. One of the PBB's leaders, Ahmad Sumargono, was very angry with his party's decision to support Yudhoyono. He publicly stated that he supports Amien Rais of Partai Amanat Nasional (PAN). It should be noted, however, even Sumargono's position here could be questioned since PAN took the substantive *shari'a* approach during the 1999–2002 constitutional reform, whereas Sumargono and PBB supported the formal approach particularly when examining the proposal to amend Article 29. Of course, Amien Rais, the former General Chairperson of Muhammadiyah, the second largest Islamic organization in Indonesia, could be considered as more "Islamic" than Yudhoyono. However, Amien Rais only obtained 14.94 per cent of the vote in the first round and therefore failed to go on to the second round of presidential election in 2004.

8. More information can be found in Yusril Ihza Mahendra, *Modernisme dan Fundamentalisme dalam Politik Islam: Perbandingan Partai Masyumi (Indonesia) dan Partai Jama'at-i-Islami (Pakistan)* (Jakarta: Paramadina, 1999).

9. Article 9(1), Law No. 12 of 2003 on General Elections.

10. See Aay Muhammad Furkon, *Partai Keadilan Sejahtera: Ideologi dan Praksis Politik Kaum Muda Muslim Indonesia Kontemporer* (Bandung: Teraju, 2004), p. 182.

11. Gary F. Bell, "Obstacles to Reform The 1945 Constitution: Constitutions do not Perform Miracles", *Van Zorge Report on Indonesia — Commentary and Analysis on Indonesian Politics and Economics* III, no. 6 (2001).

BIBLIOGRAPHY

1981 Universal Islamic Declaration of Human Rights (UIDHR). Available at http://www.al-bab.com/arab/docs/international/ hr1981.htm#III.

Abdillah, Masykuri. *Responses of Indonesian Muslim Intellectuals to the Concept of Democracy (1966–1993)*. Hamburg: Abera Verl, 1997.

Abramski-Blig, Irit. "The Judiciary (Qadis) as a Governmental-Administrative Tool in Early Islam". In *The Formation of Islamic Law*, edited by Wael Hallaq. Burlington: Ashgate, 2004.

Adiwijoyo, Suwarno. *Amandemen UUD 1945*. Jakarta: Intermasa, 2000.

Adji, Oemar Seno. "An Indonesian Perspective on the American Constitutional Influence". In *Constitutionalism in Asia: Asian Views of the American Influence*, edited by Lawrence Ward Beer. Berkeley: University of California Press, 1979.

———. *Peradilan Bebas Negara Hukum*. Jakarta: Erlangga, 1980.

Ahmad, Mumtaz, ed. *State, Politics and Islam*. Washington, D.C.: American Trust Publications, 1986.

Alatas, Syed Farid. *Democracy and Authoritarianism in Indonesia and Malaysia: The Rise of the Post-Colonial State*. Houndsmill: Macmillan, 1997.

Ali, Parveen Shaukat. "Equality as a Basic Human Rights in Islam". In *Human Rights in Islamic Law*, edited by Tahir Mahmood. New Delhi: Genuine Publications, 1993.

Ali-Karamali, Shaista P. and Fiona Dunne. "The Ijtihad Controversy". *Arab Law Quarterly* 9 (1994): 238.

Alrasid, Harun. *Naskah UUD 1945 Sesudah Tiga Kali Diubah oleh MPR*. Jakarta: UI Press, 2002.

Alwani, Taha Jabir al-. *The Ethics of Disagreement in Islam*. Herndon, VA: International Institute of Islamic Thought, n.d. Available at http://www.usc.edu/dept/MSA/ humanrelations/alalwani_disagreement/chapter3.html.

———. *Usul Al Fiqh Al Islami: Source Methodology In Islamic Jurisprudence*. Herndon, VA: International Institute of Islamic Thought, 1990. Available at http:// www.usc.edu/dept/MSA/law/alalwani_usulalfiqh/ch3.html.

———. "The Crisis of Thought and Ijtihad". *American Journal of Islamic Social Sciences* 10, no. 2 (1993): 237.

———. "Globalization: Centralization not Globalism". *American Journal of Islamic Social Sciences* 15, no. 3 (1998): vii.

Alyubi, M. Sa'd b. Ahmad b. Mas'ud al-. *Maqasid al-Shari'a al-Islamiya wa Alaqatuha bi Adillah al-Shar'iyyah*. Riyadh: Dar al-hijrah li al-Nasyr wa al-Tawzi', 1998.

Amidi, Sayf al-Din al-. *al-Ihkam fi Usul al-Ahkam*, vol. 4. Cairo: Dar al-Kutub al-Khidiwiya, 1914.

Amir, Zainal Abidin. *Peta Islam Politik: Pasca-Soeharto*. Jakarta: LP3S, 2003.

Anshari, Endang Saifuddin. "The Jakarta Charter of June 1945: A History of the Gentleman's Agreement between the Islamic and the Secular Nationalist in Modern Indonesia". M.A. thesis, McGill University, Montreal, 1976.

Arifin, Busthanul. *Pelembagaan Hukum Islam di Indonesia*. Jakarta: Gema Insani Press, 1996.

Arjomand, Said Amir. "Religion and Constitutionalism in Western History and in Modern Iran and Pakistan". In *The Political Dimensions of Religion*, edited by Said Amir Arjomand. Albany: State University of New York Press, 1993.

Armstrong, Karen. "The Curse of the Infidel". *The Guardian*, 20 June 2002.

Asad, Muhammad. *The Principles of State and Government in Islam*. Kuala Lumpur: Islamic Book Trust, 1980.

Ashmawi, Muhammad Sa'id al-. *al-Shari'a al-Islamiya wa al-Qanun al-Misri*. Cairo: Maktabah Madbuli al-Shaghir, 1996.

Aspinall, Edward, and Gerry van Klinken. "Chronology of Crisis". In *The Last Days of President Soeharto*, edited by Edward Aspinall, Herb Faith, Gerry van Klinken. Clayton: Monash Asia Institute, 1999.

Asshiddiqie, Jimly. "Telaah Akademis atas Perubahan UUD 1945". *Jurnal Demokrasi & HAM* 1, no. 4 (2001): 17.

Audah, Abd al-Qadir. *al-Islam wa Awda'tuna al-Siyasiyah*. Beirut: Mu'assasat al-Risalah, 1980.

Awa, Mohamed S. El-. *On the Political System of the Islamic State*. Indianapolis: American Trust Publications, 1980.

———. *Punishment in Islamic Law: A Comparative Study*. Indianapolis: American Trust Publication, 1982.

Awa, Muhammad Salim al-. *Fi al-Nizam al-Siyasi li al-Dawla al-Islamiyya*. Cairo: al-Maktab al-Misri al-Hadis, 1983.

Ayoub, Mahmoud. "Religious Freedom and the Law of Apostasy in Islam". In *Islamochristiana*, No. 20. N.p.: Pontificio Istituto di Studi Arabi d'Islamistica, 1994.

Azhari, Aidul Fitriciada et al. *Dari Catatan Wiranto Jenderal Purnawirawan Bersaksi di Tengah Badai*. Jakarta: IDe Indonesia, 2003.

Azhary, Tahir. *Negara Hukum*. Jakarta: Bulan Bintang, 1992.

Azra, Azyumardi. "The Indonesian Marriage Law of 1974". In *Shari'a and Politics in Modern Indonesia*, edited by Arskal Salim and Azyumardi Azra. Singapore: Institute of Southeast Asian Studies, 2003.

Baderin, Mashood A. *International Human Rights and Islamic Law*. Oxford: Oxford University Press, 2003.

Bagby, Ihsan Abdul. "Utility in Classical Islamic Law: The Concept of *Maslahah* in *Usul al-Fiqh*". Ph.D. thesis, University of Michigan, 1986.

Barton, Greg. "Neo-Modernism: A Vital Synthesis of Traditionalism and Modernism in Indonesian Islam". *Studia Islamika* 2, no. 3 (1995): 1–75.

———. "Islam, *Pancasila* and the Middle Path of *Tawassuth*: The Thought of

Achmad Siddiq". In *Nahdlatul Ulama, Traditional Islam and Modernity in Indonesia*, edited by Greg Barton and Greg Fealey. Clayton: Monash Asia Institute, 1996.

———. "Indonesia's Nurcholish Madjid and Abdurrahman Wahid as Intellectual *Ulama*: The Meeting of Islamic Traditionalism and Modernism in Neo-Modernist Thought". *Islam and Christian-Muslim Relations* 8 (1997): 3.

——— and Greg Fealy, eds. *Nahdlatul Ulama: Traditionalist Islam and Modernity in Indonesia*. Monash: Monash Asia Institute, 1996.

Basalim, Umar. *Pro-Kontra Piagam Jakarta di Era Reformasi*. Jakarta: Pustaka Indonesia Satu, 2002.

"Basic Principles on the Independence of the Judiciary", adopted by the seventh United Nations Congress on the Prevention of Crime and the Treatment of Offenders, held at Milan on 26 August – 6 September 1985, and endorsed by General Assembly Resolutions 40/32 of 29 November 1985, and 40/146 of 13 December 1985.

Baso, Ahmad. "UU NO.1/PNPS/1965 dan Soal 'Agama Resmi' Itu: Sebuah Tatapan untuk JPS". Paper for Rakernas "Perencanaan Strategis Jaringan" Pokja-pokja Jamaah Persaudaraan Sejati di Puncak, Ciloto, 28–31 July 2004.

Baswedan, Anies Rasyid. "Political Islam in Indonesia: Present and Future Trajectory". *Asian Survey* (forthcoming).

BBC News. "Muslim leader moves to block Megawati", 20 June 1999. Available at http://news.bbc.co.uk/1/hi/world/asia-pacific/373658.stm.

Bell, Gary F. "Obstacles to Reform The 1945 Constitution: Constitutions do not Perform Miracles". *Van Zorge Report on Indonesia: Commentary and Analysis on Indonesian Politics and Economics* III, no. 6. (2001).

———. "Minority Rights and Regionalism in Indonesia: Will Constitutional Recognition Lead to Disintegration and Discrimination?". *Singapore Journal of International and Comparative Law* 5 (2001): 784.

Belliotti, R. A. "The Rule of Law and the Critical Legal Studies Movement". *University of Western Ontario Law Review* 24, no. 1 (1986): 67–78.

Benedanto, Pax, ed. *Pemilihan Umum 1999: Demokrasi atau Rebutan Kursi?* Jakarta: LSPP, 1999.

Berger, Maurits. "Public Policy and Islamic Law: The Modern *Dhimm* in Contemporary Egyptian Family Law". *Islamic Law and Society* 8, no. 1 (2001): 88.

Berger, Peter. "Secularism in Retreat". *The National Interest*, Winter 1996/1997, pp. 3–12.

———. "Epistemiological Modesty: An Interview with Peter Berge". *Christian Century* 114 (1997): 974.

———. "Protestantism and the Quest for Certainty". *Christian Century* 115, no. 23 (1998): 782.

Berkes, Niyazi. *The Development of Secularism in Turkey*. Montreal: McGill University Press, 1964.

Beyer, Peter. *Religion and Globalization*. London: Sage Publication Ltd, 1994.

Bielefeldt, Heiner. "Muslim Voices in the Human Rights Debate". *Human Rights Quarterly* 17, no. 4 (1995): 602.

Billings, Dwight B. and Shaunna L. Scott. "Religion and Political Legitimacy". *Annual Review of Sociology* 20 (1994): 173.

Bird, Judith. "Indonesia in 1998: The Pot Boils Over". *Asian Survey* 39 (1999): 29.

Biro Pusat Statistik (BPS). 2000. Available at http://www.bps.go.id/sector/ population/ pop2000.htm.

Black, Antony. *The History of Islamic Political Thought: From the Prophet to the Present.* Edinburgh: Edinburgh University Press, 2001.

Boland, B. J. *The Struggle of Islam in Modern Indonesia*. The Hague: Martinus Nijhoff, 1982.

Botiveau, Bernard. *al-Shari'a al-Islamiya wa al-Qanun fi al-Mujtami'at al-'Arabiya*, translated from *Loi Islamique Et Droit Dans les Sociétés Arabes*. Cairo: Sina li al-Nasyr, 1997.

Bourchier, David. "Lineages of Organicist Political Thought in Indonesia". Ph.D. thesis, Monash University, 1996.

Boyle, Kevin and Adel Omar Sherif, eds. *Human Rights and Democracy: The Role of the Supreme Constitutional Court of Egypt*. London: Kluwer Law International, 1996.

Brown II, Scott Kent. "The Coptic Church in Egypt: A Comment on Protecting Religious Minorities from Nonstate Discrimination". *Brigham Young University Law Review* 2000 (2000): 1049.

Brown, L. Carl. *Religion and State: The Muslim Approach to Politics*. New York: Columbia University Press, 2000.

Brown, Nathan J. "Islamic Constitutionalism in Theory and Practice". In *Democracy, the Rule of Law and Islam*, edited by Eugene Cotran and Adel Omar Sherif. London: Kluwer Law International, 1999.

———. *Constitutions in a Non-Constitutional World: Arab Basic Laws and the Prospects for Accountable Government*. Albany, NY: State University of New York Press, 2002.

Bruce, Steve. *Religion and Modernization: Sociologists and Historians Debate the Secularization Thesis*. Oxford: Clarendon Press, 1992.

Bukhari, Abu 'Abd Allah Muhammad b. Isma'il b. Ibrahim b. al-Mugirah b. *Sahih Bukhari*. Beirut: Dar al-Qalam, 1987.

Bureau of Democracy, Human Rights, and Labor. "Indonesia". International Religious Freedom Report 2004, 15 September 2004.

Cammack, Mark. "Islamic Law in Indonesia's New Order". *International and Comparative Law Quarterly* 38 (1989).

———. "Islam, Nationalism, and the State in Suharto's Indonesia". *Wisconsin International Law Journal* 17 (1999): 27.

———. "Indonesia's 1989 Religious Judicature Act: Islamization of Indonesia or Indonesianization of Islam". In *Shari'a and Politics in Modern Indonesia*, edited by Arskal Salim and Azyumardi Azra. Singapore: Institute of Southeast Asian Studies, 2003.

———, L. Young and T. Heaton. "Legislating Social Change in an Islamic Society: Indonesia's Marriage Law". *American Journal of Comparative Law* 44 (1996): 45.

Carpenter, R. Charlie. "Surfacing Children: Limitations of Genocidal Rape Discourse". *Human Rights Quarterly* 22 (2000): 428–77.

Casanova, Jose. *Public Religions in the Modern World*. Chicago: University of Chicago Press, 1994.

Cassel, Doug. "Universal Rights and Asian Culture: Indonesia Converts". *Worldview Commentary*, No. 2, 19 August 1998.

Castiglione, Dario. "The Political Theory of the Constitution". In *Constitutionalism in Transformation*, edited by Richard Bellamy and Dario Castiglione. London: Blackwell Publishers, 1996.

Chaidar, Al. *Pemikiran Politik Proklamator Negara Islam Indonesia S.M. Kartosoewirjo: Fakta dan Sejarah Darul Islam*. Jakarta: Darul Falah, 1999.

Chaudhry, Zainab. "Myth of Misogyny: A Reanalysis of Women's Inheritance in Islamic Law". *Albany Law Review* 61 (1997): 511.

Clark, Dana L. "The World Bank and Human Rights: The Need for Greater Accountability". *Harvard Human Rights Journal* 15 (2002): 205.

Clark, David. "The Many Meanings of the Rule of Law". In *Law, Capitalism and Power in Asia*, edited by Kanishka Jayasuriya. London: Routledge, 1999.

Close, David, ed. *Legislatures in the New Democracies in Latin America*. London: Lynne Rienner Publishers, 1995.

Connolly, Jennifer. "Becoming Christian and Dayak: A Study of Christian Conversion among Dayaks in East Kalimantan, Indonesia". Ph.D. thesis, New School University, 2004.

Constitution of the Arab Republic of Egypt, available at http://www.uam.es/otroscentros/medina/egypt/egypolcon.htm.

Constitution of the Islamic Republic of Iran. Available at http://www.iranonline.com/iran/iran-info/Government/constitution.html.

Constitution of the Republic of Indonesia. Available at http://www.law.unimelb.edu.au/alc/assets/1945_Indo_Constitution.pdf.

Constitution of the Republic of Turkey. Available at http://www.mfa.gov.tr/grupc/ca/cag/I142.htm.

Cotran, Eugene and Adel Omar Sherif, eds. *Democracy, the Rule of law and Islam*. London: Kluwer Law International, 1999.

Coulson, Noel J. "Doctrine and Practice in Islamic Law". *Bulletin of the School of Oriental and African Studies* 18, no. 2 (1956): 211–26.

———. *A History of Islamic Law*. U.K.: Edinburgh University Press, 1964.

Crone, Patricia. *Medieval Islamic Political Thought*. Edinburgh: Edinburgh University Press, 2004.

Crouch, Harold. "Masjumi". In *The Oxford Encyclopedia of the Modern Islamic World*, vol. II, edited by John L. Esposito. New York: Oxford University Press, 1995.

Damanik, Ali Said. *Fenomena Partai Keadilan: Transformasi 20 Tahun Gerakan Tarbiyah di Indonesia*. Jakarta: Teraju, 2002.

Darmaputera, Eka. *Pancasila and the Search for Identity and Modernity in Indonesian Society: A Cultural and Ethical Analysis*. Leiden: E.J. Brill, 1988.

———. "Aspek-aspek Etis Teologis Hubungan Gereja-Negara". In *Hubungan Gereja dan Negara dan Hak Asasi Manusia*, edited by Weinata Sairin and J. M. Pattiasina. Jakarta: BPK Gunung Mulia, 1996.

———. "Prinsip-prinsip Hubungan Agama-Negara". In *Pergulatan Kehadiran Kristen di Indonesia: Teks-teks Terpilih Eka Darmaputera*, by Trisno Sutanto et al. Jakarta: BPK Gunung Mulia, 2001.

Dawalibi, Muhammad Ma'ruf al-. *al-Madkhal ila 'Ilm al-Usul al-Fiqh*. Damascus: Matba'ah Jami'ah Damsyq, 1959.

Dicey, Albert. V. *Introduction to the Study of the Law of the Constitution*. London: Macmillan, 1959.

Dietze, Gottfried. *Two Concepts of the Rule of Law*. Indianapolis: Liberty Fund, 1973.

"Documents of Kongres Mujahidin". Yogyakarta, 5–7 August 2000. Available at http://www.geocities.com/kongresmujahidin/.

Douzinas, Costas. *The End of Human Rights*. Oxford: Hart, 2000.

Dworkin, Ronald. "Political Judges and the Rule of Law". *A Matter of Principle*. Cambridge: Harvard University Press, 1985.

Effendy, Bahtiar. *Islam and the State in Indonesia*. Singapore: Institute of Southeast Asian Studies, 2003.

Eklof, Stefan. *Indonesian Politics in Crisis: The Long Fall of Soeharto, 1966–98*. Copenhagen: Nordic Institute of Asian Studies, 1999.

Emmerson, Donald K. "Islam in Modern Indonesia: Political Impasse, Cultural Opportunity". In *Change and the Muslim World*, edited by Philip H. Stoddard. Syracuse: Syracuse University Press, 1981.

Emon, Anver. "Reflections on the 'Constitution of Medina': An Essay on Methodology and Ideology in Islamic Legal History". *UCLA Journal of Islamic and Near Eastern Law* 1 (2002): 103.

Enayat, Hamid. *Modern Islamic Political Thought*. London: Macmillan, 1982.

Engineer, Asghar Ali. *The Islamic State*. New York: Advent Books, 1980.

———. *Theory and Practise of the Islamic State*. Lahore: Vanguard Books, 1985.

Esposito, John L. and James P. Piscatori. "Democratization and Islam". *Middle East Journal*, 45, no. 3 (1991): 428.

Esposito, John L. and Azzam Tamimi, eds. *Islam and Secularism in the Middle East*. New York: New York University Press, 2000.

Estiko, Didit Hariadi, ed. *Amandemen UUD 1945 dan Implikasinya terhadap Pembangunan Sistem Hukum Nasional*. Jakarta: Tim Hukum Pusat Pengkajian dan Pelayanan Informasi Sekretariat Jenderal DPR-RI, 2001.

Fadl, Khaled Abou El. "Constitutionalism and the Islamic Sunni Legacy". *UCLA Journal of Islamic & Near Eastern Law* 1 (2002): 67.

———. "Islam and the Challenge of Democracy: Can Individual Rights and Popular

Sovereignty Take Root in Faith?". *Boston Review*, April/May 2003. Available at http://bostonreview.net/BR28.2/abou.html.

Falaakh, Mohammad Fajrul. "Komisi Konstitusi dan Peran Rakyat dalam Perubahan UUD 1945". *Analisis CSIS: Di Ambang Krisis Konstitusi?* No. 2, 2002, pp. 189–90.

Faris, M. Abd al-Qadir Abu. *al-Nizam al-Siyasi fi al-Islam*. Beirut: Dar al-Qur'an al-Karim, 1984.

Farrell, David M. *Comparing Electoral Systems*. London: Prentice Hall/Harvester Wheatsheaf, 1997.

Faruqi, Shad Saleem. "Constitutional Law, the Rule of Law and Systems of Governance in Islam". Paper presented at the Conference on Islamic Law and the West: Can Secular Laws and Syari'ah Co-Exist?, Asian Law Centre, University of Melbourne, 19 September 2002. Available at http://www.law.unimelb.edu.au/alc/assets/faruqi%20paper.pdf.

Fasi, Muhammad bin al-Hasan al-Hajawi al-Sa'alibi al-. *al-Fikr al-Sami fi Tarikh al-Fiqh al-Islami*. Medina: al-Maktabah al-'Ilmiyah, 1396H.

Federspiel, Howard M. *Persatuan Islam: Islamic Reform in Twentieth Century Indonesia*. Ithaca: Cornell University, 1970.

Feith, Herbert, and Lance Castles, eds. *Indonesian Political Thinking, 1945–1965*. Ithaca: Cornell University Press, 1970.

Ferencz, Benjamin B. "From Nuremberg to Rome". May 1998, Available at http://www.benferencz.org/bonnlec2.htm.

Fluehr-Lobban, Carolyn, ed. *Against Islamic Extremism: The Writings of Muhammad Sa'id al-Ashmawy*. Gainesville: University Press of Florida, 1998.

Freedom House Report. Available at http://www.freedomhouse.org/research/freeworld/2003/countryratings/iran.htm.

Furkon, Aay Muhammad. *Partai Keadilan Sejahtera: Ideologi dan Praksis Politik Kaum Muda Muslim Indonesia Kontemporer*. Bandung: Teraju, 2004.

Gallagher, Nancy. "Apostasy, Feminism, and the Discourse of Human Rights". 2003. Available at http://repositories.cdlib.org/uciaspubs/editedvolumes/4/1058.

Gaudron, Mary. "Reply to Professor Michel Troper 'The Limits of the Rule of Law' ". Rule of Law Lecture Series, The Centre for Comparative Constitutional Studies, University of Melbourne, 10 April 2001.

Geertz, Clifford. *The Religion of Java*. Chicago, University of Chicago Press, 1979.

Ghazali, Abu Hamid al-. *al-Tibr al-Masbuk fi Nasihat al-Muluk*. Available at http://www.al-eman.com/Islamlib/viewchp.asp?BID=167&CID=2#s10.

———. *Fada'ih al-Batiniyya wa Fada'il al-Mustazhiriyyah*. Available at http://www.ghazali.org/works/fadiah.pdf (in Arabic) and at http://www.ghazali.org/books/mz-4.pdf (in English).

Ghazali, Abu Hamid Muhammad al-. *al-Mustasfa min 'Ilm al-Usul*. Medina: al-Jami'ah al-Islamiyah, n.d.

Ghunaimi, Mohammad Talaat al-. *The Muslim Conception of International Law and the Western Approach*. The Hague: Martinus Nijhoff, 1968.

Gill, Robin. "The Future of Religious Participation and Belief in Britain and Beyond". In *The Blackwell Companion to Sociology of Religion*, edited by Richard K. Fenn. Oxford: UK and Malden, MA: Blackwell Publishers, 2001.

Gindy, Gamil Mohammed El-. "The Shura and Human Rights in Islamic Law: The Relevance of Democracy". In *The Rule of Law in the Middle East and the Islamic World*, edited by Eugene Cotran and Mai Yamani. London: I.B. Tauris, 2000.

Glenn, H. Patrick. "The Capture, Reconstruction and Marginalization of 'Custom' ". *American Journal of Comparative Law* 45 (1997): 613.

———. *Legal Traditions of the World*. New York: Oxford University Press, 2000.

Goldziher, Ignaz. *Introduction to Islamic Theology and Law*. New York: Princeton University Press, 1981.

Gonggong, Anhar. *Amandemen Konstitusi, Otonomi Daerah dan Federalisme: Solusi untuk Masa Depan*. Yogyakarta: Media Presindo, 2001.

———. *Menengok Sejarah Konstitusi Indonesia*. Yogyakarta: Ombak and Media Presindo, 2002.

Goodroad, Scott L. "The Challenge of Free Speech: Asian Values v. Unfettered Free Speech, an Analysis of Singapore and Malaysia in the New Global Order". *Indiana International and Comparative Law Review* 9 (1998): 259.

Gould, Ron, Christine Jackson, and Loren Wells. *Strengthening Democracy: A Parliamentary Perspective*. Aldershot: Dartmouth, 1995.

Griffel, Frank. "Toleration and Exclusion: al-Shafi'i and al-Ghazali on the Treatment of Apostates". *Bulletin of the School of Oriental and African Studies* 64 (2001): 3.

Grote, Rainer. "Rule of Law, *Rechtsstaat* and *Etat de Droit*". In *Constitutionalism, Universalism and Democracy: A Comparative Analysis*, edited by Christian Starck. Baden-Baden: Nomos Verlagsgesellschaft, 1999.

Habibie Centre, The. *Naskah Akademis dan Draf Rancangan Naskah Undang-Undang Dasar Republik Indonesia*. Jakarta: The Habibie Centre, 2001.

Hague, Rod and Martin Harrop. *Comparative Government and Politics*. Hampshire: Palgrave, 2001.

Haidar, M. Ali. *Nahdatul Ulama dan Islam di Indonesia: Pendekatan Fikih dalam Politik*. Jakarta: Gramedia Pustaka Utama, 1994.

Hakim, Muhammad Taqi al-. *al-Usul al-'Ammah li al-Fiqh al-Muqarin*. Beirut: Dar al-Andalas, 1963.

Hallaq, Wael. "Was the Gate of Ijtihad Closed?". *International Journal of Middle East Studies* 16 (1984): 3.

———. "On the Origins of the Controversy about the Existence of Mujtahids and the Gate of Ijtihad". *Studia Islamica* 63 (1986): 129.

———. "From *Fatawa* to *Furu*: Growth and Change in Islamic Substantive Law". *Islamic Law and Society* 1, no. 1 (1994): 29.

Halliday, Fred. "The Politics of Islamic Fundamentalism: Iran, Tunisia and the Challenge to the Secular State". In *Islam, Globalization and Postmodernity*, edited by Akbar S. Ahmed and H. Donnan. London: Routledge, 1994.

Harding, Andrew. "The Keris, the Crescent and the Blind Goddess: The State, Islam and the Constitution in Malaysia". *Singapore Journal of International and Comparative Law* 6 (2002): 154.

Harjono, Anwar. *Perjalanan Politik Bangsa*. Jakarta: Gema Insani Press, 1997.

Hartono, Sunaryati. *Apakah Rule of Law Itu?* Bandung: Alumni, 1982.

Harun, Lukman. *Muhammadiyah dan Pancasila*. Jakarta: Pustaka Panjimas, 1986.

Hasan, Ahmad. "The Political Role of Ijma". *Islamic Studies* 8 (1969): 136.

————. *The Early Development of Islamic Jurisprudence*. Islamabad: Islamic Research Institute, 1970.

Hasan, Husain Hamid. *Nazariya al-Maslahah fi al-Fiqh al-Islami*. Cairo: Dar al-Nahdah al-'Arabiyah, 1971.

Hassal, Graham and Cheryl Saunders. *Asia-Pacific Constitutional Systems*. Cambridge: Cambridge University Press, 2002.

Hassan, Mohammad Kamal. "Contemporary Muslim Religio-Political Thought in Indonesia: The Response to New Order Modernization". Ph.D. dissertation, Columbia University, 1975.

Hayek, F. A. *The Rule of Law*. California: Institute for Humane Studies, 1975.

Hayek, Friedrich von. *The Political Ideal of the Rule of Law*. Cairo: National Bank of Egypt, 1955.

Hazairin. *Demokrasi Pancasila*. Jakarta: Tintamas, 1970.

Heclo, Hugh and Wilfred M. McClay, eds. *Religion Returns to the Public Square: Faith and Policy in America*. Washington, D.C.: Woodrow Wilson Center Press; Baltimore, MD: Johns Hopkins University Press, 2003.

Hefner, Robert W. "Islam, State and Civil Society: ICMI and the Struggle for the Indonesian Middle Class". *Indonesia* 56 (1993): 1–35.

————. "Modernity and the Challenge of Pluralism: Some Indonesian Lesson". *Studia Islamika* 2, no. 4 (1995): 37.

————. "Secularization and Citizenship in Muslim Indonesia". In *Religion, Modernity, and Postmodernity*, edited by Paul Heelas. Oxford: Blackwell Publishers, 1998.

————. *Civil Islam: Muslims and Democratization in Indonesia*. Princeton, NJ: Princeton University Press, 2000.

Henkin, Louis. "Elements of Constitutionalism". Occasional Paper Series, Center for the Study of Human Rights, 1994.

Hermann, Rainer. "Political Islam in Secular Turkey". *Islam and Christian-Muslim Relations* 14, no. 3 (2003): 265–76.

Hibri, Azizah Y. al-. "Islamic and American Constitutional Law: Borrowing Possibilities or a History of Borrowing?". *University of Pennsylvania Journal of Constitutional Law* 1 (1999): 492.

————. "Islamic Constitutionalism and the Concept of Democracy". In *Border Crossings: Toward a Comparative Political Theory*, edited by Fred Dallmayr. Maryland: Lexington Books, 1999.

Hobink, M. *Two Halves of the Same Truth: Schacht, Hallaq, and the Gate of Ijtihad*. Amsterdam: Middle East Research Associates, 1994.

Hollenbach, David. "Contexts of the Political Role of Religion: Civil Society and Culture". *San Diego Law Review* 30, no. 4 (1993): 878.

——. "Politically Active Churches: Some Empirical Prolegomena to a Normative Approach". In *Religion and Contemporary Liberalism*, edited by Paul J. Weithman. Notre Dame: University of Notre Dame Press, 1997.

Hooker, M. B. *Islamic Law in South-East Asia*. Singapore: Oxford University Press, 1984.

——. "The State and *Shari'a* in Indonesia". In *Shari'a and Politics in Modern Indonesia*, edited by Arskal Salim and Azyumardi Azra. Singapore: Institute of Southeast Asian Studies, 2003.

Hosen, Ibrahim. "Fiqh Siyasah dalam Tradisi Pemikiran Islam Klasik". *Jurnal Ulumul Qur'an* 2, no. 4 (1993): 58–66.

——. "Taqlid dan Ijtihad: Beberapa Pengertian Dasar". In *Kontekstualisasi Doktrin Islam Dalam Sejarah*, edited by Budhy Munawar-Rachman. Jakarta: Paramadina, 1995.

Hosen, Nadirsyah. "Can a Woman Become the President of the World's Largest Muslim Country? Megawati — an Indonesian Political Victim". Paper presented at Women in Asia Conference, Australian National University, Canberra, 23–26 September 2001.

——. "Human Rights and Freedom of Press in the Post-Soeharto Era: A Critical Analysis". *Asia-Pacific Journal on Human Rights and the Law* 3, no. 2 (2002): 1–104.

——. "Revelation in a Modern Nation State: Muhammadiyah and Islamic Legal Reasoning in Indonesia". *Australian Journal of Asian Law* 4, no. 3 (2002): 232–58.

——. "Fatwa and Politics in Indonesia". In *Shari'a and Politics in Modern Indonesia*, edited by Arskal Salim and Azyumardi Azra. Singapore: Institute of Southeast Asian Studies, 2003.

——. "Indonesian Political Laws in Habibie Era: Between Political Struggle and Law Reform". *Nordic Journal of International Law* 72, no. 4 (2003): 483–518.

——. "Reform of Indonesian Law in the Post-Soeharto Era (1998–1999)". Ph.D. thesis, University of Wollongong, 2003.

——. "Behind the Scenes: Fatwas of Majelis Ulama Indonesia (1975–1998)". *Journal of Islamic Studies* 15, no. 2 (2004): 147–79.

——. "Collective *Ijtihad* and Nahdlatul Ulama". *New Zealand Journal of Asian Studies* 6, no. 1 (2004): 5–26.

Human Rights Watch Report. "Indonesia: The Damaging Debate on Rapes of Ethnic Chinese Women". Available at http://www.hrw.org/hrw/reports98/indonesia3.htm.

Human Rights Watch. "Indonesia: Soeharto-Era Abuses Must Go". 1998. Available at http://www.hrw.org/reports98/indonesia2/.

Huwaydi, Fahmi. *Muwatinun la dhimmiyun*. Cairo: Dar al-Syuruq, 1985.

Indarayana, Denny. "Menguji Kesehatan Capres". *Kompas*, 19 April 2004.

International Commission of Jurists. *The Dynamic Aspects of the Rule of Law in the Modern Age*. Report on the Proceedings of the South-East Asian and Pacific Conference of Jurists, Bangkok, 15–19 February 1965.

International Crisis Group (ICG). "Afghan's Flawed Constitutional Process". Kabul and Brussels, ICG Asia Report No. 56, 12 June 2003.

―――. "Iraq's Constitutional Challenge". Baghdad and Brussels, ICG Middle East Report No. 19, 13 November 2003.

Isma'il, Ibnu Qayim. *Kiai Penghulu Jawa Peranannya di Masa Kolonial*. Jakarta: Gema Insani Press, 1997.

Ismail, Faisal. "*Pancasila* as the Sole Basis for All Political Parties and for All Mass Organizations: An Account of Muslims' Response". Ph.D. dissertation, McGill University, 1995.

Jacob, Herbert et al. *Courts, Law, and Politics in Comparative Perspective*. New Haven: Yale University Press, 1996.

Jawad, Ahmad Fuad 'Abd al-. *al-Bay'ah 'inda Mufakkiri Ahl al-Sunnah wa al-'Aqd al-Ijtima'i fi al-Fikr al-Siyasi al-Hadith: Dirasah Muqaranah fi al-Falsafa al-Siyasiya*. Cairo: Dar Quba', 1998.

Johns, A. H. "Indonesia: Islam and Cultural Pluralism". In *Islam in Asia: Religion, Politics and Society*, edited by John L. Esposito. Oxford: Oxford University Press, 1989.

Johnson, Elaine Paige. "Streams of Least Resistance: The Institutionalization of Political Parties and Democracy in Indonesia". Ph.D. dissertation, University of Virginia, 2002.

Juergensmeyer, Mark. *The New Cold War? Religious Nationalism Confronts the Secular State*. Berkeley and Los Angeles: University of California Press, 1993.

Jung, Al-Haj Mahomed Ullah Ibn S. *The Administration of Justice of Muslim Law*. Delhi: Idarah-I Adabiyat-I Delhi, 1977.

Juwana, Hikmahanto. "Special Report: Assessing Indonesian's Human Right Practice in the Post-Soeharto Era". *Singapore Journal of International and Comparative Law* 7 (2003): 644–77.

Kadir, Suzaina Abdul. "Traditional Islamic Society and the State in Indonesia: The Nahdlatul Ulama, Political Accommodation and the Preservation of Autonomy". Ph.D. dissertation, University of Wisconsin-Madison, 1999.

Kahin, George. *Nationalism and Revolution in Indonesia*. Ithaca: Cornell University Press, 1952.

Kamali, Mohammad Hashim. *Principles of Islamic Jurisprudence*. Cambridge: The Islamic Text Society, 1991.

―――. "Appellate Review and Judicial Independence in Islamic Law". In *Islam and Public Law*, edited by Chibli Mallat. London: CIMEL, 1993.

Kansil, C. S. T., Christine Kansil and Engeline Palendeng. *Konstitusi-Konstitusi Indonesia Tahun 1945–2000*. Jakarta: Pustaka Sinar Harapan, 2001.

Kenney, Charles D. "Reflections on Horizontal Accountability: Democratic Legitimacy, Majority Parties and Democratic Stability in Latin America". Paper presented at the Conference on Institutions, Accountability, and Democratic Governance in Latin America, Kellogg Institute for International Studies, University of Notre Dame, 8–9 May 2000.

Kerr, Malcolm H. *Islamic Reform: The Political and Legal Theories of Muhammad 'Abduh and Rashid Rida*. Berkeley: University of California Press, 1966.

Khadduri, Majid. *The Islamic Law of Nations: Shaybani's Siyar*. Baltimore, MD: Johns Hopkins Press, 1966.

Khaldun, Ibn. *Muqaddimah*. Mecca: Dar al-Bazi, 1978.

Khallaf, 'Abd al-Wahhab. *Al-Siyasa al-Shar'iyya*. Cairo: Salafiyah, 1350H.

Khan, Muhammad Zafrullah. *Islam and Human Rights*. Islamabad: Islam International Publication Ltd, 1999.

Khatab, Sayed. "The Concept of Jahiliyyah in the Thought of Sayyid Quthb". Ph.D. thesis, University of Melbourne, September 2002.

Kim, Hyung-Jun. "The Changing Interpretation of Religious Freedom in Indonesia". *Journal of Southeast Asian Studies* 29, no. 2 (1998) 357.

King, Blair A. "Empowering the Presidency: Interests and Perceptions in Indonesia's Constitutional Reforms, 1999–2002". Ph.D. thesis, Ohio State University, 2004.

Kompas. "Semangat PAH I BP MPR Pemilihan Presiden Langsung". 11 September 2001.

———. "Beda Prinsip di Putaran Kedua Pemilihan Presiden". 10 November 2001.

———. "Pemilihan Presiden Didesak Masuk UU Pemilu". 13 June 2002.

———. "Jadi Pilar Demokrasi, Pers Tuntut Budaya Hukum". 11 October 2002.

Kurzman, Charles. *Liberal Islam: A Source Book*. New York: Oxford University Press, 1988.

———. "Liberal Islam: Prospects and Challenges". *Journal Middle East Review of International Affairs* 3, no. 3 (1999). Available at http://www.biu.ac.il/SOC/besa/meria/journal/1999/ issue3/jvol3no3in.html .

Lambton, Ann K. S. *State and Government in Medieval Islam*. New York: Oxford University Press, 1991.

Lane, J. *Constitutions and Political Theory*. Manchester: Manchester University Press, 1996.

Lange, David L. "The Speech and Press Clauses". *UCLA Law Review* 23 (1975): 77.

Lapidus, Ira M. *A History of Islamic Societies*. Cambridge: Cambridge University Press, 1993.

———. "State and Religion in Islamic Societies". *Past and Present* 151 (1996): 3.

Latif, Asad, ed. *Walking the Tightrope: Press Freedom and Professional Standards in Asia*. Singapore: Asian Media Information and Communication Centre, 1998.

Laver, Michael and Kenneth A. Shepsle, eds. *Cabinet Ministers and Parliamentary Government*. Cambridge: Cambridge University Press, 1994.

Legrand, Pierre. "The Impossibility of 'Legal Transplants'". *Maastricht Journal of European and Comparative Law* 4 (1997).

Lev, Daniel S. *Islamic Courts in Indonesia: A Study in the Political Bases of Legal Institutions*. Berkeley: University of California Press, 1972.

————. "Reformasi Hukum Dimulai dari Penggantian Hakim Agung". *Kompas*, 27 October 1999.

————. *Legal Evolution and Political Authority in Indonesia: Selected Essays*. Boston: Kluwer Law International, 2000.

Liddle, R. William. *Leadership and Culture in Indonesian Politics*. Sydney: Allen & Unwin, 1996.

————. "Indonesia's Democratic Transition: Playing by the Rules". In *The Architecture of Democracy*, edited by Andrew Reynolds. Oxford: Oxford University Press, 2002.

————. "New Patterns of Islamic Politics in Democratic Indonesia". In *Piety and Pragmatism: Trends in Indonesian Islamic Politics*. Asia Special Report No. 10. Washington: Woodrow Wilson International Center, 2003.

Lijphart, Arend. *Electoral System and Party Systems: A Study of Twenty-Seven Democracies 1945–1990*. Oxford and New York: Oxford University Press, 1994.

————, ed. *Parliamentary Versus Presidential Government*. New York: Oxford University Press, 1992.

Lindsey, Timothy. "Paradigms, Paradoxes and Possibilities: Towards Understandings of Indonesia's Legal System". In *Asian Laws Through Australian Eyes*, edited by Veronica Taylor. Sydney: Law Book Company, 1997.

————. "From Rule of Law to Law of the Rulers — to Reformation?". In *Indonesia: Law and Society*, edited by Timothy Lindsey. Sydney: The Federation Press, 1999.

————. "Indonesian Constitutional Reform: Mud Towards Democracy". *Singapore Journal of International and Comparative Law* 6 (2002): 244.

————. "Legal Infrastructure and Governance Reform in Post-Crisis Asia: The Case of Indonesia". *Asian Pacific Economic Literature* 18 (2004): 1.

————. "Indonesia: Devaluing Asian Values, Rewriting Rule of Law". In *Asian Discourses of Rule of Law: Theories and Implementation of Rule of Law in Twelve Asian Countries, France, and the U.S.*, edited by Randall Peerenboom. London: RoutledgeCurzon, 2004.

Linnan, David K. "Indonesian Law Reform, or Once More Unto the Breach: A Brief Institutional History". *Australian Journal of Asian Law* 1 (1999): 27.

Lombardi, Clark Benner. "Islamic Law as a Source of Constitutional Law in Egypt: The Constitutionalization of the Sharia in a Modern Arab State". *Columbia Journal of Transnational Law* 37 (1998): 81.

————. "State Law as Islamic Law in Modern Egypt: The Amendment of Article 2 of the Egyptian Constitution and the Article 2 of Jurisprudence of the Supreme Constitutional Court of Egypt". Ph.D. thesis, Columbia University, 2001.

Lubis, Nur Ahmad Fadhil. "Institutionalization and the Unification of Islamic Courts Under the New Order". *Studia Islamika* 2, no. 1 (1995): 1–52.

Lubis, Todung Mulya. *In Search of Human Rights: Legal Political Dilemmas of Indonesia's New Order 1966–1990*. Jakarta: Gramedia Pustaka Utama, 1993.

———. "Constitutional Reforms". In *Governance in Indonesia: Challenges Facing the Megawati Presidency*, edited by Hadi Soesastro et al. Singapore: Institute of Southeast Asian Studies, 2003.

Luhulima, James, ed. *Hari-hari Terpanjang: Menjelang Mundurnya Presiden Soeharto dan Beberapa Peristiwa Terakit*. Jakarta: Kompas, 2001.

Ma'arif, Ahmad Sayfi'i. *Islam dan Masalah Kenegaraan: Studi tentang Percaturan dalam Konstituante*. Jakarta: Lembaga Penelitian Pendidekan dan Penerangan Ekonomi dan Sosial, 1985.

Madjid, Nurcholish. "The Issue of Modernization among Muslims in Indonesia: From a Participant Point of View". In *Readings on Islam in Southeast Asia*, edited by Ahmad Ibrahim, Sharon Siddique, and Yasmin Hussain. Singapore: Institute of Southeast Asian Studies, 1985.

Madkur, Muhammad Salam. *Manahij al-Ijtihad fi al-Islam*. Kuwait: al-Matba'ah al-'Ashriyah al-Kuwait, 1974.

Magnis-Suseno, Frans. "Beberapa Dilema Etis antara Agama dan Negara". In *Kuasa dan Moral*. Jakarta: Gramedia, 2000.

Magnis-Suseno, Franz. "Seputar Rencana UU Peradilan Agama". *Kompas*, 16 June 1989.

Mahendra, Yusril Ihza. *Modernisme dan Fundamentalisme dalam Politik Islam: Perbandingan Partai Masyumi (Indonesia) dan Partai Jama'at-i-Islami (Pakistan)*. Jakarta: Paramadina, 1999.

Mahfud, Moh., Sidik Tono, and Dadan Muttaqien, eds. *Peradilan Agama dan Kompilasi Hukum Islam dalam Tata Hukum Indonesia*. Yogyakarta: UII Press, 1993.

Mahmood, Tahir, ed. *Human Rights in Islamic Law*. New Delhi: Genuine Publications, 1993.

Majah, Abu 'Abd Allah Muhammad b. Yazid b. *Sunan Ibn Majah*. N.p: Dar al-Turas al-Arabi, 1975.

Majelis Ulama Indonesia. *Himpunan Keputusan dan Fatwa*. Jakarta: Sekretariat MUI, Masjid Istiqlal, 1995.

Makdisi, George. "Ash'ari and the Ash'arites in Islamic Religious History". *Studia Islamica* XVII and XVIII (1962 and 1963).

Makka, A. Makmur. *B.J. Habibie: His Life and Career*. 5th ed. March 1999.

Malik, Abu 'Abd Allah. *al-Muwatta'* (book al-Haj). Beirut: al-Syirkah al-'Alamiyah, 1993.

Malik, Adam. *Riwajat dan Perdjuangan Sekitar Proklamasi Kemerdekaan Indonesia 17 Agustus 1945*. Jakarta: Penerbit Widjaya, 1956.

Mallat, Chibli, ed. *Islam and Public Law: Classical and Contemporary Studies*. London: Graham & Trotman, 1993.

———. *The Renewal of Islamic Law*. Cambridge: Cambridge University Press, 1993.

Manin, Bernard. *The Principles of Representative Government*. Cambridge: Cambridge University Press, 1997.

Mardjono, Hartono. *Negara Hukum yang Demokratis*. Jakarta: Yayasan Koridor Pengabdian, 2001.

Masters, Edward. "Indonesia's 1999 Elections: A Second Chance for Democracy". Available at http://www.asiasociety.org/publications/indonesia/.

Masud, Muhammad Khalid. *Shatibi's Philosophy of Islamic Law*. Pakistan: Islamic Research Institute, 1995.

Maududi, Abul A'la al-. *Human Rights in Islam*. London: The Islamic Foundation, 1983.

———. *First Principles of the Islamic State*. Lahore: Islamic Publications, 1983.

———. *Political Theory of Islam*. Lahore: Islamic Publications, 1985.

Mawardi, Abu al-Hasan 'Ali bin Muhammad bin Habib al-. *al-Ahkam as-Sultaniya*. Cairo: Mustafa Babi al-Halabi wa Auladuh, 1996.

Mayer, Ann Elizabeth. *Islam and Human Rights: Tradition and Politics*. Boulder: Westview Press, 1991.

———. "The Fundamentalist Impact on Law, Politics, and Constitutions in Iran, Pakistan and Sudan". In *Fundamentalisms and the State*, edited by Martin E. Marty and R. Scott Appleby. Chicago: University of Chicago Press, 1993.

———. "Conundrums in Constitutionalism: Islamic Monarchies in an Era of Transition". *UCLA Journal of Islamic and Near Eastern Law* 1 (2002): 183.

McHugh, James T. *Comparative Constitutional Traditions*. New York: Peter Lang, 2002.

Media Indonesia. "PDI-P Isyaratkan Tolak Pemilihan Langsung". 30 June 2002.

Mernissi, Fatima. *Women and Islam: An Historical and Theological Enquiry*. Basil: Blackwell, 1991.

———. *Islam and Democracy: Fear of the Modern World*. London: Virago Press, 1993.

———. *The Forgotten Queens of Islam*. Minneapolis: University of Minnesota Press, 1993.

———. "A Feminist Interpretation of Women's Rights in Islam". In *Liberal Islam: A Source Book*, edited by Charles Kurzman. Oxford: Oxford University Press, 1998.

Mietzner, Marcus. "Godly Men in Green". *Inside Indonesia*, No. 53, January–March 1998.

Miller, Michelle Ann. "The Nanggroe Aceh Darussalam Law: A Serious Response to Acehnese Separatism?". *Asian Ethnicity* 5, no. 3 (2004): 333.

Millie, Julian. "The *Tempo* Case: Indonesia's Press Laws, the Pengadilan Tata Usaha Negara and the Indonesian Negara Hukum". In *Indonesia: Law and Society*, edited by Timothy Lindsey. Sydney: The Federation Press, 1999.

Mitha, Farouk. *Al-Ghazali and the Ismailis: A Debate on Reason and Authority in Medieval Islam*. Ismaili Heritage Series no. 5. London: I. B. Tauris and Institute of Ismaili Studies, 2001.

Molavi, Afshin. *Persian Pilgrimages: Journeys Across Iran*. New York: WW Norton, 2002.

Moustafa, Tamir. "Law versus the State: The Judicialization of Politics in Egypt". *Law and Social Inquiry* 28 (2003): 833–69.

MPR. "Pendapat Akhir Fraksi Partai Bulan Bintang MPR". Sidang Tahunan MPR

2000. Reprinted in *Amandemen UUD 1945 Tentang Piagam Jakarta*, edited by Ramlan Mardjoned and Lukman Fatullah. Jakarta: DDII, 2000.

————. "Pendapat Akhir Fraksi Persatuan Pembangunan MPR RI". Sidang Tahunan MPR, 15 August 2000. In *Risalah Sidang Tahunan MPR Tanggal 7 Sampai Dengan Tanggal 18 Agustus 2000*, by Sekretariat Jenderal MPR, Buku Ketiga Jilid 9. Jakarta: Setjen MPR, 2000.

MPR Decree No. III/MPR/1978.

MPR Decree No. IV/MPR/2003.

Muhsin, Amina Wadud al-. "Qur'an and Woman". In *Liberal Islam: A Source Book*, edited by Charles Kurzman. Oxford: Oxford University Press, 1998.

Mujani, Saiful. "Mu'tazila Theology and the Modernization of the Indonesian Muslim Community: Intellectual Portrait of Harun Nasution". *Studia Islamika* 1 (1994): 1.

————. "Religious Democrats: Democratic Culture and Muslim Political Participation in Post-Suharto Indonesia". Ph.D. thesis, Ohio State University, 2004.

———— and R. William Liddle. "Politics, Islam and Public Opinion". *Journal of Democracy* 15, no. 1 (2004): 113.

Mujiburrahman. "Islam and Politics in Indonesia: The Political Thought of Abdurrahman Wahid". *Islam and Christian–Muslim Relations* 10, no. 3 (1999): 344.

Mulder, Nies. *Inside Indonesian Society*. Bangkok: Editions Duang Kamol, 1994.

Mulia, Musdah. *Negara Islam: Pemikiran Politik Husain Haikal*. Jakarta: Paramadina, 2001.

Müller, Christian. "Judging with God's Law on Earth: Judicial Powers of the Qur'an, al-Jama'a of Cordoba in the Fifth/Eleventh Century". *Islamic Law and Society* 7, no. 2 (2000): 159.

Murad, Hasan Qasim. "*Jabr* and *Qadr* in Early Islam: A Reappraisal of their Political and Religious Implications". In *Islamic Studies Presented to Charles J. Adams*, edited by Wael Hallaq and Donald P. Little. Leiden: Brill, 1991.

Musa, Muhammad Yusuf. *Tarikh al-Fiqh al-Islami*. Cairo: Dar al-Ma'rifah, n.d.

Muslim, Abu al-Husain al-Qusyari al-Naisaburi. *Sahih Muslim*. Cairo: Dar Ihya al-Turast al-'Arabi, 1972.

Muti'i, Muhammad al-. *Haqiqah al-Islam wa Usul al-Hukm*. Cairo: Maktabat al-Nahdah al-Hadisah, 1344AH.

Nabhani, Taqiyuddin al-. *Nizam al-Islam*. Available at http://www.hizb-ut-tahrir.org/arabic/kotobmtb/htm/01ndam.htm .

Na'im, Abdullahi Ahmed an-. *Toward an Islamic Reformation*. New York: Syracuse University Press, 1990.

Naim, Mochtar. *The Nahdlatul Ulama Party (1952–1955): An Inquiry into the Origin of its Electoral Success*. M.A. thesis, McGill University, Montreal, 1960.

Nasution, Adnan Buyung. *The Aspiration for Constitutional Government in Indonesia: A Socio-Legal Study of the Indonesian Konstituante 1956–1959*. Jakarta: Pustaka Sinar Harapan, 1992.

National Democratic Institute for International Affairs (NDI). "Advancing Democracy In Indonesia: The Second Democratic Legislative Elections since the Transition". June 2004, available at http://www.accessdemocracy.org/library/ 1728_id_legelections_063004.pdf .

Natsir, Mohammad. "Pengorbanan Umat Islam Sangat Besar". (interview). *Panji Masyarakat*, 11 June 1987.

Ndulo, Muna. "Globalisation and Empire: The Democratization Process and Structural Adjustment in Africa". *Indiana Journal of Global Legal Studies* 10 (2003): 350.

Noer, Deliar. *The Modernist Muslim Movement in Indonesia 1900–1942*. Singapore: Oxford University Press, 1973.

————. *Administration of Islam in Indonesia*. Ithaca: Cornell Modern Indonesia Project Southeast Asia Program Cornell University, 1978.

————. *Pancasila dan Asas Tunggal*. Jakarta: Yayasan Perkhidmatan, 1983.

O'Rourke, Kevin. *Reformasi: The Struggle for Power in Post-Soeharto Indonesia*. Sydney: Allen & Unwin, 2002.

Ohnesorge, John K. M. "On Rule of Law Rhetoric, Economic Development, and Northeast Asia". (English version of "Etat de droit (rule of law) et developpement economique"). *Critique Internationale* 18 (2003): 46–56. Available at http://www.law.wisc.edu/facstaff/download.asp?ID=73.

Ohnesorge, John K. M. "The Rule of Law, Economic Development, and the Developmental States of Northeast Asia". In *Law and Development in East and Southeast Asia*, edited by Christoph Antons. London: RoutledgeCurzon, 2003.

Osman, Fathi. "The Contract for the Appointment of the Head of an Islamic State". In *State, Politics, and Islam*, edited by Mumtaz Ahmad. Indianapolis: American Trust Publications, 1986.

Patterson, C. Perry. "The Evolution of Constitutionalism". *Minnesota Law Review* 32 (1948): 427–57.

Peerenboom, Randall. "Varieties of Rule of Law: An Introduction and Provisional Conclusion". In *Asian Discourses of Rule of Law: Theories and Implementation of Rule of Law in Twelve Asian Countries, France, and the U.S.*, edited by Randall Peerenboom. London: RoutledgeCurzon, 2004.

Piliang, Indra J. "Konstitusi Elit versus Konstitusi Rakyat". *Analisis CSIS: Di Ambang Krisis Konstitusi?* No. 2, 2002.

Pink, Johanna. "A Post-Qur'anic Religion between Apostasy and Public Order: Egyptian Muftis and Courts on the Legal Status of the Baha'i Faith". *Islamic Law and Society* 10, no. 3 (2003): 409.

Powe, Lucas A., Jr. *The Fourth Estate and the Constitution: Freedom of the Press in America*. California: University of California Press, 1991.

Powers, David S. *Studies in Qur'an and Hadith: The Formation of the Islamic Law of Inheritance*. Berkeley: University of California Press, 1986.

Pratiknya, Ahmad Watik, Umar Juoro, Indria Samego et al. *Reform in Indonesia: Vision and Achievements of President Habibie*, vol. 1. Jakarta: The Habibie Centre, 1999.

Price, Daniel. *Islamic Political Culture, Democracy, and Human Rights: A Comparative Study*. Westport: Connecticut, Praeger, 1999.

Primariantari, Rudiah. "Women, Violence, and Gang Rape in Indonesia". *Cardozo Journal of International and Comparative Law* 7 (1999): 245.

Quthb, Sayyid. *Ma'alim fi al-Tariq*. Cairo: Dar al-Syuruq, 1987.

Rabi', Muhammad Mahmoud. *The Political Theory of Ibn Khaldun*. Leiden: EJ Brill, 1967.

Rahman, Fazlur. *Islamic Methodology in History*. Lahore: Central Institute of Islamic Research, 1965.

———. "A Recent Controversy Over the Interpretation of Shura". *History of Religions* 20 (1981): 291–301.

———. *Islam and Modernity: Transformation of an Intellectual Tradition*. Chicago: University of Chicago Press, 1982.

———. "The Principle of Shura and the Role of the Ummah in Islam". In *State, Politics, and Islam*, edited by Mumtaz Ahmad. Indianapolis: American Trust Publications, 1986.

Rahman, S. A. *Punishment of Apostasy in Islam*. Kazi Publications, 1986.

Rais, M. Amien. "The Moslem Brotherhood in Egypt: Its Rise, Demise, and Resurgence". Ph.D. dissertation, University of Chicago, 1984.

Ramadireksa, Hendarmin. *Visi Politik Amandemen UUD 1945 Menuju Konstitusi yang Berkedaulatan Rakyat*. Jakarta: Yayasan Pancur Siwah, 2002.

Ratuperwiranegara, Alamsjah (Minister for Religion Affairs). Statement in *Pelita* (Indonesian daily newspaper), 12 June 1978.

Raziq, 'Ali 'Abd al-. *al-Ijma' fi al-Shari'a al-Islamiya*. Beirut: Dar al-Fikr al-'Arabi, 1948.

Reynolds, Noel B. "Grounding the Rule of Law". *Ratio Juris* 2, no. 1 (1989): 3.

Ricklefs, M. C. *A History of Modern Indonesia, c. 1300 to the Present*. London: Macmillan, 1981.

Rosenbaum, Alan S., ed. *Constitutionalism: The Philosophical Dimension*. Connecticut: Greenwood Press, 1988.

Roy, Olivier. *The Failure of Political Islam*. Cambridge: Harvard University Press, 1996.

Rusyd, Ibn. *Bidayah al-Mujtahid*, vol. 2. Beirut: Dar al-Fikr, 1995.

Sabili. "UUD Bukan Kitab Suci" [The Constitution is not the Holy Book]. No. 23, 16 May 2002.

Sachedina, Abdulaziz Abdulhussein. *The Just Ruler (al-Sultan al-Adil) in Shiite Islam: The Comprehensive Authority of the Jurist in Imamite Jurisprudence*. New York: Oxford University Press, 1988.

———. *The Islamic Roots of Democratic Pluralism*. New York: Oxford University Press, 2001.

Saeed, Abdullah. "Ijtihad and Innovation in Neo-Modernist Islamic Thought in Indonesia". *Islam and Christian-Muslim Relations* 8 (1997): 3.

Safi, Louay M. "The Islamic State: A Conceptual Framework". *American Journal of Islamic Social Sciences* (1991): 233.

Salim, Arskal. "*Shari'a* From Below' in Aceh (1930s–1960s): Islamic Identity and the Right to Self-Determination with Comparative Reference to the Moro Islamic Liberation Front (MILF)". *Indonesia and the Malay World* 32, no. 92 (2004): 80.

Samson, Allan A. "Conceptions of Politics, Power, and Ideology in Contemporary Indonesian Islam". In *Political Power and Communications in Indonesia*, edited by Karl D. Jackson and Lucian W. Pye. Berkeley: University of California Press, 1978.

Sanasarian, Eliz. *Religious Minorities in Iran*. New York: Cambridge University Press, 2000.

Saphiro, Ian. *The Rule of Law*. New York: New York University Press, 1994.

Sasongko, H. D. Haryo. *Pemilu'99: Komedi atau Tragedi*. Jakarta: Pustaka Grafiksi, 1999.

Sato, Shigeru. *War, Nationalism and Peasants: Java under the Japanese Occupation 1942–1945*. Sydney: Allen & Unwin, 1994.

Schacht, Joseph. *An Introduction to Islamic Law*. Oxford: Clarendon Press, 1998.

Schedler, Andreas P. "Taking Electoral Promises Seriously: Reflections on the Substance of Procedural Democracy". Paper prepared for presentation at the XVIth World Congress of the International Political Science Association (IPSA), Berlin, 21–25 August 1994.

Schirazi, Asghar. *The Constitution of Iran: Politics and the State in the Islamic Republic*. London and New York: I.B. Tauris, 1997.

Schlesinger, Rudolf B. et al. *Comparative Law: Cases, Text, Materials*, 6th ed. Mineola, NY: Foundation Press, 1998.

Schultz, Julianne. *Reviving the Fourth Estates: Democracy, Accountability and the Media*. Cambridge: Cambridge University Press, 1999.

Secall, M. Isabel Calero. "Rulers and Qadis: Their Relationship During the Nasrid Kingdom". *Islamic Law and Society* 7, no. 2 (2000): 235.

Sekretariat Jenderal MPR. *Risalah Rapat ke-6 Badan Pekerja MPR RI*. 23 May 2000. Jakarta: Setjen MPR, 2000.

———. *Risalah Sidang Panitia Ad-Hoc I, Badan Pekerja MPR-RI*. Jakarta: MPR, 2000.

———. *Risalah PAH I BP MPR 2000*. Rapat Ke-3, 6 December 2000.

———. *Risalah PAH I BP MPR 2000*, Rapat Ke-4, 7 December 2000.

———. *Risalah Rapat Panitia Ad Hoc I Badan Pekerja MPR RI ke-21 s.d 30 Tanggal 28 Maret 2002 s.d 19 Juni 2002*. Jakarta: Setjen MPR, 2002.

Sekretariat Negara Republik Indonesia. *Risalah Sidang BPUPKI-PPKI 28 Mei 1945– 22 Agustus 1945*. Jakarta: Sekneg, 1995.

Shadid, Anthony. *Legacy of the Prophet: Despots, Democrats, and the New Politics of Islam*. Boulder, CO: Westview Press, 2002.

Shepard, William E. "Muhammad Said al-Ashmawi and the application of Sharia in Egypt". *International Journal of Middle East Studies* 28, no. 1 (1996): 39.

Sherif, Adel Omar. "Separation of Powers and Judicial Independence in Constitutional Democracies: The Egyptian and American Experiences". In *Human Rights and*

Democracy: The Role of the Supreme Constitutional Court of Egypt, edited by Kevin Boyle and Adel Omar Sherif. London: Kluwer Law International, 1996.

Sherkat, Darren E. and Christopher G. Ellison. "Recent Developments and Controversies in the Sociology of Religion". *Annual Review of Sociology* 25 (1999): 363.

Shihab, Alwi Abdurahman. "The Muhammadiyah Movement and Its Controversy with Christian Mission in Indonesia". Ph.D. thesis, Temple University, 1995.

Shihab, Habib Rizieq. "Jika Syariat Islam Jalan, Maka Jadi Negara Islam". Interview in *Tashwirul Afkar* 12 (2002): 104.

Shinoda, Hideaki. *Re-examining Sovereignty: from Classical Theory to the Global Age.* New York, St. Martin's Press, 2000.

Shklar, Judith N. "Political Theory and the Rule of Law". In *The Rule of Law: Ideal or Ideology*, edited by Allan C. Hutchinson and Patrick Monahan. Vancouver: Carswell, 1987.

Sidjabat, W. B. *Religious Tolerance and the Christian Faith.* Jakarta: Badan Penerbit Kristen, 1965.

Simanjuntak, Marsilam. *Pandangan Negara Integralistik: Sumber, Unsur dan Riwayatnya dalam Persiapan UUD 1945.* Jakarta: Pustaka Utama Grafiti, 1994.

Simatupang, T. B. "Sebagai Penutup: Sepuluh Dalil". In *Iman Kristen dan Pancasila.* Jakarta: BPK Gunung Mulia, 1985.

Simons, Kenneth W. "Equality as a Comparative Right". *Boston University Law Review* 65 (1985): 387.

Sinanovic, Ermin. "The Majority Principle in Islamic Legal and Political Thought". *Islam and Christian-Muslim Relations* 15, no . 2 (2004): 237–56.

Singh, Bilveer. *Habibie and the Democratisation of Indonesia.* Sydney: Book House, 2001.

Sitompul, Einar Martahan. *NU dan Pancasila.* Jakarta: Pustaka Sinar Harapan, 1989.

Stark, Rodney. "Secularization, R.I.P.: Rest in Peace". *Sociology of Religion* 60, no. 3 (1999): 249–73.

Steenbrink, Karel A. *Beberapa Aspek tentang Islam di Indonesia Abad ke-19.* Jakarta: Bulan Bintang, 1984.

———. *Dutch Colonialism and Islam in Indonesia: Conflict and Contact 1596–1950.* Amsterdam: Rodopi B.V., 1993.

———. "Itinerant Scholars". *Inside Indonesia*, no. 52, October–December 1997.

Suara Hidayatullah. "Piagam Jakarta Terganjal Lagi". September 2000.

Subekti, Valina Singka. "Electoral Law Reform as Prerequisite to Create Democratization in Indonesia". In *Crafting Indonesian Democracy*, edited by R. William Liddle. Bandung: Mizan, 2001.

Sugiarto, Bima Arya. "Sidang Tahunan MPR 2002: Menuju Institusionalisasi, Menyelamatkan Transisi". *Analisis CSIS: Di Ambang Krisis Konstitusi?* no. 2, 2002.

Sugiono, Sukiati. "Islamic Legal Reform in Twentieth Century Indonesia: A Study of Hazairin's Thought". M.A. thesis, McGill University, 1999.

Suharizal. *Reformasi Konstitusi 1998–2002: Pergulatan Konsep dan Pemikiran Amandemen UUD 1945*. Padang: Anggrek Law Firm, 2002.

Sukardja, Ahmad. *Piagam Madinah dan Undang-Undang Dasar 1945: Kajian Perbandingan tentang Dasar Hidup Bersama dalam Masyarakat yang Majemuk*, 1st ed. Jakarta: UI-Press, 1995.

Sulami, Mishal Fahm al-. *The West and Islam*. London: RoutledgeCurzon, 2003.

Sumartana, Th. et al. *Agama dan Negara Perspektif Islam Katolik, Hindu, Buddha, Konghucu, Protestan*. Yogyakarta: Interfidei, 2002.

Summers, Robert S. "A Formal Theory of the Rule of Law". *Ratio Juris* 6, no. 2 (1993): 127–42.

Sundhaussen, Ulf. "The Military: Structure, Procedures, and Effects on Indonesian Society". In *Political Power and Communications in Indonesia*, edited by Karl D. Jackson and Lucian W. Pye. Berkeley: University of California Press, 1978.

Sunny, Ismail. "Hukum Islam dalam Hukum Nasional". *Hukum dan Pemabungan*, XVII/4, August 1987.

Suny, Ismail. *Mekanisme Demokrasi Pancasila*. Jakarta: Aksara Baru, 1978.

Susanti, Bivitri. "Constitution and Human Rights Provisions in Indonesia: An Unfinished Task in the Transitional Process". In *Constitutions and Human Rights in a Global Age: An Asia-Pacific Perspective*, edited by Tessa Morris-Suzuki. Canberra: Australian National University, 2003.

Syadzali, Munawir. *Islam and Governmental System: Teachings, History, and Reflections*. Jakarta: INIS, 1991.

Syalabi, Ahmad. *al-Hukuma wa al-Dawla fi al-Islam*. Cairo: Maktabah al-Nahdah al-Misriyah, 1958.

———. *al-Siyasa fi al-Fikr al-Islami*. Cairo: Nahdah al-Misriyah, 1983.

Syaltut, Mahmud. *Al-Islam Aqidah wa Shari'a*. Cairo: Dar al-Syuruq, 1988.

Syamsuddin, M. Sirajuddin. "Religion and Politics in Islam: The Case of Muhammadiyah in Indonesia's New Order". Ph.D. thesis, University of California Los Angeles, 1991.

Taher, Tarmizi. *Aspiring for the Middle Path: Religious Harmony in Indonesia*. Jakarta: CENSIS-IAIN Jakarta, 1997.

Tahhan, Mahmud al-. *Taysir Mustalah al-Hadith*. Cairo: Dar al-Turas al-'Arabi, 1981.

Taimiyah, Taqi al-Din Ibn. *Enjoining Right and Forbidding Wrong*. Available at http://www.ymofmd.com/books/erfw/.

———. *Majmu' al-Fatawa*, vol. 2. Beirut: Mu'assasah al-Risalah, 1398AH.

Taj, 'Abdurrahman. *al-Siyasa al-Shar'iya wa al-Fiqh al-Islami*. Cairo: Dar al-Ta'rif, 1953.

TAPOL. *Indonesia: Muslims on Trial*. London: TAPOL, 1987.

Thaba, Abdul Azis. *Islam dan Negara dalam Politik Orde Baru*. Jakarta: Gema Insani Press, 1996.

Thoolen, Hans, ed. *Indonesia and the Rule of Law: Twenty Years of "New Order" Government*. London: Frances Pinter, 1987.

Tibi, Bassam. *The Challenge of Fundamentalism: Political Islam and the New World Disorder*. Berkeley: University of California Press, 1998.

Tobing, Robert Lumban. "Christian Social Ethics in the Thoughts of TB Simatupang: The Role of Indonesian Christian in Social Change". Ph.D. thesis, University of Denver, 1996.

Troper, Michel. "The Limits of Rule of Law: The Rechtsstaat and the Problem of Obedience to the Law". Rule of Law Lecture Series, Centre for Comparative Constitutional Studies, University of Melbourne, 10 April 2001.

Tsadik, Daniel. "The Legal Status of Religious Minorities: Imam, Shia, Law and Iran's Constitutional Revolution". *Islamic Law and Society* 10, no. 3 (2003): 376.

Tyan, E. "Bay'a". In *The Encyclopaedia of Islam*, vol. I, edited by B. Lewis, Ch. Pellat and J. Schacht. Leiden: E.J. Brill, 1965.

U.S. Department of State. "Indonesia: Country Reports on Human Rights Practices — 2000". Bureau of Democracy, Human Rights, and Labor, 23 February 2001.

Unger, Roberto M. *Law in Modern Society*. New York: Free Press, 1976.

van Bruinessen, Martin. "Islamic State or State Islam? Fifty Years of State-Islam Relations in Indonesia". In *Indonesien am Ende des 20. Jahrhunderts*, edited by Ingrid Wessel. Hamburg: Abera-Verlag, 1996.

van der Kroef, Justus M. *Indonesia After Soekarno*. Vancouver: University of British Columbia Press, 1971.

van Dijk, Kees. *A Country in Despair: Indonesia between 1997 and 2000*. Jakarta: KITLV Press, 2001.

van Klinken, Gerry. "The Chinese Rapes, Economic Depression and Indonesian Communalism". *Inside Indonesia*, digest 68, 31 August 1998.

Vatikiotis, Michael R. J. *Indonesian Politics under Suharto*. London: Routledge, 1994.

Vatikiotis, P. J. *Islam and the State*. London: Routledge, 1991.

Venkatraman, Bharathi Anandhi. "Islamic States and the United Nations Convention on the Elimination of All Forms of Discrimination Against Women: Are the Shari'a and the Convention Compatible?". American University Law Review 44 (1995): 1949.

Venter, Francois. *Constitutional Comparison: Japan, Germany, Canada and South Africa as Constitutional States*. Cape Town: Juta & Co., 2000.

Vogel, Frank E. "The Closing of the Door of Ijtihad and the Application of the Law". Paper presented at the American Oriental Society Conference, Cambridge, Massachusetts, 13 March 1992.

Vogel, Frank Edward. "Islamic Law and Legal System Studies of Saudi Arabia". Ph.D. dissertation, Harvard University, 1993.

Wahid, Hidayat Nur. "Mewujudkan Konstitusi yang Adil dan Demokratis (Kasus Amandemen Pasal 29 Ayat 1 UUD 1945)". Available at official website of *Partai Keadilan*, http://www.keadilan.or.id.

Wahyono, Padmo. *Guru Pinandita: Sumbangsih untuk Prof. Djokosoetono, SH*. Jakarta: Lembaga Penerbit Fakultas Ekonomi Universitas Indonesia, 1984.

————. "Konsep Yuridis Negara Hukum Indonesia". Unpublished paper, September 1988.

Watson, Alan. *Legal Transplant: An Approach to Comparative Law*, 2nd ed. Athens: 1993.

Watt, W. Montgomery. *The Formative Period of Islamic Thought*. U.K.: Edinburgh University, 1973.

Weeramantry, C. G. *Islamic Jurisprudence*. Basingstoke: Macmillan, 1988.

Wehr, Hans. *A Dictionary of Modern Written Arabic*. London: Macdonald & Evans Ltd, 1974.

Weiss, Bernard. *The Spirit of Islamic Law*. Athens: University of Georgia Press, 1998.

Widiatmoko, Dono. "Kriteria Sehat Calon Presiden". *Kompas*, 19 April 2004.

Widjojanto, Bambang et al. *Konstitusi Baru Melalui Komisi Konstitusi Independen*. Jakarta: Pustaka Sinar Harapan, 2002.

Williamson, John. "What Should the World Bank Think about the Washington Consensus?". *World Bank Research Observer* 15, no. 2 (2000): 251–64.

Wormuth, Francis D. *The Origins of Modern Constitutionalism*. New York: Harper & Brothers, 1949.

Ya'qub, Ahmad Husayn. *al-Nizam al-Siyasi fi al-Islam: ra'y al-sunnah, ra'y al-syi'ah, hukm al-syar'*. Iran: Mu'assasah Ansariyan, 1312AH.

Yamin, H. Muhammad. *Naskah Persiapan Undang-Undang Dasar 1945*. Jakarta: Yayasan Prapanca, 1959.

Yasuko, Kobayashi. "*Kyai* and Japanese Military". *Studia Islamika* 4, no. 3 (1997): 65.

Yusuf, Slamet Effendy and Umar Basalim. *Reformasi Konstitusi Indonesia: Perubahan Pertama UUD-1945*. Jakarta: Pustaka Indonesia Satu (PIS), 2000.

Zamboni, Mauro. "'Rechtsstaat': Just What is Being Exported by Swedish Development Organisations?". *Law, Social Justice and Global Development Journal (LGD)* 2 (2001). http://elj.warwick.ac.uk/global/issue/2001-2/zamboni.html.

Zuhaili, Muhammad al-. *Tarikh al-Qada' fi al-Islam*. Beirut: Dar al-Fikr al-Mu'asir, 1995.

Zuhaili, Wahbah al-. *al-Wasit fi Usul al-Fiqh al-Islami*. Beirut: Matba'ah Dar al-Kitab, 1977.

————. *Usul al-Fiqh al-Islami*, vol. 2. Beirut: Dar al-Fikr, 1986.

Zweigert, K. and H. Kötz. *An Introduction to Comparative Law*, 3rd ed. Oxford: Clarendon Press, 1998.

Interviewee

Hamdan Zoelva, 15 December 2003.

Hidayat Nur Wahid, 1 December 2003.

Lukman Hakim Saifuddin, 10 November 2003 and 10 December 2003.

Mutammimul Ula, 5 September 2003.

Mujib Rakhmat, 13 October 2003.

Saifullah Ma'sum, 29 November 2003.

T. B. Soemandjaja, 30 November 2003 and 7 December 2003.

INDEX

About the Author

Dr Nadirsyah Hosen is a Lecturer at the Faculty of Law, University of Wollongong, Australia. He is also Adjunct Fellow of the Key Centre for Ethics, Law, Justice and Governance at Griffith University. He was previously a Postdoctoral Research Fellow attached to the Centre for Public International and Comparative Law, T.C. Beirne School of Law, University of Queensland.

Nadir has a Bachelor's degree (UIN Syarif Hidayatullah), a Graduate Diploma in Islamic Studies, and Master of Arts with Honours (University of New England), as well as a Master of Laws in Comparative Law (Northern Territory University). He completed his first Ph.D. (Law) at the University of Wollongong and a second Ph.D. (Islamic Law) at the National University of Singapore.

He has experience in teaching Islamic law at UIN Syarif Hidayatullah, Institut Ilmu al-Qur'an (IIQ) and University of Wollongong. He also teaches Comparative Anti-Terrorism Law and Policy at University of Queensland. Nadir also acts as a referee for *LAWASIA, Australian Religion Studies Review*, and *University of New England Law Journal*. He was Visiting Research Fellow at the Institute of Defence and Strategic Studies (IDSS) in Singapore. In Australia, he serves the Muslim community as Rais Syuriah for Special Branch of Nahdlatul Ulama (NU).

His articles have been published in internationally recognized and refereed journals such as the *Nordic Journal of International Law* (Lund University), *Asia Pacific Law Review* (City University of Hong Kong), *Australian Journal of Asian Law* (University of Melbourne), *European Journal of Law Reform* (Indiana University), *Asia Pacific Journals on Human Rights and the Law* (Murdoch University), *Journal of Islamic Studies* (Oxford University Press), *The Muslim World* (Hartford Seminary), and *Journal of Southeast Asian Studies* (Cambridge University Press).

www.ingramcontent.com/pod-product-compliance
Lightning Source LLC
Chambersburg PA
CBHW020404100426
42812CB00001B/187